Race,
Women
&
Rock n' Roll

John Laughter   Neil F. Sharpe

"Race, Women & Rock n' Roll": Copyright: Neil F. Sharpe, John Laughter 2023.

Excerpts from "History Of The Saxophone: Blues, Jazz, R&B, Jump, Rock n' Roll, Soul, Funk, Hip-Hop, Country, Metal, EDM and more: 1920-2021": Copyright: John Laughter, Neil F Sharpe 2021.

Excerpts from: "History of Top 40 Saxophone Solos, 1955-2021"; Copyright: John Laughter, 2021.

All rights reserved: No part of this book may be reproduced in any form by any print or electronic or mechanical means, including information storage or retrieval systems, without permission from the authors except by a reviewer/historian who may quote passages.

Our intent is not to provide a comprehensive review of artists, solos, regional styles and technology developments- that is beyond the scope of this book. What we will do is provide a musical analysis and context for each decade.

Due to the dynamic nature of the Internet, any web addresses or links contained in the book may have changed since the date of publication and may no longer be valid.

All photographs are courtesy of the authors unless credited otherwise.

While the authors have made every reasonable effort to trace the copyright owners in this book, there may be some omission of credits. Please contact the authors with any information– jsaxlATaol.com-relating to photographs not credited.

The information presented herein represents the views of the authors as of the date of publication. This book is presented for information purposes only. Due to the rate at which conditions change, the authors reserve the right to alter and update their opinions based on new conditions. While every attempt has been made to reasonably verify the information in this book, the authors do not assume any responsibility for errors, inaccuracies, or omissions.

No copyright is claimed in content quoted and copied and to the extent that material may appear to be infringed, we assert that such alleged infringement is for informational and educational purposes and is permissible under fair use principles in U.S. copyright laws. If you believe material has been used in an unauthorized manner, please contact the authors.

Internet links have been included for historical or technical reference or as required by the artist and/or copyright holder.

Music First Publishing; Atlanta, London, Toronto
ISBN: 9798868465406

4

Prologue

Blues and Rock n' Roll almost never happened.

A single record made the difference.

So did the forbidden and the forgotten.

This is their story.

What really happened…

6

Table of Contents

Prologue-11

1. Crazy Blues-15
-Crazy Blues and Racism-33
-Remember My Name-41
-Notes/References-43

2. Some These Days I'll Be Gone-49
-Blues Mafia-49
-James McKune-50
-Robert Palmer-53
-Chris Thomas King-55
-The Almost Fate Of The Blues-59
-Covers, Racism and Rock n' Roll-63
-Led Zeppelin, Jimmy Page-63
-Bob Dylan-65
-Derrick "Big" Walker-67
-Chops Horns-Darryl Dixon, Dave Watson-72
-Over The Mountains, Across The Seas-74
-Notes-77

3. West End Blues-83
-Louis Armstrong-83
-Earl Hines-86
-Notes-91

4. Strange Fruit-93
-Billie Holiday-95
-Sidney Bichet-100
-Lester Young, Stan Getz-102
-Artie Shaw-106
-Chops Horns -Darryl Dixon, Dave Watson -111
-Notes/References-121

5. Caledonia-125
-Louis Jordan-125
-Ken Fornetran-127
-Jon R. Smith-129
-Paul Revere, Mark Lindsay-129
-Spirituals to Swing-130
-Boogie Woogie-131
-ASCAP-137
-Indy Labels-141
-Women Take The Solos-151
-Notes/References-163

6. Flying Home-167
-Illinois Jacquet-167
-Sister Rosetta Tharpe-169
-R&B-Busting Through-175
-There's No Stopping Us Now-185
-The Train Kept A' Rollin' and A' Rollin'-187
-Paranoia, ESP and Great Ears-189
-Alan Freed-190
-George "Hound Dog" Lorenz-194
-Captivity, Censorship and The Birth Of Rock n' Roll-195
-Running Wild But Not So Free-203
-Lionel Prevost-207
-Notes/References-223

7. Deacon's Hop-229
-Big Jay McNeely-230
-Red Prysock-233
-Ruth Brown; Willis Gator Jackson-235
-Who You Gonna Believe? Record Credits-241
-Chops Horns-Darryl Dixon, Dave Watson-243
-Jon R. Smith-245
-Notes/References-251

8.Tutti Frutti-253

- American Bandstand-256
- Chuck Willis-256
- The Diamonds-256
- Little Richard-263
- Lee Allen-265
- John Firmin-272
- Elvis Presley-"Hound Dog"-277
- Grady Gains-289
- Alvin "Red" Tyler-293
- Jon R. Smith-"If You Want To Play, I Mean Really Play"-301
- Credits for Jon R. Smith Interview-309
- Jimmy Wright-313
- Sea Cruise-319
- Stagger Lee-321
- Sammy Price-327
- Nancy Wright-329
- King Curtis-343
- Jimi Hendrix-355
- Soul Twist; Memphis Soul Stew-358
- Bill Haley and The Comets-365
- Whispering Bells-375
- Fats Domino; Herb Hardesty-379
- Honky Tonk; Clifford Scott-383
- Thomas "Beans" Bowle-387
- Wendell DuConge-391
- Brenda Lee; Boots Randolph-395
- Lavern Baker; Sam "The Man" Taylor-411
- Budd Johnson-418
- In The Still Of The Night; Vinny Mazzetta-421
- Influences and Legends- Sax Gordon-425
- Steve Douglas-431
- At My Front Door; Red Holloway-437
- Teen Queens; Maxwell Davis-441
- The Bobbettes; Jesse Powell-445
- Poor Boy- George "Kat" Katsakis-449
- Women In Rock n' Roll-457
- Crossfire-Johnny Paris-473

-The Circle Is Unbroken- Detroit Gary Wiggins pg. 479; Johnny Ferreira pg. 485; John Barrow pg. 491; Deke McGee-pg. 501
-Short Shorts- Bill Crandall-517
-Oh What a Night- Lucius "Little Wash" Washington; McKinley Easton-523
-Of Special Note-527
-Speedo- Jesse Powell-535
-Sil Austin-537
-Jim Horn-541
-Gil Bernal-545
-Raunchy-549
-Justin Gordon-553
-Get a Job; Rollee McGill-557
-The Big Bands During The 1950s; Count Basis-Frank Foster, Frank Wess; Jimmy Dorsey-Dick Stabile; Tommy Dorsey-Joe Lopes; Johnny Dankworth; Ernie Fields-Plas Johnson-559
-Kissing Time-George Young-569
-Buddy Savitt; Dave Appell-575
-Tall Cool One; Mark Marush-581
-Sax Kari-585
-David "Fathead" Newman-587
-Home of The Groove-589
-Collections of Blues, R&B, Rock n' Roll Sax Records-593
-Tequila-Chuck Rio-595
-Blues, R&B, Rock n' Roll Teaching Links; Jeff Harrington; Pete Thomas-601
-Sam Butera-603
-Notes/References-607

9. Stardust-613

10. The Authors-621

11

12

"Everyone has pain as well as times of joy. The rich and the poor, everyone. The ability to express beauty and its correlatives is the defining quality of all artists.

However, this is not what makes him or her an artist; you have to love it and be willing to suffer for arts' sake. Giving your time, social life, money, and life experiences, even what some people call 'soul'.

There is not one type of experience that makes an artist. It just has to be truly from your heart and soul. That's not as easy as it sounds.

First, you have to find your heart and soul. To do that, you have to find out what heart and soul is."

-Derrick "Big" Walker

14

1

Crazy Blues

By Neil Sharpe

Left over cabbage for breakfast. Winter coat pawned, riding the subway all night to duck paying the rent. A "King Kong" to "straighten up" (alcohol and sugar with a whisky flavor- 5 cents a glass). Molls, mobsters, and pimps. A "tame" Saturday night with only "six razor operations", four persons found in the morgue Sunday morning". Blueberry juice and gin.

Pairs of shoes worn clean through tramping the pavements of Broadway, pounding on the doors of record companies. Perry Bradford was driven by a vision, haunted by African spiritual songs.

A vision that record executives swore would never happen, "when the prejudice and discrimination were so thick you couldn't cut them with a butcher's knife". 1

A vision of the sound of America- "the sound of the voice of a Negro singing the blues with a jazz combination...I felt strongly it should be a girl...I was laughed at by all the wise guys in Tin Pan Alley. I had pleaded with Columbia and Victor... there was 'no dice'." 2

Even his friends thought that Perry Bradford had as much chance fulfilling his vision as a warrior trying to rip the Moon out of the sky with a single slash of a sword.

The music industry had become both the devil and the savior- oppression, fraud and theft waging eternal war on creativity, hope and freedom.

For Perry Bradford, every day seemed like battling through a cold blood rain of apathy and prejudice that threatened to eat whole the heart and soul. In the music business, people had a tendency is to push it as far as they could.

But it's easier to believe the longer you keep going. Always aiming straight ahead like an asteroid eager to fulfill its mission.

"My unadulterated nerve and determination to keep hounding the record companies to try and get them to believe...". 3

Perry had travelled all over the United States, playing songs that could take you to the place before memories and words began. He'd won tributes from exceptional musicians like Jelly Roll Morton and Fats Waller. Through these journeys, he knew that his vision could reach out to a vast, untapped market, whose people would buy if recorded by one of their own- a musical vision of a culture and a history that had been walled off by the great darkness of prejudice and hatred, of broken lives that had never been allowed to speak, but now would be born again.

"I knew the people were waiting for that sound on the record, because it was the sound of America, Negro and White."

"It is my humble belief that people were looking for something to lift them up so they could forget about the war…that's why I was busy knocking myself out and facing many insults and wise-cracking from recording managers…for our folk had a story to tell and it could be told only in vocal- not instrumental recordings…but Columbia wouldn't think of recording a colored girl at this time [1919]." 4

The music industry is dangerous for the innocent, the unprepared. But spend time in the industry and you learn how to duck and roll. See the traps. Know the ways out. At least, for those willing to put themselves at blood risk.

Perry Bradford's tenacity and determination to let the blues tell the truth, eventually guided him safe passage through.

"Bill Tracy, the white writer, gave me the key which opened the prejudice-door to my thorny problem." Tracy told Perry to use his name and recommend to Fred Hagar of Okeh Records that he give you "an audition for a colored girl." 5

But Fred Hagar of Okeh Records had received "many threatening letters" from Northern and Southern pressure groups not to deal with any colored girls in recordings. If he did, Okeh records and phonograph machines would be boycotted. 6

Perry later wrote: "May God bless Mr. Hagar, for despite the many threats, it took a man with plenty of nerve and guts to buck those powerful groups and make the historical decision which echoed aroun' the world." 7

Hagar's first choice for singer was Sophie Tucker, however, she had to turn it down (she was sick and under contract to another label). Perry convinced him to try the well experienced performer, singer Mamie Smith, who Bradford had managed and performed with in music revues, including "Made In Harlem".

The initial, tryout, record release- "That Thing Called Love" and "You Can't Keep A Good Man Down"- did better than expected. W.C. Handy wrote in "Father OF The Blues", "the sales on these number had been very large...In Chicago, large crowds of domestic servants and packinghouse workers waited outside Tate's Music Store to hear us demonstrate" the songs. With these sales numbers in hand, Okeh and Perry went for the home run and wider distribution, with the song "Crazy Blues".

But to do that, Perry first had to stop the ground from breaking open beneath his feet.

Perry already had used the tune of "Crazy Blues" for another record. Earlier, he had a situation where he'd inadvertently copied another composition and had to make a pre-emptive strike with a cash payment before it was discovered. 8 This time, if everything wasn't clean, the record companies' legal hawks, with wings the color of broken moonlight, would only be too eager to swoop down and pick him clean like the skeleton of a deer.

Add to this, Percy Bradford had booked recording studio space for a five piece jazz band to back "Crazy Blues" without knowing who would be in the band! The night before the recording, he had to run through saloons and nightclubs to put a band together.

"Crazy Blues" was officially released in November, 1920, sung by Mamie Smith with the backing band, the "Jazz Hounds" (later joined by a young saxophonist named Coleman Hawkins, who went on to create music described as "perfect art"). No one expected much, but the record reportedly sold over a million copies and forever changed the music industry.

The sales figures for "Crazy Blues" exploded high in the sky like fire rockets on a late summer night.

Some have suggested that the sales figures were exaggerated. The music industry has always been net-profit serious. Record companies operate on the assumption that their artists, and only their artists, will have the hits, and if that doesn't happen, record executives will fly in low and hard, reflexes and claws tuned to drive into extinction the outsiders who have dared to intrude.

When Mamie Smith burst into this touch-of-Dante world with "Crazy Blues", the companies' war alarms fired off in sharp bursts and jangles- their guard dogs were released.

Maintain the bottom line at all costs was the core mission of every record executive. Those who had believed that "blacks" neither had the interest nor the money to buy records, suddenly found their salaries and careers at risk, as a new form of music, the blues, slashed through their ranks. Cannibals, hustlers and con men don't always win.

Once-impenetrable walls of musical prejudice and discrimination came crashing down, not because of any newfound respect for equality and civil rights, but for the overwhelming desire to appease the reigning god of the music industry- profit. The record companies' frantic response tells us everything we need to know about how many records "Crazy Blues" sold.

Record company executives, in their battle uniforms of funeral director pearl grey hats and dark blue suits with silver buttons that gleamed under candelabras, rushed into battle with a ruthless pincers attack. They signed like-sounding singers with like-shaded skins and like-arranged music; they copied, copied, copied until- their war game plan had promised them- they could steal Perry's music, take his place and bury this newcomer deep. Three versions of "Crazy Blues" were issued by other companies (including Columbia) in the following year, 1921.

With his first royalty cheque for $2500.00, Perry Bradford and his wife Marion threw out their usual breakfast of left-over, cold cabbage and went to a restaurant, because, as Perry told his wife, "rich folks order rich food", which on this occasion translated as ham, eggs and French-fried potatoes.

Mamie Smith flew higher, performed before audiences of 18,000 with extravagant stage shows, and created a new life of diamonds, French fashion, and homes upon homes upon homes.

Female blues singers suddenly were in great demand. Dorian Lynskey cites, in a BBC article, a report from The Metronome (a music magazine that published from 1885-1961; in the late 1920s-early 1930s, its primary focus changed from classical music to jazz, a change triggered by the decision to cover the saxophone!) that found, in 1922, one company made over 4 million dollars on the Blues. "'Now every phonograph company has a coloured girl recording. Blues are here to stay.' The classic blues was African-American culture's first mainstream breakthrough and, for several years, it was effectively a female art form." 9

On September 19, 1926, The New York Times ("American Jazz Is Not African"-Pg 27, Sec. 20, p. 8; reprinted in Metronome, October, 1926) published an article that described African music as a "definite, painstakingly developed system rooted in centuries…From it…jazz sprung." However, the author of the study, Nicolas George Julius Ballanta of Sierre Leone, "was not prepared to claim jazz as African. It is essentially Western in everything except its basic principle-rhythm-which he feels is unmistakably African.…If African music had never come to this country, there would be no jazz" said Ballanta.

Ma Rainey is widely given credit for being one of the first to bring blues into her performances. In 1902, she'd heard a girl singing a "strong and poignant song" about how her man had left her.9A The music of Mamie Desdunes, an early New Orleans blues pianist of the late 1800s-early1900s, was a major influence for Ma Rainey and Jelly Roll Morton.

Ma Rainey wrote about "reactions to betrayal and rejection by men, from suicidal depression to murderous rage, but also comedy and cynicism…Ma Rainey's recorded songs constitutes a message to women…women aggressively confronting or attempting to change the circumstances of their lives." [10]

In this explosion of the blues, the record companies, thrown into sudden competition for artists and profits, may have thought it would be easy, like the teeth of winter wolves to the pale throats of innocents, but some artists knew how to cut and move too.

Black Swan Records-initially founded as the "Pace & Handy Music Company" by Harry Pace (who earlier had collaborated with W.C. Handy in song writing) who next formed the "Pace Photograph Corporation New York City", later changed to "Black Swan" (named for Elizabeth Taylor Greenfield, a famous singer during the 1800s, known as "The Black Swan" who had performed for Queen Victoria), the first major record company operated by African American owners. They released Alberta Hunter's "He's A Darn Good Man", had a big hit with Ethel Waters' "Down Home Blues", followed by "Oh Daddy" in 1921, and what some argue is the first record to refer to "rocking" and "rolling" by Trixie Smith.

However, as the recording of female blues singers became widespread, Black Swan often was outbid for artists by the major labels. In 1923, it ceased operations and was sold to Paramount Records in 1924.

[A six part podcast entitled "The Vanishing of Harry Pace" is available: https://radiolab.org/series/vanishing-harry-pace

- Broome Records (founded by George Wellington Broom) is thought to have issued at least 51 records (many pressed by Columbia) and continued to sell records into the early 1940s (e.g. "Go Down Mosses" by Harry Burleigh).
- Juanita Stinnette Chappelle, a singer, and her husband, Thomas E. Chappelle, started the third independent record company owned and operated by African Americans, Chappelle and Stinnette Records (a.k.a C&S Records); however, their label was short-lived and only issued nine records, all blues, before closing.
- A fourth, short-lived label, was Black Patti Records in Chicago, that debuted in May 1927. Founded by Mayo Williams and named after the "19th century African-American singer Sissieretta Jones". The label reportedly produced 55 records, many with limited pressings (100 or less for some) but had few sales. The company disappeared as fast as it had arrived, ceasing operations in September 1927. The scarcity of these records has made

them the "El Dorado" of the most sought-after records by collectors. 11 One record, Black Patti 8030, recorded in a Chicago studio in May 1927, is one of the most sought after. Its title, which reportedly was first discussed in 1897, that has been known under various titles such as "Stagger Lee," "Stagolee," "Stack-A-Lee", years later was a major hit for Lloyd Price in 1959 as "Stagger Lee" that hit Number One on both Billboard's R&B and Pop charts.11

- Ethel Waters initially had signed with Cardinal Records (she recorded "The New Jump Steady Ball" backed with "The New York Glide"; the exact date is uncertain, ranging from 1919-1921). She moved to Black Swan from 1921-23 with a contract that made her the "highest paid black recording artist at the time"; "Oh Daddy" sold a reported 500,000 copies; later, Paramount, who bought out Black Swan during 1924-25, signed her. She had numerous hits that included "Dinah" and one of the classic songs of the 20th Century, "Stormy Weather" (the song was inducted into the Grammy Hall of Fame in 2003) and was covered by Lena Horne in 1941, immortalized in the film "Stormy Weather", (Lena Horne's film version was Number 30 on the American Film Institute's Top 100 Songs of American Cinema).
- Victoria Hernández, a violin and piano player, opened the first Puerto Rican-owned record

store in New York City in 1927, and founded the record label *Hispano* that produced a number of hits by artists for the Puerto Rican community. During the Great Depression, she managed bookings and placement of artists for labels like Decca and Columbia, and, in 1941, opened the first Latin music store in New York City that eventually became the longest running record store in the city.
- Columbia Records signed Bessie Smith and Clara Smith. Alberta Hunter wrote the lyrics for "Down-Hearted Blues", melody composed by Lovie Austin and sung by Bessie Smith, that sold nearly 800,000 copies. Bessie Smith's record later won recognition by the National Recording Registry of the Library of Congress in 2002, by the Recording Industry Association of America and the National Endowment for the Arts in 2001, and won a Grammy in 2006. Alberta Hunter, however, only received a few hundred dollars in royalty payments due to a secret deal by the producer Ike Williams who sold the rights to Columbia Records in exchange for nearly all the royalties.
- Bessie Smith's release of "St. Louis Blues" featured Louis Armstrong, and was one of the first blues recordings to make use of "call and response" (a staple in gospel with roots in traditional Africa music), a technique that subsequently was widely applied in all genres of music.

Bessie Smith reportedly was never paid any royalties; black artists were mostly excluded from ASCAP (American Society of Composers, Artists and Performers). Those who had royalty agreements didn't have much chance of enforcing them. During the 1920s, however, Bessie Smith made life dance for her, earning a reported $2000.00 per week and even purchased a custom Pullman sleeping car to transport her and her band across the country. Bessie Smith was inducted into the Rock n' Roll Hall of Fame in 1989.

- Paramount Records, that sprang out of a failing Wisconsin company that made chairs and wooden phonograph cabinets, jumped into the record business with low quality, low price, 78 rpm shellac records. It ran print ads that boasted about "Paramount Stars", with photos- in order of appearance- Alberta Hunter, Ma Rainey (aka Gertrude Pridgett;), Ida Cox, Edmonia Henderson, Norfolk Jazz Quartette, Edna Hicks, Faye Barnes, and Trixie Smith. 12
- Aletha Mae Dickerson-Robinson, in 1928, became recording director of Paramount in Chicago where she supervised recording dates. She left Paramount sometime before 1938. Ironically, the cheap quality of Paramount records and the number of male artists they signed, who sold few records in the 1920s-30s, during the 1950s-60s drew the attention of a group of record collectors-the Blues Mafia-

who proclaimed that they and only they could identify "authentic" blues artists, lobbing artillery blasts at all that had gone before…but more on that shortly.

- Okeh Records countered with Sara Martin, Louis Armstrong, King Oliver, Fats Waller, and Sippie Wallace ("The Texas Nightingale") who had an early hit with "Shorty George" and later the blues classics "Women Be Wise" and "I'm A Mighty Tight Woman". They also opened a studio in Chicago and recorded King Oliver, Sidney Bechet, Hattie McDaniel, Duke Ellington and Louis Armstrong.
- In 1925, Victor hired away Okeh's director of recording, Ralph Peer. With Victor, Peer became a critical influence in the development of country and bluegrass music, discovering and recording artists like The Carter Family, Jimmy Rodgers and Ernest Stoneman. His interest was largely the result of a country song that Peer had recorded, on Okeh, Fiddlin' John Carson's "The Little Old Cabin In The Lane"; they had pressed only 1000 copies for the official release, but, much to everyone's surprise, it sold over 500,000 copies.

Dorian Lynskey cites a 1926 study:"…upwards of 75% of the songs are written from a woman's point of view. Among the blues singers who have gained more or less national recognition, there is scarcely a man's name to be found." 13 That didn't last long…

In the late 1920s, record company executives, with unwelcome rumors of forced career-ending farewells whispering in their ears, cut costs by phasing out female singers in favor of male country blues singers whose salaries were lower. More simple arrangements that featured only a guitar or banjo with a piano and a male singer (e.g. singer Tampa Red and his hit "It's Tight Like That") also slashed studio and tour costs compared to those for jazz bands with female singers.

Blind Willie Johnson's "Dark Was The Night, Cold Was The Ground" (1927) became popular and, 50 years later, was chosen as one of 27 songs on the "Voyager Golden Record" carried into space by the Voyager spacecraft in 1977. His version of "John The Revelator", 1930, described as one of the most powerful blues songs ever recorded, has been covered by a wide variety of artists, including the synth-driven English band Depeche Mode.

Lonnie Johnson, who is credited as the creator of the note-by-note guitar solos played with a pick, recorded over 100 songs with Okeh with excellent sales. He also recorded with Louis Armstrong and His Hot Five, Duke Ellington, Bessie Smith, Victoria Spivey, and outstanding jazz pieces with Eddie Lang. His 12 string guitar solos would prove a critical influence for future jazz greats Charlie Christian, Django Reinhardt and George Barnes. After World War II, he moved into rhythm and blues with a number of hits, including "Tomorrow Night", Number One on Billboard Race Records and Number

19 on Pop charts. Always a great vocalist, he was rediscovered in the 1960s and in 1965 moved full time to Canada. After he was hurt in an automobile accident, a benefit was held for him by a wide range of artists at Massey Hall, Toronto, Ontario Canada, including John Lee Hooker and folk singers Ian and Sylvia.

Okeh also recorded guitarist Sylvester Weaver to back Sara Martin (e.g. "Guitar Blues").

Okeh pioneered "location recording" in 1922, and in 1924 sent mobile recording trucks to tour the country twice a year including New Orleans, Chicago, Atlanta, Detroit, Kansas City, St. Louis and San Antonio.

Others like J. Mayo Williams and H.C. Spier (for Paramount), Ralph Peer (as early as 1923), John Lomax, his son John Jr. and John Work III, in the early 1930s, sought out musicians in the southern United States (especially in the city of Memphis where a reported nine different recording units visited in the late 1920s) and did field recordings, discovering, amongst others, Blind Lemon Jefferson, Charley Patton, Son House, Blind Blake, and Lead Belly. 14

Paramount employed field agents, who canvassed the states for talent, made test recordings and helped to arrange for artists to travel north for recordings, including Blind Lemon Jefferson and later Charles Patton, Son House, Blind Blake and Skip James.

Brunswick discovered and recorded artists Furry Lewis, Leroy Carr, and Charlie McCoy.

In 1936, the immortal Robert Johnson was recorded by Don Law, head of Columbia's country music division, in San Antonio in 1936, and Dallas Texas in 1937. 15

Years later, Bob Dylan wrote in his highly recommended book "Chronicles Volume One": "Johnson is serious, like the scorched earth… Robert Johnson's code of language was like nothing I'd heard before or since…" 16

32

Crazy Blues and Racism

"What blues and poetry have always offered the reader or listener is a path to relief from a reality often forced upon that person or people. The storyteller uses metaphors to sometimes say what he or she cannot or dare not say normally. This gives the writer an outlet for his pent-up emotions and a way of influencing his or her environment, sometimes even history."
                                            -Derrick "Big" Walker

The lyrics of "Crazy Blues" became phantoms that listeners carried inside them for the rest of their lives.

"I went to the railroad
Hang my head on the track
Thought about my daddy
I gladly snatched it back
Now my babe's gone
And gave me the sack.

I'm gonna do like a Chinaman
Go and get some hop
Get myself a gun, and shoot myself a cop
I ain't had nothin' but bad news
Now I've got the crazy blues."

Some critics have argued that the lyrics like those for "Crazy Blues" were "carefully coded blues for self-expression and protest", written in response to violent repression, vicious lynchings ("4,473 people were lynched in the United States between 1888 and 1968, 3,446 -72.7 percent- of them black, 73 percent of them in the South, around 150 of them women; in 1891, 11 Italians were lynched in New Orleans, the leader of that mob later became the governor 16A), the racial riots of the Red Summer of 1919 and the growth of the Ku Klux Klan. 17, 18

Today, some would prefer to ignore, cover over, or substitute other memories for these horrific events, but these faces will never be silent.

- A mother and her son reportedly were jailed in Okemah, Oklahoma after her husband had stolen a cow. At midnight, a mob broke into the jail, seized the 14-year-old son and mother, took them to a nearby bridge, tied nooses around their necks, and threw them over the rail. Photos were taken of the bodies swinging from the ropes; the mob posed above with some waving. The photos were sold as postcard souvenirs. No one was ever charged with their murder. 19

  A member of the mob was the father of Woody Guthrie, the folk singer who later wrote the song "Hangknot, Slipknot" about the lynching.

- In Ocoee Florida, "a Black U.S. citizen" attempted to vote but was turned away. "That evening, a mob of armed white men came to the home of his friend, July Perry in an effort to locate Norman. Shooting ensued. Perry was eventually lynched. An unknown number of African American citizens were murdered, and their homes and community were burned to the ground. Most of the Black population of Ocoee fled, never to return." 20

- In 1921, the Tulsa Race Massacre occurred when a prosperous "black business" and community was burned to the ground by a mob of "white vigilantes" which even included "biplanes dropping bombs." 35 city blocks were burned, 1,256 homes destroyed, another 400 were looted and at least 300-400 people killed. 21

Perry Bradford in his book "Born With The Blues" that described how "Crazy Blues" came to be written, however, never mentioned any of the above as a factor in writing the lyrics.

Which isn't to say that the overwhelming public response to "Crazy Blues", wasn't affected by these events as well as by the vicious racial riots of the "Red Summer" that raged across the USA. A brief to the U.S. Senate about these riots listed 43 lynchings and 8 incidences where people were burned at the stake, others were hanged, shot, and "one was cut to pieces". In cities like Washington D.C. and Chicago, the police were reported to have refused to take action in the burning and destruction of "black businesses and homes". 22

On October 5, 1919, at page 11, the New York Times, in an article entitled "Racial Propaganda Among Negros Growing and Increase of Mod

Violence Set Out In Senate Brief for Federal Inquiry", stated: "Even though recurring race riots have made the public aware that the negro problem has entered upon a new and dangerous phase, only those in touch with the inner forces that are playing on ignorance, prejudice, and passion, realize how great this menace is. Bloodshed on a scale amounting to local insurrection at least will be threatened in more than one section where large white and black populations face each other…influences that are now working to drive a wedge of bitterness and hatred between the two races…The States have done nothing. The Federal Government has done nothing." 22

The background to this article were reports that "negro soldiers" who had returned from World War I, were fighting back against the mob attacks. Some argued that the mob actions were triggered by the spread of false rumors the soldiers' resistance was fueled by "Bolshevik propaganda" following the Russian Revolution in 1917.

The Senate brief, entitled "Why Congress Should Investigate Race Riots And Lynchings", gave specific examples of "race riots" and mob violence across the USA where people were lynched: "a mob of white men invaded the negro residence district shooting and burning houses", and mobs "wrecked and looted shops and invaded the colored district". 22

Robert J Peer, at the time, recording director for Okeh, decided to use "Race" to describe their blues recordings. This was followed by Paramount, with "Their Popular Race Record" and other record companies, which included the later founder of Decca Records, Jack Kapp, who called the blues recordings, "Better and Cheaper Race Records".

Record companies attempted to distinguish blues from other forms of music, and, in doing so, played into the hands of a social conservative movement that objected to jazz's "vulgarity" and "depravity". "Mothers are bringing in their flapper daughters in the hope they will be horrified and stop flapping." (cited from "Some Father Opinions on 'Jazz' By Prominent Writers"-*Variety*, August 1922) [23]

"We had records by all foreign groups," says Mr. Peer. "German records, Swedish records, Polish records, but we were afraid to advertise Negro records. So, I listed them in the catalogue as 'race' records..."[24]

The "race" labels lent the impression, strongly backed by the spirit of segregation, that blues "race" records should be sold only to "'Black" audiences and "White" artists to white consumers. "Race records" remained in common use until June 25, 1949, when Billboard changed the chart name to "Rhythm and Blues" (which ended in November 30, 1963).

By the late 1920s, competition from talking movies and the radio slashed into theatre audiences with resulting closures. Ma Rainey recorded 20 songs for Paramount and had a successful tour, but was dropped by Paramount because, according to Paramount, "her down-home material was out of fashion." [25] This soon rang true for many blues/gospel performers.

As sales of blues records first stalled then collapsed, suddenly there seemed to be no work for many female blues singers. The record companies started trying other forms of music, including "swing "as played by large orchestras such as Duke Ellington' and Benny Goodman with singers like Billie Holiday. Some women artists changed their style and arrangements in order to survive, including Lottie Kimbrough and Lucille Bogan (aka Bessie Jackson). Artists who had been more obscure or were instrumentalists made their recording debuts, like the outstanding guitar player Memphis Minnie, Mae Glover (who had recorded using a wide variety of names but eventually came to be known as "the Mother of Beale Street") and guitarist/singer Elvie Thomas.

Tears would soon fill the sky with the stock market crash in 1929. One of Bessie's Smith biggest hits, a cover of Jimmie Cox's immortal "Nobody Knows You When You're Down and Out", released on September 13, 1929, sadly foretold the crash, the onset of the Great Depression, and her own future. [26]

> "Once I lived the life of a millionaire, spendin' my money I didn't have a care.
> I carried my friends out for a good time, buying bootleg liquor, champagne and wine.
> When I begin to fall so low, I didn't have a friend and no place to go..."

The song reportedly has been covered 313 times as of the date of this writing (https://secondhandsongs.com/work/13105).

The long freezing night of the Great Depression tightened like a python around the necks of blues musicians, who suddenly found themselves alone and at risk, even the most talented brought to their knees.

No one could have predicted just how far things would spin out of control with few second chances, no trumpet-blaring comebacks, only a careening head-on crash into a future that seemed unforgiving and disturbingly empty.

By 1933, blues record sales were 7 percent of what they had been in 1929. All record sales for every type of music plummeted from 106 million in the US in 1921 to 6 million by 1932.

Bessie Smith's fees bottomed out to a reported one sixth of what they used to be, her record releases were sporadic, one for Columbia in each of 1931, 1932, none in 1933, two for Okeh in 1934. She died in a car crash in 1937.

Mamie Smith was left penniless, later buried without a tombstone, until 1946, when fans raised funds to erect a memorial.

Many artists didn't make it through the Depression, careers crushed under broken pieces of once palace walls. But some, no matter how tattered and thin, continued to climb toward the sky, their grit and determination hard as a stone.

40

Remember My Name

- Alberta Hunter subsequently recorded with Perry Bradford and for various labels including Black Swan, Gennett, Okeh, Victor and Columbia. She was rediscovered in the 1970s, signed by John Hammond to Columbia Records, performed on television and nightclubs, and wrote the soundtrack, at the request of Robert Altman, for the 1978 movie "Remember My Name".
- Victoria Spivey recorded with Okeh from 1926-29 and wrote/recorded the hits "Black Snake Blues" and "Dope Head Blues". Through the 1930s and 1940s, Spivey continued to work in musical films and stage shows. Early in 1961, Spivey launched Spivey Records and recorded -to name just a few- Otis Rush, Otis Spann, Willie Dixon, and Big Joe Turner. In 1962, her label released the album "Three Kings And A Queen" with Big Joe Williams that featured Bob Dylan on harmonica and backup vocals. A photograph of her and Dylan appear on the back cover of Dylan's 1970 album "New Morning".

"I think one of the best records that I've ever been a part of was the record made with Big Joe Williams and Victoria Spivey. Now that's a record that I hear from time to time

and I don't mind listening to it. It amazes me that I was there and had done that."

-Bob Dylan
Rolling Stone Magazine, November 22, 2001

But what about the fates of other female artists, what about their historical breakthroughs and accomplishments, after the stock market crash and the Great Depression, would they still be remembered, honored, and celebrated?

Not if "The Blue Mafia", an almost exclusively male group of record collectors and their followers, had their way. They dismissed, ridiculed, and obliterated the accomplishments of the female blues singers and their landmarks recordings.

There was money to be made...

Notes

1.

1. Perry Bradford (1965) Born With The Blues. Oak Publications (January 1, 1965) pg.114
2. Ibid; pg. 13
3. Ibid; pg. 14
4. Ibid; pg. 114-115
5. Ibid; pg. 118
6. Ibid; pg. 118
7. Ibid; pg. 118
8. Ibid pg 136
9. Dorian Lynskey (2021) The forgotten story of America's first black superstars. BBC 16th February 2021. https://www.bbc.com/culture/article/20210216-the-forgotten-story-of-americas-first-black-superstars

9A. Palmer Robert (1982) Deep Blues: A Musical and Cultural History of the Mississippi Delta. Penguin Books (July 29, 1982) pg. 44.

10. Sandra R. Lieb (1982) Mother of the Blues: A Study of Ma Rainey. Univ of Massachusetts (January 1, 1982). Pg. xvi
11. Amanda Petrusich (2014) Black Patti 8030; Oxford American July 6, 2014. https://oxfordamerican.org/magazine/issue-85-summer-2014/black-patti-8030 and. https://www.factmag.com/2013/07/22/from-the-archives-black-patti-the-amazing-story-of-the-rarest-american-record-label-ever/

11A_https://www.ny1920.com/1921mar-22),

12. Perry Bradford (1965) Born With The Blues. Pg. 101

13. Dorian Lynskey (2021) The forgotten story of America's first black superstars. BBC 16th February 2021.
https://www.bbc.com/culture/article/20210216-the-forgotten-story-of-americas-first-black-superstars
Variety magazine, in January 6, 1922, argued that Frankie and Burt Leighton were the earliest singers of "blues" in vaudeville, known especially for their version of the classic "Frankie and Johnnie". A reporter who first heard their "sanitized" version said, "I thought you boys had gone balmy. If you had sung the real verses, there would be a riot. I laid 'Besty' (his revolver) on my lap and figured I'd do my best to stop you from being mobbed." Koening K (2002) Jazz In Print, 1859-1929. An Anthology of Early Source Readings in Jazz History. Pendragon Press (July 7 2002). Pg. 202

14. OKeh Historical Survey: OKeh "Remote" Recordings and Field Trips
Discography of OKeh Records, 1918-1934; compiled by Ross Laird and Brian Rust.
https://adp.library.ucsb.edu/index.php/resources/detail/212
https://www.chnm.gmu.edu/digitalhistory/links/pdf/chapter7/7.56a.pdf
https://msbluestrail.org/blues-trail-markers/paramount-records

15. Recording Studios and Developments in Recording Technology: *Brunswick Records: A*

Discography of Recordings, 1916-1931, compiled by Ross Laird.
https://adp.library.ucsb.edu/index.php/resources/detail/198

16. Bob Dylan (2004) - Chronicles: Volume One ; Simon & Schuster Ltd; (September 5, 2004). Pgs 285, 288

16A https://www.smithsonianmag.com/smart-news/new-orleans-apologizes-1891-lynching-italian-americans-180971959/
https://www.history.com/news/the-grisly-story-of-americas-largest-lynching

Chris Thomas King (2022) *The Blues: The Authentic Narrative of My Music and Culture*: Chicago Review Press; (June 8, 2021)-pgs. 80-84

17. Racing Down the Blues -An interview with Adam Gussow- https://press.uchicago.edu/Misc/Chicago/310981in.html

In 1906, a close political election and some Atlanta Georgia newspapers, competing for readers and advertising revenue published false headlines about "'Black men assaulting white women'" and called for "a vigilante patrol'." The resulting mob violence of a "group of armed white men" caused at least 25 deaths and the destruction of homes and businesses. "Mobs then went after anyone with dark skin, pulling people off streetcars and stabbing them and dragging them out of businesses and into the street".

Rick Rojas (2023) In a 'City Too Busy to Hate,' New Attention to an Overlooked Race Massacre". New York Times. 2023/8/30.

https://www.nytimes.com/2023/09/30/us/atlanta-race-massacre-1906.html

Kuhn C, Mixon G (2005; edited 2022) Atlanta Race Massacre of 1906. https://www.georgiaencyclopedia.org/articles/history-archaeology/atlanta-race-massacre-of-1906/

The Atlanta Race Massacre of 1906 https://www.gpb.org/georgiastories/stories/race_massacre_of_1906

18. Adam Gussow (2002) "Shoot Myself a Cop": Mamie Smith's "Crazy Blues" as Social Text. Callaloo. Vol. 25, No. 1, Jazz Poetics: A Special Issue (Winter, 2002), pp. 8-44) Published By: The Johns Hopkins University Press; https://www.jstor.org/stable/3300383

19. .https://bakerartist.org/file/lynching-laura-and-ld-nelson-original-lynching-postcard and https://www.abhmuseum.org/oklahoma-lynching-victims-memorial/

20. https://www.thehistorycenter.org/exhibition/the-ocoee-massacre/

21. https://www.neh.gov/article/1921-tulsa-massacre

22. "Racial Propaganda Among Negros Growing and Increase of Mod Violence Set Out In Senate Brief for Federal Inquiry" New York Times. October 5, 1919; pg. 11

23. Koening K (2002) Jazz In Print, 1859-1929. An Anthology of Early Source Readings in Jazz History. Pendragon Press (July 7 2002). Pg. 202.

24. Petrusich Amanda (2021) *Merging Lanes-The notion of genre is disappearing. What comes next?*

The New Yorker, March 15, 2021, Pg. 68. https://www.newyorker.com/magazine/2021/03/15/genre-is-disappearing-what-comes-next

25. Lieb. Op. Cit- pg 41

26. Norman Kelley Editor Dr. Reebee Garofalo (2005) R&B (Rhythm and Business): The Political Economy of Black Music. Akashic Books (Aug. 1 2005); Blakemore Erin (2019) How 'Race Records' Turned Black Music Into Big Business. https://www.history.com/news/race-records-bessie-smith-big-bill-broonzy-music-business; Cole Tom (2013) Records: The Label Inadvertently Crucial To The Blues https://www.npr.org/sections/therecord/2013/11/02/242428973/paramount-records-the-label-inadvertently-crucial-to-the-blues

References

Andersson PA (2001) Deep River: Music and Memory in Harlem Renaissance Thought (New Americanists). Duke University Press.

Banerji R (2012) W.C. Handy's Blues: the Song Of 1912. https://www.bbc.com/news/magazine-20769518

Brooks Daphne (2020) 100 Years Ago, "Crazy Mama" Sparked A Revolution For Black Women Fans. New York Times. August 19, 2020. https://www.nytimes.com/2020/08/10/arts/music/mamie-smith-crazy-blues.html

Lott Eric (1993) Love & Theft: Blackface Minstrelsy and the American Working Class. Oxford University Press.

For a background history of blues artists and the blues record market in the early 20th Century:
https://www.loc.gov/static/programs/national-recording-preservation-board/documents/CrazyBlues.pdf

2

Some These Days I'll Be Gone

Yeah, most collectors are white men who started collecting in the second half of the 20th century and have enough money to travel and buy records. It's these privileged white people collecting this music from disenfranchised African Americans. There is something uncomfortable, I think, for a lot of people, myself included, about that exchange.
-Amanda Petrusich

Not to question the Blues Mafia's love of the blues, but when it comes to collecting, profit always depends on scarcity and demand; myth and legend, invented or real, help too.

Few invented better than the Blues Mafia, who, in the late 1950s-1960s, focused on artists who had sold little in the 1920s and early 1930s, especially those who had been recorded on low quality, easy to scratch and break, shellac records that gave on 78 rpm records a crackling, haunted sound. There was gold in those failures.

A record by Tommy Johnson (the scarcity of his records may be due to the reported problems he had in the Paramount recording studio in Wisconsin, hitting wrong notes and more than the occasional shot of whiskey) was initially purchased for a few cents but later sold for a reported $37,000.00 USD. 27

The songs that Johnson did record, however, like "Canned Heat Blues" (the inspiration for the 1960s hit band "Canned Heat") later became standards, including, "Cool Drink of Water Blues", "Lonesome Ole Train" and "Big Boy Blues" (the latter was covered by Homesick James and renamed "Lonesome Blues") that was the inspiration (together with Floyd Jones' "Dark Roads") for the 1960s' hit "On The Road Again" by Canned Heat (Top 20 in 10 countries). Johnson is also the first to have told the story that he sold his soul to the devil at a crossroads, a story later associated with Robert Johnson. 28

Legend tells us that the Blue Mafia was born after James McKune happened to find a battered copy of the Paramount disc, serial number 13110, "Some These Days I'll Be Gone" by Charley Patton. McKune was so mesmerized by the song that he began to seek out other recordings by Paramount, soon triggering a wholesale rush of collectors. 29

James McKune, who has been described as "a social isolate, closeted homosexual and alcoholic", reportedly could neither sing nor play an instrument, had worked as a re-write man on the New York Times, drifted into "an itinerant life," and who was murdered in a cheap flophouse, seems a strange choice to be the anointed one in defining the history of the blues. 30

But McKune was, in many ways, the founder and catalyst for The Blues Mafia, discovering and promoting forgotten blues records that had been left to rot and drown. When Paramount went out of business in the early 1930s, workers, who had lost their jobs, threw unsold 78 rpm records into the Milwaukee River. Years later, people with diving gear dove into the river, looking for the 78s and their newfound value in cold, hard cash.

Many of these records from the 1920s and 30s, by long forgotten artists, had sold few copies at the time of their release, but for McKune and other collectors of The Blues Mafia, the lack of sales were the reigning definitions of truth and authenticity, the more obscure the record the better. They argued that Patton, Skip James, Son House and Robert Johnson were "primitive, tormented genius".

McKune would write columns for Vintage Jazz Mart (VJM) magazine, with "the clear intention to establish which singers of country blues [his term] are 'great', and which are not…If you wanted to make a case for a white man attempting to write the blues canon, you could start with McKune's VJM columns, where he wrote that he was interested in 'knowing who the great blues singers were, not the ones who sold the best'."[31]

The problem with the Blues Mafia was their definition of "authentic blues". They created the myth of men who came in from the fields, grabbed a guitar, and "sang their pain without concern for attention or financial reward". "They wanted an heroic black primitive, the authentic voice of the working man…"

These collectors argued that musicians who "stayed at home", played a more "authentic" version of blues and jazz given their day-to-day experiences with prejudice, racial violence and abuse, compared to those artists who built their musical careers in the nightclubs and the recording studios of New York and Chicago. Female blues singers who had created the blues genre, popularized it and sold well, no longer mattered in the eyes of the Blue Mafia.

One problem with this mythology is that many of the artists the Blues Mafia praise actually "were sophisticated entertainers playing in different contexts. They'd play blues in a juke at night, then gospel at a church picnic, and the following night parties…Robert Johnson and musicians like him could play polkas and jigs-they weren't limited to 'black' repertoire…There's ugly stuff about how Alan Lomax brought Leadbelly up to New York to perform and made him dress up in prison uniform when Leadbelly wanted to wear a tux and sing ballads." 32

Folklorists such as John and Alan Lomax began with a predetermination of Black inferiority, and then proceeded to screen out any talent or persons that would "taint" their "scientific" data of primitiveness.

-Chris Thomas King 33

Another problem with this great splurge of mythology, blues artists championed by the Blues Mafia often weren't recorded fresh from cotton fields, but in Paramount studios either in Chicago, Illinois, or Grafton, Wisconsin (the latter notorious for the poor quality of its recordings). These artists included

Charley Patton, Blind Lemon Jefferson, Jelly Roll Morton, Skip James and Son House.

Between 1929 and 1932 alone, it's been argued that over 1,600 songs were recorded in Grafton; the output is cited to account for about 1/4 of the so-called "race records" of the era. In contrast, it has been estimated that about 20,000 "race" records, mostly of country blues, gospel, preaching and comedy, were produced between 1922 and 1932. 34

The record labels for Paramount usually referred to "The New York Recording Laboratories" that operated between 1917 and 1933 as a subsidiary of the Wisconsin Chair Company of Port Washington, Wisconsin (as detailed by Amanda Petrusich in her fascinating book, *Do Not Sell at Any Price: The Wild, Obsessive Hunt for the World's Rarest 78 rpm Records*). 35

Sergio Gonzalez, an assistant professor at Marquette University, noted that many of the Paramount artists never received royalties for their work, and that while they could record there, Grafton was not a "safe" place to stay due to racism; to sleep and eat the artists would have to travel to Port Washington or to Milwaukee. 36

Jack White, lead guitarist for the White Stripes, through his record company "Third Man Records" together with Revenant Records, released *The Rise and Fall of Paramount Records Vols. 1 and 2*, that included 800 tracks from the early days of the Wisconsin label. 37

In Robert Palmer's much praised book "Deep Blues", he seems to have accepted the Blues Mafia definition of who and what were defined as "authentic blues" without question. Palmer surprisingly devoted only one paragraph out of 310 paperback pages to Mamie Smith and "Crazy Blues". Although he acknowledged that this record alerted "record executives to a vast untapped market" and resulted in the many blues recordings that followed, "Almost all by of them by women", he dismissed "Crazy Blues" as "more a vaudeville tune than a blues"; then wrote how, beginning in 1923, "authentic down-home blues singers found their way onto records" and identified four male and no female, singers. If you scroll down the Index of Palmer's book, the names Percy Bradford and Fred Hagar are nowhere to be found. Ma Rainey has one mention but only in reference to her first hearing the blues in 1902 (with no reference to her classic song "See See Rider" which will be reviewed shortly). Bessie Smith also receives only one mention about how she and other "jazz-accompanied women retained their popularity". Most of the other women blues singers, including Ethel Waters, discussed earlier in this book, as well as blues standards such "Stormy Monday" and "Nobody Knows You When You're Down and Out", are nowhere to be found in the Index to "Deep Blues". Which, with all due respect to Robert Palmer, given the title of his book, is bizarre. 38

Beginning in the 1960s, the "Original Jazz Library" record company, founded by members of the Blues Mafia, Pete Whelan with Bill Givens, issued a series of albums that were notable for their early focus on blues artists who had few sales during the 1920s-30s. They rationalized this focus by arguing that their selections would be based on "musical merit alone", that earlier blues reissues by other record companies that had featured quality recordings with low noise and few scratches, had missed what OJL unilaterally now declared were "great performances". As for the low sales figures of many of their OJL artists, they argued that this happened because these musicians bravely stayed home and therefore recorded the least! 39 Scarcity and mythical heroes never hurt the appeal for record collectors.

This wild, mushroom-cloud-explosion of mythological blues history blasted through the musical world, blowing away the reputations and soon-to-be-ignored-and-forgotten voices of too many female blues singers of the 1920s.

https://originjazz.com/releases/

More recent assessments of the Blues Mafia have not been kind.

- Amanda Petrusich in, her book "Do Not Sell At Any Price" quotes Ian Nagoski's assertion: 40

'Skip James does not represent pre-war blues. Skip James- who had few sales- is a weirdo. He's a freak. He doesn't really fit in, and the fact that he's such a big part of the blues canon is a direct result of the blues canon having been written by white men."

- Chris Thomas King, blues musician and author of *The Blues: The Authentic Narrative of My Music and Culture*:

> *"The Blues Mafia represents a motley crew of gatekeepers and white cultural brokers. The Blues Mafia represents the existential antagonists to my iconoclastic art."*
> *"Moreover, this motley crew, motivated by greed, purposely obfuscated the truth, replacing it with myths, fairy tales, and half truths."* 41

King does acknowledge, however, that if not for collectors and academics like Gayle Dean Wardlow, John Lomax, Alan Lomax, and Dick Waterman, [Or Robert "Mack" McCormick and Steve LaVere who were able provide an in depth look at Robert Johnson and his music] plus writers like Clyde Woods and Amiri Baraka, many blues artists may never have been rediscovered.

"The historiography of the blues was built by White sociologist, folklorists, and record collectors. Their recordings and documents are indispensable. Indeed, I commend them for preserving and documenting noncommercial aspects of my culture that may have otherwise gone unnoticed." 42

One example is the blues collection of Robert "Mack" McCormick, who, as reported in the Washington Post by Geoff Edgars in 2023, struggled with paranoia and depression, borrowed rare photographs and material but never returned them, and had to part ways with the Johnson family after trying to gain exclusive control of Robert Johnson's material. These and other questionable actions caused the Smithsonian archivist for the project, Vanessa Broussard Simmons, to conclude that she did not like Mack McCormick. McCormick, however, did collect "590 reels of recordings and 160 boxes of material" that eventually were donated to The Smithsonian Institute by his daughter and resulted in the publication of the book "Biography of a Phantom: A Robert Johnson Blues Odyssey," edited by John Troutman, Curator of music and musical instruments at the American History Museum, plus a 3-CD, six LP of McCormick's field recordings of more than 30 artists. 42

"But, in reality, the loose consortium of White record collectors and researchers were driven by egotism, power, and avarice", writes King. 43

58

The Almost Fate Of The Blues

How much of what we know today as "the blues" and those artists critical to its development and growth, would have happened if not for the record "Crazy Blues"?

If Percy Bradford had given up his vision, if Fred Hagar hadn't taken on great risk, if Mamie Smith hadn't recorded "Crazy Blues", given the discrimination in the music industry coupled with the lynchings, racial riots, the growing influence of the Ku Klux Klan and planes dropping bombs on black businesses and homes, would any major record company executive have recorded a black blues artist, would any record company have sent out scouts to find blues musicians; would artists like Bessie Smith, Charley Patton, Ma Rainey, Son House or Robert Johnson ever have been discovered, much less recorded?

What of the blues artists who emerged, during the 1930s, that included singers like Joe Turner, Big Bill Broonzy, Tampa Red, Muddy Waters, Jimmy Rushing, Teddy Bunn, Jack Teagarden, Hot Lips Page and great blues instrumentalists like Memphis Minnie. Would they have been recorded, would they have had anywhere near the same impact on the development of rhythm and blues and rock n' roll?

However, Blues Mafia collectors who travelled to southern states, did find old 78 records and interviewed the artists who made them-e.g. Robert

Johnson, Son House, and Charley Patton, who proved a critical influence in the 1960s for English artists like Eric Clapton and Keith Richards; who, in turn, helped to popularize, and reintroduce, blues musicians like Muddy Waters, Sonny Boy Williamson and Buddy Guy to American audiences. This included once obscure artists such as singer/guitarist Blind Willie McTell whose song "Statesboro Blues" became a breakthrough hit for the Allman Brothers.

However, before history gets sucked into the whirling blades of the Blues Mafia's self-created myths, could any of this happened without the release of "Crazy Blues"?

"They [British players like Eric Clapton, Jeff Beck, Keith Richards] helped all of us in America...Black people looked bonded to a certain amount of music. And I don't bite my tongue, I think a lot of whites here in America didn't want their children to hear blues, but when the British guys started playing the blues and started coming here...

We had a television show in the '60s called Shindig. And the Rolling Stones were getting so big. They were taking over the world with music. And the television wanted to bring them on Shindig, and Mick Jagger said, 'I'll come if you let me bring Muddy Waters.' And they said, 'Who the hell is that?' Jagger said, 'You mean to tell me you don't know who Muddy Waters is? We named ourselves after his famous record, Rollin' Stone." 44

-Buddy Guy

"'Before the Rolling Stones', said Muddy Waters, "People over here (America) didn't know nothing about me *and didn't want to know anything about me. I was making race records, and I'm gonna tell it to you the way older people told it to the kids. If they'd buy my records, their parents would say, 'What the hell is that. Get that nigger record out of my house'. But then the Rolling Stones and those other groups come over here from England playing this music, and now, today, kids buy a record of mine, and they listen to it,...I play in places now don't have no black faces in there but our black faces....Those records I'm making now, that Johnny Winter producin', they're selling better than any of my old records ever did...This is the best point of my life that I'm living right now.' "* 45

"*One day in the early sixties, after Muddy Waters performed at the Newport Jazz Festival, Leonard Marshall was called into his dad's office. 'We're getting all these sales from white kids', Leonard Chess said, perplexed. "What's going on?" His son, hip to the British Invasion, knew.*"46

62

Covers, Racism and Rock n' Roll

Not all share this sentiment about cover versions of blues songs by English musicians.

Chris Thomas King, in his book *"The Blues: The Authentic Narrative of My Music and Culture"* wrote: "White middle class musicians quicky realized extraordinary wealth and fame awaited any White musicians who could rewrite and perform blues songs with an electric guitar and a rock n roll beat." 47

In an interview for his book, King said about Led Zeppelin's covers of blues songs:

"Zeppelin represents capitalism colonizing blues, mining for Gold records. We were barred from partaking in capitalism. We were reduced to miners. We couldn't rent castles and hire million-dollar gear and expert sound engineers for an hour, let alone months. That huge tone took capital and lots of it…Zeppelin wouldn't be Zeppelin if they had recorded in archaic conditions and with inferior equipment. Don't get me wrong, they still would have sounded pretty good, but not much better than Slim Harpo, Magic Sam, or Buddy Guy. Zeppelin and all those white capitalist blues bands sounded like a million dollars on FM radio. That heavy bombastic sound was drilled into the public with payola and cocaine until they submitted." 48

Re the allegation about "castles, million-dollar gear and expert sound engineers", Led Zeppelin's first album (that broke the band wide open around the world, hitting the Top Ten in the USA, United

Kingdom, Australia, and Top Twenty in 5 other countries) was recorded in Olympic Studios, Barnes (a district in London), England. BB King, Ray Charles and Ella Fitzgerald also recorded there.

Zeppelin's sessions for the first album were completed *before* Led Zeppelin had a recording contract, and were *produced, and paid for,* by the band's guitarist Jimmy Page. The total costs for the 36 hours of studio time was a reported £1,782.

Page had been a much-called-upon full time session musician before he joined the band The Yardbirds; after The Yardbirds broke up without honoring a tour contract, to avoid being sued, Page assembled musicians to complete The Yardbirds' contractual tour in Scandinavia. When that tour went surprising well, he decided to find a recording studio and to record the songs worked on during the tour. This group of musicians became "Led Zeppelin". 50

[Although blues musician and songwriter Willie Dixon was credited as the song writer on two songs of Zeppelin's first album, as well as on later albums, lawsuits subsequently claimed that Dixon was not given credit for "Bring It On Home" and "Whole Lotta Love." Both cases were settled out of court, and songwriting credit was given to Dixon on those songs; however, the repetitive opening guitar riff on "Whole Lotta Love" is Jimmy Page's alone.] 49

When King writes about the English "white capitalist blues bands" he often chooses to ignore the positive impact, as noted in the above, some of those bands had on American blues artists and the American record buying public.

As well, given King's comments about the "heavy bombastic" production of blues songs by English bands like Led Zeppelin, although King cites Jimi Hendrix as a critical influence, he chooses to ignore Jimi Hendrix's "huge tone" cover version of Bob Dylan's song "All Along The Watchtower". Musicologist Albin Zak argues, "The song itself owes...debt to Robert Johnson's fatalism in "Me And The Devil Blues" from 1938.

"The song itself draws together elements of ballad and blues traditions; and the two recordings treat this synthesis in very different ways even as they share the common ground of late 1960s rock. Dylan's is a spare, acoustic folk-rock rendition, while Hendrix's is an opulent electric spectacle whose sonic and syntactic conception unpacks the latent drama only suggested by the original. In the process, Hendrix offers an alternative answer to the song's existential dilemma implied in its lyrics and emphasized in its musical setting." 51

-Albin J. Zak

Chris Thomas King also writes that Bob Dylan's "Blowing In The Wind" is "based on the slave song 'No More Auction Block For Me. Many Thousands Gone'" as sung by Odetta and earlier by Paul Robson 52. A few pages later, King elevates this claim even higher, writing that "Blowing In The Wind" had been lifted from "the sentiment and melody" of "Auction Block". 52

Dylan certainly was familiar with the song and performed it at the Gaslight Café New York in 1962. The inspiration for the opening melody of "Blowing In The Wind" is clear, and Dylan has publicly acknowledged that "Blowing" follows "the same feeling" as "Auction" 52A. However, the lyrics, line lengths and rhythmic meter, are significantly different. Dylan's lyrical ability was one of the reasons that the outstanding record producer Tom Wilson - Sun Ra, Cecil Taylor, Frank Zappa, Lou Reed, Simon and Garfunkel, Dion, The Animals, Velvet Underground, Nico, and many more-agreed to work with Dylan. 53

Sam Cooke later cited Dylan's "Blowing in the Wind" as a critical inspiration for his inspirational song "A Change Is Gonna Come"; Dylan early songs had protested injustice like *The Death of Emmett Till, The Lonesome Death of Hattie Carroll* as well as the later *Hurricane*.

King can provide an invaluable perspective, which his book certainly does, however, at times, he fails to acknowledge the contributions of some of the musicians he has criticized with his argument that "a new wave of White Americans musicians who, for the first time, had the audacity to promote themselves as blues musicians…within blues…redefined by the Blues Mafia", and then proceeds to list John Hammond Sr. and Jr., Mike Bloomfield, Paul Butterfield of the Paul Butterfield Blues Band, Al Kooper, and Charlie Musselwhite. 54

King fails to mention that Mike Bloomfield was the lead guitar (other than Muddy Waters' guitar work) on Muddy Waters' highly successful album, "Fathers and Sons", released by Chess Records, and that Paul Butterfield was part of the backing band (that also included Otis Spann and Sam Lay). 55

In an interview he did for our book "Ride The Wild Wind-History of the Saxophone-1920-2021", **Derrick "Big" Walker** (sax and harmonica; who has played with artists such as Lowell Fulson, Percy Mayfield, Big Mama Thornton, Sonny Roads, Jimmy McCracklin, Jimmy Dawkins, Zora Young, and Sugar Pie De Santos) said 56:

https://www.youtube.com/watch?v=9wkdeakYMCs)

"The Paul Butterfield Blues Band did three iconic albums. The first was 'The Paul Butterfield Blues Band' with mostly classic blues songs, a couple of originals, but the next album 'East-West' was a revolution. They managed to mix jazz, blues and popular into something unique.

The title song 'East West' had elements of Dave Brubeck and John Coltrane, Eastern music, a spectacular solo by Michael Bloomfield and Paul Butterfield's harmonica playing, sometimes sounding like a saxophone, sometimes like a trumpet…something I had never heard before.

A lot of harmonica players around the world were inspired by that album, including me. I think Paul Butterfield is the most imitated harmonica player in history, along with Little Walter and Sonny Boy Williamson.

The third album, 'The Resurrection of Pig Boy Crabshaw' used more of a '50s style of blues song writing, like 'One More Heartache'- one of my favorite albums to date.

I would say if you want to play 'modern blues', that is not from the Mississippi Delta or strictly Chicago, you have to listen to these three albums. Paul also was a great singer with a wide range, and excellent songwriter. If you want to hear the iconic Paul Butterfield, listen to Muddy Waters' album 'Fathers and Sons', you can't get better blues than that album."

Sam Lay, an exceptional drummer to many- e.g. Little Walter, Willie Dixon, Howlin' Wolf, John Lee Hooker- a vocalist (e.g. "I Got My Mojo Working" with Paul Butterfield) and a member of both the Blues Hall of Fame and the Rock n' Roll Hall Of Fame, explained that due the popularity of Paul Butterfield and the enormous respect he earned from the music community, "venues opened that previously didn't feature blues music, venues now open to *all* musicians."

Chris Thomas King also questions the "real blues appropriations"[56A] of Mike Bloomfield and John Hammond because they had grown up in "wealthy homes", but largely fails to note their important contributions in music.

Bloomfield was born in Chicago and his parents, Harold and Dorothy did run a successful manufacturing business. Mike Bloomfield, described "As an indifferent and underachieving student at New Trier High School, …began to haunt South Side clubs where he heard and would eventually play with such giants as Muddy Waters and Howlin' Wolf…Muddy Waters praised Mike Bloomfield: 'When I first heard Michael, I knew he was gonna be a great guitar player… One of the greats' " [57]

Bloomfield played and was a co-producer of James Cotton's outstanding 1967 album "James Cotton Blues Band" (Gene Barge on tenor sax) on Verve Records.

https://www.youtube.com/watch?v=mO7WxQvwHjw

Derrick Walker joined Mike Bloomfield's band and played on Bloomfield's last album "Cruisin' for a Bruisin". Derrick's memories of Mike Bloomfield include: "One of the tours, the tour bus broke down, Michael got out, flagged down a big semi-truck, an 18-wheeler, told the driver the situation and convinced the driver to help us out. We loaded all our equipment, P.A. system, drum sets, the amplifiers, and instruments; the guy drove us all the way to the gig. Michael had this influence with people, they trusted him, liked him.

I ended up living with Michael for a while at his house in Mill Valley, due to a relationship problem I was having. He had an old broken down, dilapidated

Impala car with bald tires and he had me drive down to buy wine and groceries. When I was there, he did not do drugs. Michael liked to live very simply, had no interest in wealth or fame.

He had a large record collection that filled one wall of his house, lots of books, and often would be up all night playing the piano due to chronic sleep problems. Other musicians dropped in all the time after gigs because they knew he would always be up, like Bob Dylan (the only musician who ever intimidated me).

He and the record producer Norman Dayron also played a trick on me. They put me in a recording booth to play the harmonica on a song called 'Country Mechanic' (written by Nick Gravenites). Said they were going to run the track by me to warm up on it a little bit before we start to record. Track starts, I play around a little bit on it, track ends. I say: 'O.k. I'm ready. Are you going to record the track now?'

They say, 'Thank you'.

I say, 'For what?'

They say, 'We got it'.

Michael told me, 'Your first impression of the track is the real one. The first thing that you play is your real inspiration, 'cause after that you're just trying to copy yourself.'

I've used that, used that way of thinking, in all my subsequent recording sessions. Plus, Michael and Norman told me after, 'You're the best and you can tell people we said that' and I didn't know what to say because I didn't really believe that, but that has stayed with me. I realized that what they meant is that I was sincere, honest, and that I played traditional, didn't just play licks but listened to the music and found myself in it."58

John Hammond Jr. came from a wealthy family but was a critically important record producer, including Count Basie and Billie Holiday, and was regarded as a strong proponent of racial integration in the music business. He organized the first of two historic "Spirituals to Swing" concerts (discussed later), which chronicled the history of "Black jazz and blues" and was Hammond's effort to break the segregation that prevented "black musicians" from appearing in major entertainment centers.

Mr. King also doesn't discuss the impact of YouTube.

Darryl Dixon, Dave Watson-Chops Horns

Alicia Keys, Bob Dylan, Usher, George Clinton's Parliament- Funkadelic, The Rolling Stones, Maceo Parker, The Police, Grandmaster Flash and The Furious Five, Mariah Carey, Boyz II Men, Fred Wesley, Lionel Hampton, Bonnie Raitt, Chaka Khan, Lenny Kravitz, Gladys Knight, Stevie Wonder, Luther Vandross are just a few of the musicians they have played with) said in their interview for the book "Ride The Wild Wind; History of The Saxophone 1920-1921" 58:

DW: "In February, we had Black History month, it's not black history, it's American history. There are some people who want to know the truth, but there are people who don't want to change the way things have been."

DD: "We didn't have YouTube when we were growing up. When we were growing up, to hear the music we liked, you had to go to clubs, but a lot of young kids couldn't get into clubs. Like a lot of white kids who liked jazz and blues couldn't get into clubs because they were black clubs, but now with YouTube, it transcends the race issue. Now, you can look and hear the kind of music you want to hear, the race issue rarely comes up.

Now, you get 10 year old drummers who can play like Billy Cobham and they don't give a damn if he's black, they just like what's he's doing. And that is what they hone in on. That's really good for young kids and their whole attitude when it comes to race and who did what first and so on, because they see what they want to see without being tainted by the race issue as it was back in the day."

Over The Mountains, Across The Seas

Thanks to cover versions, blues songs and artists continue to reach across decades and inspire new generations.

Ma Rainey recorded the traditional blues song "See See Rider Blues" for Paramount Records, in 1924, with a band that included Louis Armstrong on cornet and Fletcher Henderson on piano (Lena Arent wrote the first three rhymed couplets at the beginning of the song). 59

- "See See Rider", and its alternative versions and titles, has been covered by artists nearly 380 times in blues, rock, r&b, folk, country, and jazz, with the title and lyrics occasionally changing.
- In the 1950s, a version by Chuck Willis - entitled "C.C. Rider"- reigned as the initial theme song for the most popular rock and roll television show in the USA, "American Bandstand".
- A Grammy Hall Of Fame Award was given in 2004 and the song and has been recognized by National Recording Registry of The Library of Congress U.S.A. and The Blues Foundation as" a classic of blues recording". 60

Artists who have covered this song include:
-Lead Belly-1940,
-Wee Bea Booze-1943- Number One on Billboard's Harlem Hit Parade,

-Chuck Willis' "C.C. Rider", 1957, Number One R&B charts, Number 12 Billboard's Top 100 (Gene Barge tenor)

-LaVern Baker, "See See Rider" (Buddy Lucas tenor) 1963 –Number 9 R&B charts, Number 34 on Billboard's Top 100

-B. B King on the album "Confessing The Blues", 1965

-"Jenny Take A Ride" by Mitch Ryder and The Detroit Wheels, 1965- Number 10 Billboard's Top 100,

-The Animals, 1966, Number 10, Billboard's Top 100,

-Plus, country music's Charlie Rich, folk music's Ian and Sylvia, Ella Fitzgerald, Archie Shepp, and Regina Carter to name just a few.

Cover versions of recordings remain a staple of the music industry. In each year of the 20th and 21st Century to date (2023), lists have been published of "The Best Cover Songs".

In 2023, Elvis Costello when asked to comment on a song by Olivio Rodrigo that some thought was influenced by a Costello song. He replied: "This is fine by me…It's how rock and roll works. You take the broken pieces of another thrill and make a brand new toy. That's what I did…", referring to the Bob Dylan and Chuck Berry songs ("Subterranean Homesick Blues" and "Too Much Monkey Business") that influenced Costello's song "Pump It Up". 61

Perry Bradford's, 1920s, "Keep A Knockin'" became a cornerstone hit in the early days of rock n' roll when covered by Little Richard (earlier and *very* different covers had been done by Louis Jordan and Jimmy Dorsey).

Although Little Richard's version only referred to himself ("Richard Perriman") as the songwriter, Little Richard said, "Everything happens for a reason. Who knew that the style Perry was developing in the Twenties would lead to Rock and Roll."

Notes

27. Wardlow Gayle D. (1988) Chasin' That Devil Music: Searching For The Blues. Backbeat Books, 1988. Pg. 51

28. Ibid. pg 187-189

29. Amanda Petrusich; *Do Not Sell at Any Price: The Wild, Obsessive Hunt for the World's Rarest 78 rpm Records.* Scribner; Reprint edition (June 9, 2015); Lisa Hix (2014) Why Nerdy White Guys Who Love the Blues Are Obsessed With a Wisconsin Chair Factory. August 8th, 2014 https://www.collectorsweekly.com/articles/why-nerdy-white-guys-who-love-the-blues-are-obsessed-with-a-wisconsin-chair-factory/

30. Brown Mike (2007) Fairy tales of happy slaves-a Book *Review* of "In Search of the Blues: Black Voices, White Visions" by Marybeth Hamilton. The Telegraph. Feb 4, 2007. https://www.telegraph.co.uk/culture/books/3662955/Fairy-tales-of-happy-slaves.html

31. https://genius.com/Greil-marcus-the-old-weird-america-excerpt-annotated; https://www.bobdylan-comewritersandcritics.com/pages/books/invisibleUS97hb.htm

32. "http://www.bluesandrhythm.co.uk/wp-content/uploads/2014/08/Pages-from-BR-305-Final-Proof-TB-2.pdf

33. https://www.songfacts.com/blog/writing/debunking-blues-history-myths-with-author-chris-thomas-king

34. https://medium.com/@Vinylmint/history-of-the-record-industry-1920-1950s-6d491d7cb606

35. Amanda Petrusich (2014) *Do Not Sell at Any Price: The Wild, Obsessive Hunt for the World's Rarest 78 rpm Records* Op. cit.

36. https://www.collectorsweekly.com/articles/why-nerdy-white-guys-who-love-the-blues-are-obsessed-with-a-wisconsin-chair-factory/
https://spectrumnews1.com/wi/milwaukee/news/2022/02/18/the-paramount-records-story--how-grafton-left-an-unlikely-legacy-on-american-blues-music
https://statetrunktour.com/paramount-records
https://www.bbc.com/culture/article/20210216-the-forgotten-story-of-americas-first-black-superstars

37. https://thirdmanrecords.com/products/the-rise-and-fall-of-paramount-records-1917-1932-volume-1 Also see: Nick Perls's "Yazoo Records" that focused largely on 78 rpm records from the 1920s from artists such as Charly Patton and Blind Blake as well as his second label "Blue Goose Records". https://www.wirz.de/music/yazoo.htm

38. Palmer Robert (1982) *Deep Blues: A Musical and Cultural History of the Mississippi Delta.* Penguin Books (July 29, 1982) pg. 106.

39. Templeton R (2014) Original Jazz Library http://www.bluesandrhythm.co.uk/wp-content/uploads/2014/08/Pages-from-BR-305-Final-Proof-TB-2.pdf

40. Ibid and Petrusich Op. Cit.

41. Chris Thomas King, blues musician and author of *The Blues: The Authentic Narrative of My Music and Culture*: Chicago Review Press; (June 8, 2021)-*page xiii*

42. Ibid. pg. xiii; Edgars G (2023) "He spent a lifetime collecting the blues. The Smithsonian listened." Washington Post (October 14, 2023). https://www.washingtonpost.com/entertainment/music/2023/10/14/smithsonian-folkways-robert-mccormick/

43. Ibid. xvi; https://www.songfacts.com/blog/writing/debunking-blues-history-myths-with-author-chris-thomas-kin

https://www.chicagoreviewpress.com/blues--the-products-9781641604444.php?page_id=21

44. Horsley Jonathan (2021) *Buddy Guy: "When you pick up a guitar, you have something of your own, even if you don't recognize it."*

https://www.guitarworld.com/features/buddy-guy

45. Palmer Op.cit. pgs 259-260

46. John Seabrook (2023) Chess Records, Revived; New Yorker. Sept. 11, 2023

47. King Op cit. pg 181

48. https://www.songfacts.com/blog/writing/debunking-blues-history-myths-with-author-chris-thomas-king

49. https://www.loudersound.com/features/how-the-blues-was-stolen

https://www.rollingstone.com/politics/politics-lists/songs-on-trial-12-landmark-music-copyright-cases-166396/led-zeppelin-vs-willie-dixon-1972-64390/

50. https://www.rollingstone.com/music/music-features/how-led-zeppelin-formed-718697/

51. Albin J. Zak, III (2005) Bob Dylan and Jimi Hendrix: Juxtaposition and Transformation "All along the Watchtower"; *Journal of the American Musicological Society* (2005) 57 (3): 599–644.

52. King Op. cit.pg. 175, 179

52A. https://secondhandsongs.com/work/2673

53. https://www.texasmonthly.com/arts-entertainment/the-greatest-music-producer-youve-never-heard-of-is/

https://www.producertomwilson.com/

https://musicaficionado.blog/2021/06/30/tom-wilson-producer-part-1/

For a review of relevant musical forms http://www.lipscomb.umn.edu/rock/ReviewForms.htm

54. King Op. cit. pg. 179

55. Havers R (2023) How Muddy Waters' 'Father And Sons' Reinstated The King of the Blues". April 21, 2023.

https://www.udiscovermusic.com/stories/rediscover-muddy-waters-fathers-and-sons/

56. Sharpe N, Laughter J (2022) Ride The Wild Wind-History of the Saxophone-1920-2021"

https://www.amazon.com/Ride-Wild-Wind-History-Interviews-ebook/dp/B09L79RQ4G

56A. King Op. cit. pg. 179

57. Rick Kogan (2016) *Michael Bloomfield's life captured in new biography.* Chicago Tribune Sep 12,

2016; the article quotes from Ed Ward's biography of Mike Bloomfield.

58. Sharpe Op. cit.

59. Lieb Op. cit. pg.64.

60. https://blues.org/blues_hof_inductee/see-see-rider-blues-ma-rainey/ https://www.bbc.com/culture/article/20210216-the-forgotten-story-of-americas-first-black-superstars

61. https://www.billboard.com/music/rock/elvis-costello-reacts-olivia-rodrigo-brutal-comparison-9594517/

https://www.nytimes.com/2023/04/27/arts/music/music-copyright-lawsuits-ed-sheeran-blurred-lines.html

3

West End Blues
By Neil Sharpe

New Orleans, 1913. Late spring. The soft aroma of magnolia trees. Blossoms drifting free on the warm air, heavy and sweet. Banana boats. Gin mills. Night clubs. Friends singing in the nights.

Daddy's old '38' pistol. Fired loud above the racket of firecrackers, honky tonks, and hot jazz. A turning point that launched a music career.

Louis Armstrong had begun to feel the music inside him, a new style they called "jass". At thirteen years old, he sang in a quartet that was, he wrote, "big" for the new jazz songs.

New Year's Eve. 1913. "A heap of noise" filled the air. Young Louis would show them all up. With his dad's .38. Fired it off. Cop hears, arrests Louis. Everything changes.

"I do believe that my whole success goes back to that time I was arrested at the age of thirteen. Because then, I had to quit running around and learn something. Most of all, I began to learn music." 62

"Jazz was the grandaddy of swing music. Came out of old negro songs and spirituals. The regular beat of jazz

syncopation probably came out of the strumming of the banjos slaves learned to play before the Civil War".

Louis Armstrong took special note of, "...Buddy Bolden. So far as any of us know and just about saw jazz born, this boy was really the first of them all. He blazed himself into New Orleans with his cornet, as early as 1905...undoubtedly the first great individual jazz player...just a one man genius that was ahead of 'em, all-too good for this time." 63

Louis listened to Buddy Bolden, blowing so loud and strong "you could hear him a mile away", playing what they would call "Swing" thirty years later.

"Buddy Bolden, a key figure in the development of New Orleans' ragtime music. a.k.a. "jass"...whose legend and scattered first-person accounts credit as the earliest jazz musician...By the time Bolden and Bechet began playing jazz, the Americanization of African music had already begun, and with it came the Africanization of American music...This dynamic, so essential to the history of jazz, remains powerful even in the present day..." 64

Jazz began to spread via the excursion boats that would call at ports along the Mississippi River. From New Orleans to St. Paul. To Chicago, New York, San Francisco...

"Many of the old plantation songs...were being played in the new jazz rhythms and new tunes were being composed that were hotter and better- "Memphis Blues" and "St. Louis Blues"...written by W.C. Handy. He had caught jazz from some on the players on the Mississippi River boats." 65

Some, however, take angry issue with use of the term "jazz". Chris Thomas King, in his book "The Blues- The Authentic Narrative of My Music and Culture", writing more than a hundred years later, argues that jazz was a "mindless" word and what "White folks called the blues", and that Miles Davis "often would scold critics for using the word jazz to describe his music". [66]

King writes: "White superiority is an Anglo-Saxon creation to which Black achievement, or equality, is wildly supressed as though it were kryptonite." He argues that labels like "Dixieland jazz", "swing", "rock n' roll" are a "rebrand and whitewash of the blues". "Relabeling those blues pioneers' music as *jazz* or *Dixieland* neither captured the essence of their music nor its cultural significance." [67]

Imani Uzuri, composer and vocalist, however, has argued that "Jazz comes out of spirituals and the blues, and is embedded with codes of escaping enslavement." "There's always been an understanding about resistance in jazz and creative music."[68]

King acknowledges that he has read Armstrong's "Swing Time" but chooses to ignore Louis Armstrong's comments on "jazz" and "swing" or to acknowledge that Armstrong had no issues with the use of these terms.

The new music style, jazz, with its core roots in blues and ragtime that also incorporated French musical influences like biguine, found full flower in the 1920s-1930s.

But what some thought was the promised land of a recording contract, in the 1920s, could be more like trying to wade through swamp lands with alligators eager to rip and tear than what recorded companies promoted as a gold-plated road to fortune and flash-bulb flashing glory.

In a Chicago recording studio, in the late 1920s, artists got one shot, one take, period. Then they waited. Waited for two or three weeks to see if their playing made the grade. If it didn't, they were done and gone, unless they had the money to go back into the studio and pay, pay, and pay, but again with no guarantee of success. No exceptions to the rule, even for the greats like Louis Armstrong.

In 1928, 78 rpm records couldn't play back a take without affecting the wax master to such a point that it would be "unusable for commercial release". That's why the Louis Armstrong and his band "His Hot Five", featuring the great Earl Hines on piano, did not hear the first recorded version of "West End Blues" until it was finished by the studio a few weeks later. [69]

"When it first came out, Louis [Armstrong] and I stayed by that recording practically an hour and a half to two hours and we just knocked each other out because we had no idea it was gonna turn out as good as it did." [70]

"Louis was surprised when the record came out, 'cause…you know, we'd forgotten we'd recorded it' …." [70]

The immortal "West End Blues", on Okeh Records, (originally recorded by King Olivier), was released on

June 28, 1928. It would become, "The most well-known record in the history of jazz".

- *"It's like another whole concept of a fanfare. Armstrong goes into two different times...uses arpeggios all these chromatic notes, he uses the sound of the blues, everything is in there, but is so natural it sounds very simple, but let me tell you it's hard to hit that D...When you hear him play it, its brilliant but so natural too."* - Wynton Marsalis

- *"I heard a record Louis Armstrong made called the 'West End Blues'...and I thought, this is wonderful! And I liked the feeling I got from it...Sometimes the record would make me so sad I'd cry up a storm. Other times the same damn record would make me so happy"*. Billie Holiday 71

- West End Blues *"starts with a surprise, ...four biting quarter notes by way of fanfare then vaults upward through a chain of interlocking triplet arpeggios to a fiery high C...the most technically demanding passage to have been recorded by a jazz trumpeter up to that time..."* 72

Eli Oberstein, who, four years later, signed Armstrong to an exclusive contract with Victor Records, said that "West End Blues" "was the first record that really made a wide inroad...

"When I say, made him well known, I mean to the country at large...". However, *"...the people who bought his records in 1928, consisted mainly of Armstrong's fellow

*musicians and 'college students, who right now are crazy about 'hot' music...the average layman does not understand this type of work."*73

Ethel Waters released a cover version within days of the release.

Strangely, the one person who did not view "West End Blues" as his greatest recording was Louis Armstrong. In his book "Swing That Music", Armstrong acknowledged that although "West End Blues "was a favorite of his, the solo that he really wanted to talk about was from the Broadway show "Hot Chocolates".

"I introduced the song Ain't Misbehavin', playing a trumpet solo in the high register. From the first time I heard it, that song used to "send" me. I wood-shedded it until I could play all around it...I believe that great song, and the chance I got to play it, did a lot to make me better known all over the country." 74

Louis wasn't the only one who didn't forever fall in love with West End Blues. When selecting the 27 pieces of music to send out into the immortal cosmos on the satellite Voyager, "Melancholy Blues," recorded by Louis Armstrong and his Hot Seven a year earlier, in 1927, was selected instead of "West End Blues".

After recording "West End Blues", Earl Hines left for gigs in New York. When he returned, he discovered that he had been replaced. No problem! With Chicago nightclubs -at least 100 number- in full roar, Hines was destined to send radiant clouds of musical inspiration across the land via national radio, his angelic chords bringing newly born light to eyes haunted by the brutal grinding of the Great Depression. Hines' orchestra (which, from time to time, included Dizzy Gillespie, Charlie Parker, Sarah Vaughn, Nat King Cole and Teddy Wilson) and his popular radio show, during the 1930s, helped to give relief and rescue to a United States that had gone into a harsh, financial, deep freeze.

Jazz artists (in no particular order) included Kid Ory's Original Creole Jazz Band, Louis Armstrong and the Fletcher Henderson Dance Band (which included tenor sax player Coleman Hawkins), Lovie Austin and Her Blues Serenaders, Duke Ellington, Paul Whiteman Orchestra, Jelly Roll Morton and the New Orleans Rhythm Kings later named Jelly Roll and the Red Hot Peppers (the source for the name of the rock band "Red Hot Chili Peppers" formed in the 1980s).

Jazz salvaged and soothed those nervous, jabbering years, kept weary hearts dreaming of summer blue with songs that quickly became classic standards in the American Song Book.

Valaida Snow was an exceptional trumpet player who Louis Armstrong called the "second best jazz trumpet player" next to him.

Louis' wife, Lil Hardin Armstrong, was a jazz pianist, band leader, composer, and arranger whose songs were covered and even became hits later in the 1950s and 1960s for Ray Charles ("Just A Thrill") and Ringo Starr of The Beatles ("Bad Boy"). [75]

Louis Armstrong's influence would prove far reaching. One of the great tenor sax players of rock n' roll, Lee Allen, said that Armstrong's use of quarter notes affected his style of phrasing (according to Armstrong, the sax came into general use about 1917).

Far more importantly, music began to attack the senseless screaming and blood wars of prejudice and blind hatred.

The fight was on...

Notes

62. Armstrong Louis (1936; 1993) Swing That Music. DaCapo Press Armstrong Louis (1936) Swing That Music. De Capo Press Edition 1993. Unabridged republication of the edition published in New York in 1936 with a new Introduction by Dan Morgensterm (original Introduction by Rudy Vallee)-pg 5;

Teachout Terry (2009) Pops-A Life of Louis Armstrong; Houghton Mifflikeep; Harcourt, New York

63. Ibid Pg. 12
64. Gioia T (1997) The History of Jazz. https://archive.nytimes.com/www.nytimes.com/books/first/g/gioia-jazz.html
65. Armstrong op cit. pg. 13
66. King op. cit. pg. xiv
67. King op. cit. pg. 71
68. Michelle Mercer (2018) Imani Uzuri. https://www.npr.org/sections/therecord/2018/04/30/607142770/a-map-to-the-line-and-how-not-to-cross-it-a-code-of-conduct-for-the-performing-a
69. Armstrong op cit. Pg 115
70. Ibid. pg. 112
71. Billie Holiday (2006) Lady Sings the Blues: originally printed 1956; Harlem Moon and Broadway Books paperback edition 2006: pg. 115
72. Armstrong op. cit. pg 112
73. Ibid. pg. 91
74. Ibid. pg. 14

75. Alexandra Daoud (20170 Women In Jazz: 10 Ladies Who Changed Music Forever https://projectrevolver.org/features/articles/women-jazz-10-ladies-changed-music-forever/

4

Strange Fruit
By Neil Sharpe

"No one is going to give you the education you need to overthrow them. Nobody is going to teach you your true history, teach you your true heroes, if they know that that knowledge will help set you free."
— Assata Shakur

Percy's vision of a jazz band to back Mamie Smith foreshadowed the immense growth of jazz during the 1920s-30s, the time period known as "The Jazz Age". As argued by Whitney Balliett, "Stripped to the essentials, the blues, which are a highly malleable form, had no set melody…and specifically designed for jazz improvisation".

Duke Ellington's "It Don't Mean a Thing If It Ain't Got That Swing" (released in 1932, with Johnny Hodges on alto sax- named one of Time Magazine's Top 100 songs of the 20th Century; inducted into the Grammy Hall of Fame in 2008), followed by Benny Goodman's "Ain't Cha Glad" clearly announced to all that a new kid was in town with a made-for-the-wounded music for those suffering in the Great Depression.

With its "notes like cosmic kisses", swing promised that no matter what had been ripped away due to greed and indifference, if people gave the music a chance, whether on a dance or kitchen dirt floor, swing could lift their hearts high above the Depression and set sail towards a new horizon shimmering with the promise of summer blue. 76

Although Louis Armstrong had heard the music that they now called "swing" in New Orleans in the early 1900s, what was new were the 16-25 piece big bands and their hits that quickly became part of The Great American Song Book.

Charles Gillette, in his exceptional book "Sound of the City" (page 4), writes that between 1937-1941, of 43 records that sold over a million, twenty nine were by the bands.

- Artie Shaw- "Begin the Beguine" (1938) and "Stardust" (1940) Frank Sinatra the vocalist (1941)
- Benny Goodman- "Stompin' at the Savoy" (1936); "Sing, Sing, Sing (With a Swing)" (1938)
- Count Basie- "Lady Be Good" (1936); "One O'Clock Jump" (1937)
- Cab Calloway- "Minnie the Moocher (The Ho Do Ho Song)" (1931); Jump and Jive (1939)
- Duke Ellington- "Sophisticated Lady" (1932); "In A Sentimental Mood" (1934); "I Let A Song Go Out Of My Heart (1938); "Take The A Train" (1939)

- Fats Waller- "Ain't Misbehaving"- 1929
- Glenn Miller- "In the Mood" (1939); "Moonlight Serenade" (1939); "Pennsylvania 6-5000" (1940)
- Harry Richman with Earl Burtnett and His Los Angeles Biltmore Hotel Orchestra- "Puttin' on the Ritz" (1930)
- Jimmy McHugh and Dorothy Fields "On the Sunny Side of the Street" (1930)- "I'm in the Mood for Love" (1935)
- Guy Lombardo and His Royal Canadians whose hit, "Auld Lang Syne", became a New Year's tradition from 1929 until the late 1970s. This band sold an estimated 100-200 million records.
- Tommy Dorsey- "I'm Getting Sentimental Over You" (1932)
Tommy Dorsey with Frank Sinatra- "I'll Never Smile Again" (1940)
- Woody Herman- "At the Woodchoppers' Ball" (1939)
- George Gershwin's- "Rhapsody In Blue" in 1924.

The creative and production processes of the big bands varied considerably.

Billie Holiday wrote: "I still say the greatest thing about the Basie band…was that they never used a piece of music…"77

"Benny Goodman always had big arrangements…But with Basie…we had a book of hundred songs and every one of us carried every last damn note of them in our heads." 78

The sound of influential early "pre-jazz" players like "Rudy" Wiedoeft, who had helped to popularize the saxophone using a C-Melody sax, by the 1930s, had fallen out of popular favor. A new generation of players, like Coleman Hawkins, who, Whitney Balliett argued "achieved the impossible-perfect art" with the record "Body and Soul" (1939) anticipated the improv of bebop music. 79

Lester Young had his first breakthrough in competition against Chu Berry, "playing his little old saxophone held together by adhesive tape and rubber bands" 80. Lester Young "championed nothing", his tone light with and melodic improvisation that matched the "new coolness of Billie Holiday and Teddy Wilson." 81

Coleman Hawkins© William Gottlieb

In his book, "Collected Works- A Journal of Jazz", Whitney Balliett's fondest praise is reserved for Ben Webster (first taught by Lester Young's father), whose warm, embracing tone "touched you in a way that Hawkins and Young, for all their genius, rarely did."81

But then came the jackhammer attack of Charlie Parker who "exploded" through the world of jazz, passionately ripping through arpeggios with "avalanches of eighth notes", helping to trigger, together with Dizzy Gillespie, the bebop movement, that forever changed jazz from a dance-oriented music to one defined by extended solos and a new form of harmonic language. 82

This revolutionary new jazz style and its players challenged the traditional jazz establishment. In Chicago, prior to 1945, jazz had been perceived as primarily dance music and jazz musicians were forbidden by the musicians' union from jamming and were fined if they did!

Many jazz saxophonists were great blues men; for example (in no particular order): Coleman Hawkins, Johnny Hodges, Charlie Parker, Hank Crawford, Benny Carter, Hilton Jefferson (who played with King Oliver Orchestra, Cab Calloway Band), Stanley Turrentine, Gene Ammons, Al Sears, David "Fathead" Newman, Dexter Gordon, Eddie Cleanhead Vinson, and Cannonball Adderley.

Ben Webster© William Gottlieb

Many of these players would accompany the immortal Billie Holiday on songs that soon became classic standards, soft, golden light pulsing behind the clouds of notes that encircled the world.

Songs like "What a Little Moonlight Can Do" and "I've Got My Love To Keep Me Warm" with Ben Webster,

"Mean To Me" with Billie Holiday, Johnny Hodges on alto and Lester Young (who called her "Lady Day") on tenor saxophone; in the 1940s:

"The Man I Love" with Coleman Hawkins and Lester Young on tenor.

In 1952, "Tenderly" with Flip Phillips on tenor solo.

Jazz had an important influence on rock and roll. Coleman Hawkins' approach helped to shape the tones of rock saxophonists Lee Allen and Red Prysock, as did Joe Thomas with Jimmie Lunceford Big Band; King Curtis and Illinois Jacquet pointed to the rhythmic sense of Lester Young; Joe Houston called Charlie Parker his main man; Jimmy Forrest was a great admirer of Ben Webster; King Curtis admired Louis Jordan and Charlie Parker for his phrasing and technique as well as Red Connor who King Curtis called (on the liner notes of an album), "a Coltrane ahead of his time".

Special note must be made of Sidney Bechet, an important pioneer in jazz saxophone, who was described by Duke Ellington as "the very epitome of jazz" and by Whitney Balliett as "probably the most lyrical and dramatic of all American jazz musicians". Bechet's blues-drenched sound, on songs like "Blue Horizon", was a seminal influence on many players including Johnny Hodges, the famed alto saxophonist with Duke Ellington.

Sidney Bechet © William Gottlieb

But waiting to torpedo these voyages of love and rescue was a conservative social movement that called jazz "The Devil's music", an accusation often fueled by underlying racism and segregation.

What does a Japanese haiku, written nearly 200 years ago have to do with the Big Bands of the 1930s-1940s?

"Never forget:
we walk on hell,
gazing at flowers."

— Kobayashi Issa (1763 –1828)

A reminder that no matter how sweet and saving the music may have been, racism was close at hand, a knife and rope gripped tightly in hand, always ready to strike.

Membership in the Klu Klux Klan rose to a reported 4 million in the early 1920s. At a Fourth of July rally outside Kokomo, Ind., in 1923, the Klan attracted a reported 200,000 people. Membership and influence, however, later declined due to activities of some its leaders, such as D. C. Stephenson, grand dragon of the Indiana Klan, who was convicted of the rape and the murder of Madge Oberholtzer in 1925. [83, 84]

But it didn't end there:

- A Boston restaurant wouldn't let Billie Holiday in the front door.

- Chuck Peterson, the famous trumpet player, was jumped by four men and beaten deliberately in his face to try and prevent him from ever playing the trumpet again, for trying to bring Billie Holiday into a Detroit bar.

- In 1945, Cab Galloway decided to visit Lionel Hampton who was playing in Kansas City. After purchasing a ticket, Cab was refused entrance by a doorman who claimed Galloway pushed him to the floor. The doorman took his revolver and struck Cab a number of times on his head. After being treated in a hospital, Cab Galloway was charged by the police for resisting arrest. 85

Drummer Connie Kay famous for his work in the Modern Jazz Quartet, comments: "Was Lester [Young] depressed? Lester was depressed like all black musicians in the States that are talented and not appreciated, man. If you're not strong enough, it'll get to you. You go around the world and see how other artists are appreciated and accepted and you wonder. 'Here's a guy who is talented, who is considered a genius, and what is he getting out of it? He's got to work like a dog to keep two cents in his pocket and feed his family and keep a roof over this head. And you see people less talented, and they're out there making it' ."-86 as quoted in Henry Ferrini's fine website: https://lesterlives.com/roy-hanyes/

"In the *Tragedy and the Triumph of Lester Young*", Ron Tabor writes: "Lester was also disturbed by the racist nature of the popular music business, in which Blacks are often the innovators...Lester was especially irked by the fact that many of his imitators (Stan Getz and Paul Desmond?) were getting more work, were making much more money, and were so much better known than he was.'" 86

On the other side of it...

In an interview with John Cooper of the New York Times, Stan Getz spoke about his early love of music: "the age of 13, there was only music. 'I became a music kid,' he says, [practicing eight hours a day]'." Getz grew up in a tenement that was so close to other apartments that when the windows were open, and he was practicing in the bathroom, people would yell for him to shut up. However, his family was poor and needed money, [87] the reason Getz left school in grade nine to become a professional musician.

"My father was a mostly out-of-work printer and at that time in the 30's they didn't allow Jews into the printers' union, so we had a hard time…I used to go around 52nd Street and hear them Bird, Diz, Billie Holiday. None of them would let me sit in. The only two who would were Ben Webster and Erroll Garner, and then it was lovely.'…"[87]

Getz did note that for years critics persisted in seeing him as "just a pale shade of Lester Young" but acknowledged that Young was his stylistic mentor.

Musicians have always been influenced by other musicians, no matter who those influences are, As musician Roy Frasen remarked: "The past is there for a cat to take what he needs from it. Paul Desmond listened to Lester Young and Gil Evans to Brahms and they wouldn't be what they are if they didn't."[88]

Any number of saxophone players were influenced by Lester Young who reinvented the saxophone both tonally and melodically [89] but, over time, it is argued, Getz's style became closer to Coleman Hawkins, Ben Webster and Johnny Hodges; however, these players "were grounded in the blues…a subtle underpinning to everything they played." Getz's highly personal style "grew partly out of the skewed emotional freight he carried with him"[89], a litany of alcoholism and drug addiction, legal troubles, battles with the I.R.S., and his two attempted suicides. 89

Given Getz's own considerable abilities as a musician, "who", it is argued, "at his best, he could play rings around God", 90 it is reasonable to ask whether some critics reduced him to a stereotyped stick figure on which questionable, negative labels were stuck, while ignoring the practical realities of the person they had stigmatized and trapped inside.

Let us take for example the perception of…a person. In order to perceive them fully, we must first fight our tendency to classify, to compare, to evaluate, to need, to use. The moment that we say that man is a 'foreigner', in that moment, we have classified him…and to some extent cut ourselves off from the possibility of seeing him as a unique and whole human being, different from any one in the whole world…It is this ability to perceive the whole and to rise above its parts which characterizes cognitions in the various peak [exceptional performance] experiences.

Abraham H. Maslow
Towards a Psychology of Being (2nd edition)

***

Freedom from hate.
Freedom from self-pity.
Freedom from fear.
Freedom from pride.

Billy Strayhorn
"Four Moral Freedoms":
https://www.phillytrib.com/lifestyle/the-life-music-of-

<u>billy-strayhorn/article_c4e061fc-bcc3-5a84-8ce2-a2fee346872d.html</u>

***

"Racial categories, assigned to people based on their appearance, geographic origin and other supposed attributes, got their start during the dawn of Western science in 18th century Europe. White Europeans, who then had no knowledge of human genetics and little meaningful contact with other cultures, placed themselves at the pinnacle. For centuries now, the categories have been used to divide and perpetuate every version of harm — enslavement, violence, an eclipse of opportunity...

In 2003, the completion of the Human Genome Project — which found that humans globally share 99.9 percent of their DNA — gave waste to the notion of "race" among the vast majority of scientists. But the public appears barely to have noticed. The idea still lives everywhere — in discrimination and criminal profiling, in the rise in hate speech and acts, in the recent Supreme Court decision ending affirmative action in college admissions, in the rhetoric of social justice advocates and the new capitalization of Black and White in the media."

Trent Sydney ((2023) "Race isn't real, science says. Advocates want the census to reflect that." Washington Post. October 16, 2023.

For an America increasingly fractured and torn apart at the heart, it was seemingly impossible to even speak to another without provoking rage and hatred.

Which isn't to say that no one tried.

Heroes emerged.

"There aren't many people who fought harder than Artie [Shaw]" wrote Billie Holiday, "Against the vicious people in the music business or the crummy side of second-class citizenship with eats at the guts of so many musicians…" 91

Recordings such as Duke Ellington's "Black, Brown and Beige", his movie "Symphony In Black- A Rhapsody of Negro Life", and Fats Waller's "Black and Blue", led the way forward, as did a song, now recognized as one of the greatest of the 20th Century, Billie Holiday's searing, powerful "Strange Fruit". 92

Inspired by a poem written by Abel Meeropol who set it to music (he used the pen name Lewis Allan):

"*Southern trees bear a strange fruit,*
Blood on the leaves and blood at the root,
Black body swinging in the Southern breeze,
Strange fruit hanging from the poplar trees."

It was during her performances at Café Society that the song was born. Strange Fruit was "my personal protest…It seem to spell out all the thing that had killed Pop."

Billie's father had pneumonia that gradually had worsened. He went from hospital to hospital in Dallas, Texas. None would take him in. He eventually hemorrhaged and died. When his body was brought to Billie and her mother, her father's white shirt was still covered in his dry blood.93

"I worked like the devil on [Strange Fruit) because I was never sure…that I could get across to a plush night-club audience the things that it meant to me. I was scared people would hate it.

The first time I sang it I thought it was a mistake and I had been right being scared. There wasn't a patter of applause when I finished. Then one lone person began to clap nervously. Then suddenly everyone was clapping."94

She first performed at Café Society (she worked at the Café Society for two years, seven nights a week, no nights off for $75.00 a week), New York city's only fully integrated night club. Her label, Columbia Records, had refused to record "Strange Fruit". When Columbia passed, she went to an independent jazz label, Commodore Records. The record, recorded in 1939, sold a million copies (another version was released in 1944), even though many radio stations in the USA blacklisted it.

"The version for Commodore became my biggest selling record. It still depresses me every time I sing it, though. It reminds me of how Pop died. But I have to keep singing it…because…the thing that killed him are still happening in the South." 95 When I sing it, it affects me so much I get sick. It takes all the strength out of me".95

Billie had become involved with narcotics and went to a sanatorium to try and kick the habit. Someone tipped off the FBI who began to follow her.

Harry Anslinger the head of the Federal Bureau of Narcotics, made her a target for her drug use.

She was reportedly framed by federal agents who sold her heroin, arrested her for possession and jailed her, after a trial where she didn't have legal representation. When she was released, her cabaret performer's license was cancelled, effectively ending her career in nightclubs. But when you've been pushed down again and again and you finally rise up, nothing can stop you…even when staring into the cross hairs of a prejudice and savagery disguised by the authorities as "justice".

She was still able to perform in concerts, such as Carnegie Hall, and when again charged with possession, this time was represented by a lawyer and acquitted at trial. However, she eventually was hospitalized with heart and liver problems. Federal agents were sent to the hospital in New York City, handcuffed Holiday to the bed and prevented further treatment. She died on July 17, 1959, at the age of 44.

There in an ongoing debate about whether Billie Holiday was targeted because she refused to stop singing "Strange Fruit" or whether it was due to the narcotics investigation. In her autobiography, "Lady Sings The Blues", Billie never mentions any connection with the song, only her difficulties with drugs and the FBI.

Time Magazine named "Strange Fruit", the "Song Of The Century", The Grammy Lifetime Achievement

Award was awarded in 1987, and she was inducted into the Rock and Roll Hall of Fame in 2000.

Ahmet Ertegun, who co-founded Atlantic Records, called "Strange Fruit", "a declaration of war ... the beginning of the civil rights movement".

Something was stirring, restless, impatient, filled with a defiance that called like a rebel's voice from high on the mountain , clear, pure...and ready to fight.

From this point on, every sunset would be smeared with the blood of those who fought for the American ideals of civil rights, equality and freedom-for what had been first promised in the Declaration of Independence (July 4, 1776) and The Pledge of Allegiance (1892, amended 1954).

We hold these truths to be self-evident, that all men are created equal, that they are endowed by their Creator with certain unalienable Rights, that among these are Life, Liberty and the pursuit of Happiness...

"I pledge allegiance to the flag of the United States of America, and to the republic for which it stands, one nation under God, indivisible, with liberty and justice for all."

Chops Horns

By Neil Sharpe

© David Watson, Darryl Dixon
http://www.chopshorns.com/

DD. As a kid I couldn't buy a record, I had to listen to what was in the house and that was jazz records-singers, instrumentalists, like the Lee Morgans, sax players like Gene Ammons, Coleman Hawkins' "Body And Soul".

My father bought me an alto sax and I knew there were notes in the sax, so I get on the saxophone, and

I'm 8 years old in Grade 3, and I'm pressing the keys, but it doesn't sound the same as I hear on the records, and I had no idea how to make it sound like that. I'm blowing into the horn and I'm hearing these sounds coming out and it's not what I'm hearing on the records, so I say to myself "What's the use?"

At that point, the teachers were only doing the very basics, and nobody said anything about long tones [a technical exercise that develops tone] or anything, so I quit for a year. But then I couldn't get away from it, kept listening to the records my father was playing, and I picked it back up and kept going.

I remember listening to Duke Ellington who inspired me to try arranging. And my high school teacher Ron Dolce really helped with my attitude toward music and having creative freedom.

DW. The record collection that Darryl is talking about is now mine. I inherited that collection because I asked for it. Three and a half crates of pure gold. Went out and bought a turntable and I'm listening to them like Darryl when he was 8.

Now in my case, my father was a saxophone player. He would come in off the road, stand in a corner and he would practice. I was like 4 and 5, and I would sit on the couch and listen, because I knew when he was finished, he would let me come over and put one finger, 'but only one finger' he'd say, to push the keys. I was fascinated by how they opened and closed. I got that sound in the fabric of my listening, and I wanted to play more. That's what got me started.

I started playing out when I was 14 and remember how excited I was to get paid for the first time, playing r&b in a club for $60.00 a night.

People always want to know if what we play today is different from back then.

So yea, to answer the question, we play both the old and new. Tone is tone, feel is feel.

But how we learned back then is completely different from today. Today, they have YouTube! I saw a 14 year old jazz guy when I was teaching in Newark. My school was part of the "Jazz House" program.

https://jazzhousekids.org/

Once a week, a guy would come in and help me with my jazz band. When he found who I was, he asked me to help with his band, which I did. That's where I saw this 14 year old player who had the sweetest tone and could outplay me on the horn- beautiful phrases. So, you know I had to talk to him!

"Man" I asked him, "How do you play like this?"

Said that he had private teachers for 5-6 years and copied the players on YouTube. We used to have to listen to records over and over again to figure out what they were doing and if you couldn't afford the record, you couldn't copy anyone.

DD. YouTube is fine, and you can sit in a room by yourself and practice and that's fine too, but you wouldn't get the real knowledge until you actually play with musicians. It's like a drummer, you can learn all the techniques, but you can't really learn real time until playing with other musicians. When you sit in a room all by yourself, you don't really have to focus on time. You can play a beat and go off time-wise, slow down, speed up-it doesn't matter. But when you're playing with other musicians, as a drummer you're the time keeper, so you have to focus on what everyone is doing; you have to learn to listen to everyone and that's what creates your discipline, because that is the essence of playing- being disciplined and focused. You only get that way by playing with others.

DW. Music is composed of many different languages-for example, funk, rock, jazz... sometimes you emphasis different parts of the phrase, different parts of the word, depending on what language you're speaking. And you got to stay true to the style, the context of what you're playing. You can't drop a bebop riff into a pop song and expect it to work.

DD. What notes are accented and which beats are really makes a difference. Like come in a split second just before the first beat–called "Something on the one"- and that has a bigger impact.

Also, listen how the guitar or drummer is approaching and put the horn parts exactly on that rhythm but use counterpoint. By that I mean, a lot of horn sections play the same parts as the rhythm section but I'll throw licks in counterpart to what they're doing for a different feel and sound.

DW. You have to use your ears and spend a lot of time getting that down. When I was teaching with my jazz band, I would emphasize how you listen, like you've got to listen to this part and not that. Darryl and I are disciples of Fred Wesley and Maceo. We listened to a lot of stuff that they did. There is stuff that Darryl and I do so tightly that people can't tell it's two horns. To get like that takes time and then more time.

James Brown and Maceo Parker were big influences on me. Maceo could do a solo using only four notes but how he played those four notes, the accents, the phrasing, the tone were everything- less is more.

Kids today they concentrate on how learning how to solo and being a front man, they don't spend a lot of time playing in sessions. There's lot of players who are great soloists but when we put them is sessions, they stick out badly, so we don't use them.

DD. Same with singers. Some are great lead singers, but lousy background and vice versa. And there are some who are both. If you solo all the time, you are so used to hearing your own voice, it's hard to shift and blend in with other people. Some can, some can't.

DW. The other problem is that young players have a wealth of knowledge at their fingertips and there are players on YouTube who can teach you how to play the horn. But what they don't do is tell you how to market yourself, how to go to the right open mike, to give yourself the opportunity to be "in the right place at the right time". You hear that phrase a lot in this business. There are terrific players and bands out there, but no one has ever heard of them because of that.

DD. "Being in the right place" and all that is fine, but you can't wait around for it. You've got to go out and create your own opportunities.

DW That's one thing about this business you have to understand. You've got to be able to play different styles in both music and the business, to know what is the right language at the right time, to know when to push and when to flow.

Credit happens in a lot of different ways. Not to belabor it. For me, it's about a level of respect. If you push back at producers and musicians about not getting credit on arrangements and recordings, they say, "You guys are a dime a dozen, do you know how lucky you are to be doing this!"

DD. Yea, that's the classic line.

DW. And some people will steal from you. When we first started, we thought our music spoke for itself and we wanted to be treated honestly. But when your lawyer walks in and they realize they can't steal something from you, the classic thing used to be, they'd go out and find guys they can steal from.

We hired a lawyer when we first broke out on own and learned that certain things can happen and if you push too hard, you may not get that much work again. You got to know who's hiring you, their rep, what language to speak and when.

DW. When we were touring in America with The Police, Sting brought in Black Uhuru to open for them. He did that because that was kind of how The Police got their reggae vibe. Sting told me those were the guys he'd listened to. That was such an honourable thing to do. How many musicians acknowledge who they got their vibe from, or stole it, and became super famous but never gave them any credit?

Back in those days, this was the truth. We had a black professor at Jersey City State named Paul Jeffries who said to a history class, mostly white except for me and Darryl, that if you named *any* white jazz musician, he could tell you what black musician they copied from, who was their influence.

DD. Michael Brecker's was Ernie Watts and he admitted that. Stan Getz's was Lester Young, Phil Wood's was Charlie Parker and so on. If you asked them, they'd tell you, "That's true."

But in the class, someone was insulted, went down to the head of the department and complained. Things went back and forth until Paul Jeffries was asked to resign. But he knew what he was talking about, he'd been on the road with all the heavyweights like Ellington, Basie, Lionel Hampton. He had the credentials.

"Music is your own experience, your own thoughts, your wisdom. If you don't live it, it won't come out of your horn. They teach you there's a boundary line to music. But, man, there's no boundary line to art."
– Charlie Parker

***

Ernie Watts

…released the album "To The Point" with one track entitled "For Michael", a tribute to the late Michael Brecker.

http://erniewatts.com/

A reviewer, William Rhulmann, wrote: "seems to evoke Charles Mingus' tribute to Lester Young".

https://erniewatts.com/discography/to_the_point.html

***

Lester Young

" Lester's [Young] love for Lady Day was plain. Her voice and his tenor were 'of the same mind.' Just listen and look at the 1957 CBS *Sound of Jazz* with Billie singing *Fine & Mellow.* On Sunday, March 15th 1959, Lester Willis Young passed. Four months later, Billie Holiday died." -Roy Haynes

https://lesterlives.com/roy-hanyes/

Lester Young Quintet : Jesse Drakes (tp) Lester Young (ts) Gil Coggins (p) Aaron Bell (b) Connie Kay (d); NBC radio broadcast, "Birdland", New York, August 2, 1952

Bio-https://www.knkx.org/post/originator-cool-lester-young-played-purest-blues-ever-heard

Lester Young 1958
Lester Young complained bitterly about racism in popular music.

https://lesterlives.com/roy-hanyes/

***
Stan Getz

The following articles review Stan Getz's career and the influence of Lester Young:

"Lester Young was Stan Getz's great stylistic mentor"... "'Lester had a catholic way of playing', Getz says. 'It was so right and pure and unassuming.'"

https://www.nytimes.com/1991/06/09/magazine/stan-getz-through-the-years.html

http://www.azuremilesrecords.com/Transcendental_Consolidation_The_Music_of_Stan_Getz.html

Kevin Whitehead wrote: "You can really hear his influence at quick tempos, when Getz does his take on Young's pet move, riding one barely changing note on 'Feather Merchant' ".

https://www.npr.org/2011/03/18/134652613/before-ipanema-stan-getzs-exquisite-quintets

For Getz's influences, see the website operated by Stan Getz's daughter Beverly- these included Jack Teagarden, Benny Goodman and Woody Herman, in addition to Lester Young.

http://www.stangetz.net/

***
Art Pepper

Laurie Pepper has done tremendous work restoring many of Art Pepper's released and previously unreleased live performances and albums.
https://artpepper.bandcamp.com/

***

Phil Woods
https://www.philwoods.com/discography/item/410-phil-woods-on-meeting-charlie-parker-in-1954

Charlie Parker also had a strong influence on Miles Davis: (at the 7:00 mark):
https://www.youtube.com/watch?v=7U0gDkriczc

***

Billy Strayhorn
"…was my right arm, my left arm, all the eyes in the back of my head, my brainwaves in his head, and his in mine."-Duke Ellington
http://billystrayhorn.com/

Notes

76.https://entertainment.time.com/2011/10/24/the-all-time-100-songs/slide/it-dont-mean-a-thing-if-it-aint-got-that-swing-duke-ellington/

https://swingandbeyond.com/2016/09/01/it-dont-mean-a-thing-if-it-aint-got-that-swing-1932-duke-ellington/

77 Billie Holiday (2006) Lady Sings the Blues: originally printed 1956; Harlem Moon and Broadway Books paperback edition; 2006: pg. 69
78 Ibid. Pgs. 69-70
79 Balliett Whitney (2002) *Collected Works: A Journal of Jazz 1954-2001.* (St. Martin's Press, New York, New York). 89. Norma Ganz racial discrimination, pg. 6, Johnny Hodges, pg. 129, jazz perceived as dance music pg. 147; "Dexter" pg. 483-484; Sidney Bechet pg 757: "Big Ben" pg. 863-866
80 Holiday op cit. pg 52
81 Balliett op. cit. Johnny Hodges, pg. 129, jazz perceived as dance music pg. 147; "Dexter" pg. 483-484; Sidney Bechet pg 757: "Big Ben" pg. 863-866
82 Gold J (2020) Sittin' In: Jazz Clubs Of The 1940s and 1950s. Harper Design. Worsley J (2020) Sittin' In: Jazz Clubs Of The 1940s and 1950s.

Interview https://www.allaboutjazz.com/sittin-in-jazz-clubs-of-the-1940s-and-1950s?width=1920

83 https://www.washingtonpost.com/opinions/2023/04/03/kkk-midwest-jan6-indiana/
https://www.famous-trials.com/stephenson/74-home

84 Timothy Egan (2023) A Fever in the Heartland: The Ku Klux Klan's Plot to Take Over America, and the Woman Who Stopped Them. Viking (April 4, 2023)
https://www.washingtonpost.com/books/2023/05/18/fever-heartland-ku-klux-klan-timothy-egan-review/

85 Shaw Arnold (1986) Honkers and Shouters: The Golden Years of Rhythm and Blues. Macmillan Pub Co; (March 1, 1986) pg. 125

86 R Tabor (2008) The Tragedy and Triumph of Lester Young
https://theanarchistlibrary.org/library/ron-tabor-the-tragedy-and-triumph-of-lester-young

87 Cooper J (1991) Stan Getz Through The Years. N. Y. Times. June 9, 1991, Section 6, Page 30
https://www.nytimes.com/1991/06/09/magazine/stan-getz-through-the-years.html

88 Balliett op. cit. pg 346

89 Ibid pg. 846

90 Ibid pg. 848

91 Holiday op. cit. Pg. 92

92 https://www.npr.org/2019/02/22/697075534/a-sprawling-blueprint-for-protest-music-courtesy-of-the-jazz-duke
https://umbc.edu/stories/duke-ellingtons-message-of-social-justice/

93 Holiday op. cit. pg. 78
94 Ibid pgs 90-95.

References

Gottlieb, W. P. (1946) *Portrait of Coleman Hawkins, Spotlite (Club), New York, N.Y., ca. Sept. 1946.* Monographic. [Photograph] Retrieved from the Library of Congress, https://www.loc.gov/item/gottlieb.04011/.

Gottlieb, W. P. (1947) *Portrait of Sidney Bechet and Lloyd Phillips, Jimmy Ryan's Club, New York, N.Y., ca. June.* United States, 1947. Monographic. [Photograph] Retrieved from the Library of Congress, https://www.loc.gov/item/gottlieb.00551/.

Gottlieb, W. P. (1946) *Portrait of Lionel Hampton and Arnett Cobb, Aquarium, New York, N.Y., ca. June.* United States, 1946. Monographic. [Photograph] Retrieved from the Library of Congress, https://www.loc.gov/item/gottlieb.03831/.

Gottlieb, W. P. (1947) *Portrait of Ben Webster, Eddie (Emmanuel) Barefield, Buck Clayton, Benny Morton, Joe Marsala, and Cozy Cole, Famous Door, New York, N.Y., ca. Oct. 1947.*
Monographic. [Photograph] Retrieved from the Library of Congress, https://www.loc.gov/item/gottlieb.03681/.

Balliett Whitney (2002) Collected Works: A Journal of Jazz 1954-2001. (St. Martin's Press, New York, New York).

Hansen Liane: (2005) "Saxophone's History as the Devil's Horn": In the interview, Michael Segell discusses his book, <u>The Devil's Horn: From Novelty to King of Cool</u>. It follows the history of the saxophone through more than 160 years as a controversial classical, jazz and rock instrument. The interview can be heard here: <u>https://www.npr.org/templates/story/story.php?storyId=4991482?storyId=4991482</u>

5

Caledonia
By Neil Sharpe

Being dumped over the side of a yacht into shark-filled waters wasn't the most promising start for a musical career...unless your name was Louis Jordan.

In 1937, in a preplanned, much publicized, battle of big bands, Benny Goodman's (the immortal Gene Krupa on drums) went head-to-head against drummer Chick Webb's band. They attracted a wildly cheering, sold out, audience. Chick was declared the surprise winner. From the winner's share of the box office, $4550.00, most went to management fees and to Chick Webb; a young sax player, Louis Jordan, saw only about $75.00 of it.

Was that the trigger that first made Jordan think, "Is there a better way?"

Or did the American Dream yank Louis Jordan off to one side and explain that the only way to escape the musical system, that sooner or later would try to crush him, was to do what everyone told him not to do. It wouldn't be a smooth ride, but it would be *his* ride, and that's when the magic happens- those moments where it feels like you don't have to search for notes, but the musical gods reach down and say, "Try these". 95

After he was fired from Webb's band (when he tried to leave with Ella Fitzgerald and two musicians), Louis Jordan quickly learned how tough the music business could be. He knew, however, that to survive and be noticed, he had to be different. Knew that he might only get one shot, one chance to impress, to surprise. His idea of a small band of 5-6 players wasn't going to do it alone. Well-known musicians like Louis Armstrong and Fats Waller and His Rhythm already had that covered.

His way forward was to tear down his world. Rip apart every performance and send it flying in the air to see what lands and what rises higher into the light. Do this over and over again until he was sure that his musicianship, stage image and movement, his how to smile and how to connect with an audience, were pinned down tight.

Louis Jordan also knew that he had to know old to be new.

"I wanted to play music on stage that made people forget about what they did today."

Explained Lous Jordan. "Generally, a black artist at that time would either stick to the blues or do pop. I did everything.' 96

Jordan had a vision that felt like instinct, a vision that would fill his heart during the corrosive years of the Great Depression and World War II like the last bit of flickering, stubborn sunlight that refused to surrender to a merciless winter. A vision that led him into bits of notes, fragments of voice, and snatches of phrasing that came flying together inside him to give birth to a new style of music called "jump".

Where 16-25 piece big bands featured orchestral jazz compositions with star vocalists, Jordan's "Tympany Five" revolutionized the music industry with short, punchy songs.

But Jordan knew that that to be the best, he would have to compete against the best. He may get blown off the stage again and again, but he also would get the opportunity to hear, see and learn.

"Overnight success", however, has never been the practical reality of the blood sport of music, although that's the dream the music industry has always pushed and what young musicians want to believe in- a dream that can be inspiring, but also blinding, one with no guarantees, no matter how talented you may be.

Like Louis Jordan, a musician has to commit all, both emotionally and psychologically, which can seem easy to do when you're young, when every part of your being is music and practicing six to eight hours a day seems both a joy and your true destiny.

But when you move up to the next level, reality comes crashing in; a reality where every musician is talented, where every musician is sure that the promised land is theirs and theirs alone. You may meet musicians who are on a far higher level from you; however, that doesn't mean you can't be the best performer. Downbeat award winner **Ken**

Fornetran in an interview for the book "Ride The Wild Wind: History Of The Saxophone: 1920-2021" advises: "I used to think that if I made a mistake, the entire set was messed up and horrible. But, if you really break it down to the first song, then the second, and so on, some will be good, some less so, and you suddenly realize that out of two hours, maybe only 5% wasn't that good. But that 5% shouldn't be the only part that you remember and therefore make you feel bad about your playing. The memories of that negative emotion can carry over to the next gig, and after a while you're in trouble. You don't have to sound like Coltrane or Brecker to be good. Players like Coltrane and Brecker are at a completely different level than other players, but that doesn't mean that the other players are lesser players. Each of us has our own distinct voice and tone. That's what's important. Sound like yourself! Be yourself! You can learn licks and passages and eventually your own sound will emerge out of that."[97]

You can win big in music, but you can lose big too. Some will have a career and maybe even become stars, some will have to stop because they can't pass auditions, can't find work, some will have to take other jobs just to make a living, some will have to sell their instruments to pay debts, some will commit suicide.

It's important to keep things in perspective. The biggest fear that can paralyze even the strongest of performers, is the fear of not meeting expectations.

Performers can be trapped in the expectations of others, including family, friends, and mentors. If you perceive an upcoming event as a validation of your reputation and self-worth, this is putting far too much pressure on your shoulders. It is critical to distinguish between who you are as a person from who you are as a performer. A great result does not make you a great person; a disappointing result does not make you a failure as a person. The ability to distinguish between what you can and can't control is critical.

If a musician falls short, it's often not a matter of talent or a lack of discipline or perseverance, it often can be a matter of "luck".

Legendary saxophonist **Jon R. Smith** said: "This business is all about luck, about being in the right place at the right time, and that if doesn't sound too encouraging, welcome to the cold, hard facts about the music business… I've seen so many great, great players never get the opportunity they deserved. There are a lot of terrific sax players no will ever know about, because those players weren't lucky enough to be in the right place at the right time." [97]

Paul Revere of Paul Revere and The Raiders, who (with Mark Lindsay, vocals, saxophone) had a long list of Top 40 hits in the 1960s-early 1970s) and in 2021 were featured on the soundtrack for Quentin Tarantino's hit movie "Once Upon A Time In Hollywood", said in an interview with Domenic Priore:

"We got lucky, lucky, lucky. That's the one thing that no one should leave out of their story, whether they're a movie star, television star, recording star, there's a huge thing called 'luck,' and if you're in the right place at the right time, and take advantage of it, that's the deal.

I don't care how good you are, I don't care how great the band is, how great your singer is, I don't care how great the songs are, if you don't get 'em out on the right label, and they don't get played on the right station, you don't get involved with the right people, you could spend the rest of your life spinnin' your wheels, and ending up being nobody…because I know a lot of acts that sure as hell didn't deserve to be stars, and I know a lot of acts that sure as hell should have been, so that's the way I look at it, a lot of luck involved."[98]

What introduced Louis Jordan to Lady Luck, what put him in the right place at the right time? What kept him on the road, no matter how many times reality sent him careening off the road, especially when everyone was screaming that all he was doing was carving his own name in his tombstone?

What put Jordan in the right place at the right time was hard work and a telephone call that he never heard.

In 1938, John Hammond telephoned Don Law, who had supervised gifted blues artist Robert Johnson's last recordings, to ask whether Johnson would be interested in appearing in "Spirituals to Swing", a two night concert in Carnegie Hall that would "feature largely black performers". The concert was Hammond's answer to nightclubs and bars that "still prevented black musicians" from appearing in major entertainment centers.

Don Law had to say "No" because Johnson had passed away, but the playbill was still loaded-Lester Young, Count Basie, Buck Clayton, Big Bill Broonzy, James P. Johnson, Sister Rosetta Tharp, Jimmy Rushing, Helen Humes, blues pianist Albert Ammons, and Meade Lux Lewis, jazz guitarist Charlie Christian, Lionel Hampton, and Sonny Terry. 99

Plus, at the time, a lesser known act made up of the hard driving, boogie woogie pianist Pete Johnson paired with singer Joe Turner on "It's All Right Baby", their version of Johnson's earlier tune, "Roll 'Em Pete".

Their performance at Carnegie Hall had an explosive impact that helped to trigger a national craze and led to an extended booking at the New York club "Café Society Downtown". Together with Albert Ammons and Meade Lux Lewis, they launched boogie woogie into the music business' stratosphere (and formed a critical root of rock n' roll as we shall see later, especially with Jerry Lee Lewis and Little Richard). 100

Boogie woogie helped people, ground down by the Depression, to remember what hope and joy felt like. But there was nothing new in this, just an updating.

- Lead Belly, Blind Lemon Jefferson, Jelly Roll Morton, W.C. Handy, and T-Bone

Walker all said they had heard versions of boogie woogie going back to the late 1800s and early 1900s. Meade Lux Lewis recorded "Honky-Tonk Train Blues" in 1927, followed by Clarence "Pinetop" Smith's "Pine Top's Boogie Woogie" (who had been influenced by the song "Cow Cow Boogie" that he'd heard in 1924 in a bar at Pittsburgh). 101

- Depression house parties were fueled by songs like "Pine Top Boogie Woogie" and Blind Roosevelt Graves' "Crazy About My Baby".
- "Boogie Woogie Stomp" (recorded two weeks after the concert "From Spirituals to Swing") and "Boogie Woogie Prayer" by Albert Ammons both charted
- the Will Bradly Orchestra had a hit with "Beat Me Daddy (Eight To The Bar)", in 1940;
- Count Basie released "Basie Boogie" in 1941;
- the Andrew Sisters soared to the top with "Boogie Woogie Bugle Boy", also in 1941;
- Tommy Dorsey covered Pine Top's song with the title "Boogie Woogie" and had a massive hit in both 1943 and 1945.
- Freddie Slack with vocals by Ella Mae Morse came full circle with the hit "Cow Cow Boogie".

Then came the sonic angel, with lightning for wings -whether sent by God or the Devil, at the time, a matter of great dispute- came swooping down, screaming out its true name "Amplification", a deep-gutted, rumble-filled musical engine revving like thunder, ready to run.

In the 1940s, amplifiers became common, especially on the streets of Chicago, where guitar players, like Muddy Waters and Hound Dog Taylor, could set up on a corner and play for tips, their amplified guitars cutting through the noise and clatter of street traffic with songs like "Dust My Broom" and "Rollin' and Tumblin'".

John Lee "Sonny Boy" Williamson turned the harmonica into a powerful solo voice and was featured on records destined to become blues/rock standards like "Good Mornin' Little School Girl" (as of the date of this writing, 91 covers have been recorded including a hit in the 1960s by the English rock band "Ten Years After". https://secondhandsongs.com/work/12833)

Record companies like Columbia, Vocation, Decca, and Victor's "Bluebird" label began to record blues artists again (e.g. producer Lester Melrose), including Peetie Wheatstraw (an important influence for Robert Johnson) with his "You Can't Stop Me From Drinkin'" that also featured the harmonica.

The recording studio became Louis Jordan's shelter from the competition's harsh desert sun that lashed down day after day.

Jordan had formed the small combo, "The Tympany Four", that had little initial success until he heard a tip that the popular Elks Rendezvous club was looking for a resident band. Passing the audition, Jordan was able to turn that gig into his recording debut with Decca. 102

These recordings, which included "So Good" and "Away From You" sold enough for Decca to recover all of its costs and take a chance on a second session. Louis Jordan and his expanded "Tympany Five", did a recording session which produced a version of Percy Bradford's "Keep A Knockin' " that became a local hit (with a cover by Jimmy Dorsey).

But all the talent in the world doesn't count for much if a musician can't escape local gigs. Sometimes, dancing with the skeleton of what seems like a plan- moving from city to city, chasing the sun, learning how to play to empty rooms, driving through the no one returning your calls, the minor failures, the minor successes, can leave the heart and soul hovering near empty.

Jordon's career stalled. Members of his band began to take better paying gigs. For Jordan, there seemed only one way forward to go back into the recording studio. As they say in boxing, "what matters isn't how many times you get knocked down but how many times you get back up."

"A Chicken Ain't Nothing But A Bird" which combined swing, a 4-in-the-bar blues shuffle rhythm, and boogie woogie, had record sales of 62,000 (Cab Calloway released a cover version a month later in

October 1940). Although not a chart hit, the sales showed enough promise to keep Decca interested, including a new recording contract with improved royalties especially from juke box sales (an estimated 400,000 were in the USA by 1941.)

Jordan remained true to his roots. "I tell you playing the blues was my basic idea of music. Pick out some of my tunes that made it for millions-all of them based on 12 bar blues."

These roots led to the highly successful "I'm Gonna Move To The Outskirts of Town" the first of Jordan's R&B Chart hits, backed with "Knock Me A Kiss". The record featured a raw, gut kicking, sound of the saxophone that got even the oldest in the room up and moving.

But Jordan still had to wonder why that wasn't enough to kick-start his career. By early 1942, although his record sales were climbing, Jordan couldn't escape his regular gig at the cabaret.

Robert Johnson's mythology of selling his soul to the devil at a crossroads has become part of blues music's colorful lore. However, Louis Jordan's decision to *actually hire* the devil, in 1942, proved the breakthrough that he'd been searching for.

Don Robey, "whose longtime business partner and mistress, Evelyn Johnson, described him as a 'one-dimensional gangster with a gun and a gambling problem'". "He was very real and very dangerous...liked to bundle his cash in burlap sacks, pop two shells into his 12-gauge shotgun, and head downtown" to the bank. But Robey knew how to promote…no matter what it took. Club and radio station owners quickly learned not to stand in his way. 103

Lous Jordan and the Tympany Five started in Louisiana and Texas, playing, what eventually came to be known as the "chitlin' circuit" (followed by Little Richard, Bobby "Blue" Bland, T-Bone Walker, B.B. King, Little Junior Parker, Big Mama Thornton), with often segregated gigs, however, the crowds grew larger and crazier at every stop. They triggered mountains of joyously broken beer bottles from cheering audiences in Houston and something close to hysteria in New Orleans.

Next up came Chicago, and gigs that even Billboard had to take special note of. Louis Jordan's 1943 release of the smash breakthrough hit "Five Guys Named Moe" that peaked at Number 3 on Billboard's Race Records chart, featured a tenor sax solo by Jordan that was later described as "the prototype for the whole school of rhythm and blues saxophonists". This song established Jordan as a major recording star.

Jordan had a badly needed edge over the competition-his sax solos boiled in champagne and barrel whiskey that could sweep through an audience and wash away every fear and worry.

If, however, Jordan wanted to launch himself up into permanent residence in the stars, he still needed Lady Luck to put him in the right place at the right time, a Lady Luck that came disguised as a strike, a bargain, and arrogance.

By 1938, annual record sales in the US had climbed back to 40 million and hit 130 million by 1941.

Jukeboxes and radio stations played an increasingly important role. For live radio play, however, "black musicians" were banned from radio performances" (with the exception of prominent artists like Duke Ellington, Earl "Fatha" Hines, and Chick Webb). Since most of these were free plays, the American Society of Composers, Authors and Publishers (ASCAP) on behalf of songwriters, producers and musicians, try to triple the licensing fees for radio stations. The radio stations retaliated by forming, in 1940, The Broadcast Music Inc. (BMI) to compete with ASCAP for performing rights royalties. With its formation, what had been the monopoly of Tin Pan Alley music publishers and song writers was broken open, creating new opportunities for independent publishers and songwriters.

The radio stations quickly discovered that ASCAP, which had been formed in 1914, held copyright on almost all popular types of music. If the radio stations wanted to survive, to keep people listening and the advertising revenues flowing in, they had to turn to music that ASCAP didn't have locked up, namely "race" and "hillbilly".

ASCAP executives were quoted as saying that these types of music were "Garbage music, terrible music…" 105. Radio stations, however, began to broadcast far more "race" and "hillbilly" music (The Grand Old Opry was one of the most popular radio shows) to the public via jukeboxes and the radio.

Since radio was the most efficient way to promote music, increased play brought new found exposure with resulting popularity to the point that the name "hillbilly" (which, by the late 1940s, was being used to describe a wide variety of styles, including honky tonk, western swing and bluegrass records) was changed, on June 25, 1949, to "country and western" music and "race records" was changed to "rhythm and blues".

"BMI is really a great story for what eventually turned into rock n' roll" said song publisher Irv Lichtman.105

"Country and western" music had broad roots and influences with covers of gospel (e.g. Red Foley on songs written by Thomas Dorsey) the Delmore Brothers with their version of boogie woogie, the phenomenal Hank Williams and Jimmie Rodgers with blues, western swing with Bob Wills and the Texas Playboys (whose sound grew closer to Louis Jordan), bluegrass with Bill Monroe, Roy Acuff and Flatt and Scruggs, country with Eddie Arnold, and the band that reinvented the art of stage performance, the "Maddox Brothers and Rose" a family band who described their music as "country boogie" (other examples include Tennessee Ernie Ford, George Jones and Hank Snow).

Although ASCAP subsequently dropped the increase in licensing fees due to a lack of support, in 1942, with German bombs raining down out of the sky and American battleships rotting at the bottom of Pearl Harbor, the American Federation of Musicians

(AFM) chose that moment to go on strike, its members refusing to perform on any new records in Canada or the USA. They demanded higher royalty fees from record companies, that sales to jukebox operators be stopped, and that radio stations no longer broadcast records, only live performances. Which was nothing new. When RCA (Radio Corporation of America) first started producing in the 1920s, (KDKA in Pittsburgh, Pa. was the first commercial radio station), record companies changed recording contracts to forbid major artists from working on radio.

Singers, however, were not covered by AFM strike mandate. Record companies began to shift from big band arrangements to singers backed only by vocal groups. When the strike ended in 1944, singers were now listed first on the record label and became more popular than their big band former employers.

The big band era was soon under siege. War time curfew and blackouts affected attendance for live gigs, tire and gas rationing made it difficult to travel and band members were called up to serve in the Armed Forces.

Although big bands would continue after the war, they would never regain the popularity of the 1930s. Record sales on the pop charts declined by more than 50 percent.

As discussed in John Broven's fine book "Record Makers and Breakers-Voices Of The Independent Rock n' Roll Pioneers", although in the early 1940s, Columbia, Decca and RCA Victor controlled the music industry. and practically every aspect of the record making process, with the end of World War II, the price of shellac dropped significantly and magnetic recording tape was introduced that dramatically reduced the costs of recording.105

The formation of Broadcast Music Inc. (BMI) to compete with ASCAP, had resulted in the promotion of rhythm and blues and country and western records. BMI's start-up network of 256 radio stations, coupled with the substantial drop in recording costs, the explosive growth of jukeboxes, and war time restrictions on live entertainment, opened the door for the growth of "Indy" record labels. When the going gets tough, the tough turn pro.

Indy Labels

Small, independent labels exploded, often competing with the major labels by releasing cover versions of hit songs. Due to war time shortages in shellac, the major labels had focused on artists with the broadest market appeal, with the result that artists on the subsidiary "race" labels of major music companies weren't recorded or given little time or promotion. The indie labels quickly moved in.

Close to a thousand new labels were formed between 1948 and 1954, targeting specific genres of music and regional markets. This focused approach kept overhead low and promoted sales to niche audiences.

That's when, some would later claim, the demons first started to gather, but the coming collective paranoia and palace revolts in the music business were well underway.

> *"Toto, I have a feeling we're not in Kansas anymore…"*
> Dorothy arriving in Oz
> (from the movie The Wizard of Oz)

A few of the notables:

Chess was founded by Leonard Chess and Phil Chess, original names Lejzor and Fiszel Czyn. Chess Records developed out of Aristocrat Records. Leonard had bought a liquor store in Chicago and when that went well, opened a small nightclub the Macomba Lounge. Leonard became involved with

Aristocrat when he introduced nightclub singer Andrew Tibbs to the owners. Initially, Aristocrat's record releases disappeared quickly, however, Leonard's partner at Aristocrat, Evelyn Arons (who had founded the label in 1947; she and her husband were divorced in 1948 and Leonard became involved), convinced Leonard that an untapped market of southerners had moved to Chicago and the electric blues of artist Muddy Waters would appeal to them. They initially pressed 3000 singles and when those quickly sold out, they went into overtime pressing more records and distributed them widely. Suddenly and dramatically, they were a force in the music business. Chess Records would become a critically influential blues label recording Howlin' Wolf, Muddy Waters, Gene Ammons, Little Walter, Bo Diddley, Chuck Berry, Willie Dixon and many more ("Checker" later was an associated label).

The name was changed to Chess Records in 1950 after Evelyn Arons decided to focus on record distribution and left Aristocrat.106

Beacon, Savoy (started by Herman Lubinsky who ran a record store in New Jersey) plus National Records (founded by A.B. Green in New York City; the promotion leader was Herb Abramson, later a co-founder of Atlantic Records), Varsity, and Keynote labels targeted Harlem and Newark, New Jersey.

Meteor (Memphis Tennessee, supervised by Lester Bihari, one of the four Bihari brothers), Modern (Beverly Hills California, founded in 1945 by Joe, Jules and Saul Bihari whose associated labels included Blues & Rhythm, Flair, Crown, Kent and RPM), King in Cincinnati, the blues label Excello Records (Nashville), Sun in Memphis (which gave artists the opportunity to create their own recordings for relatively little money; Sam Phillips recorded B.B. King, Howlin' Wolf, Bobby Bland, Junior Parker and James Cotton), Imperial out of New Orleans that initially became popular with Fats Domino, Modern and Specialty (Little Richard) in Los Angeles, MGM and Mercury, plus specialized labels like Electra and Folkways for folk music, Blue Note, Prestige, Verve, Pacific Jazz and Fantasy for jazz artists, were just a few of the many labels that smashed down the palace walls of the music world after World War II.

Another indie that eventually became a critically influential major label, was Atlantic Records. Founded in New York City by Ahmet Ertegun and Herb Abramson (his wife Miriam ran the label's publishing company), and partly financed by Vahid Sabit, a Turkish dentist. Two critically influential new partners who joined in the early 1950s, were Gerald Wexler (widely credited for being one of the first, if not the first, to use the term "rhythm and blues" to replace the term "race") and the older brother, Nesuhi Ertegun. Ahmet and Nesuhi reportedly had a collection of twenty-five thousand jazz and blues records, earlier had promoted jazz concerts in Washington D.C. in the early 1940s and when Atlantic was first launched, focused on jazz recordings; however, when those sales disappointed, they moved into rhythm and blues.

What were those early days like? In an article for the New Yorker by George W. S. Trow entitled *"Eclectic, Reminiscent, Amused, Fickle, Perverse"*, a profile of Ahmet Ertegun, Jerry Wexler said: "…at 234 West Fifty-sixth Street, next door to Patsy's Restaurant, 'That was our office, man, and our studio. When we wanted to record, we moved the furniture against the wall'." 106A In their early years, Chess used a toilet as an echo chamber.

Atlantic, in its early years, made a point of reintroducing established artists like Joe Turner and Tiny Grimes with new arrangements and innovatively produced/promoted artists such as Ruth Brown. LaVern Baker, The Clovers, Willis Jackson, Ray Charles, Clyde McPhatter, The Gospeleers, and Professor Longhair (Henry Roeland Byrd) (Ahmet walked through the dark and threatening fields and streets of New Orleans, only to discover that the Professor had just signed with Meteor Records; however, the Professor eventually signed with Atlantic).

Ahmet, however, commented on the practical realities of the music business: "It is like a marriage. I mean, the relationship between an artist and the label. There is the initial excitement, you know, and it goes on for a while, but it is very rare that it goes on *forever*. Either the artist finds someone richer or the label finds someone younger."106B

Atlantic's, 14 LPs, collection, *Atlantic Rhythm and Blues 1947-1974*, issued in 1985, is highly recommended. In Volume 1 of that collection, Joe

Turner's "Sweet Sixteen" is described as the "unique and identifiable" "Atlantic Sound" (Budd Johnson and Freddie Mitchell on tenor saxes, Arlem Kareem on baritone sax).

Louisiana's J.D. Miller (see the following interview with Lionel Prevost who played on nearly 800 recordings) started with Fais Do Do Records that later became Feature Records, founded a long list of labels- e.g. Zynn, Cajun Classics, Tribute, and expecially Excello-each designed for a specific type of music such as Swamp Pop, Cajun and Swamp Blues,.

Billboard recognized the indies growing importance and impact. In 1942, Billboard established "Harlem Hit Parade", followed in 1945, with formation of other "race" charts that included "Juke Box Plays".

Earl Hines had a hit on the budget label Bluebird (a subsidiary of RCA Victor known for its low cost blues/ r&b recordings and often cited as an early influence for rock n' roll) with the song "Jelly Jelly" featuring the vocals of Billy Eckstein (later covered in 1967 with a great interpretation by the James Cotton Blues Band-Verve Records-with Gene Barge on tenor sax):

Arnold Shaw, in his excellent book "Honkers and Shouters-The Golden Years of Rhythm and Blues" argues that the success of Cecil Grant's hit, "I Wonder", on Gilt-Edge Records from L.A. that soared to Number 1 on Jukebox Race Charts and Number 20 on the pop charts in 1944, then repeated in 1945 at Number One on Jukebox, only this time featuring

Roosevelt Sykes (Louis Armstrong and Warren Evans also did cover versions), proved that indie labels could financially compete with the major labels, setting the stage for the post-war explosion in jump and rhythm and blues. 107

For Louis Jordan, the end of World War Two was emphatically "the right place at the right time". Few hit it bigger.

In 1946, record sales boomed to 350 million. Courtesy of the AMF strike, his music was more widely played on the radio. Jordan's music could dance away the blues and kiss every pain.

Jordan combined blues, swing and boogie music into a hard driving, new sound called "jump blues", that influenced musicians, throughout the 1950s and 60s, including Sonny Rollins who said that: "I listened to Louis Jordan a lot. I meant he gassed me." 108

Jordan's records swept the charts with songs like "Is You Is or Is You Ain't My Baby", "Caledonia", "Choo Choo Ch'Boogie" (estimated to have sold over 2 million copies!) and "Saturday Night Fish Fry" (originally written by Ellis Walsh and recorded by Eddie Williams and His Brown Buddies; Jordan changed the arrangement in jump blues style; Chuck Berry later acknowledged copying this).

Louis Jordan had nearly 60 Top Ten hits on the US Race/R&B Charts , 12 Top Ten Hits on US Pop Charts and even 3 Top Ten on US Country, plus he hit #1 twice between 1942-1948, including the cross over hit "Open The Door Richard" that also featured Jack McVea on sax.

These hits opened the door for other artists to break through, including Haddie Brooks ("Swinging The Boogie"), Nellie Lutcher ("Hurry On Down"), and Julia Lee ("King Size Papa"). 109

The success of "Caledonia" (originally recorded by Woody Herman and his Orchestra in March 1945, Jordan's was release in April 1945) led to a world tour in 1946. Jordan's new promotional campaign, created by his manager Berle Adams, helped to break new ground in marketing. For "Caledonia", Adams struck a deal with film company and distributer, Astor Films, to make two short films per year.

Astor was an independent distributor with 26 offices across the USA. They made Jordan's short films available to movie theatres for only $25-50.00, compared to the major film distributors who "always demanding block deals, never guaranteeing timing of the film's booking" in order to coincide with the appearance of the musicians. That's why indies theatre operators broke "their backs to get the promo film for 'Caledonia', but stayed away from musical shorts produced by major film studios."

[Editor's Note: Singer Ursula Greville was part owner of Synchrophone and the label Octacros 110 The label released private recordings cinemas would play against films. Decca purchased the label in 1937].

"Caledonia", the film short, would open a few days before Jordan arrived and he would make personal appearances at theatres to sign autographs and plug his records.

{Billboard on June 8, 1946 at page 38. Featured an advertisement of that promoted "The No. 1 Race Record Of The Nation" with 'Voo-it Voo It' by the Blues Woman with Buddy Banks Sextet, 'Milton's Boogie Groovy Blue' by Roy Milton and his Solid Senders, plus "Other Big Juke Box Hits" that included 'Pine Top's Boogie Woogie' by the Bailey Swing Group"]

Downbeat noted Jordan's success, writing that he had become "one of the highest paid, if not the highest paid cocktail combo in the business". 111

Louis Jordan would influence players for years to come, including some of the greatest saxophonists in r&b, rock and jazz. His version of Caledonia, for example, has been covered 122 times (https://secondhandsongs.com/performance/83536/) as of the date of this writing, including by Bill Haley, James Brown, Downchild Blues Band, Pinetop Perkins, Willie Nelson & Wynton Marsalis, Powder Blues Band, Little Willie Littlefield, Roy Clark and Gatemouth Brown.

Forces, however, were at work, invisible at first but beginning to take shape and gain momentum, forces that would soon lift the darkness from many eyes.

1960: #3 R&B #28 HOT 100 *Ooh Poo Pah Doo-Part II* **Jessie Hill**
DAVID LASTIE - TENOR

Photo courtesy George Porter, Jr.

According to Jessie Hill; "We started playing 'Ooh Poo Pah Pah Doo' as a gimmick, but it got really big, everywhere we went". With Allen Toussaint on the piano and David Lastie on tenor saxophone, Jessie Hill created an irresistible song loosely based on the rhythms of carnival singing. It was recorded in New Orleans on December 12, 1959. Minit Records rushed it out to coincide with the local carnival, and the recording quickly spread from New Orleans to other markets. Jessie Hill (vocal, tambourine), Nat Perilliat, David Lastie (ts), Clarence Ford (bs), Allen Toussaint (p), Roy Montrell (g), Richard Payne (b), John Boudreaux (d).

Bio courtesy *Up From The Cradle Of Jazz-New Orleans Music Since World War II*- Berry, Foose & Jones:

As a child, David Lastie watched Louis Jordan on the nickelodeon performing "Caledonia," feet stomping, knees high, and an irrepressible smile as he sang. The image stayed in David's head. Leroy Sergion, who played alto in Roy Brown's band, showed David the key finger placements on the horn. David drew the sax keys on a small, flat board and would play along with Sergion. Buddy Hagan, Fats Domino's saxophone player, gave David formal lessons. David was influenced by national recording artists Jimmy Liggins, Jimmy Forest and Louis Jordan. David's first band was called the Houserockers.

    Lastie worked with just about every artist in New Orleans during the fifties while playing in house bands. He also joined the pool of session men working periodically at Matassa's studio in the 1960s. He became a valuable sideman on early Minit recordings by Alen Toussaint.

Women Take The Solos

During World War Two, with many all-male big bands brought to their knees by rationing and departures for the armed forces, all-female bands quickly formed to keep the music alive. Big bands including:

- The International Sweethearts of Rhythm with saxophonist Rosalind Cron (the first integrated all women band; named "America's No. 1 All-Girl Orchestra" by *Downbeat* magazine in 1944),
- Darlings of Rhythm The All American Girl Band
- Hour of Charm, featuring musicians like the great pianist Hazel Scott (who later had her own television show)
- Blanche Calloway and Her Joy Boys
- Ina Rae Hutton and her Melodears.

Today, some female musicians criticize these bands, arguing "all-female groups tend to marginalize women musicians" and "that gender shouldn't play any role in the music".

That's one of the problems with look-back criticism, imposing modern day values and standards on situations decades old.

We can't help but live in the times that we are born in with its modern values, standards and perceptions.

However, when we try to apply these to earlier time periods, we need to do this with a real understanding of those eras. This type of criticism too often reveals a fatal lack of understanding of the practical realities of the 1930s-1940s, where women musicians -aside from singers- who tried to find the opportunity to play, often were confronted with gender and racial bias.

It has been acknowledged that "Women did contribute to the early formation of jazz genre" but "women instrumentalists, especially 'horn' players (saxophones, trumpets, and trombone) often go unheard, and unknown. They have been made invisible." 113

Have things changed in the 21st Century? In rock, r&b and hip hop, female artists top the charts, and approximately half of classical orchestras are composed of women musicians; however, when it comes to brass players, it's a different story. Trombonist Hillary Simms is the first woman to become a member of the prestigious American Brass Quintet. As reported in the New York Times, when she first started her career, she quickly discovered that she was working in a male-dominated field.

She was told to disguise the fact she was a woman. For blind orchestra auditions, when playing behind a screen, "Don't breathe too shallow, you'll sound like a girl" or "Don't wear high heels, so they won't know you're a woman…"

"But in all-female groups, there's just this comfort level of knowing that everything that I've gone through in my career, the other members have had similar experiences...I don't have to put on a mask to play."114

The World War II impact on big bands provided women instrumentalists with the previously rare opportunity to be seen and heard.115

With millions of men enlisted in the armed forces of the United States, Canada and Great Britain, their absent created openings in every aspect of the music business. Following are a few examples of the important contributions of women in the music business.116

Outstanding musicians who emerged in the 1930s and 1940s include:

- The legendary jazz composer, arranger and pianist extraordinaire **Mary Lou Williams** who worked with Duke Ellington, Benny Goodman, Thelonious Monk, Cecil Taylor, Louis Armstrong, Charlie Parker, Miles Davis, Dizzy Gillespie, to name just a few. Her musicianship and influence was such that she has been **described as the "Mount Rushmore" of jazz**.

  In 2021, new performances of her "Zodiac Suite" were presented including by the New York Philharmonic; in 2023, a chamber orchestra version was released on the Mack Avenue record label by Aaron Diehl & The Knights.

- the great jazz guitarist **Mary Osborne**;

- **Dorothy Donegan**, pianist, a protégé of Art Tatum ("the only person who made me practice" said Art Tatum)

- saxophonists **Fran Gaddison** (jazz piano and saxophone; played with Lionel Hampton, Billie Holiday, Wes Montgomery

- Margaret Backstrum, tenor sax

- trombone player **Sammy Lee Jett**
https://libguides.uky.edu/AAWPMI/Trombone
https://www.wbur.org/npr/130915265/the-mosaic-project

Also, see Lara Pellegrinelli (2013) A DIY Guide To The History Of Women In Jazz
https://www.npr.org/sections/ablogsupreme/2013/05/10/182885860/a-diy-guide-to-the-history-of-women-in-jazz

Songwriters

- **Irene Higginbotham** (she reportedly sometimes used the name "Glen Gibson" to disguise that she was a woman)-songs include: "Good Morning Heartache" for Billie Holiday, "This Will Make You Laugh" recorded by Nat King Cole Trio, Carmen

McRae and Marvin Gaye to name a few, and "It's Mad, Mad, Mad" for Duke Ellington;

• **Dorothy Fields** who wrote lyrics for more than 400 songs, including the Oscar winner "The Way You Look Tonight" for Jerome Kern, co-wrote with Jimmy McHugh "On the Sunny Side of the Street and I Can't Give You Anything But Love Baby.")

Singers
(in addition to those discussed earlier)

• **Ella Fitzgerald** (Queen Of Jazz")

• **Peggy Lee**

https://projectrevolver.org/features/articles/women-jazz-10-ladies-changed-music-forever/

Owners, Producers, Engineers, Executives

• **Ethel Gabriel** started working, in 1940, at RCA. Camden. New Jersey. Promoted to record tester for quality control, she learned quickly from studio engineers. Later, as the first female record producer for a major label, she not only produced 2500 records but also selected songs, arrangers and studio musicians for artists like Elvis Presley and

Chet Atkins. In 1955, she produced the Number One hit Perez Prado's *Cherry Pink And Apple Blossom White*. After producing six Grammy winning albums, including *Tommy Dorsey / Frank Sinatra The Complete Sessions*, in 1959, she was the first female music producer to receive an RIAA Gold Record. Women in Music Inc. In 1997, she was awarded the title of First A&R Producer in the Industry. After becoming vice-president of RCA, she retired from the company in 1983.

> **Daphne Oram** was a pioneering electronic music composer and performer. She got her start by refusing to go to the Royal College of Music in 1942. Instead, she went to work for the BBC as a Junior Studio Engineer. Promoted to studio manager in the 1950s, she established the BBC Radiophonic Workshop in 1958. She left the BBC in 1959 and became the first full-time electronic music composer in Britain.

• **Evelyn Blanchard** was the engineer of the Number One hit, in 1947, 'Smoke! Smoke! Smoke! (That Cigarette)' by Tex Williams. at Radio Records. Los Angeles California. Evelyn also performed disc dubbing and tape editing. Radio Records has been declared an historical site primarily due to the artists who recorded there, including Billie Holiday, Charlie Parker, Sam Cooke, Louis Armstrong, Patti Page, Elvis Presley, and Jimi Hendrix.

- **Estelle Axton**, with her brother Jim Stewart created the important and critically influential Stax Records. A second mortgage on her home enable them to covert an old movie theatre into a recording studio. Their artists and hits became a critically important musical voice. The Grammy Awards honored her with the Trustee's Award in 2006.
The rediscovery of demos performed by the songwriters of the legendary Memphis recording studio reveals a hidden history of soul. See: Bilger Burkhard (2023) The Secret Sound of Stax.
https://www.newyorker.com/magazine/2023/06/05/the-secret-sound-of-stax?utm_source=nl&
https://staxrecords.bandcamp.com/album/written-in-their-soul-the-stax-songwriter-demos

- **Lillian Shedd McMurry** (December 30, 1921 – March 18, 1999) An important influence in the development of blues music. She discovered Elmore James and Sonny Boy Williamson II. She'd heard about

Williamson's playing, was able to contact his wife, Mattie. He signed a recording contract and she set up the first session (in a little studio about ten by twelve feet), on January 4, 1951, that feature Elmore James and Joe Willie Wilkins on guitar, pianist Willie Love and Joe Dyson on drums. Eight songs were recorded, but only two were released, "Eyesight To The Blind" and "Crazy About You Baby". The former record subsequently had to be recut due to a fire in a Chicago warehouse that destroyed the masters, this time without Elmore James on guitar. It became a big hit. In 1950, she founded Trumpet Records and the parent company Diamond Record Company. Although their first releases featured gospel music, she recorded Elmore James' original recording "Dust My Broom" and Sonny Boy Williamson's "Nine Degrees Below Zero". 117 She also is credited with writing Williamson's "Red Hot Kisses".

> Some have argued that Elmore James only did one recording for Trumpet because he was "tricked" into recording "Dust My Broom". Lilliam McMurray angrily denied this. The real reason is that Elmore couldn't come up with another song for the reverse side of "Dust My Blues". "Elmore was supposed to have

been getting another side to record but he just couldn't come up with it...he couldn't even cut another song for the back of his record."117

Musicians recorded by her include Arthur "Big Boy" Crudup, Big Joe Williams and Willie Love. She hired B.B. King and Little Milton Campbell to play on the productions.

She refused to follow the segregationist polices of the musicians' union and faced financial issues throughout her recording career, eventually forced to close Trumpet in 1955, but tried to continue with her new label Globe Music. She later paid for Sonny Boy Williamson's tombstone in 1965 and was inducted into the Blues Hall Of Fame in 1998.

- **Bess Berman**- together with her husband Isaac "Ike" Berman, Herman "Hy" Siegel and Sam Schneider, they established Apollo Records, in New York City in 1944, with a focus on gospel and rhythm and blues. Her artists included Mahalia Jackson, Champion Jack Dupree, Wynonie Harris, and Solomon Burke. She took sole control of the business in 1948.

- **Miriam P. "Mimi" Trepel**-a radio broadcaster and pioneering record industry distribution manager, described by writer John Broven as "an unseen heroine of rock 'n' roll."118

She started at WLIB in 1944 with music programming and production, broadcasting shows by artists that included Ella Fitzgerald and Ethel Waters.

In 1946 she moved to WMCA, became interested in the work of music publishers and copyright responsibilities. She soon became head of music programming at WLIB in 1947. She joined London Records, in 1954, a subsidiary of Decca Records. She was appointed head of the company's music publishing subsidiaries, for both ASCAP and BMI copyrights, and managed the company's foreign distribution department.

She was responsible for negotiating releases by the American artists in Britain and elsewhere including records by Atlantic, Monument, and Dot. Those records helped to practically define rock & roll and rhythm & blues, including labels such as Imperial (e.g. Fats Domino), Specialty (e.g. Little Richard), Sun, Atlantic, Chess, and Vee-Jay (e.g. Jimmy Reed, John Lee Hooker and The Spaniels), and later Motown (e.g. The Supremes).

- **Vivian Carter-** She and her husband James C. Bracken who started out in Chicago radio and had their own record shop in Gary Indiana, founded Vee Jay Records in 1953, and used their initials for the name of the company. The first record they released, The Spaniels' "Baby It's You" hit the Top Ten of America's national rhythm and blues charts.

  Her brother Calvin Carter was instrumental in signing artists like Jimmy Reed, Five Blind Boys, Staple Singers, the El Dorados, Dee Clark, John Lee Hooker, Jerry Butler, Betty Everett and jazz sax great Eddie Harris.

  They discovered Jimmy Reed who was working in Chicago stockyards cutting up cattle but also was playing harmonica for the singer King David. In the recording studio, he would sit on a drum case with his wife seated next to him. He would ask her to recite the song lyrics. For most of his sessions, he reportedly was drunk with the result his voice was slurred, but this gave his records a relaxed sound.119

  In 1962, Vee Jay heard a record by an English artist Frank Ifield, "I Remember

You". They offered to trade a song by The Four Seasons to acquire the American rights to the song but had to also take a "package" of other artists. One group they had to take to make the deal work was by an unknown band with the strange name "The Beatles" and their record "Love Me Do", which became their first American release. The Beatles flopped in North America…The soon-to-be greatest band of the 1960s, and still influential in the 21st Century, flopped in the United States of America…on their first try.

Notes

95. Proust (2009) "Le Temps Retrouve" Peter Lang AG, Internationaler Verlag der Wissenschaften; Bilingual - New edition (August 31, 2009).

96 – Popa C (2008) Louis Jordan "Jump and Jive With The Tympany Five."
http://www.bigbandlibrary.com/louisjordan.html

97 Sharpe op. cit.

98. Domenic Priore. (2011) The Tall Cool Tale of Paul Revere & the Raiders: A conversation with Mark Lindsay and Paul Revere. March 24, 2011. Permission courtesy of Jay Millar Sundazed Music / Modern Harmonic, Nashville.
https://sundazed.com/a-conversation-with-mark-lindsay.aspx

99 Balliett op. cit. pg. 92

100 Palmer op. cit. pg. 130; Balliett op. cit pgs 54-55; Clarence "Pinetop" Smith pg. 52;

Silvester PJ. (1989) A Left Hand Like God. The Story of Boogie Woogie. Da Capo (Jan. 1 1989)

101 . Chilton J (1997) Let the good times roll : the story of Louis Jordan and his music. University of Michigan Press; Reprint edition (Oct. 30 1997). Pgs 48-49; 101A 67-69.

Kock S (2014) Louis Jordan: Son of Arkansas, Father of R&B; pg.17; The History Press.

102. Kock Ibid. pg. 17

103. Lauterbach Preston (2015) *Sympathy For The Devil*. Oxford American. A Magazine Of The South.

A fascinating look at the segregated recording industry, life on the "chitlin' circuit" with artists like Johnny Acey, Little Richard, Bobby "Blue" Bland, T-Bone Walker, B.B. King, Little Junior Parker, Big Mama Thornton".https://main.oxfordamerican.org/magazine/item/1040-sympathy-for-the-devil

104. Ibid.

105. Broven J (2010) Record Makers and Breakers: Voices of the Independent Rock 'n' Roll Pioneers. University of Illinois Press; First Edition (Jan. 13 2010)

106. https://www.spontaneouslunacy.net/aristocrat-records/

https://www.discogs.com/label/667134-The-Aristocrat-Record-Corporation

https://78rpm.club/record-labels/aristocrat-2/

106A Trow GWS (1978) *Eclectic, Reminiscent, Amused, Fickle, Perverse',* New Yorker, May 22.1978.

https://www.newyorker.com/magazine/1978/05/29/eclectic-reminiscent-amused-fickle-perverse-i

106B

https://www.newyorker.com/magazine/1978/06/05/eclectic-reminiscent-amused-fickle-perverse-ii

107. Shaw op. cit. pgs. xvii and 129-130.

108 Balliett op. cit. pg. 154.

109. Whitburn, Joel (1996). Top R&B/Hip-Hop Singles: 1942–1995. Record Research. pp. 621, 235.

110. https://www.discogs.com/label/835073-Octacros.

111. Chilton op. cit. pg. 98

112. Tim Price

http://ricoreeds.blogspot.com/2015/08/tim-price-bloggin-for-daddario.html

113. https://alumni.duke.edu/magazine/articles/swing-shift-all-girl-bands-1940s

https://www.vintageinn.ca/2016/03/women-of-the-big-band-era/

114. Javier C. Hernández (2023) A Trombonist on a Mission to Break Barriers in Classical Music. New York Times July 30, 2023. https://www.nytimes.com/2023/07/30/arts/music/hillary-simms-american-brass-quintet.html?action=click&module=Well&pgtype=Homepage&section=Music

115. https://www.researchgate.net/publication/263229324_Jazzwomen_music_sound_gender_and_sexuality

116. https://apriltucker.com/timeline-women-1930/

https://www.womeninmusic.org/
https://www.womeninmusic.ca/en/

April Tucker (2022) Finding Your Career in the Modern Audio Industry. Focal Press; (July 29, 2022)

117. Franz S (2003) The Amazing Secret History of Elmore James. Wolsworth Publishing Company. Marceline, Missouri. pgs. 20-22; pgs. 33-34

118. Broven op. cit. pgs. pp. 401–411.

119. *The Vee-jay Story 1953-1993; Collector's Edition;* Liner Notes

References

Broven J (2010) "Record Makers and Breakers-Voices Of The Independent Rock n' Roll Pioneers", University of Illinois Press; (January 13, 2010) https://www.press.uillinois.edu/books/?id=p077272

6

Flying Home
By Neil Sharpe

Big bands continued to tour after World War II, however, a new sound was rolling across the country, radio stations and jukeboxes couldn't get enough of it.

It was happily fueled by a 19 year old tenor sax player who, on May 26, 1942, blew the world away. During a recording session for Decca records, by Lionel Hampton's big band, tenor sax player Illinois Jacquet…

Illinois Jacquet © William Gottlieb

...stepped forward and ignited a spark that would fuel a revolution, with his seminal 64 bar, wailing R&B solo on "Flying Home". While that solo lit the fuse, it was Illinois Jacquet's "incredible, screaming" performance during the "Jazz At The Philharmonic Concert In Los Angeles", in 1944, on the song "Blues" that creatively set afire a breakthrough generation of musicians who helped to invent a revolutionary, surging, gritty, raucous, new form of music.

Jazz At The Philharmonic - Philharmonic Auditorium, Los Angeles, July 2, 1944.

https://www.youtube.com/watch?v=1iktZrraWQg'

Once other musicians heard this new sound, they tried to push it as far as they could. Which led them back to where it all began- "boogie woogie". The music that people had long looked to for escape; a music born out of road gangs, driving rail, plowing fields, dying-on-your-feet factory jobs and out of a hardship and despair that brought tears to the failed angels of the soul. 120

"If anything can truly be said to be the philosophical core of the blues, it is this: when you suffer you can at least boogie, and when you boogiein', you ain't suffering. But first you got to face the fact you're suffering. Once you acknowledge you pain, you can get to dealing with it." 121

Although the debate about what was the first rock n' roll record and the first rock n' roll artist will forever drone on, blues, gospel, New Orleans jazz, and boogie woogie are a good place to start.

Sister Rosetta Tharpe took these styles and fused them into a distinctive sound that became a critical influence on what soon would be known as "rock n' roll", with hits like "Rock Me" (1938), "The Train" (1939, "Down By The Riverside" (1944) and "Strange Things Happening Every Day" (on Decca 1944;1946).

Chuck Berry once said his entire career was "one long Sister Rosetta Tharpe impersonation." On stage, she did an early version of Berry's duckwalk, but all you needed to hear is the guitar introduction to Sister Rosetta's 1947 hit "The Lord Followed Me" to recognize Chuck's musical debt to her.

Compare her record "The Train" to Little Walter's 1955 No.1 R&B hit, "My Babe,"

One of the first to use distortion on an electric guitar, she became a critical influence, especially for British blues and guitar players in the 1960s, including Eric Clapton and Keith Richards

She also is credited with playing a critical role in the career of Little Richard. On what is now recognized as one of the Top 100 albums of the 20th Century, "Here's Little Richard", his left hand playing on those songs owed to a large debt to boogie woogie. 122

If we look to boogie woogie for the heart of rock n' roll, what about its soul? At this point, the fierce debate begins once again, the debaters' glasses filled with ice and demon whiskey, names recited like Chuck Berry, Fats Domino, Elvis Presley, Little

Richard, Joe Turner but what about the flamboyant, jump blues sax players, who reinvented stage image and presence, when they lay on their backs under blistering strobe lights and drove rapturous audiences into "frenzy" and "delirium", with explosive, honking, screaming solos.

"Joe Houston and Big Jay McNeely were some of the wildest of the honkers. Their unique approach to driving riffs and musical mayhem is a constant source of inspiration for me. While he may be best known for his wild honking workouts, sometimes very appropriately named after natural disasters (Earthquake, Hurricane, Thunderstorm)...

Joe Houston could also nail a low-down blues like 'Hog Maws', handle a ballad like 'I Cover The Waterfront' as well as blast through the swing-to-bop encyclopedia on 'Lester Leaps In'.

He played smooth with vocal groups on 'Blues After Hours' and 'Troubles and Worries' and rocked through stomping tunes like 'The Hully' and a whole series of dance craze LP's like the 'Twist' and the 'Limbo'. His relentless energy, brawny tone, and willingness to explore the extremes make Joe Houston one of the all-time greats of Rhythm & Blues Saxophone.

Big Jay also took the honking approach to the extreme in performance and recording. In his live shows he's been known to drop to his knees, lay on his back, walk through the crowd, or play out in the street. I've seen him come out in a darkened club with a fluorescent sax! His recorded music ranges from more understated Jump-Blues instrumentals to novelty vocal tunes ('Insect Ball') to complete glorious musical chaos ('Real Crazy Cool').

Big J's '3-D' is a masterpiece featuring the intricate interplay between Jay and his brother Bob who played background, answers and counter lines on the baritone sax often spontaneously with Jay's frantic riffs and ideas."

Sax Gordon Beadle
https://saxgordon.com/

In 1947 and early 1948, Roy Brown (his record label termed it "Rocking Blues") and Wynonie Harris both had hits with "Good Rockin' Tonight". Brown's featured tenor sax player Earl Barnes, alto sax O'Neil Jerome; Wynonie Harris' version had Hal Singer on tenor sax and included handclapping to give it a "rockin" rhythm, a feature of gospel music".

- Muddy Waters incorporated electric guitars and harmonica (e.g. "The Blues Had A Baby And They Named It Rock n' Roll").

- Paul Williams climbed to Number One on R&B Charts with "The Huckle-Buck" in March 1949.

- Frank "Floorshow" Culley's "Coleslaw" hit Number 11 R&B, battling it out with covers by Louis Jordan and Jesse Stone

- Tenor sax man Wild Bill Moore had the hit singles "We're Gonna Rock" and "Rock and Roll".

- Arnett Cobb earned the title the "Wild Man of the Tenor Sax" with singles like "Dutch Kitchen Bounce".

- Eddie Chamblee hit Number 1 on Billboards' R&B charts with "Long Gone".

- Jackie Brenston & His Delta Cats did the vastly influential "Rocket 88" (actually performed by Ike Turner and the Kings of Rhythm).

- Roy Brown "Rocking At Midnight" - [Led Zeppelin's Robert Plant formed a "roots" band "The Honey Dippers", covered Roy Brown's "Rockin' At Midnight" and hit #25, in 1984, on Billboard's Top 100]

- Ike Turner and the Kings Of Rhythm's "Box Top" and Jimmy Forrest's "Night Train" were smash hits. "Night Train" inspired musicians for generations to come, including a ferocious version in the 1960s by James Brown that featured (J.C. Davis solo on tenor; Alfred Corley alto, Al "Brisco" Clark baritone; more on this shortly).

Even the world of jazz felt the impact. Whitney Balliett wrote that, in the early 1950's, famed alto jazz saxophonist Johnny Hodges had become "a leader of a small semi-rock-and-roll group", with titles like "Castle Rock" (which also featured "Big Al Sears" on tenor, "You Need To Rock" and "Early Morning Rock". However, what Balliett chose to describe as rock n' roll, more of a blend of swing, jump and r&b, was a far cry from what would soon explode across the pop and r&b charts.

Al Sears
Courtesy http://userserve-ak.last.fm/serve/252/5988132.jpg

Al Sears American jazz tenor saxophonist and bandleader. Replaced Johnny Hodges in Chick Webb's ensemble, played with Elmer Snowden (1931-32), led his own groups between 1933 and 1941. Move on to Andy Kirk (1941-42) and Lionel Hampton (1943-44) before he became a member of Duke Ellington's Orchestra in 1944, replacing Ben Webster until 1949.

He played as a studio musician on a variety of R&B albums in the 1950s and recorded two albums for Swingville Records in 1960.

R&B- Busting Through

Major label record executives who tried to bury the ever-growing influence of rhythm and blues, soon found themselves buried in soggy and stained-soaked sales as the record buying public gave pallid pop tunes and feather weight classics an emphatic kick in the balls. In the late 1940s, a tiny minority of records (one in 25 per one estimate) released by the majors turned a profit. 121A

Radio stations and Indies labels increasingly turned to "Race" records which were proving popular with all types of audiences.

To add to the confusion, a 1948 musicians' strike prevented the major record labels from recording their main stars, some of whom moved to independent labels. With this new growth in popularity, indie labels started their own distribution channels with better dollar margins for the record stores.

For too many record executives, inbred racism and insistence on wallowing in past styles and formats (the style of many rhythm and blues records seemed, for them, to contradict every rule that had led to mainstream success), blinded them to the fact that the game was rapidly changing. Their traditional battle plan of cover, cover, cover would buy a little time (including cover of country songs such as the multi-million seller "Tennessee Waltz" by Patti Page #1 Pop #2 Country) but for those who couldn't or refused to adapt, they were fated to wake up one morning to find themselves curled up among carnage of their careers, the red lights of too-late ambulances filtering in through the windows, rock n' roll vibrating through their still-refusing-to-believe bones.

In the 1950s, major labels were heavily penalized by their failure to provide rock n' roll records. Between 1954 to 1959, record sales nearly tripled from $213,000.00 to $603,000.00. "A large proportion of the increase in sales accrued to independent companies".121A Although the major labels still had a large majority of the top ten hits in 1955, "the independents doubled their top ten hits from 1955 to 1956 then doubled them again in 1957."

One major label, however, did feel the ground moving beneath its feet. Although, at the time, r&b music made up only an estimated 5.7 percent of the total American record market 121A, Decca Records signed Bill Haley who in one session recorded "Rock Around The Clock" and "Shake, Rattle and Roll", that would both hit the Top Ten of Pop in 1954-55.

In Chicago, after the fledgling label, "Aristocrat" had an unexpected hit record with Muddy Waters' "I Can't Be Satisfied", they quickly followed with "I Feel Like I'm Going Home" and harmonica great Little Walter's "I Want My Baby" (with Muddy Waters both on vocals).

In 1950, Aristocrat changed its name to Chess Records (from 1957-1965 located at what became one of music's most famous addresses, 2120 South Michigan Avenue, Chicago, the label's main office and studio). The first release from Chess was by tenor sax great Gene Ammons "My Foolish Heart" which was their big seller for the year 1950.

They subsequently signed a distribution agreement with Sam Phillips' Sun Records and promoted "Rocket 88" by Jackie Brenston and his Delta Cats (Ike Turner and His Rhythm were the musicians who actually did the track), plus the sensational Howlin' Wolf (his "Moanin' at Midnight" and "How Many More Years" were released in 1951 and became all time blues classics).

The Moonglows followed with the hit "Sincerely" (#1 R&B, #20 Pop; subsequently covered by the McGuire Sisters who hit #1 on the Pop charts)

Muddy Walters, Little Walter and Jimmy Rodgers formed a band and started hitting national r&b charts on a regular basis, with songs like "Louisiana Blues", "Honey Bee" and the critically important "She Moves Me" that featured Little Walter using an amplifier for the first time with a solo that forever changed the recorded sound of the harmonica. All proof that small indie labels could not only survive but go head-to-head with the major labels.

"I'm Your Hoochie Coochie Man", "Just Make Love To Me" and "I'm Ready" soon followed from Muddy Waters (whose guitar phrasing influenced later groups like "The Coasters"), while Little Walter recorded the monster hit "Juke", again backed by Muddy.

After Little Walter left to form his own band, Junior Wells replaced him on harmonica. Wells had previously recorded with State Records who also represented Big Walter Horton, Robert Nighthawk, The Danderliers and Cozy Eggleston on tenor sax (to name just a few) who cut one of the instrumental classics from the early 1950s, "The Big Heavy".

If it was a Saturday night with a glass of beer or whiskey and your hand was turning the radio dial trying to find a spark to get the night going, here are a few examples of jump, blues and r&b classics that served as the birthplace for rock n' roll. Which is fitting in that rock n' roll which emphasizes the 2nd and 4th beats of each measure, finds it roots in "polyrhythmic African-derived music."123

- **T Bone Walker** "I'm Still In Love With You". 1945 Comet Records (Bumps Myers sax)

- **Charles Brown** "Drifting Blues" -Best R&B record of 1946 (Cash Box) and "Trouble Blues"- Number 1 R&B 1949

- **Amos Milburn** "Down The Road Apiece". Aladdin 1946
    and "Chicken Shack Boogie" 1948. Aladdin 1949 Number 9 R&B

- **Anne Laurie/Paul Gayten** "Since I Fell For You"   De Lux Records 1947 (cover of original by Buddy Johnson and Ella Johnson 1945)

- **John Lee Hooker** "Boogie Chillen" Modern Records 1948

- **Lowell Fulson**
  - "3 O'clock Blues" Down Town Records 1948 and "Blue Shadows" Swing Time 1950

- **Jimmy Witherspoon**
 "Ain't Nobody's Business" Modern 1949- originally done by Bessie Smith and Alberta Hunter- Otis Spann's later cover is especially powerful.

  - "Bad Bad Whiskey". Aladdin 1950 Number 1 R&B

- **Lightnin' Hopkins** (who was discovered by Lola Anne Cullum in 1946) "T-Model Blues" Gold Star Records 1949 "Don't Think 'Cause You're Pretty" Herald Records 1954

- **Elmore "Elmo" James**
 "Dust My Broom" Trumpet Records 1951

Although "Dust My Broom" has been widely accredited to Robert Johnson, some have argued that the real author was Elmore James. The argument goes the James and Johnson played together and James taught Johnson how to play "Dust My Broom". 124

Johnny Winters, in "Raisin' Cain: The Wild and Raucous Story of Johnny Winter" by May Lou Sullivan, said "Elmore played the same licks on a lot of his songs. His one little lick that he played over and over again—I picked that up. Can't really describe it, but I liked him a lot. He was similar to Robert Johnson—his stuff sounds the same too a lot of times."

- "I Believe"   Meteor   1952

Elmore James' recordings with his band "Broomdusters", usually featured J.T. Brown tenor sax; also credited as sax players were Boyd Atkins, Maxwell Davis, Oliver Sain, Raymond Hill, Danny Moore, and Elmore James (!). On the Chess album "Whose Muddy Shoes", John Brim plays tenor.

- **Howling Wolf**
  "How Many More Years" and "Moaning at Midnight" Chess 1951

- **Willie Mabon**
  "I Don't Know Chess" 1952 #1 R&B

- **Eddie Boyd**
  "Five Long Years" J.O.B. Records 1952

- **B.B.King**
"You Know I Love You"   RPM Records 1952 (Ike Turner piano)

  - **Ray Charles**
  "Midnight Hour "-Atlantic 1952 (Charles had recorded with Swing Time but with that label's pending demise, after a payment of $2500.00, he was signed by Atlantic)

- **Charley Booker**
"I Walked All Night". Sun Records 1952

- **Little Walter** -two all time classics: "Juke"   Checker Records 1952.
and "My Babe" Checker 1954

- **Guitar Slim**
"The Things I Used To Do"   Specialty Records 1953

- **Big Walter Horton**
Easy"   Sun Records 1953 (inspired by "I Almost Lost My Mind" by Ivory Joe Hunter)

- **Big Maybelle**.
"Gabbin' Blues"   Okeh 1953.

- **Jimmy Reed**
  "You Don't Have To Go" Vee-Jay Records 1954 #5 R&B
  and "Ain't That Loving You Baby " Vee-Jay Records 1955 #3 R&B.

Jimmy Reed was widely covered, including The Rolling Stones, The Yardbirds, Elvis Presley, The Animals, Van Morrison and The Grateful Dead.

- **Sonny Boy Williamson**
  "Don't Start Me Talking" Checker (a subsidiary of Chess) 1955

- **Big Joe Turner**
  "Flip Flop & Fly"   Al Sears tenor sax Atlantic 1955.

(As of the date of writing this song has been covered 79 times including by The Blues Brothers, Downchild Blues Band and Powder Blues Band.
https://secondhandsongs.com/performance/65275/all

- **Ivory Joe Hunter**.
  "I Almost Lost My Mind" MGM Records 1955   #1 R&B
  Pat Boone did a cover that was #1 on Pop

- James Brown And The Famous Flames.
"Please, Please, Please" #6 R&B Federal 1956

The promo "Dee Jay Special" record label shows Naspendle Konx on tenor sax for "Please, Please, Please". When the final version was released, however, saxes weren't featured! What happened and why?

https://www.youtube.com/watch?v=7S3r_s-ZaGE (33 second mark)

"At first, the record labels were spooked by the rawness of the song and no one would sign Brown. Then King Records A&R man Ralph Bass heard the song in January 1956 and loved it on first listen. He wired owner Syd Nathan about a new act that he wanted to sign to the Federal subsidiary and flew the group to the King studios in Cincinnati to cut a *new* version of "Please, Please, Please." Bass was promptly fired by Nathan because the boss thought the song was "a piece of s--t." Bass eventually rehired, once the single started selling."-John Laughter

- **Little Richard**
"She's Got It" #9 R&B. U.K. #15

Hi John,

"According to the discographical information given in the box set *The Specialty Sessions*, "She's Got It" (Sp- 584) was cut with the Upsetters in Los Angeles on September 6, 1956, with Wilbert Smith, Grady Gaines and Clifford Burks (tenor sax) and Jewell Grant (baritone sax)."

-Best wishes,
Michael Robinson,

North Perth, Western Australia
**GRADY GAINES (SOLO) TENOR SAX
CLIFFORD BURKS. TENOR SAX
WILBERT SMITH A/K/A LEE DIAMOND - TENOR SAX
SAMUEL PARKER, JR. – BARITONE SAX**

The original Upsetters on their first Specialty Records tour, 1955. From upper left to right: Nathaniel Douglas, lead guitar; Charles Connor, drums; Olsie Robinson, bass; Wilbert Smith, saxophone; Clifford Burks, tenor saxophone; Little Richard, lead vocals and piano; Grady Gaines, tenor saxophone.

There's No Stopping Us Now

In the early 1950s, indie labels challenged the major labels in local markets. The strategy worked well. At one point, the major labels lost half their market share to indie labels.

Elvis Presley, Chester Burnett a.k.a Howlin' Wolf were first launched by Sun, James Brown on King, Sam Cooke on Specialty, Ray Charles on Swing Time and Atlantic, Everly Brothers on Cadence, Specialty, Imperial and Aladdin recorded Fats Domino.

Chess countered with Muddy Waters, Chuck Berry (who was signed by Chess on Muddy Waters' recommendation). Chuck brought with him the great boogie woogie pianist Johnny Johnston -who earlier had hired Berry for Johnny's band- and worked on many of Berry's hits-the song "Johnny B. Goode" was a part tribute to Berry's mother, Johnny Johnson and Bo Diddley.

Delmark Records was founded by Robert G. Koester in St. Louis, Missouri in 1953, originally under the name "Delmar." In 1958, the label relocated to Chicago and added a "k" to its name. Although its initial home was in the basement of a record store, "Delmark has become the oldest continuously operating jazz and blues (e.g. Sun Ra, Jimmy Forrest, Junior Wells, the Art Ensemble of Chicago, Anthony Braxton, Little Walter, T-bone Walker, Sleepy John Estes, Arthur Crudup, Otis Rush to name just a few) independent record label in the United States". Julia A. Miller is the President and CEO. The 70th Anniversary Blues Anthology that features Buddy Guy, Dinah Washington, Junior Wells, Otis Rush, Little Walter Magic Sam, to name just a few, is highly recommended.

https://delmark.com/

The Train Kept A' Rollin' and A' Rollin'

Like a right hook punch that comes out of nowhere to blast a big time shot of adrenaline right into the brain, covers showed their power to keep creative visions alive for decades.

The song "The Train Kept A' Rollin'" was first recorded in 1951 by Tiny Bradshaw's band with Red Prysock on tenor.

"The Johnny Burnette Trio covered it in 1956, featuring Paul Burlison's distorted guitar which he claimed was the result of a loose tube in his amplifier." He had noticed the sound after accidentally dropping his amplifier, which dislodged a power tube. "Whenever I wanted to get that sound, I'd just reach back and loosen that tube." (Robert Palmer argued it "strikingly resembles the sound of Willie Johnson" on early Howling Wolf's records on Chess in 1951 such as "Moaning at Midnight") 125.

The Yardbirds, in 1965, recorded the song as "psychedelic blues", that later was retitled as "Stroll On" when featured in Michelangelo Antonioni's classic movie "Blow-Up", with Jeff Beck and Jimmy Page on guitar. Their version has been cited as an early influence for heavy metal musicians.

This song was one of the first songs that Led Zeppelin worked on, while touring Scandinavia, that convinced them their band could be something special.

Jimmy Page, Joe Perry and Jeff Beck helped to perform the song live at The Rock n' Roll Hall of Fame in 2009.

Paranoia, ESP and Great Ears

Protective paranoia, ESP and great ears became occupational necessities in the music industry of the 1950s.

Megalomanics, sword waving lawyers, magical shamans, and miracle working producers/ engineers had become the norm. To keep from being sucked into the howling, chop-chop-chop turbines of the rock and roll music business, you had better be able to clearly see which direction the music was about to go, because when decision time suddenly appeared and the competitions' jealousies, plots and traps swirled around like starving barracuda, you had to be able to predict those musicians that were going to be the next musical gods, or the business was going to run over you without a glance behind.

A massive musical storm was brewing on the horizon that didn't really give a damn whether anyone surrendered, it just gripped the wheel tightly, set the radio music at screaming volume, pointed straight ahead, and stomped the gas pedal to the floor, ready to become the new American Dream.

Two disc jockeys, who showed just how important a radio d.j. could be, were only too happy to pour fuel into this deep-gutted, full chromed, hot rod engine that kept thinking it was a tidal wave.

Alan Freed

In 1951, Alan Freed created a musical oasis with a new radio show, "The Mood Dog House: Rock n' Roll Party" in Cleveland radio station WJW. He is credited as being the first radio disc jockey to call r&b "rock n' roll".

A visit a record store in downtown Cleveland, Ohio was the first domino to fall that led to the radio show…

https://www.youtube.com/watch?v=s19HmcLeTtQ (Alan Freed Rock n' Roll Show)

https://www.youtube.com/watch?v=dGWLaS8-bJY (Alan Freed Rock n' Roll Party)

"I heard the tenor saxophones of Red Prysock and Big Al Sears. I heard the blues-singing, piano playing Ivory Joe Hunter. I wondered. I wondered for about a week. Then I went to the station manager and talked him into permitting me to follow my classical programme with a rock n' roll party" which started in 1951.125

To put that change in perspective, in Arnold Shaw's excellent book, "Honkers and Shouters", Bobby Shad, producer and label owner (Mainstream Time Records) said that when he first started working with Dinah Washington, he wanted to get her out of the R&B category, because, in 1952-53, "If you brought a record by a black artist to a pop disc jockey, you were dead. They would refuse to play them."126

This protective paralysis of the music business was about to be swamped with too-late accusations of incompetence and failing careers while rock n' roll merrily hammered away on every front door.

Early in 1952, Freed promoted a concert at the Cleveland area that had a capacity of 10,000- 21,000 people showed up. The concert featured r&b records and helped to promote "Sixty Minute Man" by the Dominos, the first r&b song to cross over to the national pop charts where it was listed for twenty-three weeks, alongside Billboard's usual concoction of dance bands, novelty tunes and crooners; the revolution had begun.

Alan Freed argued: "Rock 'n roll is really swing with a modern name. It began on the levees and plantations, took in folk songs, and features blues and rhythm."

Freed was an important part of a series of movies that featured r&b and rock n' roll artists.

1956: *Rock Around the Clock*
1956: *Rock, Rock, Rock*
1957: *Mister Rock and Roll*
1957: *Don't Knock the Rock*
1959: *Go, Johnny Go!*

The television show "The Big Beat" was launched by Freed in 1957. Although the early ratings were strong, the show was suddenly cancelled, reportedly because Frankie Lymon was dancing with "a "white" audience member.

However, in television, ratings are king and viewer numbers conquer all. The show was relaunched two years later…

https://www.youtube.com/watch?v=er-Dv-tvcd8

Freed also put together "package" tours that featured both r&b and rock n' roll musicians that toured nationally.

August 30 – September 5, 1957: King Curtis played in Alan Freed's Big Rock'n'Roll Orchestra with Al Sears and Sam Taylor at the Brooklyn Paramount on Alan Freed's "Holiday Rock'n'Roll Stage Show". Artists appearing: The Five Keys, Jimmie Rodgers, The Cleftones, The Moonglows, The Del-Vikings, The Diamonds, Mickey & Sylvia, Little Richard, Larry Williams, Buddy Holly & The Crickets, JoAnn Campbell, Shaye Cogan, O.C. Smith.

ALAN FREED ROCK'N'ROLL SHOW: Probably: Taft Jordan, Leon Merian (tpts), King Curtis, Sam "The Man" Taylor, Lowell "Count" Hastings (tens), other brass, Ernie Hayes (pno), Kenny Burrell (gtr), unk. bs, dms. Arrangers probably Ernie Wilkins and/or Sammy Lowe.

New York. November 13, 1957

103662	Lady Whistle Bait	Coral LP 57213
103663	Fandango Rock	Coral LP 57213
103664	Cool Papa	Brunswick LP 54043
103665	Teenage Strut	Coral LP 57213

Same.

New York. November 15, 1957

103681	Two Good Guys	Brunswick LP 54043
103682	Tuxedo Junction	Brunswick LP 54043
103683	In A Little Spanish Town	Coral LP 57213
103684	Pushing	Brunswick LP 54043

ALAN FREED ROCK'N'ROLL SHOW: Probably: Taft Jordan, Leon Merian (tpts), King Curtis, Sam "The Man" Taylor, Lowell "Count" Hastings (tens), other brass, Ernie Hayes (pno), Kenny Burrell (gtr), unk. bs, dms. Arrangers probably Ernie Wilkins and/or Sammy Lowe.
New York. November 22, 1957

103746	Split Level	Coral LP 57213
103747	A Stomping Good Time	Coral LP 57213
103748	Tow Head	Brunswick LP 54043
103749	Campus Rumpus	Brunswick LP 54043

Dec.1958/Jan.1959: Chuck Berry noted in his autobiography "I flew off Xmas day, 1958 to New York to...Alan Freed's Christmas Jubilee, eleven days at the Loews Theater. The festive holidays were spent with Jackie Wilson, Bo Diddley, the Everly Brothers, Frankie Avalon, Jo-Ann Campbell, Eddie Cochran, King Curtis, The Flamingos, The Crests, The Cadillacs, Dion & The Belmonts, Johnnie Ray and others.

-Roy Simonds- "King Curtis Sessionography"

Alan Freed's career, however, later sank beneath accusations of payola (payments made by record companies to promote specific songs) and royalties paid to him for songs that he did not write.

George "Hound Dog" Lorenz

In the 1950s, on radio station WKBW of Buffalo, New York, with a fan club of over 100,000 paid members, the George "Hound Dog" Lorenz strongly promoted R&B and Blues artists often ignored by Top 40 radio stations. He is credited as being the first to promote and play Little Richard together with many artists that other radio stations had wished would just go away.

The theme songs for his shows became standards, such as Cozy Eggleston's *Big Heavy*,
and…
The Crawford Brothers' *Midnight Happenings*.
https://www.youtube.com/watch?v=rENzRhou6kI

His shows were later syndicated around the world as "The Great George L", including his famous blues segment, "And it's that time of night…when we take a walk down a long, long, lonely corridor…down to the end of the hall. The door on the left. Open that door…and…step… into the Blue Room. Close the door…and get the blues…with The Hound."
https://www.youtube.com/watch?v=J9Loh8UP0hE

Captivity, Censorship and The Birth Of Rock n' Roll

Fats Domino had a massive 1950 hit with "Fat Man" that sold over a million records however, due to segregated record charts, it wasn't recognized in Billboard's Top 100 (it was recognized by The Grammy Hall Of Fame in 2015).

The Dominoes' (whose members included the sent-from-heaven singers Clyde McPatter-who left in 1954 to join the group, The Drifters and the incomparable Jackie Wilson, who replaced McPhatter in the Dominoes) controversial song "Sixty Minute Man", which blended jump, gospel, and blues, became a smash hit in 1951 (featured the lyrics, "I'll rock 'em, roll 'em all night long, I'm a Sixty Minute Man"), spent 14 weeks at Number One on the R&B Charts, crossed over and hit Number 17 on Billboard's Top 100.

They followed in 1952 with the joyous, r&b smash hit "Have Mercy On Me Baby", Number One on the R&B charts for 10 weeks.

Johnnie Ray, in 1951, triggered an early example of wild audience hysteria, later common with Elvis Presley, with tears-wrapped hits like "Cry".

Lloyd Price's highly influential "Lawdy Miss Clawdy", recorded at Cosimo Matassa's J&M Studios in New Orleans that featured Fats Domino's distinctive piano triplets, was released in 1952 and sold nearly a million records. The song hit Number

One on Billboard's R&B chart, however, again, Billboard refused to list it in the Top 100 (this song was later named to The Rock And Roll Hall Of Fame's list of "500 Songs That Shaped Rock And Roll").

Joe Houston's wailing "All Night Long" (inspired by Rusty Bryant), released in 1954, with its relentless, hypnotic beat (backed by Harry Allen on baritone sax) ripped the music world wide open, inspiring other sax players like Chuck Higgins and Bill Haley's Joey Ambrosio, to leave career paranoia to the enemy and let the music fly, on early records like "Pachuko Hop" and "Strait Jacket".

Big Joe Turner had a 1954 powerful, influential, cross-over hit with "Shake Rattle and Roll" (written by Jesse Stone using the pseudonym "Charles Calhoun" the name of the contractor who had built his home) with Sam The Man Taylor tenor, Mickey Baker on guitar, Lloyd Trotman on bass, and Connie Kay on drums, Wilbur DeParis on trombone, and Haywood Henry on baritone sax, and reportedly Jesse Stone, Ahmet Ertegun and Jerry Wexler on backup vocals! Its driving, infectious, beat, like well-aimed, syncopated, sledgehammers, smashed gaping holes in the racist walls of the Pop Charts, and when taken with its "scandalous lyrics",

Way you wear those dresses, the sun come shining through
Way you wear those dresses, the sun come shining through
I can't believe my eyes all that mess belongs to you

made it a ground breaking record that crossed over to the Pop charts. (Number One on Billboard R&B chart, Number 22 on Billboard Top 100) clearing paths for the revolution to come...although not just yet. Bill Haley and the Comets released a "clean" cover version the same week Turner's record was released that rose to Number 7 on the Pop charts.126

Teddy McRae's 1955 hit, "Mr. Bear Comes To Town", featured Sam "The Man" Taylor and King Curtis on tenor.

Bill Haley and the Comets' "Crazy Man Crazy" burned up the 1953 charts (some argue this was the first "rock n' roll" record, at least in terms of being the first to be featured on Billboard's Top 100, hitting #12).
This was followed by the monster, world-wide hit (Milt Gabler who had produced Louis Jordan, modeled Haley's sound after Louis Jordan's jump beat) "Rock Around The Clock" in 1955 that stayed at Number One for two months on Billboard's Top 100, is estimated to have sold over 3 million records, and peaked at #3 on Billboard's R&B chart.

"Rudy's Rock" in 1956 featuring Haley's new tenor sax Rudy Pompilli continued to crash every party and spread the fever.

"Among the wide-eyed youngsters who saw Haley performing 'Rock Around The Clock'- Paul McCartney...and The Who's Pete Townshend who said: " 'The birth of rock and roll for me? Seeing Bill Haley and the Comets...God, that band swung!' "127 An example of the impact of "Rock Around The

Clock" is this clip from the excellent movie "Cold War".

https://www.youtube.com/watch?v=kCuEXWMh5Vo&t=10s

Chuck Berry, widely regarded as the "Father Of Rock n' Roll", was an exceptional songwriter (who was heavily influenced by Louis Jordan 128) who has been described by Adam Gopnik ("From Minor To Major"; New Yorker. Jan 20, 2020) as one of America's "great lyricists together with Cole Porter" with songs like "Promised Land" and many chart hits including:

-"Maybellene" in 1955 ("Leonard Chess had suggested that Berry change the name from 'Ida Mae', after spotting a box of Maybelline-brand mascara on a windowsill) the song reached Number One on Billboard's R&B charts, Number 5 on Billboard's Top 100, with sales of over a million;

-"Roll Over Beethoven" in 1956 (Number One Billboard R&B, Number 29 Billboard Top 100)

-"Johnny B. Goode". For the opening, Berry borrowed the opening solo of Louis Jordan's "Ain't That Just Like a Woman (They'll Do It Every Time)"128. This song, was, in part, a tribute to the great pianist Johnny Johnston but also to Berry's mother (with the lyric "His mother told him"). In his autobiography, Berry wrote that his mother was the real inspiration for the song; Number 2 on Billboard R&B, Number 8 on Billboard Top 100) to name just a few of his many hits.

"Johnny B. Goode" was one of 27 songs on the "Voyager Golden Record" carried into space by the Voyager spacecraft in 1977!

> *"My momma always said, 'You and Elvis are pretty good, but y'all ain't no Chuck Berry'."*
>
> — Jerry Lee Lewis

Fats Domino had 11 Top Ten Billboard hits between 1955-1960, including "Ain't That A Shame", "I'm In Love Again" (Lee Allen tenor), "Blueberry Hill", "Walking To New Orleans", and "I'm Walking" with the exceptional sax solo on the latter by Herb Hardesty on tenor.

"Bartholomew and Matassa put more thought into the production than was normal at this time. When mastering Domino's records, now that Matassa's studio had finally switched to tape from cutting directly on to wax, they would speed up the tape slightly -- a trick which made Domino's voice sound younger, and which emphasised the beat more. This sort of thing is absolutely basic now, but at the time it was extraordinarily unusual for any rhythm and blues records to have any kind of production trickery at all. It also had another advantage, because as Cosimo Matassa would point out, it would change the key slightly so it wouldn't be in a normal key at all. So when other people tried to cover Domino's records 'they couldn't find the damn notes on the piano!' "-John Laughter

"K.C. Lovin'" by Little Willie Littlefield, that featured Maxwell Davis' great work on tenor sax, was originally entitled "Kansas City" on Federal, but the title was changed to appeal to "African-American record buyers". It failed to chart in 1952, but when rerecorded and released in 1959 by Wilbert Harrison, hit Number One on Billboard's Top 100 charts (recognized by The Grammy Hall Of Fame in 2001).

"In an interview with Charlie Gillett in April, 1971, King Curtis claimed to have been present at Wilbert Harrison's "Kansas City" session: Harrison, interviewed by Norbert Hess in 1983 stated that "Kansas City" was recorded at the tail-end of a session by his brothers, Jim and Bob – 'The Harrison Brothers' – who were accompanied by King Curtis' band, although only the rhythm section played on "Kansas City"/"Listen My Darling". There was a single by The Harrison Brothers on Everlast, but the release dates from the mid-60s, and probably has no connection with this session. However, Fury files show two unissued titles by 'Harrison Duet' – "Till The End Of Time"/"Come On Back Where You Belong" which may be the unknown titles."

THE HARRISON BROTHERS (HARRISON DUET??) *(vcls)/* **WILBERT HARRISON** *(vcl/pno),* King Curtis (ten) on –1?, Jimmy Spruill (gtr), Jimmy Lewis (bs), "Fat Duck" (dms), unk. Male bkgnd vcls (Harrison Brothers?) on –2. Prod. Bobby Robinson.

New York. February, 1959

? (Harrison Brothers/Duet recordings) –1 unissued?

F-1045   *Kansas City*   Fury 1023
F-1046   *Listen My Darling* –2 Fury 1023

-Roy Simonds-"King Curtis Sessionography"

A version by Sam Butera on tenor sax had an earlier release in 1957.

Running Wild But Not So Free

Everyone loves a David and Goliath story. Hollywood has made a fortune with movies where the underdog comes out of nowhere to defeat the heavy favorite. Indie labels tried to fulfill that role, their record sales flooding out across the land.

John Broven writes, in his invaluable "Record Makers and Breakers-Voices Of The Independent Rock n' Roll Pioneers", that on the first ballot for the Rock n' Roll Hall Of Fame, of the 41 names on the final ballot, 39 artists had started their careers on independent labels.

The music industry's traditional attack dogs of greed, fraud and abuse of power, however, once again served as compulsive assassins, only this time for the indies. In his exceptional book "The Sound Of The City", Charlie Gillet wrote that "many of the artists who recorded for independent companies…came back to report tales of fraud, deception and unpaid royalties. It was common practice to deny artists their entitlement as songwriters by buying their songs outright for twenty-five or fifty dollars, or simply by falsely claiming co-writing credits."

Jimmy Witherspoon recorded the hit "Ain't' Nobody's Business" on the Supreme label, owned by a dentist Al Patrick, "But I didn't get one penny royalty. Patrick paid me a flat fee for the session. I was supposed to be so much on each record, which he never paid me." 129

Not all members of the AFM were treated equally. For years, "black musicians too often were paid less", and some locals remained racially segregated until the early 1970s. That was why bmusicians had created the National Association of Negro Musicians in 1919. When rock n' roll became popular in the 1950s, the AFM refused to recognize the new artists who came out of "black communities", some arguing that they weren't true musicians!

Musical artists and the audiences, however, continued to attack the walls of greed, segregation and prejudice. Marc Myers writes (*Anatomy Of A Song: The Oral History Of 45 Iconic Hits That Changed Rock, R&B and Pop*130) that in Southern California during the summer of 1952, white teens were buying 45 percent of all R&B records sold, due to the growth of independent labels, radio stations, and the influence of sax players like Red Prysock, Big Jay McNeely and Joe Houston.

Billy Boy Arnold said that when he was on tour with Fats Domino and Johnny "Guitar" Watson, "white people" wanted to see Fats Domino and wouldn't let segregation stop them. 131

Jazz too played an important role; Norman Granz who produced, in the 1940s and 1950s, jazz concert tours called "Jazz at the Philharmonic", would book- as Whitney Balliett described- "into those parts of the country where racial bias still exists" with a contract rider that if any discrimination was practiced with the audiences, the tour would be cancelled.132

By the end of 1955, writes Preston Lauterbach in the fascinating article published in Oxford American Magazine, entitled *Sympathy For The Devil*:

"Toward the end of 1955, *Billboard* marked a major turning point in American music history. The recording industry recognized that black music had become the driving creative force not just of the segregated rhythm and blues market, but for the business as a whole...By 1956, *Billboard* had desegregated its charts..."133

In January 1957, *Billboard* marveled at the sudden diversity of the once-homogenous mainstream record market. "The most numerous invasion force . . . came right out of the pure area of rhythm and blues. As the adulterated product known as rock and roll caught on, the deejays led the kids in the appreciation of the true, original article. This led to the pop success of such performers as Little Richard, the Teen-Agers and many more."

Rock n' roll- the new language for a new world.

As a political weapon, it (music) has helped me for 30 years defend the rights of American blacks and third-world people all over the world, to defend them with protest songs. To move the audience to make them conscious of what has been done to my people around the world.

Nina Simone

206

© Paul Harris

Lionel Prevost

By Paul Harris

Blues piano legend Katie Webster said, "He was only the best saxophone player in the world."

Gord "Sax Gordon" Beadle: "I suppose really Lee Allen epitomizes early Rock & Roll sax...but Lionel Prevost is right there with him in sound and feel..."

Johnny Ferreira writes that Lionel Prevost "just might be the biggest, richest sax tone you ever heard!"

John Broven, in his seminal book on regional blues, South To Louisiana, described Lionel Prevost as "a saxophonist of cherishable individuality with the tone, emotion and creativity of a top jazzman".

*****

Lionel Prevost (who also recorded as "Lionel Torrence") was at the forefront of the Louisiana music scene, and the emergence of Zydeco, Cajun and Swamp Pop in the 50's and 60's, as a frequent recording partner with Clifton Chenier (with whom he took all the lead solos), Katie Webster, Warren Storm, and many of the artists featured by Chess (in New Orleans) and Jay D. Miller Studios.

https://www.youtube.com/watch?v=yplucSzF5Z0 (Moscow Twist)

Lionel also performed and/or recorded with a wide array of artists including Ray Charles, James Brown, T-Bone Walker, Etta James, Fats Domino, Bobby 'Blue' Bland, Little Junior Parker, and Sam Cooke. It's estimated that by the early 60's, he had played on nearly 750 45 rpm recordings.

Renowned writer/professional photographer Paul Harris was asked to prepare the liner notes for an album. This led to a visit with Lionel Prevost and the following interview, first published in Juke Blues Magazine (Part 1- Issue 19; Part 2- Issue 20- Obituary-

Issue 51). Photograph of Lionel Prevost was kindly contributed by Paul Harris.

This article has been updated with an interview with Mrs. Bessie Prevost (conducted by Neil Sharpe). *The interview and editorial notes have been placed in italics.*

A special thanks to "Sax Gordon" Beadle who first brought this great artist to my attention.
For information about the availability of copies of Juke Blues please e-mail Juke@jukeblues.com.

*****

"Lionel Prevost is best known for his work in the J.D. Miller house band in the studios in Crowley, Louisiana. Back in the Fifties, he was a member of Clifton Chenier's band where, according to Rockin' Sidney, 'he took all the solos, he was the main man'.

Lionel recalls, 'While doing some recording with Clifton Chenier at J.D.'s studio, Miller took my phone number and address. He said, 'When I need somebody to do some recording and when you're not busy, would you be interested?' I told him I would. So just about every time he had somebody in there to do any recording, he would call me up. As long as I was in the area I… recorded with him… After I left Clifton Chenier, I recorded with Miller on a steady basis for quite some time. We would come up with these original tunes like some of that stuff that I did, 'Rooty Tooty' [*Sax Gordon said of " 'Rooty Tooty': That's the one where his awesome tone and effortless rockin' really come out"*], and 'Moscow Twist'. I've played just about every type of music you can imagine from zydeco to jazz. I've played rhythm & blues, swamp pop, country & western.'

https://www.youtube.com/watch?v=JxV5mDSHJwA (Rooty Tooty)

EARLY DAYS

Lionel was born to Clarence and Ora Prevost (his real surname) on 4 December 1935 on the Oxford sugarcane plantation near Franklin, Louisiana. He was one of twenty-three children, eight boys and fifteen girls. As a child he heard the music of saxophone players Louis Jordan and Illinois Jacquet. 'Louis Jordan had this real growling type style on his alto saxophone, and Illinois Jacquet used to squeal all the time. I guess you could say my style would be a combination of the two.'

Lionel's parents moved to Port Arthur, Texas whilst he remained with his grandmother in Louisiana. At the age of 12 he rejoined his parents in order to continue his education, but his obsession with the saxophone was becoming more and more obvious. 'I used to imitate a saxophone player all the time with a dish towel or bath towel or something and one day my father came home from the pawn shop with this alto saxophone and he say, 'Do you want to try and play this thing?'. I say, 'I sure would'. Needless to say, I made some terrible noises on this saxophone ... I used to go in the back room and close the door, man, I would make some of the horriblest sounds I imagine you would ever get out of a saxophone'. Unable to stand the shrieks and grunts, Lionel's father decided that some music lessons were in order. After the 'professor' absconded with advance fees from twenty-five to thirty students, another teacher was found who advised Lionel to purchase a specific saxophone 'method' book. Obtaining the $5 or $10 necessary entailed cutting grass both before and after school. Soon Lionel had learned the basics of reading music — the whole notes, the half notes, the breathing steps and the fingering — and he made plans to join the school band.

IMPROVISATION

At this time Lionel's father was working at a Texaco oil refinery and one day he brought home a bottle of mercury. Lionel found that if he painted a coin with it, 'It made it look tremendously beautiful, I mean it shined like brand new minted, gold or something, so I got this wild idea that I would put this stuff on my saxophone that was so ragged and beat up that they used to laugh at me all the time. It was a silver Buescher and, man, I spent about two or three hours putting this quicksilver on this saxophone and it looked so pretty, I put a covering over it and put it in the case. When I got to music class and I opened my saxophone case, lo and behold, this mercury that I had put on this saxophone had turned it pitch black. It had begun to eat away at the welding parts and the keys went to falling off, the pads started falling off and, not having any money to buy a new horn, I had to improvise some kind of way, so I started using rubber bands, chewing gums, the outer wrappings off a cigarette package to hold the pads in. I would use the rubber bands to make the springs work where there wasn't any springs, or put chewing gum to cover the leaks.'

Amazingly, Lionel continued to use this Heath-Robinson contraption [*a byword for a design or construction that is 'ingeniously or ridiculously over-complicated'-The New Oxford Dictionary of English*] until he began playing on the road. 'College musicians and guys that were way over my head would just wait for a youngster like me to come to town so they could get up there on the bandstand and just cut me to pieces. But after the first time this happened, I figured out a way that I could give myself a little extra enhancement.' So, before passing over his saxophone, Lionel 'would take two or three rubber bands off and a couple of pieces of paper, a plug of this chewing gum, and I'd give 'em the saxophone and tell 'em to have a go at it. And man, I'd stand back in the side and watch the fireworks, that's the word for it, because they'd get to hustlin' and scufflin' and workin' and tryin' to find out what was wrong, why couldn't they get anything goin' on this horn? Finally, they'd call me, give me my horn back and I would get on the bandstand [having secretly made the running repairs] and man, I'd be smooth sailing from then on. They'd just shake their heads and walk away in amazement or disgust, one or the other.' Harry Simoneaux confirms Lionel's ability on this patched-up instrument: 'Yes, I remember his saxophone had many rubber bands holding it together — but you couldn't tell by the sound 'cause he sounded great, oh yeah!'

Katie Webster recalls another skill: 'He was the only person that I know could play with a reed that had those little chips in it, but it was something he could do, if he had a reed and he didn't have time to change it, you never knew that something was wrong with the reed ... he always kept extra ones, but he could play with it like that. There were only two people that could tell, and that was me and J.D. Miller, 'cause J.D. Miller had amplifiers in his ears and he could hear dust flit across!'

SCHOOL BAND

Another important aspect of Lionel's development whilst still at school came when his mother was running a night club. 'The guy would come by to put new records on the juke box and I would talk him into giving me all of his old records which I would take home and put 'em on the hi-fi when I was at home alone or with my sisters, and I'd play along with these records, I'd listen to the notes, I developed a pretty good ear for music and I had the basic fundamentals of what I needed and I would practice on hours on hours on hours with these records. I would hear a song two or three times and I would pick it up in no time at all and I would play it exactly like the record.' Some months later Lionel entered a talent competition at the school house where his old music teacher 'was amazed at what I did that particular day with that old raggedy saxophone full of rubber bands and chewing gum. It was one of Louis Jordan's songs called 'There Ain't Nobody Here But Us Chickens' and I played that song note for note and I literally tore the auditorium up that day . . .

Later, I became a member of the school band.' There, he received more formal training but always retained the ability to play by ear. Despite making good grades in the band, there were very few scholarships available at the time and as his parents could not afford to send him to college, his musical training had to be completed, in practice rather than theory, among the local musicians.

TEENAGE EXPERIENCE

Whilst still at school, Lionel played with Nap Henry and 'there was this guy named Lackey [Shelby Lackey], he played tenor sax. He was a wiz, he was the fastest thing I'd ever heard. He did a lot of staccato notes, tonguing, and I liked that so I sort of added that into my style too. Whatever I heard that I liked I was fortunate enough to be able to copy these people and develop my style.'

During the weekend breaks from school Lionel 'picked up a little extra money ... by playing with these musicians in Texas and Louisiana, I guess you would call that the chitlin' circuit, and I got to be pretty good. When I went out there at 16 years old I was quite green, I was still in high school, wasn't drinking, wasn't doing too much of anything. I can remember one of my first jobs was in a place called Darrow, Louisiana and whenever the band took an intermission, the older guys in the band would go out and mingle with the crowd and they'd get 'em something to drink, they'd sit at the table with 'em. My being 16 years old, I used to stay on the bandstand quite often until the intermission was over and the guys would bring me up a Coke or whatever cold drink. This particular night as I was sitting there on the bandstand, this young lady decided to come up and talk with me. Well, this was all interesting to me being my first dance in a public place. I really didn't know too much what to expect, that is until her jealous boyfriend or husband or whomever it was, decided to come up with a .38 and clear out the joint. Man, I was scared to death! I jumped out the window and started running. The band caught up with me down the street somewhere and I went back, we finally played the dance. Needless to say I was shaking in my breeches the rest of the night. These things happened time and time again.'

CLIFTON CHENIER

'Clifton Chenier was a neighbour of mine when I was a young kid and I used to watch him all the time sittin' on the front porch playin' on the accordion. Sometimes I would play the rubbin' board for him. One day [in 1955] he came through town, he had recorded these new songs, 'Ay-Tete-Fee'...

https://www.youtube.com/watch?v=L6u90Q_283s

...and a couple of others [for Specialty Records] and he happened to need a saxophone player and I wasn't doin' anything at the time so I started workin' with his group. The quality of the band, called The Playboys, was improved and 'Cliff sort of put me in charge of things. I was in charge of learnin' all of the songs because we did the first hour before he ever came on the stage to do his show, and the band did the entertaining. I'd do a little singing and playing and we had all the latest songs that was on the radio at that time. I played with Cliff over a period of about five or six years. [By then] it seemed to me that Cliff was a little harder to get along with. We never lost any friendship, but it just got to the point where I felt I couldn't stay there any longer, that I had to move on a little bit further.'

J D MILLER

It was around 1958 that Lionel first became involved with Jay Miller's house band where, along with the likes of Warren Storm, Katie Webster, Lazy Lester, Harry Simoneaux, Al Foreman on guitar and bassist Bobby McBride, he backed innumerable artists on a multitude of record releases. According to Katie Webster: 'He was

in the studio as much as I was. The two of us were on just about everything that came out of that studio and I know I must have played on about 750 45s by age 18 and I didn't know how many albums between Goldband and J.D. Miller. We played together many, many years on many songs out of the Jay Miller sessions for Excello Records and … just about everything that came out of there, Lionel Torrence was playing [on].'
  https://www.youtube.com/watch?v=chqNiQco91o

    Lionel recalls one specific session when, 'We stayed in the studio for two or three days. Just as you drove into the city limits of Crowley coming from Texas, there was a liquor store called Huck's House Of Spirits and at this time everybody was drinking Ripple Wine and we went into the studio and at the end of these three days of recording, when they decided to clean up the studio, they picked up 110 empty wine bottles and I think Jesse Domingue [a guitarist at that time] and myself drank most of 'em, and Warren Storm.'

    At one point it was decided to record some of Lionel's original tunes and Miller asked what was his last name. 'I told him, 'My last name is Prevost — Lionel Prevost'. And he says, 'Ain't nobody gonna be able to remember the name Prevost, we gonna have to change your name. Do you have a middle name or a nickname or anything?' Well, my grandfather's name was Terrance and they sorta hung that name on me because my family said I favoured him, a lot of them called me Terrance, and I told him my name was Lionel Terrance Prevost so he said, "Well, we'll use Lionel Terrance'. Somewhere in the spelling and in the pressing, they got mixed up and they wind up being Torrence. It didn't make any difference at that time, I just wanted to get some type of music on a record.'

In fact, only three singles appeared under this name: the much praised 'Moscow Twist'/'Rooty Tooty', Zynn 1023; 'Rockin' Jole Blonde'/'Anytime', Zynn 1008; and 'Flim Flam'/'Saka', Excello 2218. A previously unissued version of 'Flim Flam', recorded for Goldband under the pseudonym "Lionel Prevo", and later appeared on a Charly/Goldband compilation album, GCL-120.

https://www.youtube.com/watch?v=k46YxMVHGbE (Flim Flam)

https://www.youtube.com/watch?v=Vd6mYFf_1ZY (Saka)

Despite differences over money, both Lionel and Katie Webster had respect for J.D. Miller's professional abilities. Lionel: 'J.D. Miller's a businessman. In the studio he knew what he wanted. I guess he had him something going.' Katie: 'I always admired Miller, always had the greatest of respect for him 'cause he was a good producer back in those swamps. You had to do it over until you got it right, that's just the way he was — 'OK, take number 160'! That's why he made such remarkable records 'cause everything was so clean. If it was just the piano and my voice or somebody beating on a cardboard box with brushes — Lester used to do that — it always sounded great.' Harry Simoneaux confirms that, 'J.D. had a very keen ear and if something didn't sound right — 'Stop, start all over again' — 'cause we didn't have the electronics that we do now, so it was not unusual to do one song twenty, twenty-five times — very often.'

RACIAL PROBLEMS

'I was travelling on the road with Lowell Fulson, Clifton Chenier and Etta James, we had a package together, we were doin' some touring. We were on our way back from Chicago, back down to the South and we had some cooking utensils and things. We would stop on the side of the road, we found it cheaper to eat this way. We'd stop in a store somewhere and buy us a bunch of food, stop with this camping stove and we'd make sandwiches or fried chicken or pork chops or what have you. As we got into Mississippi, we spotted a roadside park after we left the grocery store and we pulled in. There was this couple sitting way on the other side of the park, a man and a lady, a white couple. So when we drove through we spoke to them and when I asked the lady, 'Mind if we share the roadside park with you?' she said, 'It's a public place, go right ahead'. About two or three minutes passed, and they got in their car and they left. About five minutes later, here we were cooking hot eggs and hot chicken on the fire and these two carloads of State Troopers pulled up and they asked Etta, 'What are you doin' ridin' around with these black guys?' —

well they used some other language! She say, 'Well, I'm black too' — you know Etta James is a very fair-skinned young lady, blonde hair — and he asks us, 'Are you boys about ready to leave?'. So we mentioned the fact that we'd just gotten there, we'd been drivin' for a couple of days and we decided to stop and have a little rest and get somethin' to eat and we'd be on our way after a while. He say, 'Well, you can eat in the car or you can eat in jail, but you gonna have to get out of this roadside park!'

'Then there was that time with Jimmy McCracklin's group over in East Texas. We was travelling in a bus and we stopped about 1.30 that mornin' to gas up, and after we'd filled the bus up with gasoline, one of the guys went over to the water faucet to get a drink of water and the guy told him, 'We don't have any water here for niggers'. So the guy said, 'Hey man, we just bought over thirty gallons of gas, the least we can do is get a drink of water'. And he says, 'What are you fellas doin' here anyway?'. We told him we were musicians just drivin' through on our way to Houston. By this time, a couple of other cars had drove up and one of these guys came out of the station with a shotgun — double-barrelled — and he says,' If you guys are musicians, you ought to be able to play some music'. And they commenced to making us set up right then and there on the service station lot and we had to play seven or eight songs — either that or create a whole lot of problems.

'I usually find myself in a situation where I'm the only black guy with a bunch of white musicians in these predominantly white night clubs and I never really have any problems with the customers, but it seems the club owners themselves always assume that I'm gonna cause a problem, or that I *am* a problem because I stand out like a sore thumb among the rest of the crowd. Sometimes this gets a little tedious — not wantin' you to mix with the crowd. They hire you to play good music and entertain their customers, but some of them feel you shouldn't mix with the people which is pretty hard to do and at the same time satisfy them out there on the dance floor. The more intimate you are with your people, the more you are able to get 'em in some type of groove because it's easy to get on the same wavelength . . . Then there's some clubs you go in and there's no problem whatsoever.'

BACKING MUSICIAN

Whilst recording behind artists such as Tabby Thomas, Charles 'Mad Dog' Sheffield, Clarence Garlow, Clifton Chenier, Leroy Washington, Katie Webster and Warren Storm, Lionel was also doing live shows. Rockin' Sidney remembers him backing Ervin Charles and Barbara Lynn.

Lionel recalls, 'I worked with different guys like T-Bone Walker, Fats Domino, Jimmy Wilson — we were on shows behind Etta James, Ruth Brown. I remember when Ray Charles came to Dallas once. His whole band had got busted in Pittsburgh, Pennsylvania. Our band was behind the show, so Ray Charles worked with us for quite a while. When James Brown first started, he was working with us. We worked with some other great artists like The Clovers, The Cadillacs, The Dells, Cal Green & The Midnighters, Clarence Garlow. I did some shows with Bobby 'Blue' Bland, Little Junior Parker, Sam Cooke. I recorded a couple of songs with Rosco Gordon over in Memphis, Tennessee' ['Shoobie Oobie'/'Cheese And Crackers', Sun 257, 25 October 1956]."

https://www.youtube.com/watch?v=y0AsbBUQD60

Although not listed in *Blues Records,* Lionel said that he recorded with Etta James on Chess, Clifton Chenier's 'My Soul' and tunes like that'. [*Lionel Prevost is credited on "My Soul"- Chess (originally Checker single 939) 1957- See "Chess New Orleans"- CD- 9355*].

https://www.youtube.com/watch?v=yyjWSBF0xXY

NOTES

Photographs have been generously donated by Paul Harris, who was a regular contributor to *Juke Blues* magazine, Bristol, England and to *Now Dig This* magazine, Gateshead, England.
paulharrisphotography.blogspot.com

120. Silvester PJ (2009) The Story of Boogie Woogie-A Left Hand Like God.
Scarecrow Press Inc. of Rowman and Littlefield Publishing Group Inc. Latham Maryland, USA.
121. Murray CS (2000) Boogie Man: The Adventures of John Lee Hooker in the American Twentieth Century. St Martin's Press; Franz S op. cit. pg. 131.
121A. Charles Gillette (1996) The Sound Of The City: The Rise Of Rock And Roll.
Da Capo Press; 2nd edition (March 22, 1996) pg.14. With regard to record sales in the mid-1950s and the independent labels increasing share from 1956-1959, see pgs 39-40.
https://medium.com/@Vinylmint/history-of-the-record-industry-1920-1950s-6d491d7cb606
122. Ruggieri M (2018) Sister Rosetta Tharpe; *Singer influenced key rock n' roll figures.* Atlanta-Journal Constitution-

https://www.npr.org/2017/08/24/544226085/forebears-sister-rosetta-tharpe-the-godmother-of-rock-n-roll

https://www.udiscovermusic.com/stories/sister-rosetta-tharpe-rocknroll-pioneer/

123. Norman Kelley Editor Dr. Reebee Garofalo (2005) R&B (Rhythm and Business): The Political Economy of Black Music. Akashic Books (Aug. 1 2005); pg. 133

124. Franz S (2003) The Amazing Secret History of Elmore James. Wolsworth Publishing Company. Marceline, Missouri. pgs. 20-22; pgs. 33-34

125. Charles Gillette (1996) The Sound Of The City: The Rise Of Rock And Roll. Da Capo Press; 2nd edition (March 22, 1996) pg.13

Palmer op. cit. pgs 235-236.

126. Gillette op cit.

126A. Caitlin Vaughn Carlos (2023) "Shake Rattle and Roll by Joe Turner"- Songs That Changed Music; https://producelikeapro.com/blog/shake-rattle-and-roll/

127. Lindsay Zoladez (April 2021) *Rock n' Roll Arrives in Cold War.* The Criterion Collection- Songbook]
https://www.criterion.com/current/posts/7348-rock-and-roll-arrives-in-cold-war?

128. Shaw op cit. pg. 64

129. Norman Kelley Editor Dr. Reebee Garofalo op cit. pg. 139

130. Marc Myers *Anatomy Of A Song: The Oral History Of 45 Iconic Hits That Changed Rock, R&B and Pop*. Grove Press; Reprint edition (November 21, 2017)
https://www.billboard.com/articles/columns/chart-beat/8014043/fats- dominos-biggest-billboard-hits-from-aint-that-a-shame-to

131. Dunas Jeff, Ferris William, Hooker John Lee (2005) *State of the Blues: The Living Legacy of the Delta* p. 103,105, 140, Aperture Foundation. Highly Recommended

132. Balliett Whitney (2002) *Collected Works: A Journal of Jazz 1954-2001*. (St. Martin's Press, New York, New York). Norma Ganz racial discrimination, pg. 6
https://medium.com/@Vinylmint/history-of-the-record-industry-1920-1950s-6d491d7cb606

133. Lauterbach Preston (2015) *Sympathy For The Devil*. Oxford American. A Magazine Of The South.".
https://main.oxfordamerican.org/magazine/item/1040-sympathy-for-the-devil

References

Broven J (2010) "Record Makers and Breakers-Voices Of The Independent Rock n' Roll Pioneers", University of Illinois Press; (January 13, 2010) https://www.press.uillinois.edu/books/?id=p077272

Broven J (2019) "South to Louisiana: The Music of the Cajun Bayous"; Pelican Publishing; 2ed. (March 2019).

https://www.pelicanpub.com/products.php?cat=15192 019)

Dawson Jim, Propes Steve (1992) What Was The First Rock 'n' Roll Record? Boston: Faber & Faber, 1992.

Dawson Jim (1994): Nervous Man Nervous: Big Nickle productions; Milford, New Hampshire; 1994 A fascinating review of the flamboyant swing, jump blues saxophonists and their critical influence on rock n' roll and rhythm and blues. This book includes bios of Big Jay McNeely, Joe Houston, King Curtis, Chuck Higgins, Hal Singer, Big Al Sears, Sam "The Man" Taylor, and more, with a special look at Big Jay McNeely and his influence on future generations of musicians, including Jimi Hendrix.

Discography Of American Historical Recordings: "…a database of master recordings made by American record companies during the 78 rpm era. It is part of the American Discography Project (ADP)—an initiative of the University of California, Santa Barbara and the Packard Humanities Institute that is edited by a team of researchers based at the UCSB Library."
https://adp.library.ucsb.edu/index.php/mastertalent/detail/109150/Jefferson_Hilton

Dunas Jeff, Ferris William, Hooker John Lee (2005) State of the Blues: The Living Legacy of the Delta p.

103,105. Quotes by Rufus Thomas, Billy Boy Arnold. Aperture Foundation. Highly Recommended. https://www.amazon.com/State-Blues-Living-Legacy-Delta/dp/0893817996/ref=sr_1_4?dchild=1&keywords=blue+aperture+foundation&qid=1621137356&s=books&sr=1-4

Gottlieb, W. P. (1947) *Portrait of Illinois Jacquet, New York, N.Y., ca. May.* United States, 1947. Monographic. [Photograph] Retrieved from the Library of Congress, https://www.loc.gov/item/gottlieb.12591/.

Lukasavitz Brian (2014) "Blues Law; Hound Dog vs. Bear Cat". http://www.americanbluesscene.com/2014/03/blues-law-hound-dog-vs-bear-cat/ https://www.linkedin.com/pulse/most-litigated-song-rock-history-brian-lukasavitz

Porter Bob (1986) Atlantic Honkers: Rhythm & Blues Sax Anthology (2 LP set) Liner notes- Atlantic Records 78 1666-1-F: Also see: Jazz At The Philharmonic: The First Concert; CD. Issued: Mar 22, 1994: Verve (USA) 731452164629

Spörke, Michael (2014). Big Mama Thornton: The Life and Music. McFarland Inc. p. 43, p 70. As cited in: https://en.wikipedia.org/wiki/Ball_and_Chain_(Big_Mama_Thornton_song)#cite_note-13

Thomas Pete: R&B saxophone players in the 1940's-1950's who contributed significantly: https://tamingthesaxophone.com/saxophone/players/blues-saxophone

Walker Steve- The Dominoes-The Clyde McPhatter Years.
http://tims.blackcat.nl/messages/dominoes1.htm

Ward Ed (2016) The Rocking, Rollicking R&B Of Billy Ward And His Dominoes. NPR Radio. March 11, 2016. https://www.npr.org/2016/03/11/470007011/the-rocking-rollicking-r-b-of-billy-ward-and-his-dominoes

7

Deacon's Hop

"Rock & roll is not an instrument; rock & roll is not even a style of music.

Rock & roll is a spirit…It's been going since the blues, jazz, bebop, soul, R&B, rock & roll, heavy metal, punk rock and yes, hip-hop.

And what connects us all is that spirit…

Rock & roll is not conforming to the people who came before you,

but creating your own path

in music and in life…"

-Ice Cube*

*https://icecube.com/ice-cubes-rock-and-roll-hall-of-fame-speech/

*With permission of Kennedy Gerrick (2017) *Parental Discretion Is Advised: The Rise of N.W.A and the Dawn of Gangsta Rap.* Atria Books. pg. 5

Big Jay McNeely ©Paul Harris

DEACON'S HOP- **Big Jay McNeely**
#1 R&B

THERE IS SOMETHING ON YOUR MIND—
LITTLE SONNY WARNER

BIG JAY MCNEELY   TENOR
#5 R&B #42 Pop

"Big Jay McNeely's explosive improv "3D" coupled with his stage performance of lying flat on his back, horn pointed high at the ceiling, strobe lights blasting away, announced to all in the music industry that a new kid was taking over.

"He took the honking approach to the extreme in performance and recording. In his live shows, he's been known to drop to his knees, lay on his back, walk through the crowd, or play out in the street. I've seen him come out in a darkened club with a fluorescent sax!"

-Sax Gordon
Live With Detroit Gary Wiggins
https://www.youtube.com/watch?v=F8QIsQO7DIg

https://www.youtube.com/watch?v=tmiZEZJoxGQ

Big Jay was an important influence for a young guitar player-Jimi Hendrix-who closely studied his stage act and solos, especially the way Big Jay's sax "cut through the rhythm section", his "bent notes", and how he used feedback and soared and swooped through the climax of the song.

"I have often contended if Elvis Presley or John Lennon had a saxophone in their bands then Big Jay McNeely would be one of the biggest icons in American music. Instead, he has to settle for mere 'legendary'" status..." 140

John Firmin*"I have always been a Big J fan. When I was about 14 years old, I was accused of attempting to cover J! The bebop guys thought they were insulting me. So I got a couple of J's records and went for it. Being the only teenage sax player in Anchorage, I fit in with the surf bands of the era. Of course, "Tequila" was mandatory. "Night Train"..."Harlem Nocturne" (which could most often be difficult to navigate)..."Wild Weekend" and the rest of them.*

Unfortunately, as we horn players all know, a half assed vocalist can keep an audience enchanted with a lot less effort than the greatest tenor man, hence King Curtis insisted on singing a few tunes.

I was fortunate over the years to put Big J's backup band together when he played this area and got to know him fairly well. He was a good guy. His sound dwarfed mine! Played the Monterey Jazz Fest with him! We paraded all over and around the audience. He'd make me get down on my knees and back sort of imitating him...it was a blast and the ol' dude would exhaust me and the band. Steve Douglas was sort of envious that I got to do the Big J gigs. He was towards the top of Steve's list of favorites. There was hope that when J returned at some point (if I got the gig) Steve would have the opportunity to play with him."

HANDCLAPPIN'

Red Prysock Tenor Sax

Red Prysock ©William Gottlieb

Gottlieb, W. P. (1946) *Portrait of Red Prysock, Hugues Panassié and Tiny Grimes, New York, N.Y., Between 1946 and 1948*. United States, 1946. Monographic. [Photograph] Retrieved from the Library of Congress, https://www.loc.gov/item/gottlieb.06731/.

Red Prysock's "Handclappin'" is cited as one of the critical breakthroughs in the birth of rock n' roll.

"Prysock's rocking sax work could make the hairs on your neck stand on end and often set the tone for the wild, early package tours...Red Prysock was not a star of the magnitude of Little Richard, Fats Domino or Chuck Berry," writes Bob Bell in the AVI album's liner notes for "Rock and Roll: The Best of Red Prysock". "Yet in many ways, his sound was the universally recognized sound of rock 'n' roll in all its primeval wildness and magnificent glory." 139

Rock And Roll/The Beat - Red Prysock (LP Mercury 20088/20307)

"It's hard for me to pick a favorite between these LP's by Red Prysock, both feature his signature driving, Jazz-influenced R&B and Rock n' Roll. Red's execution, tonguing, and ability to work rhythmic variations on one note are really unmatched. There are a few CD reissues available that draw from this mid 50's period with Mercury records. Absolutely essential...if you're feeling adventurous try *Battle Royale - Red Prysock & Sil Austin*..."

- Sax Gordon

Ruth Brown- *(Mama) He Treats Your Daughter Mean*

Willis "Gator" Jackson   Tenor

#1 R&B

Lucky Lips
#6 R&B #25 Pop

. RUTH BROWN, EARL SWANSON
Courtesy
https://cult45.wordpress.com/2012/12/06/baby-earl-the-trini-dads-back-slop/

The Queen of R&B.

Ruth Brown dominated the R&B charts to such a degree that Atlantic Records was called "The House That Ruth Built"! Atlantic, however, made her pay for touring and recording costs out of pocket. It wasn't until the late 1990s that she was able to force Atlantic Records to pay her back royalties, a settlement that led her to press for other musicians' rights regarding royalties and contracts, that led to the founding of the Rhythm and Blues Foundation in 1998.
https://www.rhythmandbluesfoundation.org/

https://www.npr.org/2017/10/23/559070707/forebears-ruth-brown-the-fabulous-miss-rhythm

Her hits, in the 1950s included "So Long"(Number 4 R&B)1

"Teardrops from My Eyes" (Number 1 R&B) and

"(Mama) He Treats Your Daughter Mean".

RUTH BROWN (vcl), Joe Wilder, Steve Lipkin (tpts), King Curtis (ten), Mike Stoller (pno), Charles Macey, Everett Barksdale (gtrs), Lloyd Trotman (bs), Joe Marshall (dms), Bradley Spinney (perc). Unk. vcl grp on −1. Orch. dir. Howard Biggs. Prod. Jerry Wexler & Ahmet Ertegun.
New York. July 30, 1958

A-3104   I Haven't Met unissued

A-3105   This Little Girl's Gone Rocking
          Atlantic 1197
A-3106   Why Me –1   Atlantic 1197

RUTH BROWN (vcl), King Curtis, Seldon Powell (alt/tens), Sy Mann (pno), Billy Mure (gtr), Everett Barksdale (bs-gtr), Wendell Marshall (bs), Belton Evans (dms), Maeretha Stewart, James Leyden, Marcia Neil, Mary-Margaret Mullen, Robert Miller (bkgnd vcls). Orch. Dir. Billy Mure.
New York. October 10, 1958

A-3169-1   Itty Bitty Girl Atlantic 2015
A-3170   I'll Step Aside Atlantic 2008
A-3171   Mama, He Treats Your Daughter Mean
            Atlantic 2008
A-3172-2   5-10-15 Hours Atlantic 2015

Note: Michel Ruppli gives date for this session as October 28, but session sheet is dated and filed at October 10.

-Roy Simonds- "King Curtis Sessionography"

Her first pop hit came with "Lucky Lips", that reached Number 6 on the R&B chart and Number 25 on the Pop. "This Little Girl's Gone Rockin" followed in 1958 and hit Number 7 on the R&B chart and Number 24 on Pop. Patti Page covered Brown's Number One R&B hit "What A Dream" and reached #10 on the Pop chart.

Willis "Gator" Jackson (April 25, 1932 – October 25, 1987) was an American jazz tenor saxophonist.

Willis Jackson joined Duke Ellington alumnus Cootie Williams' band in 1949 as a teenager, after being discovered by Eddie Vinson. During the 1950s he participated in R&B and jazz recordings, primarily as a session musician. He also toured as leader of the backing band of singer Ruth Brown, whom he married. Jackson joined Prestige Records in 1959, making a string of jazz albums which were an influence on the burgeoning soul jazz movement. During this era, Jack McDuff and Pat Martino became famous through association with Jackson. Jackson's main influences were Lester Young and Illinois Jacquet.

Courtesy:http://en.wikipedia.org/wiki/Willis_Jackson_(saxophonist)

4 R&B #4 POP   DEVIL OR ANGEL — THE CLOVERS   WILLIS JACKSON   TENOR

Courtesy of Harold J. Winley, the original bass singer of The Clovers. Willis Jackson was performing with the Erskine Hawkins Orchestra.

240

Who You Gonna Believe?
Record Credits
By Neil Sharpe

"I was looking at the jacket copy…but the 'producer's' name was in huge script on the back, and underneath it four or five other names…punks and narks and other ten-percentages who apparently had more leverage than the musicians who made the album, and so managed to get their names on the record jacket."

-Hunter S. Thompson,
The Great Shark Hunt, pg. 96.

Perry Bradford said that he played the piano on "Crazy Blues", however so did noted jazz pianist William Henry Joseph Bonaparte Bertholoff Smith a.k.a William "The Lion" Smith.

The Lion didn't stop there, claiming that he also had organized the recording session and assembled the musicians to back Mamie Smith.

Although Smith's claims have been largely discredited, they were typical of what would soon follow, with various people claiming composer credits on songs, to have played famous solos and on and on…

Unfortunately, for many years, session musicians on the 1950s hits usually were never given credit on the LP covers or CD liner notes. In some cases, had it not been for the studio musicians, a record might not have become a hit for the singer. Even in some recordings that used the singer's own band, credit was not always given to those who made it happen.

"For many years, the record companies excluded the names of all musicians on their records. There are albums that I played on where the commentary on the back cover...proceeds to describe the recording technique and equipment – nothing about the musicians...So, many thanks John Laughter...for the efforts in digging out and publishing this information."

-Plas Johnson

"John Laughter has done the near impossible... John has created a player's...Rosetta stone. What you have here is a history from the point of view of the true "unsung heroes" of the art form..."

-Dave "Woody" Woodford

If musicians complained about lack of credit, they could soon be back on the street or permanently nailed to the floor by bad contracts and royalty payments that disappeared into the pockets of executives who got rich by feasting off musical talent and claiming composer copyright on songs they didn't write.

For those with the courage to demand their rights, record executives, knowing that a recording contract was essential to have a career, would ask one nightmare question again and again, "You don't like it, leave! What're you gonna do about it?"

That attitude rarely changed over the decades.

After working on best selling albums with George Clinton, **Chops Horns Darryl Dixon and Dave Watson** moved to Sugar Hill Records and played on what became some of the most important, and pivotal, hip-hop recordings.

" 'Rapper's Delight' by the Sugarhill Gang was hip-hop's first Top 40 single and a worldwide smash hit. Then came 'The Message', a song that changed the direction and nature of hip-hop from primarily party music into a vital, creative, driving voice for equality and justice.

Dave Watson: We played on all the Sugar Hill Records between 1980-82, but Gene Chase wrote the horn arrangements. We were just the hired guns to play the stuff. We were the in-house horn section and got paid $75.00 a song, no matter how well that song did; we didn't see any residuals. Other members of the house band were: trumpets: Marvin Daniels, Bill McGee, Sly Smithers, Charles DeStefano (1 song), Bones Melvin El and Robin Eubanks. The saxes were Otha Stokes and Eric Allen.

Darryl Dixon: Grandmaster Flash and the Sugarhill Gang were really big in Europe. But it was in their contract that they didn't get any overseas royalties. When we were with The Police and we'd go through Europe, we'd see posters of them performing everywhere in Europe. They were great there, but it's unfortunate that they didn't get any royalties from it.

DW. When we were with Sugar Hill, we wanted to put out some of own music but they wanted us to change our name to the Sugarhill Horns, and when we refused, they said, "If you put some music out and don't use us, we're going to blackball you". And that's exactly what they did. Of course, they had a lot of ins with the radio stations and the stations wouldn't play our stuff. They were told: "You play their stuff and we're going to pull all of ours".

That's one thing about this business you have to understand. You've got to be able to play different styles in both music and the business, to know what is the right language at the right time, to know when to push and when to flow.

Sugar Hill gave us no credit whatsoever. Didn't bother me personally but you might need that to get more work. But that happens in this business. Credit happens in a lot of different ways. Not to belabor it. For me, it's about a level of respect. If you push back at producers and musicians about not getting credit on arrangements and recordings, they say, "You guys are a dime a dozen, do you know how lucky you are to be doing this!"

DD. Yea, that's the classic line.

DW. And some people will steal from you. When we first started, we thought our music spoke for itself and we wanted to be treated honestly. But when your lawyer walks in and they realize they can't steal something from you, the classic thing used to be, they'd go out and find guys they can steal from.

We hired a lawyer when we first broke out on own and learned that certain things can happen and if you push too hard, you may not get that much work again. You got to know who's hiring you, their rep, what language to speak and when."

In the 1950s, for a young musician, a recording contract *seemed* everything. It meant that after a lot of hard work, you had finally made it, had been accredited as a professional musician, that your recorded music would soon heard by your family, friends and the entire country, that every dream had come true.

That was the goal of every musician, what they thought a record could accomplish, why they signed whatever the record executives put in front of them. Only later, with dogs snapping at their heels, t debt collectors closing in and no sources of mercy found, that they discovered how the music industry really worked. Why being a functional paranoid could seem an occupational necessity.

Tenor saxophonist **Jon R Smith** comments:

"A musical career can be incredibly inspiring, rewarding, and satisfying.

I have been very fortunate in my career to have the opportunity to tour and to perform with a wide variety of musicians, including Keb Mo, Philip Glass, Edgar Winter, Percy Sledge, Ike and Tina Turner, Delbert McClinton, Kim Wilson and The Fabulous Thunderbirds, John Hiatt, Bonnie and Delaney Bramlett, Rick Derringer, and the Isley Brothers, to name just a few.

A musical career also can be a tough, ruthless, business.

The first thing you need to understand, there's a big difference between the music and the music industry. In an industry where burnouts and shooting stars are the norm, God-given talent helps, but no matter how gifted you may be, thinking that you can handle negotiations when dealing with high powered booking agents, record company executives, and the industry's lawyers and accountants, is a recipe for disaster…

Not knowing the contractual and legal end of the business can leave you penniless. Sharks are always lurking. That's why you must have a good music lawyer acting for you, especially in the early stages of the negotiations with a major label or agency. Unless you want to get run over, never let the lawyer for the company or the agency act for you. Hire a lawyer and an agent who will be truly independent and act in your best interests. How do you find that out? By knowing how to ask the right questions. By educating yourself about the business, about recording contracts, about where and how to tour, and so on. You do this so that when you're talking to a lawyer or an agent, you'll know what he/she is talking about, whether he/she is just blowing smoke, what you're entitled to, and when you're getting screwed.

You need enough savvy to know what's good advice and what's isn't."

[These aren't Jon's thoughts alone. In 2021, Rapper IDK has linked up with Harvard University to teach financial literacy, contract negotiations, networking, social media strategy, and mental health; "No Label Academy." The 10-day music business course is primarily for BIPOC (Black, Indigenous, and People of Color} students at Harvard University in Boston, Mass.

https://www.rollingstone.com/pro/news/rapper-idk-harvard-university-music-business-classes-1096530/

Also, C. Keith Harrison offers graduate and undergraduate courses centered on the business of hip-hop innovation and entrepreneurship.

https://www.ucf.edu/pegasus/the-business-of-hip-hop/]

Jon R. Smith: "When I talk to young people, especially the ones from impoverished backgrounds, they ask about how much money they can make.

I went on the road in the ninth grade. That was a big mistake. I should have taken the time to get a good education, especially a degree in music, so that when the business doesn't treat you the way it should, and after beating your brains out trying to make a living out of music, you can go into the education system and teach, make a regular income, and still play music on the weekends or every night if you wish.

I never would advise anyone to depend only on music for a living. Few people have cashed in on being a musician. Being a great, great musician doesn't mean you're going to be rich and famous. Very few jazz players make it big, and the ones who do have a tendency to be more commercial players.

This business is all about luck, about being in the right place at the right time, and that if doesn't sound too encouraging, welcome to the cold, hard facts about the music business.

I've had a fair amount of success and luck in my career, but brother, I won't wish my life on anyone, not even my worst enemy. I don't try to discourage, but I don't try to encourage either. I like people to be realistic right from the beginning.

I say this because of all the things I've had to go through, and all the bad crap I've sometimes fallen into. I've seen so many great, great players never get the opportunity they deserved. There are a lot of terrific sax players no will ever know about, because those players weren't lucky enough to be in the right place at the right time.

Music is a really touchy business. You just never know how things will break, about who will get the recognition and rewards. That's why every musician must come to terms with- what 'success' really means."

When all is said and done, that is the bottom line- just go out and enjoy the music. When you have a chance to play with great musicians like Luther Kent and the Forever Fabulous Chicken Hawks…let the sax and the music be an extension of your body and your mind. Relax and just let the music flow…

Which explains how my personal CD came together. All the tunes are favorites of my family's- with a few changes in arrangements. For example, with 'Rainy Night in Georgia', I didn't like the original bridge, so I left it off and did a turn-around. We recorded that track at Larry's Sieberth's house, my friend, producer and a genius at playing great changes. The rain was coming down cats and dogs, giving us the perfect setting and mood.

https://www.youtube.com/watch?v=miFYUC_RxuY

Special guests on the CD include the great Tower of Power trumpet player Mic Gillette, Doug Belote on drums, Mark Braud on flugel horn, Bob Sundra bass, Shane Theriot guitar, Bill Solley, guitar, Michael Skinkus, percussion, and Phillip Manual and yours truly on background vocals. Engineered and Mixed by Misha Kachkachishvili, with Gary Beutler the Executive Producer.

My favorite track on the CD is 'Slow Jam', a song originally done by 'Midnight Star'. The lyrics are terrific. My kids played and danced to this when they were young, and it was featured at one of my daughter's wedding."

https://www.youtube.com/watch?v=7yVGnkd5AbE

"If there are times when I feel sorry for myself, I realize that I'm still alive, have a wonderful family, and can wake up every day with a positive attitude.

For every musician, times will come when there's not much, if anything going on. But, you must have the attitude that although you never know when that phone call will come, it will. And then…you're back on the road, doing what you love."

Notes

Gottlieb, W. P. (1946) *Portrait of Red Prysock, Hugues Panassié and Tiny Grimes, New York, N.Y., Between 1946 and 1948*. United States, 1946. Monographic. [Photograph] Retrieved from the Library of Congress, https://www.loc.gov/item/gottlieb.06731/.

Harris, Paul Portrait of Big Jay McNeely. paulharrisphotography.blogspot.com

Red Prysock: Catlin Roger (1996) When Rock Rolled In. The Hartford Courant, June 16, 1996. A great bio of Red Prysock: But, as the musician lamented in 1983, "they never call my name when they talk about the roots of rock 'n' roll on TV." https://www.courant.com/news/connecticut/hc-xpm-1996-06-16-9606140042-story.html

252

8

TUTTI FRUTTI

"Deep gutted. Full chromed.
Slammed to the floor.
Supercharged Chevy bustin' for more.
Blue smoke trailing,
Stars tumbling out of the sky,
My wild-eyed passenger screaming,
'I don't wanna die!'"

"'Have for fear', I shout,
'Cause
People soon will be yelling:
More! More! More!
As my sax gets them jumpin'
Across a jammed dance floor.
I'm not trying to kill you!
Just getting you ready for some
ROCK N' ROLL!' "

-Neil Sharpe

Back then- the 1950s. Antianxiety and inhibitors' sales skyrocketed. Mr. Gray Flannel suit and "Susie Homemaker" were choking back pills like there was no tomorrow 'cause there wasn't. Love and hope lost in the grind of suburbia, the corporate rat race, "Keeping Up With The Joneses".

Enter Rock n' Roll. Straddling the rhythm-and-blues-powered-engine of change. Ripping up, tearing down, everything in sight. The music that saved a generation. And not a moment too soon.

Which isn't to say, it went easy. Music executives, politicians, preachers and Parent-Teacher Associations condemned Rock n' Roll. Said it caused juvenile delinquency, street fights and motorcycle gangs.

Newspapers featured ads like "Don't Buy Negro Records"…The screaming idiotic words and savage music of these records are undermining the morale of white youth in America." 134

A California psychiatric board was reported to have investigated Big Jay McNeely because his young audience behaved so wildly.135

ASCAP tried to convince radio stations not to play the music promoted by BMI.

Johnnie Ray's cover of "Such A Night" (originally recorded by Clyde McPhatter and The Drifters) was banned from radio play on the basis of "sexual suggestions" as was Joe Turner's "Shake Rattle and Roll". 136

However, on November 20, 1955, the viewing public was treated to pure rhythm and blues for the first time on Ed Sullivan's popular Sunday night CBS-TV variety show, Ed Sullivan called it, "A new trend in music."

Featured were Bo Diddley, LaVern Baker and The Five Keys and Willis "Gator" Jackson's band. Jackson, a 23 year old Miami-born tenor saxophonist, tore up the stage, arching his back while ripping off the roof with his screaming sax.

December, 1955- Billboard commented on the many of new R&B records flooding the market..."'We are seeing and hearing more good records than ever before...'" 137

https://www.youtube.com/watch?v=7-is9GsxCT0 (Willis Jackson)

https://www.youtube.com/watch?v=dLcYuuljrD4&list=PLQWND5qZhbj3G24DJh0BjAEwEq8_7bivw (Bo Diddley)

https://www.youtube.com/watch?v=sq8vRci5Mi4&list=PLQWND5qZhbj3G24DJh0BjAEwEq8_7bivw&index=5 (LaVern Baker)

https://www.youtube.com/watch?v=AaosFc9Z0i4 (The Five Keys)

But for some record executives, such as Mitch Miller, head of Mercury and Columbia Records, whose "Sing Along With Mitch" albums had hit the top of the charts, rock n' roll "isn't music, it's a disease"; he kept rock n' roll out of Columbia Records for "far longer" than his colleagues wanted. Billy Rose of ASCAP claimed, "Not only are most of the BMI songs junk, but in many cases they are obscene junk, pretty much of a level with dirty comic magazines."136

Elvis Presley first appearance on a leading televisions program, The Ed Sullivan Show, had produced record ratings. During his second appearance, Elvis was only filmed from the waist up to ensure viewers didn't see his gyrating hips!

Mainstream record companies tried to bury newcomers with covers by pop artists, such as Pat Boone's of Little Richard and Fats Domino.

But how could anyone resist? Especially with a wailing sax, a red-hot band, and flame-throwing music calling your name.

"American Bandstand", a late afternoon, after school, teen dance show, (Dick Clark took over as host in 1956) quickly became the voice of music for American teenagers.

The show featured interviews, rock performances and what initially was the show's theme song, Chuck Willis' version of "C.C. Rider" (#1 R&B #12 Pop) with Gene Barge on tenor sax.

The Diamonds, while great admirers of Chuck Willis, saw the drenched-in-gold opportunity. They recorded the song "The Stroll", written by Clyde Otis and Nancy Lee, and released it in December 1957 (#4 on Billboard's Top 100). Chuck Willis, as shown in the following session notes, was just getting started.

Fats Domino's band was flown in from New Orleans to New York to back The Diamonds on this session. King Curtis took the tenor sax solo.

Dave Somerville, co-founder and original lead singer of The Diamonds:

"Dick Clark wanted us to make a record for the dance," Somerville said. "We worked on that song for a long time. Brook Benton (a famous R&B singer of that era who later sang, 'Rainy Night in Georgia') coached me on 'The Stroll'. We brought in King Curtis to play saxophone. And Fats Domino's band played the music." But the biggest factor was Dick Clark. "He loved the song and played it all the time on 'American Bandstand'", Somerville said, adding that "The Stroll" was probably the first line dance. Teenagers would form two lines, each couple would then 'stroll' between both lines."

-John Laughter

THE DIAMONDS: *Dave Somerville, Ted Kowalski, Phil Leavitt, Bill Reed (vcls), King Curtis (ten), unk. pno, gtr, bs, dms.*
New York. November 27, 1957

16416	*The Stroll*	*Mercury 71242*
16417	*Eternal Lovers*	*Mercury 71366*
16418	*Walkin' Along*	*Mercury 71366*

-Roy Simonds: "King Curtis Sessionography"

CHUCK WILLIS *(vcl), King Curtis (ten), Sam Price (pno), Al Caiola, George Barnes (gtrs), Lloyd Trotman (bs), Joe Marshall (dms), Teddy Charles (vbs), The Cues: Ollie*

Jones, Eddie Barnes, Jimmy Breedlove, Robie Kirk, Abel De Costa (bkgnd vcls). Orch. Dir. Reggie Obrecht.

New York. February 14, 1958

A-2977   You'll Be My Love   Atlantic 2005

A-2978   What Am I Living For   Atlantic 1179
#1 R&B #9 Pop

A million seller that has been covered 79 times: (https://secondhandsongs.com/performance/28741

A-2979 Hang Up My Rock & Roll Shoes Atlantic 1179
#9 R&B #24 Pop

A-2980   Keep A-Driving   Atlantic 2005.
#19 R&B

By the late 1950s, American Bandstand had become ABC's top-rated show and the most popular daytime show on the television networks.

As a genre, rock n' roll jumped from 15 percent in 1955 to 42.7 percent in 1959. 137

Although the classic period for rock n roll is generally considered to have ended in the early 1960s, the influence of sax players of the 1950s has lived on for generations.

The torrid, screaming, and what some critics charged, "demented", sax solos, powered rock n' roll to the top of the pop and r&b charts.

Unfortunately, many the great, formative, sax players of this generation have suffered the same fate. History's distorted sense of what, how and why they played have hardened impressions and memories of them into an inflexible, shallow, "soda shop" stereotypes that prevent us from hearing what really lies behind their notes- the mediations and riffs on human nature, and, more importantly, the defiance, and the calls for rebellion and freedom that are the true spirit and heart of rock n' roll.

***

Following is a highly eclectic selection of exclusive interviews, emails, texts and letters together with notes on record production and sound, women in rock, elusive interviews and recording stories that tell what really happened.

We have used Internet resources, email and text responses, and various books to finally give musicians credit where credit is due, to confirm as many dates, names, and songs as possible.

Photos have been included wherever copyright clearance has made it possible.

For a free, historical record (Pdf) of who played sax on Billboard Top 40 hits from 1955-22, complied by John Laughter, write jsaxl@aol.com

A few great sax solos by sax players have yet to be identified, even on monster hits like Paul Anka's "Diana" which sold over 10 million copies in 1957.

If you have a suggestion, please write to jsaxlATaol.com

For a comprehensive history of the saxophone, - loaded with music clips- in blues, jazz, r&b, jump, rock n' roll, soul, rock, reggae, funk, rap, hip-hop, country, metal and EDM and more- including exclusive interviews and John Laughter's complete history of who actually played on Top 40 hits from 1955-1921, please order the ebook "Ride The Wild Wind: History of The Saxophone:1920-2021" available from Amazon around the world:

The complete sessionography for King Curtis, complied by Roy Simonds, provides a fascinating overview and insight into the career of a musical legend. In 2011, Roy shared this invaluable research with members of Saxontheweb.net. Roy also sent me (Neil Sharpe) a copy and we exchanged subsequent emails. Unfortunately, Roy passed away shortly thereafter. Because this wonderfully detailed research has not been published, it is at risk of being lost forever. Selections from the years 1947-59 are included in the following profiles.

Interested in a particular song? Try this resource: the internet's largest website dedicated to the magic of the vinyl seven inch single (or **7"** or **45**).

Discuss, rate, review or simply admire some of the **1,241,044** records, or help add some more.
https://www.45cat.com/

262

Tutti Frutti

Here's Little Richard (album)- Little Richard

Lee Allen   Tenor

Alvin "Red" Tyler   Baritone

Mono LP- Specialty SP 100

#2 R&B #13 Pop

The album "Here's Little Richard" that featured the flamboyant vocals and pounding piano style of Little Richard, together with Lee Allen's unique phrasing and deep gutted tone on tenor sax, helped to define the new standard for "rock sax" and rock n' roll, with songs like "Slippin' and Slidin', "Tutti Frutti" and "Long Tall Sally".

Pat Boone's cover version of "Tutti Frutti" reached #12 on the Pop charts, Little Richard's #21. However, Little Richard's album has been cited by Time Magazine as one the Top 100 Recordings of the 20th Century.

Little Richard said that though Boone "took [his] music"…They didn't want me to be in the white guys' way. ... I felt I was pushed into a rhythm and blues corner to keep out of rockers' way, because that's where the money is. When 'Tutti Frutti' came out. ... They needed a rock star to block me out of white homes because I was a hero to white kids. The white kids would have Pat Boone upon the dresser and me in the drawer 'cause they liked my version better, but the families didn't want me because of the image that I was projecting." 141

Critical influences in the development of Little's Richard's stage image, vocal and piano styles, also include blues singer Billy Wright and Eskee Reeder. 142

Billy Wright (Neil James alto, Artie Clark, Fred Jackson, tenors)
https://www.youtube.com/watch?v=8jUwLAigD1w

Esquerita
https://www.youtube.com/watch?v=JA0xKHTkqxM

Lee Allen © Paul Harris

Lee Allen

David Bowie said: "The first record I think I bought was called 'I Got It', which Little Richard later re-wrote as 'She's Got It'. And ever since I saw that photograph, I realized he had so many saxophones in his band. So I went out and bought a saxophone intending that when I grew up, I'd work in the Little Richard's band as one of his saxophonists."

In the 1950s, Cosimo Matassa's J and M Studio in New Orleans put together one of the finest session bands in the history of rock and roll and R&B. Although various musicians were involved over the years, the main band consisted of: Lee Allen on tenor sax, Alvin "Red" Tyler on baritone sax, Earl Palmer on drums, Edgar Blanchard on guitar, Justin Adams on guitar, Huey "Piano" Smith on piano, James Booker on piano, and Frank Fields on bass. Regulars also included Doctor John, Salvador Doucette, Wendel DuConge, Clarence Ford, Edward Frank, Herb Hardesty, Ernest McLean and Allen Toussaint.

-John Laughter

Born in Pittsburgh, Kansas, on July 2, 1926, and schooled in New Orleans. Lee Allen's tenor style was a major factor in the sound of the New Orleans R&B hits of the 1950s. His solos burned and seared the 78 and 45 rpm records of Fats Domino, Lloyd Price, Little Richard, Professor Longhair, Huey "Piano" Smith, Smiley Lewis, Shirley & Lee, Clarence "Frogman" Henry, Amos Milburn, Charles Brown, Etta James, and many more.

Allen was a very important member of the studio band at Cosimo's. His solos appeared on hundreds of Crescent City classics. In 1958, Allen also recorded his own instrumental record on Ember titled "Walking With Mr. Lee" which charted at #54 on Billboard Pop.

His hard-driving solos on the Little Richard and Fats Domino hits inspired generation of sax players. His unique and distinctive tone is still respected and often copied to this day. Allen's use of note bending and the "growl" technique were key factors in his style.

In 1965 he left the road touring with Fats Domino and moved to the West Coast to take a job in an aeronautics factory; however, in 1975, Lee Allen was back with Fats Domino. Allen performed until his death from lung cancer in 1994. He was a member of The Blasters, a Los Angeles-based band of rockers.

Remembering Lee Allen
by Billy Vera
Courtesy
http://www.grindstonemagazine.com/backissues/1.html

It would be difficult to find anyone else besides Lee Allen who deserves the title of "The quintessential rock 'n' roll tenor sax soloist." In pure terms of hundreds of rock 'n' roll classics he played on, Lee outshone even the likes of King Curtis, Plas Johnson, Sam "the Man" Taylor and Big Al Sears.

Born on July 2, 1926, in Pittsburgh, Kansas, and raised in New Orleans, Lee came up at a time when any black musician who aspired to the tenor saxophone had to perform, verbatim, Illinois Jacquet's solo from the Lionel Hampton 1942 hit "Flying

Home." That one record changed forever the way the instrument was approached.

Unlike many of the "honkers & screamers," such as Big Jay McNeely, Red Prysock and Joe Houston, Lee developed a more melodic version of Jacquet's basic style. Perhaps this was due to the highly developed sense of melody inherent in New Orleans music. Allen could honk with the best, but his own style was filled with sexy cajoling, teasing slides and barks.

While a student at Xavier University, he was discovered by local bandleader Paul Gayten, who had been responsible, in 1947, for the first hit recordings of the R&B era by a New Orleans artist, "True (You Don't Love Me)."

Paul introduced Lee to the burgeoning recording scene and ultimately Lee became part of the house band at the famed Cosimo's recording studio. Other members included baritone saxist Alvin "Red" Tyler and drummer Earl Palmer. This ensemble was the rhythmic force behind such New Orleans rock 'n' roll classics as Shirley & Lee's "Let The Good Times Roll," Smiley Lewis's "I Hear You Knockin'", Professor Longhair's "Tipitina," Lloyd Price's "Lawdy Miss Clawdy," Clarence "Frogman" Henry's "Ain't Got No Home" and Huey "Piano" Smith's "Rockin' Pneumonia & The Boogie Woogie Flu."

Although Lee had long played with Fats Domino and many have believed that Lee took the solos on Domino's records, Fats actually used his road band on most of his recordings and the solos were usually by Herb Hardesty rather than Lee.

Lee Allen's greatest legacy may be the wonderful solos he took on Little Richard's greatest hits, "Tutti Frutti," "Long Tall Sally," "Rip It Up," "Good Golly Miss Molly" and many more. Those tenor sax breaks contributed as much to the mayhem of those recordings as did the psychotic vocalizing of Richard himself.

Earl Palmer defected to Los Angeles in 1957 to become the most successful studio drummer of his generation, but Lee stuck around New Orleans a little longer, cutting a hit of with "Walking With Mr. Lee," a great dance favorite on American Bandstand.

Unable to produce a follow-up hit, Lee took to the road with Fats until 1965, then following Palmer to LA. Not the greatest sight-reader, Lee did not find the success in the studios that Earl had, so he went to work in one of the many airplane factories in Southern California while performing at night with one of the organ/sax combos so popular at the time. In the seventies, he returned to Fats' touring band full-time and, in the next decade, was rediscovered by local roots bands, such as The Blasters and The Stray Cats. He occasionally sat in with my band, The Beaters.

"The last time I saw him in good health was at the funeral of our mutual friend Paul Gayten. When Lee was dying of cancer, I went to visit him at the rest home where he was staying. It was heartbreaking to see this once-vital man wasting away and going in-and-out of lucidity. I was glad, however, to be able to pay my last respects to a man who was both a hero and a friend."

https://www.youtube.com/watch?v=f2a09u2Bms4 (Driving Home)

***

"It was fascinating listening to stories about recording with Little Richard, or his early gigs in the south when he played for strip shows – he spoke about a gauze curtain between the band and the strippers so that the white customers could not see that there was black band on stage with white naked women.

Listen to those solos on the early Little Richard hits, but if possible, try to find some of his earlier recordings with Paul Gayten – shades of Ben Webster! Later stuff with Dr John (Gumbo).

You will hear how it's possible to say an awful lot with very few notes. He had a knack of making simple melodic phrases right on the beat with no syncopation sound as funky as anything. His solo on "Walking With Mr Lee" is a perfect example of how to make a solo just keep on building in intensity.

The name "Walking with Mr Lee" comes from Lee's habit of walking (more of a stomp as excitement builds) on the spot while playing. Perhaps this has some connection to his amazing ability to state the beat, his phrasing was so in the pocket he was almost part of the drum kit.

I was with Lee in LA a week before he died of lung cancer and met his wife "Tiny" who was bringing him home cooked meals into the hospital every day. I was in the process of getting legal help for him to get royalties for his music which he never received, however I'm sad to say I was too late." -Pete Thomas

https://tamingthesaxophone.com/saxophone/players/saxophone-lee-allen

Discography:

1956 *Honkers and Screamers*—Savoy
1958 *Walkin' with Mr. Lee*—Collectable
Paul Gayten, Gayten's Nightmare (1949)
https://www.youtube.com/watch?v=HnC2w2Zflvc&list=PLvVkpXKafnJs3fiKyQViw1H_MGZOv8tsU

Paul Gayten Boogie Jump (1949)

https://www.youtube.com/watch?v=HnC2w2Zflvc

Smiley Lewis, Playgirl (1953)
Professor Longhair, In the Night (1953)
The Spiders, I Didn't Want To Do It (1953)
Shirley and Lee, Feel So Good (1955)
Little Richard, Tutti Frutti (1955)
Fats Domino, I'm In Love Again (1955)
Little Richard, Long Tall Sally (1956)
Little Richard, Slippin' And Slidin' (1956)
Lloyd Price, I Yi Yi Gomen-A-Sai (1956)
Paul Gayten, You Better Believe It (1956)
Bobby Mitchell, Goin' Round In Circles (1956)
Huey Smith, Li'l Liza Jane (1956)
Bobby Charles, Take It Easy Greasy (1956)

Etta James, Tough Lover (1956)
Richard Berry, Yama Yama Pretty Mama (1956)
Little Richard, Lucille (1956)
Roy Montrell, That Mellow Saxophone (1956)
Roy Brown, Saturday Night (1956)
The Spiders, Better Be On My Way (1956)

More info :
http://tamingthesaxophone.com/saxophone-lee-allen.htm

***

"I think I was one of the few younger sax players that he [Lee Allen] personally knew that he felt understood what he was all about. Steve Douglas loved Lee's sax playing. Douglas' other favorites were Sam Butera and Big Jay.

Lee as a youngster was a fan of Illinois Jacquet. But there is a lot of Louis Armstrong quarter note stuff in Lee's playing...How do you notate the deliberate things Lee Allen constantly does with his sound and pitch? Lee was great at attacking a note somewhere in space and lipping it into the correct note/sound. He was almost like a slide guitarist!

I had the opportunity to play with Lee on many occasions. I learned all the heads to the "Walkin With Mr Lee" LP... We would stand there and I was in charge of the melody then he would play harmony and solo. I had been doing "Boppin at the Hop" for years...One night Steve Douglas, Lee and I were the featured frontline. Steve was in awe of Lee and met him for the first time that night.

Both these men were very nice guys. I don't think they got the respect from other sax players that they deserved during their lives. Now everyone recognizes their contributions and uniqueness. Big Jay is another player who has been grossly maligned…totally unique. His sound dwarfed mine! Also, a great guy. I was fortunate over the years to put J's backup band together when he played this area and got to know him fairly well.

"Steve and Lee got the calls because the people producing and wanting the sax on their records, wanted a certain style. A style that wasn't really defined. Sam The Man Taylor (early on) was the only sax in the studios making big bucks, and although both mentioned him, he was definitely more of a jazz/r&b style. We could be splitting hairs here r&b vs r&r? Jimmy Wright is another player who seems to me more a r&r sax style…Steve didn't care for so called "jazz" saxophone at all. He made me aware that there truly was a rock and roll school of sax and very few guys could do it or figured it out". -John Firmin

https://www.youtube.com/watch?v=E2K15lCaSIg
(John Firmin- Harlem Nocturne)

https://davidbromberg.net/john-firmin/

John Firmin passed away peacefully in his home in San Anselmo, CA on the morning of October 8th, 2021. He spent his final days visiting with friends and sitting in his garden, enjoying the sun and fistfuls of tomatoes. Born in Anchorage, Alaska on April 20, 1947, John was prideful of his Alaskan roots, forever cherishing the unique and fun times he had growing up with his four brothers and sister.

Passionate about music from an early age, he was taught clarinet and saxophone by his father Lewis, learning the core skills he would go on to develop into a career performing music. In his mid-twenties, after a year spent working on the construction of the Alaskan Pipeline, John decided to go to Woodstock,

New York to study at the Creative Music Studio, a school that had recently opened for the study of improvisational music. His studies were cut short when one of the instructors (drummer Jack DeJohnette) recommended him after singer/guitarist David Bromberg contacted the school looking for someone that could play both clarinet and saxophone. John moved to New York City to join the David Bromberg Band, playing the city's biggest venues and touring frequently throughout the mid/late 70s.

He would later move to the Bay Area where he played in various bands throughout the early/mid 80s. After surviving a serious spinal cord injury and nearly drowning, John worked diligently to regain his movement and strength. He would use the accident and subsequent recovery as a catalyst, motivating him to form his own group in 1989, the horn heavy Johnny Nocturne Band. Throughout the 90s and 2000s the band played locally, nationally, and internationally, some years playing Italy's Umbria Jazz Festival in the summer and then returning to play the smaller winter festival.

John married Linda Ross in 1989 and their son Jake was born in 1990. John will be remembered for his joyous sense of humor, warm-hearted generosity, and love for music, chocolate, and Coca-Cola. He is preceded in death by his father Lewis, mother Geraldine, brothers Bill and Joe, and sister Anne. He is survived by his wife Linda, son Jake, brothers Bob and Jim, and dog Mr. Meeps."

276

Elvis Presley- *Hound Dog*

1 R&B #1 Pop #1 Country

In the music industry, the knife's edge is always close to the throat. Original recordings and cover versions have a long history of battling it out on the record charts.

Cover versions of songs were common in the 1950s. Record companies routinely would produce different versions of a hit song for release in the separate pop, country, and r&b markets. Covers were also regularly used by major labels to cover originals from indie labels. The Crew Cuts for example, covered the Chords "Sh-Boom", Nappy Brown's "Don't Be Angry" and the Penguins "Earth Angel". The McGuire Sisters covered The Moonglows' "Sincerely", and The Spaniels' "Goodnight, Well It's Time To Go"…the list goes on and on.

Race was a factor, however, covers weren't the only evil eye that spoiled the fresh milk- the dollar bill was always delivering the poison or rewriting the lead.

For example, "Young Love" the original by Ric Cartey with the Jiva-Tones was covered in 1957 by country musician Sonny James, AND Tab Hunter, a Hollywood actor, AND The Crew Cuts.

"Whole Lotta Shakin' Going On" first released on Okeh 1955 by Big Maybelline was covered by Jerry Lee Lewis - #3 in the Billboard 100, #8 in the UK, and #1 in the Billboard Country Chart in 1957. Lewis' version, featuring his ferocious boogie woogie piano (inspired by the playing of Moon Mullican and Ella Mae Morse,) was far more up tempo than other versions recorded by Dolores Fredricks and Roy Hall for Decca Records 1955 143. Songwriters were David Curlee Williams and Myrian S. Davidson a.k.a. Sunny David aka James Faye Roy Hall.

In recent years, artists who recorded cover versions of blues and r&b songs have been accused of theft and cultural appropriation without giving due acknowledgment to the original artists.

While the accusations of musicians stealing the music of other musicians are many, it is important to understand that in 1950s, the main share of royalties went to songwriters and producers. In the USA, broadcast royalties were paid to publishers and songwriters *but not to the recording artists*. That's why when Elvis Presley covered a recording, the songwriter could benefit greatly (as will be seen in the following interview with Otis Blackwell) due to the dramatically increased sales and resulting royalties.

One of the more famous controversies and "one of the most litigated songs of all time" is Big Mama Thornton's version of 'Hound Dog", in 1953, that spent seven weeks at Number 1 on Rhythm and Blues Chart and became the biggest selling record in the history of the indie label Peacock Records, with estimated record sales of 600,000-800,000. Jerry Leiber and Mike Stoller, while they were still minors, wrote it specifically for her and reportedly supervised her performance. 144

Big Mama Thornton complained about the payments she received, as did the songwriters Lieber and Stoller, which may not have been a complete surprise given the owner of the label, Don Robey, had a reputation for "doing business with a gun".

Don Robey, who promoted Louis Jordan, Johnny Ace, Bobby "Blue" Bland, Ike and Tina Turner, B.B. King, Little Richard, T-Bone Walker, "Big" Joe Turner, and Wynonie Harris to name a few and threw "legendary after-parties that saw the likes of Sister Rosetta Tharpe jamming with Big Bill Broonzy and Louis Jordan, "had earned a reputation of exacting harsh discipline on his employees and associates… of being a modern-day outlaw living in a racial and moral gray area. Little Richard said he was 'almost like a dictator'. He could outsmart you and kick your ass…" An artist of the label, Johnny Ace, played Russian Roulette before every performance!145

It wasn't until 1973 that Lieber and Stoller received their full royalty payment. 146

Big Mama Thornton did enjoy touring success with "Hound Dog", travelling from coast to coast in a Cadillac. Preston Lauterbach reported, in Oxford American Magazine, that, "The Johnny Ace–Big Mama Thornton revue continually struck box office gold—they played the Apollo eight times in two years."

In January 1956, Elvis Presley stormed the charts with the blues-soaked "Heartbreak Hotel"- Number 1 Billboard Top 100 for 7 weeks, Number 1 Country and Western for 11 weeks, Number 3 Billboard Rhythm and Blues Chart. 147

This song's production and sound inspired a generation of musicians including John Cale, Keith Richards and Brian Eno (Cale recorded a praised cover of the song that was released as a promo record for Cale's album "Slow Dazzle"; this cover version was also featured in the live album -"June 1, 1974"- of songs performed at the Rainbow Theatre, London, on that date; the band included Cale, Brian Eno, Nice and Mike Oldfield).

Unsatisfied with the initial production efforts, Elvis essentially took over, including mike placement, and changing tempo to create an overall sound similar to his earlier recordings on Sun Records. Keith Richards, in his highly recommended autobiography "Life": "I'd never heard it before, or anything like it. When I woke up the next day, I was a different guy…That was the first rock n' roll I heard…It was bare, right to the roots that you had a feeling were there but hadn't yet heard. I've got to take my hat off to Elvis for that…"148

Following the release of "Heartbreak Hotel", Elvis' appearance in Las Vegas, scheduled for two weeks, unexpectedly was cancelled after only a week due to a poor reception from the adult audiences. Stung by his rejection by audiences in Los Vegas and knowing that his second hit, "I Want You, I Need You, I Love You" had been two cuts spliced together because of a fractured recording session, Elvis worried that if he didn't have a "real" follow up hit, his career might soon be over. At the time, Freddie Bell was one of the hottest acts in Las Vegas; Elvis watched their version of "Hound Dog" and saw how audiences reacted to it. 149

He started trying out "Hound Dog" to close his own stage shows. In July 1956, after a great teen reception for the song on two television shows, Elvis, decided to take a chance with "Hound Dog", performing it on the popular Ed Sullivan television show, including Freddie Bell's dancing and wiggling around the stage. Although Elvis already had been inspired by the performing styles of blues, gospel and country (e.g. the Louisiana Hayride radio/television show) performers, his decision to now include Freddie's cover version triggered controversy, as the press sharks rose up, smelling blood in the water.

Elvis Presley's version, in 1956, of "Hound Dog" was a worldwide hit, selling nearly 10 million copies. In recent years, Elvis has been accused of taking Big Mama Thornton's version of "Hound Dog" and turning it into a multi-million dollar smash hit without giving her credit. Covers, however, were the name of the game and a standard practice. When Mama Thornton first released her version of "Hound Dog", within a month, six cover versions had been released by other record companies, which didn't include Elvis' version that was released two years later. 150

https://secondhandsongs.com/performance/1730

Lieber and Stoller have said that Elvis *did not* copy Big Mama's version, his was a cover of the 1955 version by the Las Vegas group Freddie Bell and The Bellboys. Elvis' band members also reported that, as with "Heartbreak Hotel", Elvis was largely responsible for production of the song.

However, one cover of "Hound Dog" released by Sam Phillips, founder of Sun Records, titled "Bear Cat", performed by Rufus Thomas, triggered litigation. Robey sued and the court ruled against Sun Records, Phillips' small Memphis record label. Phillips was ordered to pay damages. The court found that not only was the melody and some of the lyrics the same as Mama Thornton's "Hound Dog", but also that Sam Phillips had claimed a writing credit.

The damages imposed by the court, apparently was a contributing factor in Sam Phillips' decision to sell the contract of Elvis Presley to RCA Records in 1955.

Presley is too often given little credit as an artist. John Doyle of The New York Times, on June 6, 1956 wrote: "ELVIS Presley is currently the entertainment world's most astonishing figure. The young man with the sideburns and mobile hips is the rage of the squealing teen-agers…Mr.

Presley has no discernable ability...renders in an undistinguished whine...for the ear an unutterable bore." 151

Elvis was a versatile vocalist with an emotional range that included country blues, gospel, blues, pop, and rock n' roll, he served as record producer on million selling records, and had a stage presence like few before him. Critics also have failed to recognize the high quality of Elvis' band "The Blue Moon Boys" featuring bassist Bill Black, guitarist Scotty Moore and drummer D.J. Fontana who were inducted, in 2007, to the Musicians Hall of Fame and Museum in Nashville Tennessee.

In a decision that only can be described as "strange", Rolling Stone Magazine which had listed Presley's "Hound Dog" as one of the 500 Greatest Songs of All Time, excluded it from a revised list in 2019, even though the two songs and arrangements are clearly different. Perhaps, they chose to forget or ignore that Lieber and Stoller had written the song and, at least from their account, helped to supervise the performance by Mama Thornton.

Sun Records earlier had Elvis do cover versions of other artists' songs to attract radio play and increase records sales through pop radio stations that otherwise may not have played records by the original artists. Such sales also would have benefited the original songwriters. Some have argued that Elvis acknowledged these artists, that his cover versions helped to popularize rhythm and blues and broke down the racial barrier between rhythm and blues and pop charts.

"I'd play along with the radio or photograph and taught myself the chord positions. We were a religious family, going 'round together to sing at camp meetings and revivals and I'd take my guitar with us when I could. I also dug the real low-down Mississippi singers, mostly Big Bill Broonzy and

Big Boy Crudup, although they would scold me at home for listening to them. 'Sinful music' the townfolk in Memphis said it was. Which never bothered me, I guess."

-Elvis Presley 152

Sun covers by Elvis included:
- "That's All Right Mama"- covered by Elvis in 1955.

In Deep Blues, Robert Palmer wrote about this song: "In its own odd way, it was country blues."153 The original blues song by Arthur Crudup was released in 1946, and since has been covered 238 times…and counting: https://secondhandsongs.com/work/4361/versions#nav-entity

Some have argued that Arthur Crudup did not receive his fair share of royalties. However, this has been attributed to Arthur Crudup's management 154.

- "Good Rockin' Tonight"- two months after his Crudup cover, Elvis' second release from Sun Records was a cover of the R&B hit for Wynonie Harris
- "Mystery Train"- recorded in 1954 by Elvis. The original blues song by Junior Parker was released as recorded by "Little Junior's Blue Flames", August 5, 1953- this song has been covered 184 times: https://secondhandsongs.com/work/3940/versions#nav-entity
- "Trying To Get To You"- released in 1955 by Elvis, (original was released by The Eagles in May, 1954), was written by Rose Marie McCoy and Charles Singleton; it has been covered 71 times.).

https://secondhandsongs.com/work/31533/versions#nav-entity
- "Baby Let's Play House"- Elvis' version of

Albert Gunter's original, 1954 song, hit #5 on the national country charts in 1955; a line from it- "I'd rather see you dead, little girl, than to be with another man"- was used by John Lennon, in 1965, in the song "Run For Your Life".

Some critics have claimed that Elvis "never gave credit to the black artists" whose music he covered. These critics often choose to ignore tributes to Elvis from other musicians.

Etta James: "I shared a bill with Elvis Presley. I didn't know what to expect. He turned out to be supercool and extra-respectful with his 'pleased to meet you ma'am' and gentlemanly manners. He also touched my heart many years later when my good friend Jackie Wilson was down and out, vegetating is some funky convalescent home. Elvis moved Jackie to a decent hospital-and paid for everything." 155

Jackie Wilson when asked if he could play one type of music and one type of performer for one solid hour, who would it be, had replied: "Elvis Presley".

"Any time he wanted to see me, he'd say, 'I want to talk to Mr. Blueberry Hill'. He didn't talk much, didn't brag much, all he did was smile. He had a lot of personality, but he didn't have the personality to brag about nothing, was quiet...We were just musicians. I often think about him. I think he was a wonderful man. I love him. And all I think about, every time I come to our bandstand, is to play 'Blueberry' Hill for him."

-Norm "B" Blakely- tenor sax, DJ, nickname courtesy of King Curtis.

Noah Berlatsky in an article for Atlantic Magazine (2014) "Getting Elvis' Legacy Right" wrote that Elvis "invented nothing and popularized nothing." Who is the more reliable commentator about what happened in the 1950s, Berlatsky or James Brown?156

"Elvis, Bill Haley, Little Richard, Fats Domino, Jerry Lee Lewis, Chuck Berry- all those first-generation pioneers brought something to young people nobody had ever heard before. Those cats were all into something new that wasn't already redolent in the air...Elvis, of course, is another story. In addition to all his music, he brought rebellion into teen fashion...liberating the music of a generation of uptight White kids to a few years later when those same kids-now a little older-gathered the courage to march in the streets of the South for civil rights." 157

..."I knew Elvis personally, almost from the beginning of both our careers...Offstage he was very quiet, very polite, and never arrogant or pushy. In that respect, he was one of the most pleasant people ever to be around..." 157

Elvis' covers also created the opportunity for dramatically increased royalties for the original song writers.

If you were a songwriter in the 1950s and depended on the income from your songs to pay the bills and to feed your family, who are you going to try and place a potential hit song like "Don't Be Cruel" with-Big Mama Thornton, Junior Parker or Elvis Presley?

Otis Blackwell -who wrote a large number of songs for Elvis, including the hit "Don't Be Cruel" that was released as the "A" side to the "B" side "Hound Dog". "Hound Dog" initially outsold "Don't Be Cruel", however, the latter eventually became the highest selling rock n' roll record in 1956. Presley reportedly found Blackwell's demo recording after shuffling through a stack of other demos and chose to record it. 158

After the release of the record, Elvis flew to Las Vegas to hear Jackie Wilson and The Dominoes' version of the song. Elvis praised their version and liked it so much that he returned and put together Johnny Cash, Jerry Lee Lewis and Carl Perkins to record Jackie Wilson's version, opening the recording by saying how Jackie Wilson sang the song "much better" than he did.

Blackwell also wrote the Elvis hits, "All Shook Up" and "Return To Sender", as well as "Great Balls of Fire" and "Breathless" for Jerry Lee Lewis, "Fever" for Little Willie John, "Keep It Up" for Dee Clark and hit songs for Del Shannon, Jimmy Jones and James Taylor.

Otis Blackwell provides a songwriter's perspective about song writing and the difficult decision of choosing what artist/record label to sell the songs, with the hope a major artist would record them. 159

In an appearance on David Letterman, Otis Blackwell said that he had never met Elvis Presley, "But I never wanted to meet him, I didn't want to…we had something going that was actually pretty good, as long as my songs were getting over to him and he was doing them the way I would like them to be done…in a sense we had met, and I didn't want to risk affecting the chemistry."

https://www.youtube.com/watch?v=AgzzJ-eV8JY (Otis Blackwell live on David Letterman television show)

In an interview with Bill King in The Jazz Report…159
https://www.shrout.co.uk/JazzRInt.html

…Otis spoke about his "gold wall" of songs he had written: "On my wall, I had people like Elvis Presley…People would ask, 'How come you don't have any black artists on your all?' I told them. 'That's my gold wall, and they're the ones who sold millions. I've never had a black artist do that with my songs'".

B.K: Was there more interest from black producers and artists after your first successes?

O.B: There were two gentlemen. One was Henry Glover…The other fellow, Calvin Carter, was from Vee Jay Records…Other than those two, I didn't get much interest… I used to go down every year for the remembrance of Elvis' birthday. Memphis State College invited me to sit in the auditorium and speak to the people for one of those Elvis' days."159

Otis Blackwell songwriter-
https://secondhandsongs.com/artist/3379/works

Keep A Knockin' — Little Richard

GRADY GAINES (SOLO) TENOR
CLIFFORD BURKS - TENOR
WILBERT SMITH a/k/a LEE DIAMOND - TENOR
SAMUEL PARKER – BARITONE

#2 R&B (Specialty 611-5072) Pop #8

Grady Gaines (standing on the piano) and Little Richard
From the motion picture *The Girl Can't Help It*
Photo courtesy Michael Ochs Archives

GRADY GAINES
Courtesy of Susan Criner and Gulf Coast Entertainment

In the 1950s, Grady Gaines, Houston saxophonist and recording bandleader for Don Robey, met Richard Penniman. They recorded together at Duke/Peacock Records. Richard Penniman later became Little Richard, and asked Grady to lead the Upsetters band. They recorded many classics such as "Long Tall Sally," "Send Me Some Lovin'".

Grady Gaines apparently played on subsequent recordings of these two songs, but Lee Allen played the solos on the original Specialty hit recordings (SP-572 & SP-598) recorded at J&M Studio with studio session musicians.

In the early years of rock 'n' roll, some songs and bands caused more alarm than others for the adult generation. "Keep a Knockin'" (Specialty 611-5072- Percy Bradford wrote the original song) was one of those sounds that could get the teens very excited. Listen to the power and energy in Gaines' solo on top of the band that had the perfect name, *The Upsetters*.

Regarding the "recording speed lag" around the first saxophone solo on the original 45rpm.

Some opinions:

"I've read in more than one place that "Keep A Knockin'" originally lasted less than a minute & they had to add another couple of verses at least to get it up to an acceptable length for single release. That might explain something about tape malfunctions. And, of course, you can never have too much of a good thing, either."

"I think that the strange tape speed malfunction mentioned earlier is due to the fact that the master tape is spliced together from more than one take of the song. Of course, they could've had a problem when cutting the stampers."

"The original 45 has this strange tape speed malfunction after the first sax solo starts. Some digital reissues appear to have corrected the problem."

However, Billy Vera's response to my query:

"The song, actually a demo made by Richard with his road band, was very short. Desperate for material to release as singles at this point, Art Rupe went into the studio with his trusted favorite engineer, Bunny Robyn to attempt to put together something suitable for release. You'll notice the same sax solo appears several times on the final edit. One verse, containing the phrase "Drinkin' Gin and you can't come in," had to be deleted for airplay, so other verses, sung by Richard are also duplicated. The final version, a masterful example of difficult editing, wound up being a top ten hit. Toward the end of his life, Rupe complained to me about the clumsy drumming, which resulted in the "pulling" you notice. I hope this helps." Billy, 6/3/22

Grady appeared in three movies with Richard: *Don't Knock the Rock* and *The Girl Can't Help It* (both 1956) and *Mister Rock and Roll* (1957). At Little Richard's retirement, Grady hired Dee Clark as band vocalist and continued to tour.

In the 1960s, Sam Cooke hired Grady and the Upsetters to be his band. They recorded "Bring It On Home," "Twisting The Night Away," and many more. After Cooke's death, Grady and the Upsetters continued playing at all the great houses, such as The Apollo and the Paladium, with all the great artists: Diana Ross and the Supremes, Gladys Knight and the Pips, Bo Diddley, Etta James, Jackie Wilson, and many, many others.

In the 1970s, Grady came off the road, and returned home to Houston. He recorded "There Is Something On Your Mind," and formed the House Rockers, who performed in Houston as Don Robey's house band until Robey's death.

When disco took its toll on live music in the U.S. in the 1980s, Grady toured Europe and recorded his first solo album, "Full Gain." In the late 1980s, Grady performed at blues festivals across the nation.

In the 1990s, Grady recorded "Down and Dirty, Live At Tipitina's" and "House Of Plenty." He toured Europe with Fats Domino. The Texas Blues Preservation Society honored Grady with its first annual Blues Heritage Award, citing him as a Texas Blues Ambassador Around the World and a Pioneer in the Creation of Rock & Roll. In 1993, Grady Gaines played at one of President Clinton's inaugural parties and was proclaimed Blues Artist of the Year at the Juneteenth Festival in Houston.

Discography:

1988 *Full Gain*—Black Top
1992 *Horn of Plenty*—Black Top

http://www.gradygaines.com/bio.html
Susan Criner
Gulf Coast Entertainment
P.O.Box 130026
Houston, Texas 77219 USA
Tel: 713-523-7004
Fax 713-528-0783

The Girl Can't Help It-Little Richard

LEE ALLEN (SOLO) TENOR
ALVIN "RED" TYLER-BARITONE

#7 R&B #49 Pop #9 UK

Little Richard recorded the song October 16, 1956, at J&M Music Shop in New Orleans, Louisiana, recording "The Girl Can't Help It" and "Baby Face" at the same session. Richard's backing band on the session consisted of Lee Allen (tenor saxophone), Alvin "Red" Tyler (baritone saxophone), Edgar Blanchard (guitar), Frank Fields (bass), and Earl Palmer (drums). Specialty Records owner Art Rupe produced the recording.

The movie featured The Upsetters with Grady Gaines on top of the piano appearing to play the solo. The original Specialty recording soundtrack THAT was being played was Lee Allen on sax.

Alvin "Red" Tyler is perhaps best known for his baritone sax session work with Lee Allen at J and M Studio in New Orleans in the mid 1950s; together, they recorded many hits for Little Richard and Fats Domino. Their sax sound traveled the airwaves, dance halls, bars, and sock hops from New York to Los Angeles and Europe.

Tyler is also well known for his tenor style in New Orleans circles, and he performed with Germaine Bazzle and Dr. John and was very active in the New Orleans Jazz and Heritage Festival. He played all styles, from jazz to R&B and funk. Tyler passed away on April 3, 1998, at the age of 72.

#28 A LETTER TO AN ANGEL— JIMMY CLANTON
Alvin Red Tyler -Tenor Sax

Performer Notes
All tracks have been digitally remastered.
Personnel: Earl King (guitar); **Red Tyler (saxophone);** Huey "Piano" Smith & the Clowns (piano)
Liner Note Author: Jeff Hannuschsakis

Recording information: Cosimo's Studio, New Orleans, LA.

No collection of leftovers here, this original 12-song collection featured the hits "Just a Dream," "A letter to an Angel" along with "My Love Is Strong," "Angel Face," and "It Takes a Long, Long Time," all of which turned up in the soundtrack to Clanton's film debut, "Go, Johnny, Go!" As a budget priced collection, this one's hard to turn down. More than just great 50's pop; consider it also an essential building block for any New Orleans collection. [Edsel delivered a straight up reissue of Jimmy's debut album in 1999.] ~ Cub Koda

Discography:
1960 *Rockin' and Rollin'* — ACE
1962 *Twistin' with Mr. Sax* — ACE
1986 *Graciously* — Rounder
1986 *Heritage* — Rounder
1998 *Simply Red* — West Side

Respecting 'Red' Tyler

"When we were in New Orleans two weekends ago for my

step-daughter's graduation from Loyola (we're proud - and relieved!), my wife and I got a chance to go out that Saturday night and catch a tribute to saxophonist Alvin 'Red' Tyler, a free event at the Contemporary Arts Center put on by the New Orleans Jazz & Heritage Foundation. Red, who passed away in 1998, was a talented, dependable constant on the local R&B and jazz scenes in town for some 50 years and was definitely overdue for some formal props. While living, this solid, humble gentleman was probably too much taken for granted, even overlooked, in his own hometown, not being a showboater, but rather a genuine ensemble player even as a leader of his own groups and on sessions. But the musicianship he displayed was always first rate. So, the high quality of performances presented that night at the CAC and the admiration and respect shown for Red certainly went a long way in making up for the 11 year delay in honoring him postmortem for his many accomplishments.

The evening was divided into music segments highlighting his R&B and rock 'n' roll session work as well as his long-time devotion to jazz. These were separated by discussions about and remembrances of Red by people who knew him well, such as jazz vocalists Germaine Bazzle and Ed Perkins, legendary musician and educator, Harold Battiste, and author, filmmaker, radio host and Breath Of Life blogger, Kalamu ya Salaam. Things began with a brief audio/visual overview of Tyler's career. Then the musicians took the stage. Performing over the course of the concert segments were a top of the line aggregation including drummers Albert 'June' Gardner and Johnny Vidacovich, bassists Chris Severin and George French, saxophonists Roderick Paulin and Thaddeus Richard, trumpet master Clyde Kerr, Jr., guitarist Steve Masakowski, and musical director of the program, pianist David Torkanowski (who also surprisingly got up during the rock 'n' roll segment and blew some pumpin' baritone sax!). Bazzle and Perkins also sang with the band, as did French; and all were outstanding. Most definitely, it was a memorable show that I'm glad we could attend. My thanks to David Kunian of WWOZ for hipping me to the tribute and suggesting that I do a post about Red. Duly inspired, I am more than glad to oblige.

STARTING NEAR THE TOP

From Harold Battiste's bio on Tyler in the well-done booklet included in his limited edition, four LP retrospective box set, New Orleans Heritage Jazz 1956 – 1966:
 I learned that Red did not play an instrument until he returned home from the service in the late 1940s, but had been fascinated by music since childhood, particularly jazz from brass bands to Earl Hines. Like many other musically inclined young WWII-era ex-enlisted men, Tyler used his GI-bill benefits to attend Grunewald School of Music on Camp Street in New Orleans. There he quickly learned the rudiments of the saxophone along with theory and arranging. In fact, Tyler said his studies and instrumental abilities came almost too easily for him. Soon after completing his courses, he was given the chance to play in the Clyde Kerr Band, which also allowed him entry into

the musicians' union. Clyde Kerr, Sr., an influential local musician and educator whose son later played regularly with Tyler, had a band full of serious players; and the experience of performing live in that company surely pushed Red to continually improve his skills. Union membership gave him the opportunity for other gigs and even some work on the road. Then, in 1949, he caught a real break when drummer Earl Palmer recommended him to Dave Bartholomew who had one of the most popular big bands in town. They were playing jazz and swing when Red joined, but soon began backing R&B singers such as Tommy Ridgley and Jewel King. Lew Chudd of Imperial Records had recently come to town and hired Bartholomew to scout local talent and produce records for the Los Angeles-based label; and, using his own impressive band, Dave began doing sessions on Ridgley, King, and the then unknown Fats Domino at Cosimo Matassa's first studio, a small room (10 x 12!) in the back of his record store, J&M Music Shop, on Rampart Street. That put Red in on the ground floor of the emergent New Orleans recording scene.

Those were exceptional times; and Tyler was off on a whirlwind of recording activity. In addition to tenor sax, he also played baritone, increasing his opportunities for horn section work, as more and more labels came to town to record and catch some that New Orleans magic. Much of the band on those early Imperial sessions became the core studio players in New Orleans R&B and rock 'n' roll for the next decade; and with them Red participated in countless sessions for various labels, backing Fats, Shirley and Lee,

Lloyd Price, Little Richard, Professor Longhair, Paul Gayten, and Clarence 'Frogman' Henry, among so many others. What set those studio musicians apart was their ability to contribute creatively to each project, coming up with collaborative arrangements on the spot that gave the sides a fresh, innovative sound that helped change the face of popular music. Unfortunately, their arranging skills usually went uncompensated - but session work was plentiful and paid well enough that the players did not rock the boat to demand their due. Red was particularly gifted at those "head-arrangements" and was a valuable resource on most any session.

As Jeff Hannusch relates in The Soul of New Orleans, Cosimo Matassa referred Red to Johnny Vincent, owner of Ace Records, one of the first independent labels operating in New Orleans (though technically based in Jackson, MS). Vincent was looking for someone to oversee sessions and began using Tyler, who did a lot of work for the label in the later 1950s on an informal, ad hoc basis. After providing stealth production on records by the likes of Frankie Ford, Jimmy Clanton, Joe & Ann and even James Booker, in 1959 Red was given the chance to record his own instrumental LP for Ace, Rockin' and Rollin'. Vincent probably was spurred to do so by the success Tyler's frequent saxophone partner, Lee Allen, had with his 1958 single, "Walking With Mr. Lee", and album of the same title for Ember Records (which Red contributed to), plus Allen Toussaint, who had his 1958 instrumental debut LP on RCA, The Wild Sound of New Orleans by Tousan, and also utilized Red as a player and co-arranger/co-writer. Of course, there were plenty of other instrumental releases on the radio and in jukeboxes in those days by Bill Doggett, Ernie Freeman, Plas Johnson, and a host of others; and Red certainly had the chops to run in that company."

Courtesy of Daniel Phillips
Home Of The Groove (Highly Recommended)
https://homeofthegroove.blogspot.com/2009/05/respecting-red-tyler.html

If You Want To Play, I Mean Really Play…

By Neil Sharpe

"Jon's sound is instantaneously recognized, something only a handful of players have, with a tone that's as big as a house, and a big vibrato that's characteristic of a gospel singers…If I were putting together a horn section, Jon would be my absolute first choice."

Edgar Winter
Windplayer Magazine

"I have followed him since he left Edgar Winter's White Trash…I couldn't leave Antone's until I knew he'd played his last note of the night."

Will Lee
Late Night with David Letterman Band
Austin American-Statesman

"I used to occasionally hang out with Mike Brecker in NYC. We would both be sitting in with Paula Lockhart who had Howie Wyeth playing drums…Brecker told me that two of his favorite players were Jim Pepper and Jon Smith."

John Firmin (aka Johnny Nocturne)

Brother, if you wanted to learn how to play, I mean really play, there wasn't a better spot in the world than Louisiana in the 1950s. Our gathering spot was Vinton, Louisiana, close to the border of Texas. Had a ton of clubs. Rock, rhythm and blues, 24 hours a day. The drinking age was supposed to be 18, but no one kept track. Playing in clubs at the age of 13 or 14 wasn't unusual. The club owners didn't monitor the ages of the band members. As long as you kept things straight and went into the parking lot or a backroom during breaks and not into the club, you were o.k.

Back in those days, a lot of musicians in Louisiana couldn't read music, so they'd sit down and work our 'head arrangements' while in the studio. Back in the '40s-60s, everything was recorded live on 2 and 4 track machines, with no overdubs, including the singer. So, the musicians really had to work together to get the track tight.

When I first worked at Cosimo Matassa's J & M Recording Studio in New Orleans, the set up was pretty primitive with eggshell cartons on the wall, etc., etc. But Cosimo Matassa was constantly learning and improving.

As I mentioned earlier, horn players often did all the arrangements while in studio. Rarely, did we go in with written material. That's probably why the recordings from Cosimo's Studio had such a vibrant, driving sound."

John Broven quotes Cosimo Matassa in his landmark book, *Rhythm and Blues in New Orleans*, "You made a master and a safety, and you played back the safety to see what you got. So that meant that all those performances, there was no intercutting, no tape editing, in fact those were the good performances, probably some of the best. Because they were really performances as opposed to the synthesized records you make today, when you lay down the rhythm and starting putting things on it, three months and 12 sessions later nobody knows what the original was really going to be like".

John Broven also quotes Alvin Red Tyler who described how, "Lee Allen and myself would get together and come up with the riff. We would create that song in the studio. You know it was trial and error…And we would make the thing up right then, nothing written, so we actually got by without an arrangement fee and this is why so many independents came to this city. Now in a sense this may have been why some of the things were so groovy, they were done how we felt, not how it was written…if you do it out of your head, either it lays right or it doesn't. If it grooves, it's gonna happen". 160

As Mac Rebbennack (Dr. John) described in John Broven's *Rhythm and Blues in New Orleans*, "Little Richard had things before but he was not successful until Lee Allen and Red Tyler put that sound on him and put that good hard rock feel on him. It was the New Orleans sound that got Little Richard across and since he's left that sound behind, he's never been successful." 160

Voices

The other really important thing, if you want to be any good at all, is to fit inside the music. Lee Allen, in his landmark recordings in the '50's (such as "Slippin' and Slidin'"), was a relatively 'simple' player, but his phrasing, articulation, and ability to go to the heart of a song, were perfect.

He flattered the music and didn't try to make the music flatter him. Too many players go in and try to make the solos all about them. A recent example happened at a music festival in Texas. They had a bunch of sax players up on stage. When they first started out, things were all right. Then, in the middle of the song, the leader points to one sax player, then another. Their solos had nothing to do with the song, but everything to do with them- a whole lot of 'Look at me's'. What a mess! When they finally went back into the song, it was wrecked. They were completely out of synch.

You want to pick up a vibe from another player and create a connection, a feeling, like you're having a great conversation with someone. Today, too many musicians, especially sax players, don't do that. They're so busy thinking about what they're going to say that they don't listen to what another player is saying and feeling. Fit yourself into the music and get the ego out of the way.

Group dynamics is what makes a band click. I always try to listen to what each member of the band is saying to make sure my solo fits into the song and into the band. And remember, you don't have to say a lot to say something! A great sax player may be capable of riffing off a whole ton of notes, but they also know that sometimes a very few notes is all that needs to be said.

When I go into a session for jazz, I'm going to play a solo that fits the music, sometimes a more modern sound with straight tones and sometimes no vibrato. But, if it's blues gospel, I'll use techniques like vibrato and growl. This approach has led to recordings with a wide array of musical artists such as Sarah Vaughn, Randy Newman, Peter Maffay, Rick Derringer, Junior Wells, and Sonny Landreth.

And that's another thing. Know your limitations. Great r&b players don't try to be jazz players and vice versa. I've seen some jazz players come in and play bebop riffs over r&b and rock n' roll. They're playing way outside the music and not fitting into it. It's a mess.

Fit yourself into the music and get the ego out of the way. Give space to the other musicians. Those things must always prevail over technical ability and a particular style. It's your job to keep the song alive and flowing, not to try and drown it. Players like Lee Allen, Plas Johnson, Sam Butera and Gene Ammons could say everything that needed to be said, to really push a song ahead, with just a few notes.

Plas Johnson © Jim Britt

Another great player was Plas Johnson, who always sounded a little different from any of the other Louisiana players. I fell head over heels in love with his tone. He had that huge tenor sax sound, and played on big tip openings like Berg's .160 and .170. Sound wise, I think he is one of the greatest sax players on this planet. I couldn't believe how big and huge his tone was on "Pink Panther".

King Curtis is another excellent example. The sessions he did with The Coasters were one of my favorite records.

In '62, I was touring in the Northeast and saw him with 'The King Pins', featuring Cornell Dupree, Bernard Purdy and Billy Preston on keyboards.

What a monster player! He had a big influence on me. With the Coaster records, he had that unique style that only

Boots [Randolph] came close to. I sat down and learned every one of Curtis' Coasters solos. At the time, some players thought it was too corny a style and too commercial, but it made those songs really move. That's what playing is all about. Same applies for the great Junior Walker, an enormous r&b player.

Bobby Charles

A turning point for me was Bobby Charles, one of America's all time song-writing treasures, and a true creator of that 50's rock n' roll sound, who gave me my start back in '58. I did my first recording session with him when I was 13 years old. He had a four track-recording machine and we laid down some great cuts."

Bobby's early songs for Chess often featured Lee Allen on sax, e.g. "Take It Easy Greasy".

Chart hits on Billboard's Top 100 that Bobby Charles wrote include, "Walking to New Orleans" by Fats Domino #6 Billboard; "See You Later Alligator", Bill Haley and The Comets, #6 Billboard; "I Don't Know Why I Love You But I Do": Clarence Frogman Henry, #4 Billboard

"Highly respected in the music industry, Bobby's last CD, 'Last Train to Memphis' won applause from all corners, and featured guest artists that included Neil Young, Willie Nelson, Delbert McClinton, and Maria Muldaur.

And check out his CD 'Wish You Were Here Right Now', released in 1995 on Stony Plain, which I played on.

My next gig came at 15, on the road with a Louisiana drummer named Dewey Martin, (later of Buffalo Springfield), Randy Meeks on piano, singer Dale Hawkins (who immortalized the song "Susie Q"), songwriter extraordinaire Larry Henley (e.g. "Beneath My Wings", co-written with Jeff Silbar, #1 on Billboard; writer of The Newbeats' "Bread and Butter" that went to #2).

Although we all have different influences, in the end, we are all good conscientious players expressing ourselves as best we can. That's a mistake I see too many players make. Each of us has our own unique, distinct, speaking voices. Why do we think it will be any different with the sax? That's what every player needs to do. Develop your voice as best you can. Then you're going to shine.

Some musicians only will play a specific genre of music. That's fine, but if you want to make a career out of music, the bottom line is, if you're not playing, you're not earning. I know some great, great players out there who are starving. That's because they look at music as if through a straw, with a very narrow view; if they can't play bebop, they won't play anything. Which is fine if that's your choice and you fully understand the consequences in terms of making a living and supporting a family. That's why I like playing with musicians who approach the music being played at that moment with total focus and devotion.

Talent is fine, but discipline is what makes a professional musician - together with passion, hard work, keeping your commitments, being prompt and on time. Set standards and live up to them. Do that and you'll get the calls."

Notes

Photographs have been generously donated by the late Paul Harris, a contributor to Juke Blues magazine, Bristol, England, and to Now Dig This magazine, Gateshead, England.

paulharrisphotography.blogspot.com

Quotes from Red Tyler, Cosimo Matassa and Mac Rebennack from John Broven, "Walking to New Orleans" (c) 1974 (republished in the U.S. by Pelican Books as "Rhythm & Blues in New Orleans". The expanded 3rd edition is now available. Highly recommended.
Broven J (1978) Rhythm and Blues in New Orleans; Pelican Pub Co Inc; (First Editon; January 1, 1978); 3rd Edition; Revised and Updates.
https://www.pelicanpub.com/proddetail.php?prod=9781455619511

John Broven is the author of:
Broven J (2021) "New York City Blues: Postwar Portraits from Harlem to the Village and Beyond": University Press of Mississippi (August 16, 2021).
https://www.upress.state.ms.us/Books/N/New-York-City-Blues

Broven J (2010) "Record Makers and Breakers-Voices Of The Independent Rock n' Roll Pioneers", University of Illinois Press; (January 13, 2010)
https://www.press.uillinois.edu/books/?id=p077272

Broven J (2019) "South to Louisiana: The Music of the Cajun Bayous"; Pelican Publishing; 2ed. (March 2019). https://www.pelicanpub.com/products.php?cat=15192019)

Broven John; Editor (2021) "New York City Blues: Postwar Portraits from Harlem to the Village and Beyond": University Press of Mississippi (August 16, 2021). https://www.upress.state.ms.us/Books/N/New-York-City-Blues

Note: from John Broven about "New York City Blues": "There is an entire chapter on Noble "Thin Man" Watts. Other sax players such as King Curtis, Sam "The Man" Taylor, Clifford Scott and Buddy Johnson's Purvis Henson are also featured.

KING CURTIS & HIS ORCHESTRA: *King Curtis (ten), unk. 2nd ten – poss. Noble "Thin Man" Watts or more likely KC overdubbed on –1, Herman Foster (pno), Al Casey (gtr), Jimmy Lewis (bs), Belton Evans (dms). Prod. Nesuhi Ertegun.*
New York. December 3, 1958

58C-450	King's Walk	unissued
58C-451	Jay Walk	unissued
58C-452	Night Train	unissued
58C-453	Castle Rock	Atco 6135; Atlantic LP 81666-1
58C-454	Chili –1	Atco 6135; LP 113; Clarion LP 615

https://www.youtube.com/watch?v=rvRp2h4jG5I

Note: above personnel as recalled by Belton Evans.

KING CURTIS, Noble "Thin Man" Watts (tens), Herman Foster (pno), Al Casey, Jimmy Spruill (gtrs), Jimmy Lewis (bs), Belton Evans (dms). Noble Watts omitted on –1. Prod. Nesuhi Ertegun.

New York. July 8, 1959

59C-3601 The Groove   Atco LP 113; Clarion LP 615
59C-3602 The Shake   Atco LP 113; Clarion LP 615
59C-3603 Snake Eyes   Atco LP 113; Clarion LP 615
59C-3604 Jay Walk –1   Atco LP 113; Clarion LP 615
59C-3605 Midnight Ramble –1 Atco LP 113; Clarion LP 615

note: There is a report that "Midnight Ramble" on the cd reissues (the Koch two-fer and "Hot Sax Cool Licks") is an alternate or possibly different-for-stereo take.

-Roy Simonds- "King Curtis Sessionography"

I Want You To Be My Girl—
Frankie Lymon & the Teenagers

JIMMY WRIGHT   TENOR

#3 R&B #13 POP

In a different, fairer reality, the mention of tenor saxman Jimmy Wright's name would evoke the word "cool" in the mere utterance. He'd be right there in the minds of serious rock & roll enthusiasts with Scotty Moore, Cliff Gallup, Rudy Pompili, and Franny Beecher, as maker of a sound at the heart and foundation of rock & roll.

Wright helped create a new sound that turned radio, the recording industry, and music on its head. And with Wright's honking saxophone sharing space for the lead, he was nearly as visible a musical presence as anyone on any of Elvis Presley's records from Scotty Moore, Bill Black, and D.J. Fontana on down, his instrument defining the texture and power of rock & roll on records like "Why Do Fools Fall in Love" and a dozen other Rama and Gee sides.

Near as anyone seems to know about Wright -- who, so far as we know, was never interviewed or profiled -- he was born in the late '20s, and started out in music in the '40s, conversant in jump blues, R&B, and jazz styles. And by his mid-twenties, during the first half of the '50s, he was leading his own group in New York City.

He started getting hired by George Goldner, a record producer and the founder/owner of Rama Records and various offshoot and successor labels. And for a long time, in addition to leading the band, Wright was the de facto arranger and music director on a lot of the resulting recording sessions, in effect playing a similar role at Rama and its related labels to the one that Willie Dixon played at Chess Records in Chicago.

Wright and his band showed up on practically every rock & roll session ever cut for Rama or Gee Records and gave the resulting music its drive. The sound that he and his band got was particularly compelling, a mix of elements embracing components of big-band swing, jump blues, old-style R&B, and roadhouse raunch, all carefully balanced depending upon the song -- his sax could be quietly elegant, even gently lyrical, or honk like the grossest strip joint accompaniment ever committed to record.

They were all just local jazz men making extra money on the side, usually for an afternoon when they wouldn't otherwise be engaged, playing those sessions; and part of the knack he brought to a session was a good sense for what songs worked best in which styles. Wright usually decided whether a ballad brought in by a group was better as a jump number or vice versa, often working from the most rudimentary material and building the song from scratch as far as written annotation.

Author/scholar Peter Grendysa has called Wright the equal of Red Prysock, Sam "The Man" Taylor, and Big Jay McNeely, among 1950s saxophone virtuosos. Yet Wright has always remained in the shadows, his name barely known or seen, unless you happen to be a special aficionado of the Gee or Rama labels.

Recognized or not, Jimmy Wright was one of the most influential musical figures in the history and development of early rock & roll, as well as a huge chunk of New York City-based R&B of the mid-'50s.

As the resident bandleader and, with Bert Keyes, the de facto music director for George Goldner's Rama Records and Gee Records labels from 1953 until the end of the '50s, Wright had more to say about what most of the music on those labels -- among the most successful and influential of their day, especially in New York City -- sounded like than many of the artists themselves.

The Jimmy Wright Band, also known as the Jimmy Wright Orchestra, variously included '40s jazz and jump blues veterans Skeeter Best, Jimmy Shirley, and Jerome Darr on guitar, Abie Baker and Al Hall on bass, Freddie Johnson or Jimmy Phipps on piano, and Gene Brooks on drums.

The collaboration between Wright and the Teenagers featuring Frankie Lymon was especially productive. The group never had more success in the studio than when Wright and his band were playing behind them, and it was when they stopped getting that kind of support that the group's sound softened and declined. With all due respect, the Panama Francis Orchestra, who succeeded Wright's group on later sessions, could never match the lean, lithe texture of Wright's band or the spontaneity of those early Teenagers sessions -- check out "Why Do Fools Fall in Love," the first song they cut; the arrangement is all Wright's, and the sound belongs to his band as much as it does to Lymon, Santiago, Merchant, Garnes, and Negroni on the vocals; and amid all of the activity in that one record, dig the little quotation from Roy Eldridge's "Drum Boogie" on the guitar during the quieter moments on the record. It was also Jimmy Wright, according to Grendysa, who suggested a change in name for the group, from "the Premiers" (which is how they arrived at that first session late in 1955) to the Teenagers.

Wright and his band cut a few singles on their own for Gee and Rama, but not enough, alas, to build a full LP or CD around. "2:20 A.M.," released on Rama late in 1955, is a staggering tenor sax and guitar showcase, three minutes of sharp, piercing, wailing, yet lyrical blues, while its B-side, "Move Over," is a frantic workout showcasing the bandleader, who is seemingly in a race with his drummer to see who can trip the other up with the quicker tempo, and the guitar coming in to try and nail them both about one minute in.

The beauty of Wright and his band was that they could cut two sides like that in probably under 30 minutes of studio time, sandwiched in between sessions for Valli Hinton & the Pretenders, all doing softer R&B that came out just as well, or giving the Four Chaps' pop vocal version of "Roll Over Beethoven" what snap it did have, and then getting the late Mabel King into a hot groove for "Alabama Rock 'n Roll."

More's the pity that we don't know exactly who was playing guitar, bass, or piano on a lot of those sessions. None of the group's own singles did especially well -- the public in those days wanted singers, not instrumentalists, whatever their quality -- but Wright was heard on so many Rama and Gee sides, that he and his band were practically the soul of the label; and they got heard, if not exactly known by name. Wright also cut sides at Hy Weiss' Old Town Records, providing the backing for legendary R&B pianist/singer Bob Gaddy, among other artists.

A judicious selection of the right Gee, Rama, and Old Town sides could even yield a killer tribute record to Wright, whose fate after the '70s seems to be a mystery. Jimmy Wright's principal recognized legacy as a performer or bandleader rests in the context of music director for Goldner's labels, and leader-soloist on Lymon's records in particular -- great as those sides are, he deserved (and deserves) better.

- Artist Biography by Bruce Eder

Sea Cruise-Frankie Ford

Huey "Piano" Smith,
Alvin "Red" Tyler and Robert Parker on sax,
James Booker on keys and rhythm section
Frank Fields, Charles "Hungry" Williams.
 #11 R&B #14 Pop

"In the 50s, Huey "Piano" Smith had a boisterous New Orleans band, which might be described as the low-life equivalent of Fats Domino's hit machine. Huey's band featured careening shuffle rhythms, greasy saxophones in full honk, lots of nonsense lyrics that sounded suspiciously like drug talk in Creole, and oh yes, a female impersonator on lead vocals.

But when Huey Smith and the Clowns cut "Sea Cruise" for Ace Records in 1959, it was a near- perfect example of late 50s rock and roll, destined for the charts from first listen. The problem, like many 50s recordings, it was a black record that sounded too black for the white market. Very often a "white boy" cover version would hit the street the minute a black hit broke and stomp the original back into obscurity. Ace Records was having none of that, so they scrapped Huey's vocal track and recut it with white teenager Frankie Ford whose photo they prominently displayed on the sleeve. Result: Ace Records' first top ten pop chart hit. Courtesy http://www.recallmusic.com/rootinf.htm

In the second revised edition of The Billboard Book of One-Hit Wonders (1998), Ford is quoted as saying the following (p. 70):

"Now, 'Sea Cruise' was cut to be the follow-up to Huey Smith's 'Don't You Just Know It', but Bobby Marchan [then lead vocalist for Huey's group the Clowns] was leaving. The track was cut. It was to be Huey's new release. It was cut while I was in Philadelphia promoting 'Cheatin' Woman' and singing at the George Wood Show at the Uptown Theatre. When I got home, they said 'Well, let's try Frankie's voice on it.' Huey had heard me one night in a club and said 'Hey, he sounds like Bobby'. So, I agreed and went into the studio, not knowing the song. I still have the piece of paper that Huey had written the words on for me, misspellings and all.

Now, we recorded it on this two-track Ampex. There was no punch-in. If you made a mistake, it was just there. We did about 13 takes on 'Sea Cruise', I think.

On 'Roberta', the Clowns were actually in the studio. There were two microphones. I was on one and the four of them were on the other. My manager [then, Joe Caronna] and the owner of the label [Johnny Vincent] said, 'Huey, you don't need a release now. Let's put it out on Frankie.' And it was set, I was to be the new lead singer with his group, too.

Contrary to the Monday morning quarter-backing, I was there when the agreement was made. Huey was to be listed as producer and as to what was his deal with Ace Records, I don't know. We're still friends. In a lot of books - including the first edition of One-Hit Wonders - it says that Huey was very displeased with me; and he was not with me! We worked together and collaborated on a lot of compositions. And when things got as they did, we were instrumental in bringing him over to Imperial Records". In the end, Frankie Ford never did join up with Huey Smith's Clowns.

Courtesy http://www.rockabillyhall.com/HowHits.html

Stagger Lee — Lloyd Price

? TENOR

R&B #1 #1 Pop

Hi John,
" 'Lloyd Rocks' (by Lloyd Price) on Bear Family. It has session info for 'Stagger Lee':
Recorded September 11, 1958, Bell Sound Studio, New York City. Producer: Don Costa. Lloyd Price, vocal; Clarence Johnson, bass; Sticks Simpkins, drums; John Patton, piano;
Unidentified: baritone sax; Charles McClendon, tenor sax; Eddie Saunders, tenor sax; Ted Curson, trumpet; The Ray Charles Singers, vocal group."
The flip, "You Need Love" was recorded at the same session. "Stagger Lee" entered the Billboard charts on December 8, 1958. Unfortunately, no personnel info for "Just Because"."
https://www.kcur.org/arts-life/2013-01-14/remembering-kansas-city-jazz-musician-eddie-saunders
Regards, Dik 11/15/2008
https://tims.blackcat.nl/

However, the following information gives credit to Merritt Mel Dalton; http://en.wikipedia.org/wiki/Lloyd_Price
"Merritt Mel Dalton was the lead Sax Man on the recordings of "Personality, Stagger Lee, I'm gonna get married etc..," Merritt, was in the traveling band as well and appeared on the Ed Sullivan show with Lloyd Price".
"Mel Dalton: His Life and His Music"

https://www.youtube.com/watch?v=LxD63U9Mwz0

This same site indicates, in part; "The personnel on the original hit recording of "Stagger Lee" included Clarence Johnson on piano, John Patton on bass, Charles McClendon and Eddie Saunders on tenor sax, Ted Curson on trumpet and Sticks Simpkins on drums."

Another site indicates; "With The Don Costa Orchestra, Lloyd Price: Vocals, Ted Curson: Trumpet, Charles McClendon, Eddie Saunders: Tenor saxes, "Big" John Patton: Piano, Clarence Johnson: Bass, Sticks Simpkins: Drums, Unknown: Baritone sax, A side matrix78-3415, B side matrix 78-3416, Recorded at Bell Sound Studio, New York, N.Y., Sept. 11, 1958."

Another site, https://live.kixi.com/listen/artist/d047ee24-6fac-401a-8769-34edbda52113 indicates, in part;

"In all of these early recordings by Price ("Personality", "Stagger Lee", "I'm Gonna Get Married", and others) Merritt Mel Dalton was the lead sax player; he was also in the traveling band and appeared on The Ed Sullivan Show with Price."

Martine: "I am the daughter of Merritt "Mel" Dalton. Regretfully you will not find any linear notes on these recordings or mention of my father they did not do that back in the day. You got paid for session work and no credit.

My father was Lloyd's lead Tenor Sax player for years. He traveled with the Lloyd Price Orchestra and also recorded with him. My father appeared on the Ed Sullivan show with Lloyd performing 'Personality', this film footage is also shown at the Rock n Roll Hall of Fame in the Inductees Film. I have original footage from the show.

If you Google 'Mel Dalton' you will find his Bio, posted numerous times following his death three years ago, you may also note all of his accomplishments in the music industry.

My father came from Pittsburgh Pa and went to Westinghouse High School. He formed a band then that included my father, Stanley Turrentine, Amhad Jamal, Dakota Staten and sometimes Tommy Turrentine on Trumpet as he was older than the rest and played as a sit in.

My father toured with many famous jazz personalities as Jazz was his forte 'Beebop'. There is on Video of one of his last performances on Youtube, Mel Dalton @ the Zoo Jazz Nights.

I am in contact with Lloyd Price and we do have conversations about Dad and the early days, he talks of him fondly. Something else you will not probably read about Fats Domino was one of Lloyd's early piano players. Just to Verify that is my father Merritt Dalton as he was known then playing on Stagger Lee, which he performed with Lloyd @ the Apollo Theater, also on Personality and most of his other recordings on Specialty Records. My father did not become known as Mel until he moved to Grand Rapids MI". (end of quote)

I exchanged a couple of emails with Martine and indicated that I needed confirmation that her father played the solo of the hit record that was released on the ABC Paramount 45-9972. No definitive response to date.

2/6/12

Dear Mr. Laughter—

Richard Weize from Bear Family forwarded me your e-mail--I wrote the liner notes for Lloyd Rocks and tried to help put together the sessionography, though Price's ABC sessions are very lacking in known personnel.

I've never heard of Merritt Mel Dalton--never saw his name in any discography on Lloyd or any other artist, and Lloyd sure never mentioned him when I interviewed him. There is no lead sax man on 'Personality' or 'I'm Gonna Get Married'--those are strictly ensemble horn parts, so 'Stagger Lee' would be all we have to go on to try to ID him, and without any access to possible personnel logs in ABC-Paramount's files (certainly ones that have never gone public in any publications I've ever seen), that's rather difficult. I would suggest you contact Lloyd directly to confirm that Dalton was his sax player on those sides. He's not all that hard to track down, though who knows what he remembers about individual session personnel by now. Apart from Big John Patton, Lloyd didn't mention any of his many musicians by name when I interviewed him at length a few years back. Thanks for letting us know about Merritt Mel- Bill Dahl

The following websites argue that tenor player Eddie Saunders was featured:

"Just Because" is a classic dance number sung by New Orleans Blues great Lloyd Price, nicknamed "Mr. Personality' for one of his many hits that include "Lawdy Miss Clawdy" and "Stagger Lee." Almost all feature Eddie Saunders on tenor sax.

http://northwestindianahistorianjamesblane.blogspot.com/2017/06/playlist.html

Other sources have stated that Eddie Saunders played the on "Stagger Lee" but does not indicate that he played the solo; "Saunders went off to fight in the Korean War. Later, he ended up traveling the country with singer Lloyd Price and his band. Saunders played the saxophone in the hit Stagger Lee in 1957."

The song was first published in 1911 and first recorded in 1923, by Fred Waring's Pennsylvanians, titled "Stack O' Lee Blues".

326

Back Room Rock-Sammy Price

KING CURTIS TENOR

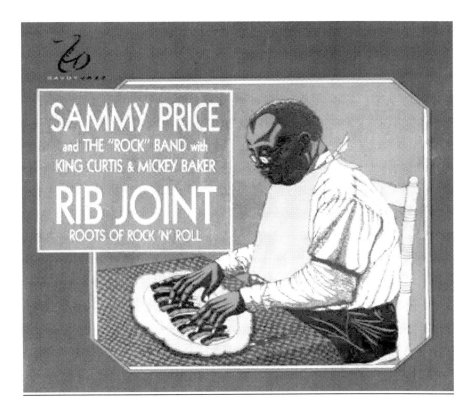

In the following interview, Nancy Wright described the impact of this exceptional album. But first, the session notes:

SAMMY PRICE & HIS ORCHESTRA: *Sammy Price (pno), King Curtis (ten), Mickey Baker (gtr), Leonard Gaskin (bs), Bobby Donaldson (dms).*
New York. October 17, 1956

SSP-6893 Rib Joint   Savoy LP 14004
          Rib Joint (alternate take)   Savoy LP 2240
SSP-6894 After Hour Swing   Savoy LP 14004
SSP-6895 Tishomingo   Savoy LP 14004
SSP-6896 Back Room Rock   Savoy LP 14004

Note: single release of "Rib Joint"/"Tishomingo", Savoy 1505, credited to
"Sam Price & His Texas Bluesicians".

SAMMY PRICE & HIS ORCHESTRA: Sammy Price (pno), King Curtis (ten), prob. Haywood Henry (bari), Mickey Baker (gtr), Leonard Gaskin (bs), Bobby Donaldson (dms).
New York. November 21, 1956

SSP-6908 Bar B.Q. Sauce   Savoy LP 14004
SSP-6909 High Price   unissued
SSP-6910 Juke Joint   Savoy LP 14004
SSP-6911 Ain't No Strain   Savoy LP 14004

SAMMY PRICE AND HIS ORCHESTRA: Sammy Price (pno), King Curtis (ten), Haywood Henry (bari), Kenny Burrell (gtr), Jimmy Lewis (bs), Bobby Donaldson (dms); Alma Simmons (vcl) on –1.
New York. January 24, 1957

SSP-6957 Rock My Soul Savoy LP 14004
SSP-6958 Chicken Out   Savoy LP 14004
SSP-6959 Jive Joint   Savoy LP 14004
SSP-6960 Gulley Stomp Savoy LP 14004
SSP-6961 Give Me Your Smile –1   unissued
SSP-6962 Love My Man –1   unissued

Nancy Wright

https://www.nancywrightmusic.com/

Nancy Wrigh has played with John Lee Hooker, Lonnie Mac, Elvin Bishop, Katie Webster, Tony Monaco to name just a few…

" I had just come off playing in the opening act for the Jimmy Buffett tour. They paid really well. Jimmy truly has the Midas touch. We got to travel around the country with handpicked musicians, they dressed us, gave us clothes to wear, it was first class all the way. We had great hotel rooms, tour buses, really nice backstage greenrooms. All the little things, like if we rolled into place at 3 a.m., you had the choice of sleeping in the bus or checking into a room, because when you go into a room, sometimes you can't get to sleep for a while.

At the same time, if you're opening for a big name act like that, whatever part of audience is already seated, they really aren't interested in you or responding to what you're doing. Plus, you're far apart on stage, you've got these monster monitors...it seems like everybody plays it really safe. You don't do experimental stuff, you play something that you know is going to sound good and get you over. It's not the same communication between musicians on stage like there is when you play a smaller club.

It was a real good view of what the top looks like.

When the tour was over, I got invited to play in Jimmy's horn section the next year. It made me really think if this is what I was all about. A tour like that can give you steady work, excellent pay, a lot more exposure, even though the music you're playing isn't speaking to you.

But I wasn't really sure if this is where I wanted to be. People can get a little nutty on the road and I wasn't being that way. For me, the music was more true when I played smaller venues- the improvisation, the emotion of the music, how it speaks to you and how that connects with the audience.

When the emotion is right, when the players are right, when the sound on stage is right, when the connection with the audience is right, you know exactly what to do. I'll play a solo and do a lick on a turnaround that's exactly the rhythm the drummer plays; that's not anything I've thought about, the music is just happening because we're all feeding off each other. For me, that's what music is all about.

Don't get me wrong. I'm not saying those tours aren't great. I just wasn't sure that's where I wanted to be.

I turned it down.

My first real influence was Lonnie Mack. When I got out of college, I was trying to make it as a musician, found myself in a Marriott Lounge band and was feeling pretty miserable about the whole thing.

One night, I hear Lonnie Mack is playing in a club in Dayton. I go there and end up standing next to this guy. We get talking a bit. On the break, he starts talking to Lonnie and asks him, 'Lonnie tell me, because I know you know, is Jim Morrison [The Doors] still alive?' and Lonnie laughs and says, 'Yea.'

Lonnie had been playing with Jim Morrison, until Lonnie's 'Memphis' and 'Wham' became big hits and he was able to start touring with his own band.

The guy introduces me to Lonnie and tells him that I'm a great horn player. Lonnie asks, 'Do you want to sit in?', and I said, 'I didn't bring my horn.' But he said, 'Why don't you come around next time?'

I started following Lonnie around. I would show up, he'd call me up on stage, I'd play a number and then go to walk off stage, and he'd yell, 'Girl, where you going?' and he'd keep me up there.

One night, I recorded a cassette of me playing with Lonnie. It wasn't anything special but he was so supportive. I was heavily influenced by the way he played guitar and the way he sang, how he ran his band. I sometimes wonder if I would have stopped playing if I hadn't met Lonnie. He means a lot to me.

Next, I got on the John Lee Hooker tour. I was young -22- and really green. We were playing with great blues artists like Willie Dixon and Big Mama Thornton. Robert Cray was the opening act, and this was before he became famous. I remember wondering why I was playing with the headline acts and I was so interested in hearing the opening act every night!

John was a really sweet guy, but when he was on stage, it was all intensity and style. He played everything in the key of E, but for the grand finale, he'd go to the key of B. For a tenor player that puts us in F# minor and then in C# minor, keys which makes things a little interesting. That tour was just an amazing experience.

I didn't start playing the tenor until relatively late. In high school, I played bassoon, piano, violin, harp, flute… In high school concert band, I'd see the sax players go off to play in the jazz band, and I thought too bad I'm not playing that, but I didn't consciously listen to sax players. It was only when I got to college and was offered a part in a 'Cabaret' but only if I played the sax; that's when I learned how to play.

I was playing bassoon with a double reed, where you have to be able to play 8 different keys with your left thumb or something ridiculous like that; a double reed is a monstrous thing to master, you have a completely different muscular structure and embouchure then for the sax. After playing sax for a few years, when I tried to play the bassoon again, I couldn't do it for more than 3 seconds without the embouchure burning.

Playing tenor sax takes a lot of diaphragm and there's a real physicalness to it. That's why my practice routines always include long tones. Some people think they're boring. In a club, I was playing in Dayton, Ohio in the 80s, they had a bulletin board, an article about Miles Davis and how he was still doing long tones. I thought if Miles Davis is doing long tones, I need to do them and I have done them forever. They really build your sound, control, and wind capacity; you learn how your body, reed and horn vibrate and work together. They really connect you with your instrument.

I also did a lot of technical exercises when I started playing tenor. In college, I decided to get a Performance Major, because I wasn't interested in teaching. I had transferred to a small liberal arts school. Because they had a small music staff, I got a local saxophonist to give me lessons. He said that I had to switch to alto, but I said, 'I don't want to switch to alto.'

'O.k. then', he said, 'but you're going to have to do it all classical.' I really wish I had put my foot down and said, 'No, I'll do classical, but you've got to teach me jazz too.'

I did a lot of work on technical exercises because, to me, the goal of technique is to allow you to do whatever you want when you improvise.

On the flip side of that, blues is a feeling, not about being a monster technician. That can be a tricky balance, because you really need to know and feel what needs to be said. That's where technique can get in the way. Blues is first about feeling and that something coming out of your soul. If you're playing a lot of notes just because you can, you start to move away from the fundamental core of the music.

That's why I really got interested in the sax- the emotion and feeling it could bring. I was classically trained on a piano and thought I was pretty good, but when I listened to someone who really had the touch for the piano, the emotion he was able to get out of the instrument was so far beyond what I could, I said to myself, 'Oh! O.k. I get it!'

When I first started singing, I thought maybe I should be like Jimmy Smith and do a couple of novelty numbers. Audiences like to be sung to and when I started fronting my own band, I thought it wouldn't work so well to do all instrumentals. I would love to be able to sing like soul singer Johnnie Taylor, [laughing at herself]. I prefer vocalists who don't sound too trained and polished and are emotional.

My love for the blues goes back to a college radio station. I met a couple of radio programmers from WYSO in Yellow Springs, Ohio [https://www.wyso.org/]. They started feeding me some great old blues and that really influenced me, those songs could really move you, like 'I Got What It Takes', a Willie Dixon tune, as in the version.

Junior Walker, King Curtis- I was very influenced by both tenors. I loved that sort of more muscular style of playing, like the Texas tenors Arnett Cobb and Illinois Jacquet. I remember the time when I was playing on stage in Dayton and all of sudden it felt like King Curtis had stepped inside me and he was playing. That's how big an influence he had.

I did a track on my CD 'Playdate' entitled 'Back Room Rock', and that came off a King Curtis cut with Sam Price on the album 'Rib Joint'. To me, that album is early rock n' roll, r&b...whatever you want to call it. Every part on that album is important and King Curtis' playing is just fabulous.

https://www.youtube.com/watch?v=UFmMRBibKIs
https://www.nancywrightmusic.com/tracks-playdate/

I used to dream that one day I'd find musicians who could play every tune on that album, it is that good.

Which brings me to my sax.

In my last year of college, the music instructor told me that for my senior recital, I needed a good horn. I looked around the music stores in Dayton, but nothing impressed.

The following Monday night- and this is in February in Dayton Ohio with freezing temperatures and a blizzard roaring away- a friend of mine was playing in a club with three floors. There were only stairs, no elevator, and I don't know that many people ever made it all the way to the third floor, but that's where she was playing.

I got up there and there was like eight of us in the whole place. During a break, a musician comes wandering up the stairs on a break and asks, 'Does anyone want to buy a saxophone?'

That was my Selmer Mark VII, the horn I've played ever since. I've tried VIs, but I don't think I can get out of a VI what I do with my VII. They were designed for a basketball player's kind of hands, but I had a guy in Boston who built up the little finger keys that helped a lot. I've always played with a metal Berg Larsen 95 O M. Once while playing a street festival, somehow I dropped the mouthpiece and the sidewalk took a little chip out of the edge, but I think it actually plays better that way! I use Rico Plasticover reeds. Have used them for years, gives me a bit more edge to my tone.

I graduated from college as a Performance Major, but when it comes to stage performing as a professional, on the spectrum of sheer entertainer on one end and sheer musician on the other, I'm more on the musician side. I'm more of an introvert but admire people who have it all, great musicians who can entertain the crowd with whatever they do or say.

As for great stage performers, how about Albert King and Vaughan?

Albert and Stevie Ray were playing at the New Orleans Jazz and Heritage Fest. I went over by the side of the stage and these two guys came over who were from Albert's horn section. One of the guys was Ed Hurley, who was from the Bay area and had played with Elvin Bishop for years. We started chatting. I don't know if they asked me if I wanted to play or I asked them, but they said, 'C'mon, let's go see what Albert says.' Albert's got this entourage around him, I get in line, they bring me up to see him, and Albert says, 'Oh do you want to play?' I said, 'Yes', then Albert asks if I do drugs or drink. I notice Ed, standing behind Albert, is shaking his head, so I say 'No.' Then Albert says, 'O.k., you can play.'

The horn section was great, they treated me with respect, and would whisper the lines to me so I could blend in. By chance, a neighbor of mine was listening and I had on black pants, a black jacket and a light pastel shirt which everyone in the band was wearing. He thought I was a member of the band!

I never worked with Stevie Ray Vaughan, but sat in a few times. First time, I was playing with Lonnie and had never heard of Stevie Ray, he wasn't a big name yet. I asked Lonnie if I should try to sit in with him, and he said, 'Sure, he's a good old boy.' When I introduced myself to Stevie, he asked for Lonnie's phone number because he'd been trying to get hold of him.

When I came back after being on tour with John Lee Hooker, Lonnie had moved to Austin and had done an album with Stevie.

I went down to see Lonnie. He was living in school bus on a campground outside Austin with his wife and two kids, and to me it looked like poverty, especially since I had grown up in the suburbs. I asked myself, 'Wow, what happened?'

Shortly after that, I was with Hot Licks touring up in Seattle, Stevie Ray's band was playing there. I'd heard that

Lonnie was really sick. I went to the bar after the gig, walked up to Stevie and said, 'What did you do to Lonnie?' Stevie throws his hands up in the air in mock surrender and says, 'I didn't do nothing, it's hereditary, his Daddy had it too.'

Lonnie eventually pulled through and the album he did with Stevie –'Strike Like Lightning'- really helped him to get back into the limelight.

Another great performer was Katie Webster, a lovely person to be with, always very bright and talkative, a real monster blues player. I first got to see that when I first moved to California to play with her backing band Hot Licks. That was a real treat to go into a recording studio with someone like Katie. I snuck in some Jack Daniels for a little inspiration and sure enough it got things moving…although I definitely don't do things like that anymore!

Of course, if you're in California, you never know where things might lead. I was playing in the musical 'Gospel at Colonus' in San Francisco-that was an amazing experience. My little band was on stage next to a full gospel choir, with Morgan Freeman, Pop Staples, The Five Blind Boys of Alabama…Night after night, we're doing our job, surrounded by this wonderful music.

After a show, a horn player tells me this agency is doing a casting call for musicians for a movie, and asked me if I wanted do to try out, because if you do, you can go with us. I said. 'Sure.' I ended up getting the job on the movie 'Dying Young', but felt really bad because the guy who had told me about it, didn't.

But there was no playing involved, just acting like you were playing. We got paid really, really well, like movie actors, but the wait is forever, you're like an extra standing around all day. We were filming in a winery, down in the basement, and you had to stand in one position. They'd say, 'Now wait', while they spent like 20 minutes puffing mist into the air. I saw those scenes afterward and I swear I don't see what that mist did or what it was supposed to be all about. When they shot the scenes, all the dancers, while dancing, had to look like they were talking to each other, and we had to look like we were playing, but all of us had to be dead silent. It was freezing down there, and I thought 'If I do much more of this. I don't know that I'll enjoy watching movies anymore.'

Guitarist Tim Kaihatsu led the house band The Rat Band at the Berkeley club 'Larry Blake's'. Members of that band eventually went on to play with Robert Cray, and keyboardist Dave Matthews now plays with Santana.

The Rat Band used to play on Monday nights, and I'd go because the best way to get better is to hang around with people who play a bit better than you, so I did some school down there.

https://www.youtube.com/watch?v=Ri7WB3HNEME

One night, at an Elvin Bishop show in Berkeley, I see Tim and he says 'C'mon backstage.' He introduces me to Elvin Bishop and says, 'This is Nancy Wright, she's a great tenor player.' Elvin says, 'Oh, well you wanna a job?' and that's how I got to play with him. If I hadn't gone there that night, it might never have happened. That's one thing you learn in this business-perseverance; if things don't work out the first time, you get right back to it until they do.

I was greatly influenced by Jackie Ivory, a Hammond organist. I used to go to this club called 'Jack's' –now the 'Boom Boom Room'- a black nightclub in the Fillmore District on San Francisco, where the Jackie Ivory Quartet played five nights a week. They had like maybe 15 sets of matching tuxes, and I just *loved* their music. I would look at their tenor player Ed Surgest and think, 'I want to be him when I grow up!'

Years later, I'm walking around on Fisherman's Wharf and up comes Jackie Ivory! He tells me that Ed has gotten too old to play, did I want to, and I said, 'Oh yea!' So my dream came true, years after I had given it up. Jackie had played with Willis Jackson and Junior Walker. Made me realize how much I loved organ music.

Whenever I took holidays, I usually went back to Dayton, Ohio. I would phone a local club owner, tell him I was going to be in town, and he would try to put together gigs for me. This one time, the owner asked, 'Have you ever heard of this guy Tony Monaco?' I said, 'No.' I started checking this guy out. Turned out he was a monster Hammond B3 player. I soon phoned back and said, 'You mean this guy would actually play with me?'

I got to sit in with him a few times, and when I got home in San Francisco, I thought, 'I got to learn just a little more stuff outside the blues, so I can have a little more to say.' I started hanging out in the soul-jazz rooms.

I kept scheming about how I could play with Tony again, because it had been such an optimum experience. This went on for a couple of years, until Tony started his own label, and he put out records by other people. That's when I wondered if he'd let me do my own record and if I could use his group as my backing band. That's what got me started recording.

https://www.nancywrightmusic.com/tracks-moanin/

After my first CD, I realized that if I did a blues record instead jazz, I'd probably make more money and get more gigs; they are just two different marketplaces. Which returned me to what I do best, the blues, and I've been doing it ever since.

Another really positive influence is Tommy Castro. I've learned to have great respect for bandleaders. I look at somebody like Tommy, who knows how to read an audience, what kind of tune to play next to keep an audience happy. As a sideman, I was blissfully ignorant of all of that. His influence has helped to teach me well.

On my first CD, I let Tony do the production, guide me through it. The next CD 'Putting Down Roots', I hired a core band to play pretty much throughout and produced it myself, which sort of means I made decisions about what was to happen and when, but Kid Andersen was a heavy advisor. He showed me how to arrange some of the tracks and I pretty much trusted him.

On 'Well, I'm Travelling' he did a Lonnie Mack-inspired solo. When I left his Greaseland studio, down in San Jose, he was working on it. When I came back the next day, he played it for me, and it was beautiful. He told me he had been up all night finishing it. That's what is nice about your own studio, you can spend time polishing.

https://www.nancywrightmusic.com/tracks-roots/

https://www.nancywrightmusic.com/store/

The next CD, 'Playdate', I asked Kid to produce it; that was the one where I had special guests. A lot of the decisions with that album were driven by Kid's take on the tunes. We knew the people we wanted. Elvin Bishop was in San Francisco, but some were in Memphis, in Minneapolis, Philadelphia...Kid realized that we were all going to be at the Blues Music Awards in Memphis year, so he got a portable record and we recorded them there.

Frank Bey and Wee Willie Walker we did in a motel room that Kid was sharing with somebody else, and Joe Louis Walker was there as well. It went fabulous. Then we went out to Victor Wainright's house and recorded him on his grand piano in breakfast nook.

https://www.nancywrightmusic.com/tracks-playdate/

https://www.nancywrightmusic.com/store/
I want to point out 'Blues For The Westside' that was recorded by Eddie Shaw on tenor and Magic Sam on guitar. When I'm teaching students about growling and greasy tones, I make them study 'Blues For The West Side', because he does amazing things, like holding a note up straight and then wagging it at the end. This song isn't about technique, it's about feeling.

https://www.youtube.com/watch?v=iItSGUeO9bI
https://www.nancywrightmusic.com/tracks-playdate/

The album was named one of Downbeat Magazine's Best Albums of 2017, and received a 2017 Blues Blast Music Awards 'Honorable Mention' in the Soul Blues Album category.

The live CD, 'Alive And Blue' was a last minute decision. Robby Yamilov from Greaseland Studio was available. You never know what you'll get with live performances, but everything worked out great playing at The Saloon. I was really glad I did it. [cited by Living Blues, Top 50 Blues Albums, 2019, Blues Bytes, Top 20 Blues Album, 2019]

I picked tunes that had influenced me early. 'Satisfied' on the 'Playdate' CD, is a tune Lonnie Mack covered that I really loved…

https://www.nancywrightmusic.com/tracks-playdate/

and 'Soul Serenade' on 'Alive And Blue', of course, was done by King Curtis.

https://www.nancywrightmusic.com/tracks-alive-blue/

https://www.nancywrightmusic.com/store/

I'm pretty selective these days about what type of gigs I'll do, and will only take one if I think it will stretch me a bit so I can learn from or that I'll really enjoy playing. But these days, being a young professional musician, you can't be selective like I am.

I worry for young players, especially in the San Francisco area, the cost of living and housing costs here are astronomical and what you get paid for playing hasn't gone up that much since I first got here back in 1983. And even though they are monster players, I don't know how they are making a living out of it.

But a whole new world has opened up that I haven't really got involved with, emerging markets like the Internet, YouTube, social media…and the musicianship of today's players is such, they know how to come together, play whatever tune it is, really connect with the audience and make it sound wonderful."

Yakety Yak — The Coasters

KING CURTIS. TENOR

#1 R&B #1 Pop

Photo courtesy Atco Records

THE COASTERS: Carl Gardner, Cornelius Gunter, Billy Guy, Will "Dub" Jones (vcls), King Curtis (ten), Mike Stoller (pno), Adolph Jacobs, Clifton "Skeeter" Best, Allen Hanlon (gtrs), Lloyd Trotman (bs), Joe Marshall (dms), Francisco Pozo (bgos). Ten, bgos, pno omitted on –1; bgos omitted on –2. Arr. Reggie Obrecht. Prod. Jerry Leiber & Mike Stoller.
New York. March 17, 1958

58C-363 Zing! Went The Strings Of My Heart   Atco 6116
58C-364 Three Cool Cats   Atco 6132
58C-365 Yakety Yak –2   Atco 6116
58C-366 Stewball –1   Atco 6168

A longer, stereo, version of "Three Cool Cats" appeared on Clarion LP 605 (stereo issue) and Uk Edsel LP 156, running 2:43 as against 2:08 for the original single. This has been identified as take 12. The same album has a slightly different version of "Stewball" featuring more echo and changed words. This runs 2:20 against the Atco single's 2:14. European (bootleg?) CD Mr. R&B cd-102, issued 2000, contains alternate takes, false starts and studio chatter from all four tracks of this session. 2008 release, Rhino cd RHM2-7740 contains all the above alternates, plus 3 different takes of "Yakety Yak", Numbered 365-3, -5, -6.

THE COASTERS: Carl Gardner, Cornelius Gunter, Billy Guy, Will Jones (vcls), Taft Jordan, Red Solomon (tpts), Eddie Bert (tbn), King Curtis (ten), Mike Stoller (pno), Adolph Jacobs, Don Arnone (gtrs), Milt Hinton (bs), Belton Evans (dms). Tpts/tbn omitted on –1. Arr. Mike Stoller. Prod. Jerry Leiber & Mike Stoller.

New York. December 11, 1958

58C-461 Charlie Brown –1   Atco 6132
58C-462 Hey Sexy   unissued

previously unused stereo take from same session:

Charlie Brown –1   Atlantic LP 8164

Note: European (bootleg?) cd, Mr R&B cd-102, issued in 2000, contains alternate takes, false starts and studio chatter from both tracks of this session, as does Rhino box set RHM 2-7740. There is also a stereo take of "Charlie Brown" on Collectors Choice cd CCM 028-2 which may be yet another outtake.

THE COASTERS: Carl Gardner, Cornelius Gunter, Billy Guy, Will Jones (vcls), King Curtis (ten), Mike Stoller (pno), George Barnes (bjo) on –1, Allen Hanlon, Tony Mottola (gtrs), Abie Baker (bs), Sammy "Sticks" Evans (dms). Jerry Leiber (vcl bridge) on –2. Prod. Jerry Leiber & Mike Stoller.
New York. March 26, 1959

59C-3418   Along Came Jones –1   Atco 6141
59C-3419   That Is Rock & Roll –2   Atco 6141

prob. from same session:

That Is Rock & Roll (alternate take) –2   Atco LP 371

Note: Rhino box set cd RHM2-7740 contains alternate takes from both tracks of this session.

THE COASTERS: Carl Gardner, Cornelius Gunter, Billy Guy, Will Jones (vcls), King Curtis (ten) on –1, Sonny Forriest, Allen Hanlon (gtrs), George Barnes (bs-gtr), Wendell Marshall (bs), Gary Chester (dms). Poss. Mike Stoller (pno), although not audible. Prod. Jerry Leiber & Mike Stoller.

New York. July 16, 1959

    59C-3606   What About Us –1   Atco 6153
    What About Us (alt. Stereo take) –1   Atco LP 135 (stereo issue)
    59C-3607   Poison Ivy   Atco 6146
    Poison Ivy (alt. Stereo take)   Atco LP 371 (stereo issue)

King Curtis is one of the best rock & roll musicians of all time. His specialty was the tenor sax. He was born Curtis Ousley in 1934 in Fort Worth, Texas, took up sax at the age of twelve, and began working in his home town in the 1940s.

Born: February 7, 1934, Fort Worth, Texas. Brought up in Mansfield, Texas – Adopted son of Mr. & Mrs. William Ousley

1947: online version of "Texas Monthly" (May 2000) magazine states that "it was in 1947 at I.M. Terrell High School in Fort Worth that young Ornette Coleman got kicked out of the marching band for improvising during "The Washington Post March", leaving fellow bandmembers Dewey Redman and King Curtis Ousley holding their woodwinds."

c. 1949-1952: Begins professional career in Fort Worth, under the wing of Aaron Watkins, a Fort Worth showman. Plays in band, under Thomas "Red" Connors leadership which possibly also included Ornette Coleman and David "Fathead" Newman. However, Coleman had left in 1949 to join the Pee Wee Crayton band (which took him to California).

1952: Visits uncle in New York. Plays on a predominantly r&b tour featuring Lester Young. Sits in on jam sessions, wins two amateur contests at the Apollo Theater. One report suggests he was in a band with Lowell Fulson at this time.

BOB KENT BAND: Bob Kent (vcl), King Curtis (ten), unk. 2nd ten, pno, bs, dms.
New York. Prior November, 1952

| 1320 | Korea, Korea | Par 1303 |
| 1321 | Oh! Baby. | Par 1303 |

note: Par was a Prestige subsidiary, 78rpm issues exist only. The label debuted in October 1951, and released just 6 singles. A&R director was Ben deCosta.

c.1953: Returns to Texas to continue schooling/musical education.

Note: 1952/3 recordings on Hummingbird and Monarch by "King Curtis" are believed to be by Eddie Curtis.

After graduating from high school in 1950, he began working with Lionel Hampton and moved to New York in 1953 to study harmony, counterpoint, and theory. In New York he had the opportunity to work with a variety of musicians in pop, soul, and jazz.

MELVIN DANIELS (RPM), **KING CURTIS** (Crown): Melvin Daniels (vcl/pno), King Curtis (ten), Vonzell Tucker?

(ten), unk. bari, Webster Armstrong (gtr), Dobbs (bs), Vernon Lewis (dms). Unk. 2nd vcl on –1.

Fort Worth, 1953

1948	I'll Be There	RPM 383; Crown LP 5294
1949	Boogie In The Moonlight	RPM 383; Crown LP 5294
	If You Don't Want My Loving	Crown LP 5294
	Hey Hey Little Girl –1	Crown LP 5294

Note: "Boogie In The Moonlight" retitled "Lean Chicks" on Crown issue. A Japanese cd, P-Vine pcd 3057, "Houston Jump Blues/The 50s"; sourced from the Modern/RPM labels, includes the above four tracks, along with four untitled instrumentals attributed to King Curtis. I am informed by Dave Penny, who has heard the 4 tracks, courtesy of Ace (who own all RPM masters) that they are in fact by pianist Pete Johnson, with Maxwell Davis on tenor sax overdubbed.

KING CURTIS & HIS TENOR SAX WITH ORCH.: King Curtis (ten), Melvin Daniels (vcl/pno) on –1, Webster Armstrong (gtr), Dobbs (bs), Vernon Lewis (dms).

Fort Worth. Prob. Prior August, 1953

6120	Tenor In The Sky	Gem 208
6121	No More Crying On My Pillow –1	Gem 208

Note: All masters of the Gem label were subsequently sold to Savoy. Label credit on 6121 reads "Melvin Daniels, vocalist" below KC's name.

c. June, 1954 Cashbox reports "TV and recording star Joan Shaw was joined by Don Hanna and tenor-man Curtis Ousley when she did a guest shot on Hanna's jazz show in Bermuda. Joan Shaw was later known as Salena Jones, and according to her self-administered website (www.salenajones.com) was bornin 1944. However, it is unlikely she was just 10 at the time of this Cashbox report! On the website she supposedly had made about 12 singles by the ageof fifteen.

c. 1954 Joins Lionel Hampton on tour for three months, and leaves tour in New York.

Leads trio there with Horace Silver and Osie Johnson (later replaced by Earl Knight and Lenny McBrowne). Initial work includes 'society' bands of Art Mooney and Lester Lanin. Also, with Buck Clayton and Charlie Shavers.
Meanwhile, studies sax under Joe Napoleon and Garvin Bushell. King Curtis discovered by Jesse Stone, whilst playing in an 8th Avenue club, and gets onto session circuit, initially with Bob Rolontz's productions for RCA subsidiaries Groove and Vik.

Curtis was naturally talented and could have pursued a career in jazz but decided that he would rather make money, so he used his talents in rock 'n' roll. With a strong work ethic and his talent, he stayed busy doing recording sessions, touring, and performing in many Harlem nightclubs.

"A strange thing happened at a December 14, 1955 date for RCA Victor's Groove subsidiary. It was unusual to book two tenor specialists for a vocal date, but that's what A&R man Bob Rolontz did for gravel-voiced blues shouter Teddy "The Bear" McRae. On McRae's hurtling rocker "Mr. Bear Comes To Town," Sam "The Man" Taylor jumped in at the halfway point with a typically spectacular 12-bar ride before handing the spotlight off to a newcomer from Fort Worth, Texas whose equally compact solo was every bit as flammable as Sam's- Curtis Ousley [who soon renamed himself "King Curtis"]

MR. BEAR & HIS BEARCATS: *Teddy McRae (vcl), King Curtis, Sam Taylor (tens) Dave McRae (bari), Ernie Hayes (pno), Mickey Baker (gtr), Al Lucas (bs), Sticks Evans (dms). Arr/dir: Leroy Kirkland. Prod. Bob Rolontz.*

New York. December 14, 1955

F5JB-8380-8 Peek-A-Boo   Groove 0138

F5JB-8381-4 Mr. Bear Comes To Town   Groove 0150

F5JB-8382-3 Radar Groove 0150

F5JB-8383-6 The Bear Hug Groove 0138

"When I first met King Curtis, I was in New York. I was in Small's Paradise. At the time, Wilt Chamberlain had taken over the ownership, and King Curtis was the house band. Well, I didn't know King was in the place. I heard he might be in there. But when I walked in, nobody was playing, and I just went through and went to the bathroom. I looked upon the bandstand and I didn't see nobody. So I went to the bathroom, and into the bathroom comes this guy. He's in the stall next to me, and it looks like, from the pictures I've seen, it looks like it could be King Curtis. So I said, 'Hey, man, what's your name?' He said, 'King.' I said, 'Yeah, my name is Gene Barge.' So he said, 'Oh yeah?' I said, 'Yeah.' I said, 'Ruth Brown told me that you were stealing my style!' He looks at me and said, 'Oh, you're the--Ruth Brown says what? Man, go get your horn! I ain't stealing your style, man!' We got into it in the bathroom. It was a friendly thing, you know, really friendly. It was quite funny."

"Reminds me of the time King Curtis was playing on Yonge St. at Le Coq D'or (Toronto Ontario Canada) and I was playing upstairs with The Majestics. At break time, Curtis came upstairs to give us a listen. We asked him if he'd like to sit in but he didn't have his horn, just his mouthpiece in his pocket. So, I invited him to put it on my sax and give it a blow. Well... it was the best I've ever heard my sax sound... amazing. I had just had the Mark VI for about two years and was wondering if it was a bit stuffy. He sure blew that notion away. Ever since then, I've tried to come up with as big a tone, but it's a life's work, I'm afraid."- Russ Strathdee

The Majestics (Russ Strathdee, tenor; earlier tenor players included John Crone and Bill Cudmore) 162
https://www.youtube.com/watch?v=WlnOMfOYfuI
http://www.canadianbands.com/Majestics.html
https://www.rstrathdee.com/bio3.htm
Wahl B (2020) King Curtis-The Soul Of King Curtis.
https://www.sunsetblvdrecords.com/blog/2020/5/7/king-curtis-the-soul-of-king-curtis

After doing some session work, Curtis struck out on his own, first as King Curtis and The Noble Knights and later as

The Kingpins. He put three songs in the Top 40 in the 1960s, but all were instrumentals at a time when instrumentals were not popular with the record-buying public.

Interesting note: when you hear Sam Cooke say, "Play that one called Soul Twist" in his 1962 hit "Having A Party," he is referring to the King Curtis song!

He had fifteen Top 100 songs from 1962 to 1971. King Curtis was very much in demand as a sax player by nearly every musician in the business.

One of his memorable sax solos can be heard on the Coasters' "Yakety Yak."

The list of people that Curtis worked for in the early days of rock 'n' roll is long and includes: Lionel Hampton, Buck Clayton, Nat King Cole, Joe Turner, The McGuire Sisters, Andy Williams, Chuck Willis, The Coasters, Buddy Holly, LaVern Baker, Bobby Darin, Brook Benton, Neil Sedaka, The Drifters, Sam Cooke, The Isley Brothers, Solomon Burke, The Shirelles, Nina Simone, The Beatles, Aretha Franklin, Herbie Mann, Wilson Pickett, Duane Allmann, Eric Clapton, The Clovers, and John Johnson.

SOLOMON BURKE (vcl): prob. Personnel: **King Curtis or Lester Young (ten)**, unk. bari on –1, unk. pno, Mickey Baker (gtr), Al Lucas (bs), Coatsville Harris (dms), Lionel Hampton (vbs).
New York. November 18, 1955

AP-3547   Christmas Presents   Apollo 485
AP-3548   ?
AP-3549   To Thee   Apollo 491
AP-3550   When I'm All Alone –1   Apollo 485
AP-3550-1 I'm All Alone –1   Apollo 491
Note: 3550-1 is a retitled alternate take of 3550.

SOLOMON BURKE (vcl), with same or similar to previous session.
New York. November 21, 1955

AP-3560   I'm In Love   Apollo 487
AP-3561   Why Do Me That Way –1   Apollo 487

Note: Michel Ruppli believes master numbers should be 3558/3559 on this track.

SOLOMON BURKE (vcl): prob. line-up: unk. tbn, **King Curtis or Lester Young (ten)**, unk. bari, Howard Biggs (pno), Mickey Baker (gtr), Al Lucas (bs), Coatsville Harris (dms), The Ray Charles Singers (bkgnd vcls). Arr. Howard Biggs.
New York. c. September, 1956

AP-3585   My Heart Is A Chapel   Apollo 527
AP-3586   This Is It   Apollo 511
AP-3587   No Man Walks Alone   Apollo 500
AP-3588   Walkin' In A Dream   Apollo 500
AP-3589   A Picture Of You   Apollo 505
AP-3590   You Can Run But You Can't Hide   Apollo 505
AP-3591   I Need You Tonight   Apollo 511

THE DRIFTERS: Benjamin Earl Nelson (= Ben E. King), Charles "Charlie Boy" Thomas, Dock Green, Elsbeary Hobbs (vcls), King Curtis (ten), Mike Stoller (pno), Sal Salvador (gtr), Wendell Marshall (bs), Belton Evans (dms), unk. Bells. Strings (4 violins, 1 cello), perc added, ten and pno omitted on –1. Arr. Stan

Applebaum on –1, or Reggie Obrecht. Prod. Jerry Leiber & Mike Stoller.
New York. March 6, 1959

    A-3396   Hey Senorita   Atlantic 2062
    A-3397   There Goes My Baby –1   Atlantic 2025. **#1 R&B #1 Pop**
    A-3398   Baltimore   Atlantic 2050
    A-3399   Oh My Love –1   Atlantic 2025

THE CLOVERS: Billy Mitchell, John "Buddy" Bailey, Matthew McQuater, Harold Lucas, Harold Winley (vcls), King Curtis (ten), unk. Pno, gtr, bs, dms. Tenor omitted on –1. Prod. Jerry Leiber & Mike Stoller.
New York. June 8, 1959

    ZTSP-2904 Love Potion No.9 (edit of takes 13&16) United Artists 180 **#23 R&B 3. #3 Pop**
    2525.   Love Potion No.9 (take 16)   United Artists LP 3099
    11335   Stay Awhile (take 19) United Artists 180
    ZTSP-62166   Lovey (edit of takes 9&13)   United Artists 209
    Noni Cosi (take 9) –1 United Artists LP 3099

BROOK BENTON (rn: Benjamin Peay) (vcl), King Curtis (ten), unk. pno, gtr, bs, dms, tamb. Strings, bkgnd vcls added, ten, tamb omitted on –1. Arr. Ray Ellis. Prod. Clyde Otis.
New York. c. December, 1958

    YW-11971 Hold My Hand   unissued

YW-11972 It's Just A Matter Of Time –1   Mercury 71394. **#! R&B #3 Pop**
YW-11973 Hurtin' Inside Mercury 71394
YW-11974 I Want You Forever   unissued
YW-11975 Tell Me The Truth   unissued

CLYDE MCPHATTER (vcl), King Curtis (ten), Clifton Smalls (pno), Sal Salvador, Carl Lynch (gtrs), Milt Hinton (bs), Belton Evans (dms), Myriam Workman, Audrey Marsh, Elise Bretton, Robert Miller, Ralph Nyland, James Leyden, Mike Stewart (bkgnd vcls). Orch. dir. Ray Ellis. Add Nigel Hopkins (bass-vocal), Brook Benton, Clyde Otis (finger snapping), ten omitted on –1. Prod. Ahmet Ertegun & Jerry Wexler.
New York. August 7, 1958

A-3117   A Lover's Question –1   Atlantic 1199
#1 R&B #6 Pop
A-3118   I Can't Stand Up Alone   Atlantic 1199
A-3119   Lovey Dovey   Atlantic 2018
A-3120   Rockin' & Rollin'   unissued

Jimi Hendrix

RAY SHARPE (vcl) with King Curtis' Orchestra: Melvin Lastie (tpt), King Curtis (ten), Willie Bridges (bari), Cornell Dupree (gtr), Chuck Rainey (bs), Ray Lucas (dms). Prod. King Curtis. (Sharpe's vocals probably dubbed over the backing track.)
New York. January 21, 1966

66C-9867   Help Me (Get The Feeling) Pt.1   Atco 6402

66C-9868   Help Me (Get The Feeling) Pt.2   Atco 6402

Notes: This is actually one continuous recording, split into two, with an overlap of about 23 seconds (making the real track length 4.05). Ray Sharpe claimed that Jimi Hendrix worked on this session, and the dates do seem to be about right. Jimi was definitely in New York on January 13, 1966, when King Curtis was looking for a second guitarist in his band, Jimi auditioned and got the job during that month. Bernard Purdie said he and Ray Lucas alternated the drum seat at the time. During the remainder of January, it is known that Hendrix was in Texas – specifically Dallas, Houston and Fort Worth. If one speculates that was with King Curtis, then a further logical speculation might be that Sharpe's vocals were recorded in one of those locations.

RAY SHARPE (vcl), King Curtis (ten), Jimi Hendrix, Cornell Dupree (gtrs), Chuck Rainey (bs), Ray Lucas, Bernard Purdie (dms).

New York. April 28, 1966.

66C-10190 Linda Lou   unissued (Atco)

66C-10191 I Can't Take it   unissued

66C-10192 Baby How About You   unissued

May 5, 1966: King Curtis' band, including Jimi Hendrix and Cornell Dupree played at an Atlantic party at the Prelude Club, New York, to mark the release of Percy

Sledge's LP. Also there and performing were Esther Phillips and Wilson Pickett.

During Hendrix's period with Curtis, (January to May 1966), Cornell Dupree remembered gigs in Wildwood, New Jersey; another with Billy Preston, and a job backing Chuck Berry at "one of the upstate New York colleges."

May 7, 1966: King Curtis' band – reportedly including Hendrix – played a gig at the Sheraton Hotel, Metropolitan Ballroom in New York City on this date.

Towards the end of May or early June, Hendrix joined Carl & The Commanders, after reportedly having been fired by Curtis for not wearing the band uniform properly.

Earlier, the importance of luck and "being in the right place at the right time" was discussed. This was never truer than with Jimi Hendrix.

Two months later, on July 5, 1966, Jimi Hendrix, now billed as "Jimmy James and The Blue Flames", was the playing the Café Wha? in New York's Greenwich Village. Chris Chandler, organist for The Animals (who had hit Number One on the Pop charts with "House of the Rising Sun"), was sitting in the audience at the insistence of Linda Keith, a girlfriend of the Rolling Stones' Keith Richards. Chandler heard Hendrix play "Hey Joe" plus a version of Dylan's "Like A Rolling Stone" and was "awestruck".

https://www.youtube.com/watch?v=rXwMrBb2x1Q

Hearing Hendrix convinced Chandler to finally make a long-planned move into record production and management. He later convinced Hendrix to move to London, England and record a single and album with British musicians. The album "Are You Experienced" was recorded between October 1966 and April 1967 when it was released.

https://www.youtube.com/watch?v=cbG7HEEPE1o&list=PL1RRNXldMeRFm7CqtN44oav-TgaWT3yt

What would have happened if King Curtis had not fired Jimi Hendrix; would Hendrix still have formed a band or played at the Café Wha?; would anyone ever have heard of Jimi Hendrix, other than session musicians?

Soul Twist & Memphis Soul Stew

KING CURTIS & THE NOBLE KNIGHTS: King Curtis (ten), Ernie Hayes (org), George Stubbs (pno), Billy Butler (gtr), Jimmy Lewis (bs), Ray Lucas (dms). Prod. Bobby & Danny Robinson.

New York. c. November, 1961

Soul Twist (alternate take)   Trip 83; LP 60-3; LP 8017; LP

9508; Upfront LP 157.

EJ2 *Soul Twist* ("Soul Time" on Trip/Upfront)   Enjoy 1000; LP 2001;

Everlast 5030;

Good Old Gold 021;

Mr.Maestro LP 1111;

Constellation LP 1;

Roulette LP 25238; LP RE-113;

Trip 83; LP 8017; LP 9508;

Upfront LP 157;

Rhino LP 70648; LP 70039;

Collectables LP 5119; LP 5156. EJ3

Twisting Time

Enjoy 1000; LP 2001;

Everlast 5030;

Collectables LP 5119.

Notes: According to Bobby Robinson, "Soul Twist" "was released in time for the Christmas market", and registration of "Twisting Time" for Kilynn took place on November 12, 1961; subsequently both it and "Soul Twist" were re-registered to Kilyn/BobDan on January 29, 1962. Original copies of Enjoy 1000 are possibly only credited to "The Noble Knights". It will be noted that the Trip/Upfront issues feature the alternate take with more prominent sax work as "Soul Twist", where the actual hit version is relegated to "Soul Time".

A further alternate take, take 7, appears on U.S. Relic cd 7102. Reverse of Good Old Gold 021 is by The Ikettes, Trip 83 by Dave "Baby" Cortez. There was apparently yet one more 'oldies' type 45 known to exist, with the flip being Bobby Freeman's "C'mon & Swim" but details are not to hand. Finally,

Frankie Lee Sims, interviewed by Chris Strachwitz in 1969, claimed to have played guitar on "Soul Twist".

KING CURTIS (ten on –1, gtr on –2, and/or vcl on –3), Ronnie Miller (gtr; vcl on –3), unk. org., Jimmy Lewis (bs), Ray Lucas (dms). Prod. Herb Abramson.

New York. June 24, 1967.

SMX-00811   Home Cookin' –1   Trip 3005; LP 9508

    Blue Man –2   unissued

    Hello Sunshine –3   unissued

Note: apparently a demo session. "Home Cookin'" (originally titled "King's Festival") is a forerunner of "Memphis Soul Stew"; "Blue Man" a forerunner of "Blue Nocturne" (see July 4, 1967 session), and "Hello Sunshine", being a tune written by Curtis and Ronnie Miller, was recorded on July 3, 1967 by Wilson Pickett (q.v.). The B side of Trip 3005 is "Sweet Georgia Brown", from The Freddie Mitchell session of January 25, 1959, q.v. A remixed version of "Home Cookin'", plus the other two, were issued in 1987 on UK Red Lightnin' RL 0074.

KING CURTIS (ten; spoken intro on –4, gtr on –3), Bobby Wood (pno/elec pno), Bobby Emmons (org), Reggie Young, R.F. Taylor (gtrs), Tommy Cogbill (bs), Gene Chrisman (dms). On –1 add: Gene "Bowlegs" Miller (tpt), Jimmy Mitchell, Charles Chalmers (tens), Floyd Newman (bari). Unk. strings on –2, prob. arr. Ralph Burns, overdubbed in New York, September 27, 1967. Unk. vbs on –5. Prod. Tom Dowd & Tommy Cogbill. Supervised Jerry Wexler.

Memphis. July 5, 1967.

67C-12768 Memphis Soul Stew –1-4   Atco 6511; Atlantic 13135;

>Atco LP 231; LP 266;
>
>Atlantic LP 8191; LP 8209;
>
>LP 18198; LP 81666-3; LP
>
>81708; LP 82198-1;
>
>Warner Special Products
>
>LP 2000-1/2.

67C-12769 When A Man Loves A Woman –2 Atco LP 231

67C-12770 Blue Nocturne –3   Atco 6511

67C-12771 C.C. Rider –1-5   Atco 6711; LP 231

Note: Date given is per main Atlantic files; but King Curtis' files read "New York, July 19, 1967", which is probably when the tapes were received in the New York Atlantic offices. "Memphis Soul Stew" is shown in Curtis' files as "Soul Recipe (Memphis Soul Stew)", and was also registered at BMI under the name of "My Father's Pot". The tune also appears on a Time/Life Records 2-LP set entitled "On The Soul Side II", the number of which is not to hand.

KING CURTIS & THE KINGPINS: King Curtis (ten/alt; spoken intro on –1); unk. pno, org, gtr, Jerry Jemmott (elec bs), unk. dms. Add unk. elec-pno on –3, vbs on –4. Prob. same or similar to other July, 1967 Memphis sessions. On –2 add Joe Newman, Melvin Lastie (tpts), King Curtis, David Newman (tens), Haywood Henry (bari), overdubbed in New York, September 26, 1967. Unk. strings on –3 arr. Ralph Burns, overdubbed in New York, September 27, 1967. Horns prob. arr. Arif Mardin. Prod. Tom Dowd & Tommy Cogbill. Supervised Jerry Wexler.

Memphis. August 24, 1967.

67C-12929 A Whiter Shade Of Pale –3 Atco 6598; LP 231

67C-12930 Cook-Out –1 Atco 6534

67C-12931 I Was Made To Love Her –2   Atco 6547; LP 231; LP 266

67C-12932 Help Me   unissued

67C-12933 I Never Loved A Man (The Way I Love You) –2 Atco 6547; LP 231

67C-12934 Ode To Billie Joe –3 Atco 6516; Atlantic 13135; Atco LP 231; LP 266 #6 R&B #28 Pop

67C-12935 In The Pocket –2   Atco 6516

67C-12936 For What It's Worth –3-4   Atco 6534; LP 231

Note: "Whiter Shade of Pale" on single (Atco 6598) is an edited version, with a renumbered matrix, 68C-14697. Editing took place on July 18, 1968. Atco 6516 "Ode To Billie Joe"/"In The Pocket" was apparently issued both as by The Kingpins (the more common) and King Curtis & The Kingpins. "In The Pocket" is co-written by Bobby Womack which may suggest his presence on the session. Also, some doubt about Jerry Jemmott's presence: he has said his first session with Curtis was "Deborah", January 4, 1968 (q.v.) for Wilson Pickett.

As a performer, King Curtis could fill a house. He continued to do session work backing Aretha Franklin and

Solomon Burke. He also appeared at the famous Fillmore West with his band playing Led Zeppelin's "Whole Lotta Love," which brought the house down.

The music world lost one of its top musicians when King Curtis was murdered in New York City on August 13, 1971. Curtis was carrying a window air-conditioning unit home to his apartment one night. There were several drug addicts on the entrance into the apartment. He asked them to move and an altercation followed in which King Curtis was stabbed to death. He is buried at Pinelawn Memorial Park, Farmingdale, Long Island, New York.

Courtesy Tom Simon, http://www.tsimon.com/curtis.htm

Discography:
1959 The Good Old Fifties—Atco
1959 Have Tenor Will Blow—Atco '
1960 King Soul—Prestige
1960 Soul Meeting—Prestige
1961 Party Time—Tru
1961 Old Gold—Tru
1962 Doin' the Dixie Twist—Tru
1962 Country Soul—Capitol
1964 Soul Serenade—Capitol
1965 Plays Hits Made by Sam Cooke
1966 That Lovin' Feelin'—Atco
1966 Live at Smalls Paradise—Atco
1967 Plays Great Memphis Hits—Atco
1967 King Size Soul—Atco
1968 Sweet Soul—Atco
1970 Everybody's Talkin'—Atco
1970 Get Ready—Atco
1971 Live at Fillmore West—Atco
1971 Blues at Montreux [live]—Atlantic

1972 Mr. Soul—Ember
1972 Soul Time—Up Front
1985 Live in New York—JSP
1995 Night Train—Prestige
It's Party Time—Ace
King Curtis & The Kingpins—Atco
One Night Stand— Sam Cooke Live at the Harlem Square Club

THE COASTERS - SESSION DISCOGRAPHY - by Claus Röhnisch
https://www.angelfire.com/mn/coasters/sessions.html

Rock Around The Clock — Bill Haley and His Comets

JOEY D'AMBROSIA TENOR

#3 R&B #1 Pop (#1 through #18 in 7 countries)

BILL HALEY

"Rock Around The Clock" (originally recorded in 1954) was the opening music in the controversial film "The Blackboard Jungle". The world was shaken as a result of "Rock Around The Clock," which went to the top of the US and UK charts. The opening rim shot on the drum would become known as "the shot heard around the world."

When the movie "The Blackboard Jungle" was shown in Britain, some teens danced in the aisles and ripped up their seats in excitement. Haley's stage show also provoked hysteria among the youth population, which soon became a serious concern to both parents and law enforcement officials.

Hello John:

Our mutual friend Joey Arminio gave me your email address. Yes--I worked with two of the greatest saxmen in Rock & Roll:

Rudi Pompilli and Joe D'Ambrosio; both of Bill Haley & his Comets (I was Bill Haley's lead guitarist from 1974 through 1976).

Joey was actually the original sax man and played on Haley's biggest hits "Shake Rattle & Roll" and of course "Rock Around The Clock" in 1954 and '55, on Decca Records. In 1955, he and two other band members left over a salary disagreement and formed The Jodimars, who recorded for Capitol Records. Joey's instrumental showpiece was "Huckleberry."

His replacement on the Comets was Rudi, who'd previously worked with the Ralph Marterie Orchestra. Rudi did get to play on the rest of Haley's Decca recordings; the later hits being "Razzle Dazzle"; "The Saints' Rock & Roll"; "See Ya Later, Alligator"; "Rock-A-Beatin' Boogie"; and "Skinny Minnie." His own show-stopping compositions were "Calling All Comets" and "Rudy's Rock" (also on Decca). Rudi remained in the Comets for the rest of his life, passing away from cancer in 1976. His final album was his own "The Sax That Changed The World" on the Swedish label, Sonet Records.

In October 1987, Original Comets' drummer Dick Boccelli and I got the original 1954 Comets back together for the Philadelphia Music Awards-the only member missing was Steel Guitarist Billy Williamson, who retired in the middle 1960's.

Anyhow, call me and we can discuss all this at length. Visit my website, our two song sample are surf-styled instrumentals featuring sax!
https://www.facebook.com/BillTurnerBlueSmoke/photos/?ref=page_internal

Your Pal, Bill Turner 3/7/07

For Bill Haley & the Comets fans;

I assume you just want to stick with US and UK charts and not include recordings like 1961's "Florida Twist", a Rudy Pompilli instrumental, which was a major Haley hit on Orfeon Records in Mexico. I don't know the chart position, but at one point it was the most successful single ever released in Mexico (or so I've heard).

One of the Bill Haley fan club newsletters from the early '60s reports that a song called 'Chick Safari' (recorded for Warner Brothers in 1961) actually made a very high chart placement in India of all places. But that's hearsay. There's sax on it (Pompilli again) but nothing too notable.

In terms of non-Top 40 recordings that are felt to have made an impact on sax players, I can't speak to what players might think, but the following Haley recordings (all of which, again, I can provide you with MP3s of for your reference) are notable:

1953: Live It Up / Farewell-So Long-Goodbye (Essex Records) - Tony Lance (baritone). This was Haley's first single using a saxophone.

1954: Straight Jacket (Essex Records) – Joey D'Ambrosia (sax). D'Ambrosia's first sax work with Haley, and a notable instrumental of the time (but non-charting).

1955: The Jodimars - Well Now Dig This (Capitol Records) - D'Ambrosia (sax). Arguably the best known recording by this Comets spin-off group. No solo, but Joey's riffs drive the song.

1955: The Jodimars – Eat Your Heart Out Annie – D'Ambrosia. Another sax-driven melody, though no solo.

1956: The Jodimars – Midnight (D'Ambrosia) - the only instrumental the band released, featuring Joey.

1956: Calling All Comets (Decca) - Rudy Pompilli. Non-single release on the Rock and Roll Stage Show LP, a saxophone instrumental that was also performed in the film "Don't Knock the Rock". This one was likely influential.

1959 (but recorded 1958): Joey's Song (Decca) - Pompilli instrumental that was a low-placing chart hit in 1959.

1960 (but recorded 1959) - Skokiaan (Decca) - Pompilli's sax plays a major role in this instrumental, which was Haley's last chart hit in America before the 1974 reissue of Clock.

1960: Tamiami (Warner Brothers) - Pompilli. I remember reading that this non-rock and roll instrumental registered on Billboard's "Bubbling Under" charts, making it the closest thing to a chart hit Haley had after leaving Decca.

In terms of the Mexican recordings, Haley recorded many instrumentals for Orfeon between 1961 and 1966 (Rudy Pompilli on all though a few might have also featured a second sax by Mike Shay). Florida Twist and a 1966 recording, Land of 1000 Dances are the only tracks I have heard referred to as chart hits down there, but there may have been others because the Comets were really popular (even hosting a TV show) for several years.

One later recording that might be of note is "Rudy's Rock: The Sax that Changed the World", an LP which was released by "Rudy Pompilli and the Comets" on Sonet Records of Sweden in 1975 or 76 (it was recorded in 1975). It was a solo album Rudy did without Haley, to give him a chance to do some final recordings before he succumbed to lung cancer. There is some great sax work by him on this album (which, sadly, did not chart and remains the only Comets-related Sonet material not to be reissued).

As always, I hope this helps.

Cheers!
Alex Frazer-Harrison
3/10/07

370

Rudy's Rock-Bill Haley and His Comets

Pop #34   #26 UK
Rudy Pompilli – Tenor

RUDY POMPILLI
Photo/bio courtesy of Rik Hull-www.billhaley.com

Joey D'Ambrosia left Bill Haley in September 1955 to form the Jodimars. "Rock-a-Beatin' Boogie" was the first session for Rudy Pompilli.

Rudy Pompilli joined the Comets in 1955. For the next twenty years, he remained at Bill Haley's side through the good times and the not-so-good times.

Pompilli was born into the Italian immigrant community of Chester, Pennsylvania. He took up the saxophone and early on it began to dominate his life. He quickly gained a reputation on the local circuit that brought him to the attention of the Ralph Marterie Orchestra. In 1953, Rudy was voted best new saxophonist by the readers of Downbeat magazine. The same year he recorded with the orchestra a cover version of Haley's "Crazy Man Crazy." Little did he realize that he would become part of the rock and roll revolution.

In 1955, Haley was looking for musicians to replace Joey d'Ambrosio, Dick Richards, and Marshall Lytle, all of whom had left the Comets to form their own group the Jodimars. Rudy, along with Ralph Jones who later became the Comets drummer, had been working on a jazz program on WPWA in Chester when he first became acquainted with Bill. Rudy was very well thought of around Chester, where his all night jam sessions were legendary. He played regularly at the Nite Cap lounge under the name of Rudy Pell; his signature tune was "When The Saints Go Marching In." This was a show stopper—Rudy would march off the stage playing his saxophone, cross the club and climb onto the bar, blowing furiously as he arch-stepped down the bar (never spilling a drink). Then he would jump to the floor and start snake dancing, with more and more of the crowd following him, while he played and marched into the ladies' room, into the men's room, finally emerging with a roll of toilet paper which he would fling across the club, out of the club itself, and into the parking lot.

Rudy's first recording session with the band came in September 1955 when the Comets cut two classic numbers, "R-O-C-K" and "Rock-A-Beatin' Boogie."

The following year they scored a big hit with the instrumental "Rudy's Rock," which was featured in the film "Rock Around The Clock". This song allowed the band to engage in some on-stage antics that became a Comets trademark—Rudy would play his sax behind his back, lift it over his head, arch his back, or lie flat on the floor while Al Rex would climb onto his bass and ride it like a horse! Audiences in the mid-1950s had never seen anything like this before.

https://www.youtube.com/watch?v=RsGgcOZWQLQ
(Rudy's Rock Live)

As well as being a superb sax player, Rudy also contributed to many of the Comets' arrangements, and as the years went by this role increased until he became Haley's right hand man. He was relied upon to audition and rehearse groups of musicians for tours and recording dates and to manage the band when it went on the road. Apart from anything else, that's why, when Rudy died of lung cancer in January 1976, it hit Bill Haley hard.

*Pompilii is the correct spelling, but Bill thought it looked odd and would appear more professional if it was changed to Pompilli. Quoted from "Bill Haley" by John Swenson(c) 1982 W.H. Allen

374

Whispering Bells-The Del Vikings

BEN SMITH TENOR

#5 R&B #9 Pop

"The Del Vikings, accompanied by a small backup band composed of base personnel, primarily appeared at the NCO Service Club [when they first formed]. Lerchey recalls the combo consisted of George Upshaw (not Gene), sax, Joe Lopes, guitar, Peoples on drums, and a long- forgotten stand-up bass." Courtesy; Carl Janusek from issue 42 of Echoes Of The Past (1997).

Quite apart from their musical achievements, the band were also one of the first 'racially integrated' groups to have success. The band included both White and Black members.

The single was originally released on the tiny Fee Bee label in December 1956. But it soon became evident that this song had major hit potential. So Fee Bee leased the rights to Dot Records, who had a big enough distribution network to handle a major national hit. The song went as high as #4 on the pop chart and remained in the Top 40 for 31 weeks.

The song was a huge seller for the time, selling more than 1 million copies by the end of 1957.

Courtesy;https://rateyourmusic.com/release/single/the_del l_vikings/come_go_with_me___how_can_i_fin d_true_love/

According to: http://www.uncamarvy.com/DelVikings/delvikings.html;

According to Marv Goldberg:

"At their next session (held in Cleveland, Ohio, at a better studio than the Penn-Sheraton had), Kripp Johnson led both "Whispering Bells" and "Don't Be A Fool." Averbach wasn't happy with the takes and had them re-record both songs at an even bigger Chicago studio (ultimately overdubbing Ben Smith's saxophone over "Whispering Bells").The tunes were released in May 1957 on both Fee Bee and Dot (mangling Kripp's name to "Krips" on both labels) and "Whispering Bells" became the Del Vikings second big smash, although not as big as "Come Go With Me": it rose to #5 (R&B) and #9 (Pop)."

Another website entry for "Whispering Bells" also gives credit to Ben Smith; Dot 15592 (original) USA, May 1957

Words & Music by: Side A – Fred Lowery, Clarence Quick; Side B – Clarence Quick Musicians: Corinthian "Kripp" Johnson (lead vocals), Norman Wright (tenor), ClarenceQuick (bass vocals), Don "Gus" Backus (second tenor), David Lerchey (baritone), Joe Lopes (guitar), Ben Smith (sax), others unknown

Recording sessions: Universal Recorders, Chicago, IL, 1957
Highest chart positions: US #9, US R&B #5

Follow up response from Marv Goldberg;
Hi, John,
"What a long and rambling reply to tell you nothing.

I managed to remember that much of what I wrote used, as its framework, an article by Carl Janusek (sadly now deceased) from issue 42 of *Echoes Of The Past* (1997).

Later in the article, Joe Lopes told him (or, at least in a section where he mentions talking to Lopes): "Averbach wasn't pleased with the Way Out session ["Whispering

Bells", recorded in Cleveland] so he rerecorded the group in Chicago at Universal International. Even with rhythmical guitar accompaniment, Averbach felt the number was still lacking a vital musical element a vital musical element a sax. Averbach took the master tape to Bell Sound in New York. There a saxophonist, named Ben Smith, dubbed in the tenor parts."

This is where I got the info from.
Hope this helps."Best,
Marv
Mon,
Dec 30, 2019 7:51 am

Come Go With Me also features one of the absolute classic openings of any doo-wop song. It goes: "*Dom, dom, dom, dom, dom-dee-doobie, dom*".

The song appeared on the movie soundtrack of *American Grafitti* and is one of the benchmark songs for inventive, melodious doo-wop. Indeed, this song is often mentioned as one of the most perfectly constructed vocal group records of all time. According to some critics, their real achievement was to mix the new rock sound with traditional R&B vocal group techniques. It is for this they are regarded as true innovators in this field.

THE DEL VIKINGS: *Kripp Johnson, Norm Wright, David Lerchey, Clarence Quick, William Blakely (vcls), prob. King Curtis (ten) on –1, unk. pno, gtr, bs, dms.*

New York? c. October, 1958

YW-10942   Flat Tire –1   Mercury 71390

YW-10943   How Could You   Mercury 71390

Note: The personnel shown is taken from what looks like the most authoritative article on the group's recordings – on the sleeve notes to Collectables cd 8809. It is acknowledged, however, that there have been sharp differences of opinion on the line-up!

I'm Walking—Fats Domino

HERB HARDESTY   TENOR

#1 R&B #4 Pop

Photo Courtesy Herb Hardesty

Herbert Hardesty was born March 3, 1925 in New Orleans, LA. His music studies began at an early age at school, private lessons and later at Dillard University. Additional training came from the musicians in big bands and small groups performing bebop and jazz along with the blues and rock and roll of the day.

Hardesty has recorded with many artists in cities such as New Orleans, New York and California. He began his first U.S. tour with Roy Brown, a famous New Orleans Blues singer who had many hits including "Good Rockin' Tonight." He returned to New Orleans and continued to work with big bands which demanded excellent readers to handle the sight-reading. After two years, Herbert decided to form his own band and, as a result of his reading ability and distinctive solo style, he was called to work in local recording studios with many new artists, including Lloyd Price. His tenor solo was featured on Prices' "Lawdy Miss Claudy." However, it is through his Top 40 hits by Fats Domino that many saxophonists know the upbeat "good feelin" solo style made famous by Herbert Hardesty.

Hardesty continues to appear as a guest soloist on many albums. He recently recorded with Al Hirt, Pete Fountain and Tom Waits. He also appears on the 1992 recording by Dr. John and is due to perform on a recording by the legendary Count Basie Band. And he continued to travel with Fats Domino serving as his band director throughout the world until the late 90's.

Hardesty was included in movie soundtracks; The Blue Brothers, Any Which Way You Can, Shake, Rattle, and Roll, The Girl Can't Help It, and Let The Good Times Roll. Television shows include The Merv Griffin Show, Ed Sullivan, David Letterman, Steve Allen, Austin City Limits, Dinah Shore, Starsky and Hutch, Andy Williams, and Perry Como.

Herbert Hardesty plays a Selmer Mark VI and a Super Action 80 which was presented to him by Selmer during a concert in Paris. He uses an Otto Link #10 mouthpiece and Rico Royal #3 and La Voz medium reeds. Asked about his approach to performance, Herb Hardesty states, "I believe in good tone and never to overblow the horn".

12/9/2007
"Dear Mr Laughter;

Thanks for your email. I would love a copy of the book. Thanks again and the best in life"

Herbert Hardesty

Photo courtesy of Palo Tung,
New Orleans Jazz Festival, 2002, Fairmont Hotel

"Honky Tonk" (Parts 1 and 2) — Bill Doggett

CLIFFORD SCOTT   TENOR

#1 R&B #2 POP

Courtesy of Polly Harrison

Clifford Scott was born December 21, 1928, in San Antonio, Texas. He began playing at the Keyhole Club in 1946. He worked with Lionel Hampton from 1948 to 1950. He performed with the R&B bands of Roy Milton and Roy Brown until 1953. He rejoined Hampton again, then left in 1954 to study music in New York and joined Bill Doggett in 1956. While with Doggett, the classic "Honky Tonk" was recorded. His four part tenor solo with the trademark intro and thumping R&B filled airwaves and dance halls across the nation for several years. It was performed in every club, bar, and roadhouse imaginable and by many bands that were fortunate to have a sax player. It also introduced many young sax players to the unique "flutter tongue" technique used in the fourth solo. Clifford Scott's tone, technique, and overall style in "Honky Tonk" would have a far reaching effect on many sax players for years to come.

In 1961, he left for Los Angeles to work at the Parisian Room. He moved back to San Antonio in 1976 and was active until his death on April 19, 1993.

"Honky Tonk" came together in February, 1956, during the many one-night stands the group played coast to coast. At first hearing, there was nothing fancy about it. However, Doggett knew he had a potential dance hit as night after night he received positive response from the crowd. "Honky Tonk" was recorded for King Records in its New York studio on June 16, 1956. The success of "Honky Tonk" was a two-edged sword. The group received offers for numerous bookings but most were to appear in rock and roll settings, and the group did not consider themselves rock and roll.

The following comes from John Broven's sleeve notes for the CD *"Honky Tonk!"* - Ace 761. "Honky Tonk" was conceived by Clifford Scott and Billy Butler (who played guitar in Doggett's combo) in an informal hotel room jam session before a dance in Lima, Ohio. That night, on stage and without rehearsal, Butler told Bill Doggett and drummer Shep Shepherd to "just play a shuffle" and when they got through the people started to applaud. They wouldn't get off the dance floor, they just continued to stand there and applaud "more, more, more." So, they did it again, played some other tunes and had an intermission, and when they came back the audience started yelling "We wanna hear that tune!" And they didn't even have a name for it. When the band got back to New York, they set up a recording session with a studio down on 31st Street. The engineer turned the machine on, he goes out to take a smoke - he wasn't regulating the controls, he wasn't doing anything - and Doggett's band went on and just played. When they started to stop, he said "Keep it up!", which they did and that's how it became a two-sided record. "Honky Tonk", parts 1 & 2, went to # 2 on the pop charts and # 1 on the R&B charts in 1956. Writing credit goes to B. Doggett, S. Shepherd, C. Scott and B. Butler.

Honey Tonk has been covered nearly 90 times, although not always with the same title.

https://secondhandsongs.com/work/3761/versions#nav-entity

King Curtis
https://www.youtube.com/watch?v=XSIJzEijOl0
Lee Allen and Paul Gayten- titled "Driving Home"
https://www.youtube.com/watch?v=brA_Gvdo2uc&list=OLAK5uy_mtDXTLxwG6jVwQuJf1gp_rCbcPBIqcDwg&index=20

R&B GOLD RECORD/BILLBOARD CHART BUSTER BILL DOGGETT'S HONKY TONK TURNS 50 [June 16th 1956-2006]

"Honky Tonk", the hugely popular 1956 R&B Instrumental Gold Record of Jazz Pianist/Hammond B2 Organ Innovator, Bill Doggett..

Recorded by King Records on June 16th, 1956 in New York, this famous R&B instrumental sold over 1 million 500 copies, topped the Billboard charts for the entire summer of 1956 and was #2 nationally, second to Elvis Presley's "Heartbreak Hotel."

"Honky Tonk" was recorded as Parts 1 and 2 of King Records 78rpm# 4950 and featured the now legendary guitar and sax solo work of Combo members, Billy Butler and Clifford Scott, the cool drum work of Shep Shepard crowned by the innovative Hammond organ work of Doggett.

Historically, "Honky Tonk" was the breakthrough crossover R&B instrumental to be etched into the Soul of an American cultural and musical earthquake of the summer of 1956, called Rock n Roll. The Rock and Roll Hall of Fame and Museum in Cleveland honors "Honky Tonk" as one of the top 500 songs that shaped Rock n' Roll.

Also earning Billboard's Top Crown Award and Top R&B Combo Award, along with Cash Box's Most Programmed Instrumental Combo, "Honky Tonk" was recently inducted into The Hall of Fame of Memphis' The Blues Foundation in May 2006.

Remembering "Honky Tonk", the top R&B instrumental of 1956, Sock Hops and High School Proms, a landmark recording that laid the foundation of inspiration for Rhythm and Blues and Jazz Organists and Combos for decades to come."

-Bill Doggett II, nephew/namesake of Honky Tonk Bill Doggett.

#35 (#11 R&B) SOFT—BILL DOGGETT
CLIFFORD SCOTT   FLUTE LEAD
THOMAS "BEANS" BOWLES (SOLO) BARITONE

Harold Thomas "Beans" Bowles
(May 7 1926 - January 29, 2000)
COURTESY: "THE MEN OF MOTOWN"

Harold Thomas "Beans" Bowles was an American baritone sax player in the session band the Funk Brothers of independent labels Motown Records.

The tall (1.88 meters or 6 feet 2 inches) Bowles began in 1935 with the clarinet, at 16 he was a professional saxophone player. He studied from 1944 at Wayne State University in Detroit, but the pharmacy study broke in favor of staying with the U.S. Navy, where he played in a U.S. Navy Band.

The jazz-oriented Bowles preferred playing his flute and baritone saxophone and was Principal Flute in Rhythm & Blues. He then worked from 1949 in the house band at the Detroit Flame Show Bar, headed by Maurice King with.

Billie Holiday came there on from 8 July 1949 and was one of the stars, which he was allowed to accompany. The cigarette license in the bar was to Gwen Gordy, sister of

Berry Gordy Jr. Through this connection, Bowles knew Berry Gordy Jr.

Bowles' first recordings were seen Bill Doggett's "Soft" and "Shindig" (Baritone saxophone solo), created on 17 July 1957 in Chicago (Instrumentation: Doggett / organ, Clifford Scott / Tenor Saxophone + Flute, Bowles / baritone, Billy Butler / guitar, Johnny Pate / bass guitar and Shep Shepard / drums).

https://www.youtube.com/watch?v=FDj8XKRcX3U (Shindig)

Bowles and his band had Marv Johnson in January 1958 in "Once Upon aTime" for the little Kudo label (# 663; "with the Band of Harold" Beans "Bowles") accompanied.

Berry Gordy had the Rhythm & Blues singer Marv Johnson as the first artist of his record label Tamla Records. Its first single, was mostly produced by Sonny Woods - "Come to Me" (Tamla # 101), which was created in December 1958 and on 21 January 1959, on the market. /Players were already played the core occupation of the Funk Brothers Eddie Willis / Joe Messina (guitar), Bowles (saxophone/flute), James Jamerson (bass), Joe Hunter (piano) and Benny Benjamin (drums). Bowles intoned a lively flute solo, the song gave it an unusual sound.

The low and fluctuating salary as a freelance musician forced Bowles to have to queue Tamla and Motown by; he was following the recommendation of Gordy's sister Esther Edwards.

He was first a member of the Swinging Tigers ("Snake Walk Pt I/II" , Tamla # 54024; June 1959)…

https://www.youtube.com/watch?v=aRzyllMExR4

…the first instrumental recording with Motown and also the first composition for Smokey Robinson (Accompaniment:

Jamerson, Benjamin Bowles). He then accompanied the Miracles in the titles The Feeling is so Fine/Bad Girl (saxophone; September 1959).

Bowles' own band "Swinging Dashikis", however, was used from 1960 with the Motown artists on tour but was not intended to be a studio band. 1960- Bowles acted as a producer for Motown's most valuable artist time Marv Johnson, for whom he was also known as Road Manager, driver and tour guide available.

Together with saxophonist Ron Wakefield, Bowles was a member of the Twistin 'Kings and opened up for the young Motown Group (Whitehouse "Twist/Twist Christmas"-

November 27, 1961 Congo Twist Parts 1 & 2, December 18, 1961).

Outside of Motown, Bowles appeared in May 1963 with the baritone sax solo in the instrumental part of the Chiffons hit "One Fine Day" on. (According to research; "ONE FINE DAY" - CHIFFONS - ARTIE KAPLAN (solo) BARITONE- Played on a Buescher bari per Artie Kaplan).

Participation in Motown Hits

At that time, he was already an integral part of the Motown session band The Funk Brothers.

He can be heard especially on the hits "I Want A Guy" (Supremes ; flute; taken in December 1960), "Do You Love Me" (The Contours ; tenor saxophone; June 29, 1962) "Stubborn Kind of Fellow" (Marvin Gaye ; piccolo ; 23 . July 1962), "You Really Got a Hold on Me" (Miracles, November 9, 1962), "Heatwave"-Vandellas, June 1963)

According to research; HEAT WAVE-MARTHA & THE VANDELLAS - ANDREW "MIKE" TERRY BARITONE),

"One More Heartache" (Marvin Gaye; January 1966) "What's Going On" (Marvin Gaye, February 1971).

He claimed to have composed Stevie Wonder's "Fingertips Part I" (21 May 1963), but never received his share of the musical song royalties. Bowles was called the main composer of the song, in particular because of the harmonica solos, which he rehearsed with Stevie Wonder. The album version features a pure Bowles Flute Instrumentation, Wonder only plays bongos.

On October 3, 1966 Bowles accompanied The Temptations , their manager, with their first live album "Temptations Live! "

Besides his work as a session musician, Bowles was Road Manager from January 1961 the "Motor Town Special" (in April 1963 renamed to "Motor Town Revue"), a tour of the Motown artists with buses across the USA. He oversaw the appointments made for hotel accommodation and advised the young artists musically. In addition, he arranged courses where the artists were taught the correct behavior in public.

Bowles was with Motown from the beginning, making it one of the longest remaininginstrumentalists of the record label. He was, next to Benny Benjamin, the oldest member of the Funk Brothers.

In June 1972, the Motown group from Detroit to Los Angeles moved, that broke the Funk Brothers apart. He passed away in 2000.

Ain't That A Shame" — Fats Domino

Wendell DuConge   Alto
Herb Hardesty (Solo) Tenor

#1 R&B. #10 Pop

The DuConge family was well-established in the music community of New Orleans. The legendary Oscar DuConge fronted his own bands. Wendell DuConge was influenced by his father, tenor saxophonist Earl DuConge as well as his uncles, pianist Adolphus DuConge, trumpeter Albert DuConge, and Peter DuConge, who played three instruments and spent the 30s in Europe. Wendell is credited on 20 different recording sessions between 1951 and 1958. After the big band music began to disappear in the 50s, Fats Domino employed talented players such as DuConge in his rock & roll music.

Another website indicates; On "Ain't That a Shame," the sax players are Herb Hardesty on lead, with Samuel Lee and Buddy Hagens; Walter "Papoose" Nelson on guitar; Billy Diamond, bass; Cornelius Tenoo Coleman, drums; and Antoine "Fats" Domino on piano and vocal.
https://www.npr.org/2000/05/01/1073610/aint-that-a-shame

Another website indicates; "Ain't It A Shame", Antoine 'Fats' Domino, (A. Domino &

D. Bartholomew) Imperial Single #5348, Session producer: Dave Bartholomew (Imperial records - Lew Chudd), Recorded: Mar 15, 1955, Pop Chart #10 Jul 16, 1955, Cosimo Matassa's Studio - New Orleans, LA. Fats Domino - piano & vocal, Joe Harris - alto sax, Herb Hardesty & Clarence Hall -

tenor sax, Alvin 'Red' Tyler - baritone sax, Ernest McLean - guitar, Frank Fields - bass, (The Great) Earl Palmer - drums. Album: 'My Blue Heaven' -The Best of Fats Domino. Imperial/Capitol-EMI, 1990 CDP-7-92808-2.
https://www.letras.com.br/Fats-Domino/aint-it-a-shame

"Bartholomew and Matassa also put more thought into the production than was normal at this time. When mastering Domino's records, now that Matassa's studio had finally switched to tape from cutting directly on to wax, they would speed up the tape slightly -- a trick which made Domino's voice sound younger, and which emphasised the beat more. This sort of thing is absolutely basic now, but at the time it was extraordinarily unusual for any rhythm and blues records to have any kind of production trickery at all. It also had another advantage, because as Cosimo Matassa would point out, it would change the key slightly so it wouldn't be in a normal key at all. So when other people tried to cover Domino's records "they couldn't find the damn notes on the piano!"

#1   Ain't That A Shame—Pat Boone   ?
     TENOR

I could not confirm the names of the recording session players for Pat Boone. His agent indicated that Mr. Boone recalled the name Justin Tubbs as being the sax soloist. However, according to a website by Don Rose:

His [Joe Daley's] career has been diverse: he was one of the "brothers" in a Woody Herman Herd of 1950—51, and worked with the Maynard Ferguson and Nelson Riddle bands. He also played tenor in the studio band that backed

Pat Boone for most of his recording sessions during the 1950s.

Daley also stated in an interview for the Jazz Institute of Chicago, "I did about 30 sides for Pat Boone on Dot—I played a lot of solos but they wouldn't let me blow. They would say, "You're playing too good, man." I needed the money, but I'm glad they didn't put my name on the records."

Another name that was suggested is Justin Gordon. Research shows that Gordon apparently recorded most of the twin sax parts on the Billy Vaughn hits.

394

Rockin' Around The Christmas Tree—
Brenda Lee

Boots Randolph Tenor

#2 Pop   (#2 through #77 in 29 countries and has charted from 1960 through 2023)

"Rocking Around The Christmas Tree" is still rocking n' rolling after more than 60 years, part of Christmas tradition for many listeners from around the world. Initially released in 1959, it wasn't until 1960 that it became a hit peaking at #3 on the Pop charts.

Brenda "Little Miss Dynamite" Lee was a hit making machine with 47 pop charts hits. Brenda's first recording session took place in July 30 and 31, 1956 when she was eleven years old. Her first chart entry was in 1957, "One Step At A Time", which peaked at # 43 pop and # 15 country.

After a long string of pop hits, Lee became a country artist, with nineteen country Top 40 hits. She was inducted into the Country Music Hall Of Fame in 1997 and into the Rock and Hall of Fame in 2002. In 2009 she received a Grammy Lifetime Achievement Award.

"Rocking Around The Christmas Tree" wasn't the only time that Brenda and Boots played together e.g.:

#7 (#4 U.K.) SWEET NOTHIN'S—BRENDA LEE
BOOTS RANDOLPH   TENOR

#6 (#19 R&B) THAT'S ALL YOU GOTTA DO—BRENDA LEE
BOOTS RANDOLPH   TENOR

#4   (#22 UK) DUM DUM—BRENDA LEE   BOOTS RANDOLPH   TENOR

BOOTS RANDOLPH

#35 YAKETY SAX
BOOTS RANDOLPH   TENOR

#2 RETURN TO SENDER—ELVIS PRESLEY
    BOOTS RANDOLPH   BARITONE

"Return to Sender" was recorded on March 27, 1962, at Radio Recorders in Hollywood and featured Presley's long-time cohorts Scotty Moore on guitar and D.J. Fontana on drums, Barney Kessel on electric guitar, Tiny Timbrell on acoustic guitar, Ray Siegal on double bass, Dudley Brooks on piano, Boots Randolph on baritone saxophone and the Jordanaires on backing vocals. The group was augmented by various session musicians including drummer Hal Blaine.

This site previously gave Bobby Keys the credit but it has since been removed; http://en.wikipedia.org/wiki/Bobby_Keys;

In Bobby Keys' book titled "Every Night's A Saturday Night", copyright 2012, Keys states on page 38 that he went to the L.A. studio with his old baritone sax and recorded the sax line on "Return To Sender". He indicates that Elvis Presley was in the studio.

This incorrect "claim" is also stated on many other websites by using the name of the song and his name.

The following statement appears on "Rolling Stones: Sax Master Bobby Keys Remembered:"

"Keys has claimed that he played the sax solo on Dion's hit "The Wanderer" (1961). If Keys did play the solo part, it was re-done on Dion's hit record on Capitol Records by tenor player Buddy Lucas. It was, in fact, Buddy Lucas who played the solo on that recording. "

Bobby Keys, claimed he performed the solo at the instigation of pianist Glen D. Hardin, in his 2012 memoir "Every Night's A Saturday Night". However, Hardin did not meet Presley until February 1970, when he joined his touring band. In addition, his claim is not supported by RCA, Ernst Jorgensen (the official archivist for Presley's recordings), or session logs".

https://en.wikipedia.org/wiki/Return_to_Sender_(song)

Other sites that mistakenly cite Bobby Keys as the sax player:

https://www.kut.org/post/sixth-rolling-stone-was-west-texan-named-bobby-keys

("He toured with Buddy Knox and pop star Bobby Vee. He put his signature sax sound on Dion's "The Wanderer," and Elvis Presley's "Return to Sender."")

Another site;

https://offthetracks.co.nz/r-i-p-bobby-keys/

("The Bobby Keys highlight reel is something to behold – working with all of The Beatles and of course The Stones, and as a teenager he played the baritone sax solo on Elvis Presley's "Return To Sender.")

Another site;

("The memorable opening bars and backing on baritone saxophone is often credited to Boots Randolph, but was in fact played by Bobby Keys.")

Another site;

http://www.classicbands.com/BobbyKeysInterview.html

("Q - When you were 18 years old, you played on Elvis' record "Return To Sender". A - Yeah.

Q - Were you an Elvis fan? That must've been a big deal for you.

A - Oh, I was an enormous Elvis fan, man. (Laughs) At one time I had Elvis pictures all over the walls of my bedroom. I wanted to be Elvis more than anything else in the world, (Laughs) but I wasn't. It didn't work out that I was ever gonna be. So, I gave up on that. It was quite an experience.

Q - Did you like Elvis when you met him?

A - Oh, yeah. He was really cool. I didn't hang around long. "Thank-you for fillin' in." They had another guy scheduled for the session, but he couldn't make it 'cause his wife's father died or something happened in the family. So, I was a last minute addition. He was just fine. A real nice feller.")

Another site;

https://www.cleveland.com/ministerofculture/2012/02/rolling_stone_sax_man_bobby_ke.html

("After following composer and performer Leon Russell to Los Angeles, he played sax on both Dion's "The Wanderer" and Elvis Presley's "Return to Sender."")

"JOHN, AS YOU MAY OR MAY NOT KNOW, STEVE DOUGLAS AND JAY MIGLIORI WERE THE SAX BASE FOR PHIL SPECTOR AND THE WALL OF SOUND. I HIRED MANY GREAT SAX PLAYERS, AND YOU HAVE COVERED THEM ALL.

I DON'T RECALL THE NAME BOBBY KEYS (PERHAPS HE WAS FROM A DIFFERENT LOCAL, AS WAS BOOTS, WHO CAME OUT FOR MANY OF THE ELVIS SESSIONS).

I DON'T SEE MR. KEYS ON MY PERSONAL CONTRACTORS LIST OR THE LOCAL 47 DIRECTORY. I DID HIRE STEVE DOUGLAS FOR THE SIDELINE OF "RETURN TO SENDER" (YOU'LL SEE US ON CAMERA WITH ELVIS). MR. KAHGAN ASKED ME TO CONTRACT THE SIDELINE MEN FOR THE FILM). I CAN'T REMEMBER IF STEVE DID THE BASIC TRACK WITH US.

THE CONTRACTOR IN THIS CASE WAS PARAMOUNT PICTURES HOUSE CONTRACTOR. THE GENTLEMAN, WHO HAS SINCE PASSED AWAY, WAS ONE OF THE GREAT CONTRACTORS IN L.A. HE DID ALL OF THE HIRING FOR FILMS IN L.A. FOR PARAMOUNT. HE WAS THE MAN THAT OWNED ALL OF THE PROPERTY THAT PARAMOUNT PICTURES SITS ON TODAY. PART OF THE SALE WAS THAT HE WOULD BE THEIR MUSICAL CONTRACTOR FOR A MINIMUM OF 50 YEARS. HE MADE IT TO
ALMOST 60 YEARS.

I HAVE NO IDEA WHO MIGHT HAVE ALL OF THOSE PARAMOUNT CONTRACTS TODAY OR IF THEY EVEN STILL EXIST. I WISH THAT I COULD HELP YOU ON YOUR GIGANTIC WORKS. IT ALL LOOKS GREAT. I CAN ONLY WISH YOU THE VERY BEST IN YOUR ENDEAVOR. LOOKING AT ALL THAT STUFF WAS A GREAT TRIP DOWN MEMORY LANE FOR ME AND I'M SURE THAT IT WILL ALSO BE FOR MANY FOLKS."

,,,, HAL BLAINE
7/9/2009

"This is Boots talking about it in an interview with the Fort Wayne Reader in
2005:
"I used to play at this place called the Blue Bar in Evansville. It was quite a watering trough, know what I mean? A friend from there took me to Nashville where Chet Atkins and a lot of folks were just getting started. I did soundtracks with Elvis Presley. The first thing I did with him, I played baritone sax on "Return to Sender." I'm the only sax player that's ever recorded a sax solo on one of Elvis

Presley's tunes — "Reconsider, Baby." Just a blues thing, you know, but I'm playing sax on it".

https://www.youtube.com/watch?v=g2Bb-KGHdgk (Reconsider Baby with extended sax part)

According to Ernst Jorgnsen; "Bobby Keys DID NOT play the sax on the "Return to Sender" track. Boots Randolph was flown to Los Angeles with Scotty Moore and D. J. Fontana a few days before recording began and rehearsed the songs that had been chosen for the movie. Elvis arrived a few days later and would record them with Boots, Scotty, D. J., and some session musicians from Radio Recorders".

#16   (UK #24) MR. BASS MAN—JOHNNY CYMBAL
ARTIE KAPLAN   TENOR

"John,

Nice hearing from you.

As far as the "Mr. Bassman" session, it was at Mirror Sound in New York. I don't recall the Sax Man you're looking for. I do remember Alan Lorber was the arranger and conductor; I produced with Allan Stanton as executive producer. Ronnie Bright sang bass, The Angels were the background voices, Gary Chester was the drummer, and then I draw a blank. I produced for 15 years in Nashville, and I can tell you all the musicians on those sessions.

Sorry, guess I'm not much help.

Jack Gale

11/10/2007

From a historical standpoint, credits can be misleading; however, Marc Wielage may have been referring to a later re-recording;

From the internet;

"I believe you mean Johnny Cymbal's 1963 #16 hit "Mr. Bassman." Here's my notes on this song: "18 year-old singer/songwriter Johnny Cymbal's first and only Top 40 hit (under this name). Boots Randolph played the sax on this session and deep-voiced Ronnie Bright ...Jul 22 1998 by Marc Wielage"

"Hi John,
I just received a copy of an email from Alan Lorber stating these facts to you. I am simply reconfirming his statement I was the Baritone Sax Player on that session. I also contracted the session. The session was done at Mira Sound. I don't believe that there is a tenor Sax solo on that Recording. Only a rhythm section, a baritone saxophone player and a bass singer (Ronnie Bright)

Al Stanton was the record's producer. And, of course, Johnnie sang the song.

John: Please confirm receipt of this email, so that I'll know that you received the proper information.

Best wishes and happy holidays,"
Artie Kaplan
11/21/07

"Thanks so much for the email. I remember Artie Kaplan WAS the sax player and it was a baritone, not a tenor.
Thanks so much."
Jack Gale 11/21/07
Mp3 sent to Mr. Kaplan;

Hi John,
You are right John. It is a Tenor sax. But it was me Artie Kaplan who played it.

Sorry I got the title confused with "Who Put the Bomp (In the Bomp, Bomp, Bomp)" by Barry Mann. I played Baritone Sax on that one."

   Artie Kaplan

When Boots Randolph starts "tootin' his horn," he does more than just play the saxophone.

More than just pop out music notes. And that's why his saxophone sounds like it cansing...can talk...can almost speak to deaf ears! His ability is awesome. His versatile style has no equal. And he's been bringing audiences to their feet ever since the early 1960s, when his signature song "Yakety Sax" first hit the airwaves. It took off like gangbusters and turned the young musician into a celebrity, probably before some of his friends in the hills of Kentucky could have even spelled it!

Boots (whose real name is Homer Louis Randolph) is a native of Paducah, Kentucky. Hisfather was also named Homer, and obviously it created confusion 'round home! As a result, young Homer's brother Bob tagged him with the nickname "Boots," never dreaming it would one day be the name of an international star! The Randolphs were always a creative clan, rich in musical talent, and their family band initially provided Boots with the first of his opportunities on stage. He learned to play a variety of instruments, but settled on the sax, at age sixteen. Years later, he was to make it his career choice while working for Uncle Sam, during which time he was privileged to perform with the Army band.

After his discharge in 1946, Boots Randolph began putting his "chops" to work professionally. However, it wasn't until 1961 that he moved to Nashville on the heels of his successful trademark tune—or, as he tells it, "that song

(Yakety Sax) is what took me out of the hills of Kentucky and put me in the hills of Tennessee!"

The song served a multitude of purposes in kicking off his early career, not only by giving him the prestige of being a hit artist, but also by opening a lot of doors to other performers. Almost instantly, the sax man was seriously being sought after as a studio musician, and he was soon playing saxophone on recording sessions for numerous stars. Boots Randolph was the first to ever play sax on recordings with Elvis, and the only one to ever play solo with him, in addition to recording on the soundtracks for 8 of his movies.

Boots also played on such diverse recordings as Roy Orbison's "Oh, Pretty Woman," Al Hirt's "Java," REO Speedwagon's "Little Queenie," and Brenda Lee's "Rockin' 'Round The Christmas Tree." In fact, he has a thirty-year history of playing on records with Lee, including "I Want To Be Wanted" and "I'm Sorry."

An array of other artists who have added the yakety sax touch to their recordings include Chet Atkins, Buddy Holly, Floyd Cramer, Alabama, Johnny Cash, Richie Cole, Pete Fountain, Tommy Newsom, and Doc Severinsen.

Randolph's unique style of sax, coupled with the tremendous popularity on Nashville sessions in the 1960s, automatically made Randolph a major player in creating the now-famous "Nashville Sound." Without question, it was Randolph's particular blend of Dixieland jazz and swinging honky-tonk that helped Nashville music makers turn hillbilly records into a hybrid sound that literally transformed Nashville into the country music capitol of the world! And to this day, Randolph still has more calls for his "Saxy" sound at studio sessions than he can handle.

While most people only associate Randolph with his self-written, multi-million seller "Yakety Sax," he also had other gold hits on "The Shadow of Your Smile" in 1966. Plus, he "hit gold" numerous other times through recordings made with others, including "Honey In The Horn," "Java," and "Cotton Candy" by Al Hirt, not to mention the countless consecutive gold records by Elvis. In addition, Randolph had smash hit singles on "Hey, Mr. Sax Man" and "Temptation." He also has over forty albums to his credit on the Monument label.

On top of that, Randolph spent fifteen years touring with The Master's Festival of Music, which teamed him with fellow instrumentalists Chet Atkins and Floyd Cramer. Another version of that group called The Million Dollar Band played for eight years on the *Hee Haw Show*. The Million Dollar Band's members were Randolph, Atkins, Cramer, and Danny Davis, Roy Clark, Jethro Burns, Johnny Gimble, and Charlie McCoy.

He also took his "Yakety Sax" to numerous network TV shows including the *Ed Sullivan Show, Kraft Music Hall, Tonight Show with* Johnny Carson, *Merv Griffin Show, Mike Douglas Show, Joey Bishop Show, Steve Lawrence Show*, and the Boston Pops. He appeared ten times on the *Jimmy Dean Show*, and he also headlined two network specials with Pete Fountain and Doc Severinsen. More recently, he's made numerous TV appearances on TNN'S *Music City Tonight* and *Prime Time Country*.

After performing all across the country in some of the most posh clubs ever built, Boots Randolph took the plunge in 1977, borrowed half-a-million bucks to restore an historic building in Nashville Printer's Alley, and opened his own dinner club, called Boots Randolph's. He performed there on a regular basis, and enjoyed a successful run with the club for seventeen years before he called it quits.

When he closed the club, Randolph had vowed to "go fishing," but it was barely a year later, in 1996, when he found himself back in business pairing up with Danny Davis, as they embarked on a brand new venture in Nashville called The Stardust Theatre, featuring both artists in concert. Two years later, they each returned to their respective on-the-road schedules. Having headlined at almost every fair, jazz festival, and convention in thecountry—as well as performed throughout Europe—definitely puts Boots Randolph in the category of being a saxophone player with experience!

Over the years, this legendary musician has written chapter after chapter of music history, forever etched in sound, and to this day, he continues to entertain audiences with the same enthusiasm he's had since day one. It's in his blood! Boots is his name. Sax is his game! His horn is a Selmer Super 80 Series II. He uses a Bobby Dukoff D-9 mouthpiece, and a #3 Rico reed.

7/3/07

BREAKING NEWS: Saxophone legend Boots Randolph dies at 80.

TENNESSEAN.COM

Boots Randolph, Nashville's most celebrated saxophonist and a member of the city's vaunted "A-Team" of session musicians, died this afternoon after suffering a subdural hematoma last week, July 3, 2007. He was 80.

Records released before 1988 are LP's. Releases since 1988 are CDs

Boots Randolph Discography by Carl G. Cederblad.

LSP-2165 *Yakety Sax* 1960 RCA Victor

SLP-18002 *Yakety Sax* 1963 Monument

AK-44356 1988 CD CBS/Sony

SLP-18015 *Hip Boots!* 1964 Monument

GS-1455 *Boots Randolph* 1964 Guest Star

SLP-18029* *B. R. Plays 12 Monstrous Sax Hits* 1964 Monument

PA-243/244 *Just a minute* 1964 SESAC

CAS- 825 *The Yakin´ Sax Man.* 1964 RCA Camden

CAD1- 825 1987 CD RCA SP

CAS- 865 *Sweet Talk* 1965 RCA Camden

SLP-1803 *Plays More Yakety Sax* 1965 Monument

| SLP-18042 | The Fantastic Boot Randolph | Monument |
| SLP-18066 | Boots With Strings | Monument |

SLP-18082 *B. R. With the Knightsbridge Strings And Voices* 1967   Monument

CCS-0135 *Chet, Floyd & Boots Play Country Favorites* 1968   RCA Camden

SLP-18092 *Boots Randolph's Sunday Sax*   1968   Monument

AK-47069   "   1991   CD CBS/Sony

SLP-18099 *The Sound Of Boots*   1968   Monument

SLP-18111 ......*With Love* 1969   Monument

SLP-18127 *Boots And Stockings*   1969   Monument

A-22175   "   1991   CD CBS/Sony

UPS- 48-T   *Yakety Sax Meets Japanese Pops vol. 1*   1969   Jap. Monument

UPS- 56-T   *Yakety Sax Meets Japanese Pops vol. 2*   1969   Jap. Monument'

SLP-18128   *Yakety Revisited*   1969   Monument

PT-1The *Nashville Sound Of Boots Randolph*   1969   Texize

UPS- 61-T   *Yakety Sax In Hawaii*   1970   Jap. Monument

SLP-18144 *Hit Boots 1970*   1970   Monument

SLP-18147 *Boots With Brass*   1970   Monument

ULS-72/73-T *Boots Randolph Show. Live Concert In Tokyo*   1971   Jap. Monument

CXS-9003 *Yakety Sax* (double album)   1971   RCA Camden

CAS-2523 *Chet, Floyd & Boots*   1971   RCA Camden

Z-30678   *Homer Louis Randolph III*   1971   Monument

AK-47070 "   1991   CD CBS/Sony

UPS-113-T *Rock Music Best Hits* 1971   Jap. Monument

UPS-134-T *Tenor Sax In Screen Mood*   1971   Jap. Monument

MG-30963 *The World Of Boots Randolph* /2-set/ 1971 Monument

DS-632 *King Of Yakety* 1972 Columbia

SP PZS-5816 *The Magic Sax Of Boots Randolph* 1972 Columbia

SP KZ-31908 *Plays The Great Hits Of Today* 1972 Monument

DRL1-0057 *So Rare* 1973 RCA Camden

KZ-32292 *Sentimental Journey* 1973 Monument

AK-44357 " 1988 CD CBS/Sony

PZ-32912 *Country Boots* 1974 Monument

AK-44358 " 1988 CD CBS/Sony

PZ-33242 *Greatest Hits* 1974 Monument

AK-44355 " 1988 CD CBS/Sony

BZ-33852 *Yakety Sax/Yakety Revisited* [2 LP set] 1975 Monument

KZ-33803 *Cool Boots* 1975 Monument

BZ-33852 *Boots With Strings/With The Knightsbridge Strings And Voices* 1975 Monument

2V-8024

The Sounds Of Boots vol. 1 1976 REALM Rec.

(*The Country Sound of Boots/The Sentimental Sound of Boots*)

1V- 8025

The Sounds Of Boots vol. 2 1976 REALM Rec.

(*The Pop Sound Of Boots*)

Jim Dandy- Lavern Baker

Sam "The Man" Taylor   Tenor

R & B #1 Pop #17

TWEEDLEE DEE—LAVERN BAKER

SAM "THE MAN" TAYLOR - TENOR

#4 R&B. #14

LaVern Baker (born Delores Evans in 1929) was the second female artist inducted (1991) into The Rock And Roll Hall Of Fame; Aretha Franklin was the first. One of the most outstanding artists of the 1950's, her career was undercut by cover versions of her songs.

Released in late 1954, LaVern Baker's "Tweedlee Dee" hit number 4 on the R&B charts and number 14 on the pop charts. A cover by singer Georgia Gibbs, that was a note-for-note cover with LaVern's, soared to number 2 on the pop chart. LaVern Baker lobbied her congressman to change the law and make this kind of "plagiarism" illegal. No law was passed but the resulting publicity helped her career.

She had had 18 pop hits during her eleven year contract at Atlantic with 18 R&B hits that went into Top 20. Her only number one was "Jim Dandy". Other notable hits were "I Cried A Tear" (# 6 Pop Charts, # 2 R&B) in 1959 and the Leiber- Stoller classic "Saved" (1961), a gospel rocker.

She was featured in Alan Freed's rock n roll shows and appeared in Freed's movies "Rock Rock Rock" (1956) and "Mister Rock and Roll" (1957).

LAVERN BAKER *(rn: Delores Williams) (vcl), Urbie Green (tbn), Leon Cohen (alt), King Curtis (ten), Ernie Hayes (pno), Al Caiola, Everett Barksdale (gtrs), Milt Hinton (bs), Panama Francis (dms), unk. Vbs, Marcia Neil, Mike Stewart, Jerry Packer, Bill Marine (bkgnd vcls). Arr. Reggie Obrecht. Prod. Jerry Wexler & Ahmet Ertegun. Tbn, alt, vcl grp omitted on –1.*
New York. September 11, 1958

A-3131   Dix-A-Billy   Atlantic 2007
A-3132   I Cried A Tear   Atlantic 2007
A-3133   Voodoo Voodoo –1   Atlantic 2119
A-3134   I'm Leaving You –1   Atlantic LP 8071
-Roy Simonds-"King Curtis Sessionography"

https://www.uncamarvy.com/LavernBaker/lavernbaker.html

Samuel Leroy Taylor, Jr. (July 12, 1916 – October 5, 1990), known as **Sam "The Man" Taylor** A certified sax legend, Sam "The Man" Taylor's non-stop drive and power worked perfectly in swing, blues, and R&B sessions. He had a huge tone, perfect timing, and sense of drama, as well as relentless energy and spirit.

Taylor was born in Lexington, Tennessee. He attended Alabama State University, where he played with the Bama State Collegians.

Taylor began working with Scat Man Crothers and the Sunset Royal Orchestra in the late '30s. He played with Cootie Williams and Lucky Millinder in the early '40s, then worked six years with Cab Calloway. Taylor toured South America and the Caribbean during his tenure with Calloway. Then, Taylor became the saxophonist of choice for many R&B dates and one of the most requested session saxophone players in New York recording studios in the 1950s. He also replaced Count Basie as the house bandleader on Alan Freed's radio series, *Camel Rock 'n Roll Dance Party*, on CBS.

He recorded with Ray Charles, Buddy Johnson, Louis Jordan, and Big Joe Turner, among others. He also did sessions with Ella Fitzgerald and Sy Oliver. During the '60s, Taylor led his own bands and recorded in a quintet called the Blues Chasers. He currently has one session available on CD, recorded in the late '50s with Charlie Shavers and Urbie Green.

Taylor played the saxophone solo on Joe Turner's "Shake, Rattle and Roll". He also played on "Harlem Nocturne"; on "Money Honey", recorded by Clyde McPhatter and the Drifters in 1953; and on "Sh-Boom" by the Chords and many more.172

https://www.youtube.com/watch?v=zPJ7N5_o-u8

During the 1960s, he led a five-piece band, the Blues Chasers. In the 1970s, he frequently played and recorded in Japan.

Taylor died in 1990 in Crawford Long Hospital, Atlanta, Georgia.

https://adp.library.ucsb.edu/index.php/mastertalent/detail/105513/Taylor_Sam?Matrix_page=5

#25 DON'T BE ANGRY — NAPPY BROWN

One of the great rocking tenor solos from the 1950s.

"Don't Be Angry" was cut on 1 February 1955 in New York by Nappy Brown (vocal), Sam Taylor and Budd Johnson (tenor saxophone), Maurice Simon (baritone saxophone), Howard Biggs (piano), Mickey Baker (guitar), Abbie Baker (bass) and Dave Bailey (drums).") Courtesy;

https://rateyourmusic.com/release/single/nappy-brown/dont-be-angry-its-really-you/

Per Stuart Colman claims that Budd Johnson took the solo on "Don't Be Angry" by Nappy Brown.

However, according to Neil Sharpe and pro players like Sax Gordon, it's Sam "The Man" Taylor.

Roy Simonds author of "King Curtis: A Discography" (1st and 2nd eds.), writes: "Re 'Don't Be Angry': The original is almost certainly Sam Taylor."

#36 R&B #2 POP   CORRINE CORRINA — JOE TURNER
SAM "THE MAN" TAYLOR   TENOR

"Corrine Corrina" was cut in New York on 24 February 1956 by Joe Turner (vocal), Jimmy Nottingham and Dick Vance (trumpet), Earle Warren (alto saxophone), Sam "The Man" Taylor (tenor saxophone), Billy Mure and George Barnes (guitar), Lloyd Trotman (bass), Panama Francis (drums) and the Cookies (backing vocals).

https://www.youtube.com/watch?v=KFCXd9NanLY

#1   R&B   YES SIR THAT'S MY BABY — SENSATIONS
SAM "THE MAN" TAYLOR   TENOR

"Hi John,

I saw the question mark for "Yes Sir That's My Baby" by the Sensations. Michel. Ruppli's Atlantic CD-ROM mentions Sam Taylor as the sax player."

Dik 10/19/2017

THE SENSATIONS:

Yvonne Mills (lead vo) Tommy Wicks (tenor vo) Alphonso Howell (bass vo) another (vo) with **Sam Taylor** (ts) & p,g,b,dm.

(2:37) My heart cries for you (2:44) Yes Sir, that's my baby Right or wrong (2:30) Sympathy

NYC, July 29, 1955

Atco 6075; CD Coll. Choice CCM 028-2 Atco 6056, LP 33-143; Cat 90132-1 CD Coll.

Choice CCM 7160-2 unissued Atco 6056; CD Rhino RHM2-7738

"At the Sensations' first Atco recording session, the group recorded "My Heart Cries For You", "Right Or Wrong", "Yes Sir That's My Baby" and the Tommy Wicks composition, "Sympathy". From these, Atco selected "Yes Sir..." and "Sympathy" for the first release.

"Yes Sir..." featured Yvonne on lead and was intended to be the "A" side. "Sympathy" featured Tommy.

Atco had picked former Ravens producer, Howard Biggs, to do the arrangements for all Sensations' songs. The standard Atlantic musicians, including guitarist Mickey Baker and sax player Sam "The Man" Taylor, were on the session.

The Sensations brought a couple bottles of wine to the recording session to "loosen up" between songs. Being new to the big business aspects of the music field, they couldn't understand why Atco was spurning their breaks between songs and rushing them through the session. They didn't realize until later that Atco was paying each musician about $65 an hour." Courtesy;

http://citeseerx.ist.psu.edu/viewdoc/download?doi=10.1.1.730.2214&rep=rep1&type=pdf

#14 (R&B) BLUE VELVET—THE CLOVERS
SAM "THE MAN" TAYLOR   TENOR
Courtesy of Harold J. Winley, the original bass singer of The Clovers.

#24 EARLY IN THE MORNING—BOBBY DARIN
SAM "THE MAN" TAYLOR   TENOR
Bobby Darin, vocals; George Barnes, guitar; Al Chernet, guitar; Sanford Bloch, string bass; Sam "The Man" Taylor, tenor saxophone; Ernie Hayes, piano; Panama Francis, drums;Phil Krause, drums; The Helen Way Singers (Helen Way, Harriet Young, Maeretha Stewart, Theresa Merritt), background vocals; Dick Jacobs (arr)
(Some sites give credit to Boomie Richman)
"Boomie Richman played on the session of October 21, 1958 ("True Love Ways" etc.),but not on any other Buddy Holly session. Personnel for the two versions of "Early In the Morning" (Bobby Darin and Buddy Holly) was exactly the same. There are dozens of websites to back this up. So it's just Sam Taylor (on tenor, I would say)."
Dik 11/27/2008

#26 Pop MARY LOU—RONNIE HAWKINS AND THE HAWKS
SAM "THE MAN" TAYLOR TENOR

#2 Pop   MY HAPPINESS—CONNIE FRANCIS   SAM "THE MAN" TAYLOR   TENOR

BUDD JOHNSON   ALTO & TENOR

Budd Johnson was born Albert J. Johnson, December 14, 1910 in Dallas Texas and died October 20, 1984 in Kansas City. Johnson played both tenor and alto sax. He also arranged scores for the studio and was a vocalist. Johnson was a very popular freelance musician and best known for associations with Earl Hines as well as Ben Webster, Benny Goodman, Coleman Hawkins, Dizzy Gillespie, Duke Ellington, Count Basie, Billie Holiday and Big Joe Turner. He was a prime influence behind modern jazz. He recorded with Frankie Laine, Buck Clayton, Jimmy Rushing and Sarah Vaughan.

Sax Gordon writes: "I had never heard these 1945 broadcast performances by the Billy Eckstine Orchestra with Sarah Vaughan (and special guest Lena Horne) recorded at the Plantation Club in Los Angeles but I'm sure the presence of 20-ish-year-old Gene Ammons is what made me acquire the LP, a bonus being that Gene is clearly visible on the cover, identifiable by his profile and the white Brilhart mouthpiece he played at that time.

The band is ASTOUNDING. While the group is well-known to Jazz/Be-Bop fans for the incredible talent that passed through its ranks, those players weren't always well-documented as soloists in the rather scant discography of the band. This live recording allows us to hear more of young Gene Ammons as well as the much-overlooked saxist Budd Johnson who doesn't get enough credit for his very significant contributions to both Jazz and early Rhythm & Blues. In fact, Budd was also instrumental in organizing the personnel for this exceptional band as well as writing many of its cutting-edge forward-looking arrangements (other arrangements are by Tad Dameron and band trombonist Jerry Valentine) that on this live recording are performed with ultra-tight swinging excellence and at times an elegant ferocity!

On top of all that we hear, incredibly inspired and high-quality sophisticated Jazz presented as entertainment with a varied program featuring both instrumentals (with great solo contributions by the aforementioned as well as Be-Bop trumpet hero Fats Navarro, altoist John Jackson and vocalist/leader Billy himself on trumpet) and excellent and unique vocal stylists while the band is rounded-out with players like trumpeter Gail Brockman (remember the solo he would play later on Gene Ammons' hit "Red Top"?), baritone saxist Leo Parker, bassist Tommy Potter, and drummer Art Blakey. The announcers/MC (including Ernie "Bubbles" Whitman) keep things moving with hip banter and jokes at each other's expense like: "The stomach that walks like a man." or "A man who's been on an 18 day diet for 18 years.."

The idea that you could walk into a club and see a show like this is beyond comprehension. Perhaps the show's budget was augmented so the broadcast (I think something for the military) could include guest star Lena Horne and other musicians that are mentioned but not heard on these recordings. In any case just the band on its own is something that will never be matched."

In The Still Of The Night- Five Satins

Vinny Mazzetta   Tenor

#3 R&B #24 Pop (#1 through #27 in 5 countries)

Fred Parris, lead vocalist wrote the song. Harmony vocals by Ed Martin, Jim Freeman and Nat Mosley. The Five Satins had only four members when recording their immortal Doo-Wop standard! Vinny Mazzetta played the saxophone. Doug Murray on bass, Bobby Mapp was behind the drum kit while Curlee Glover played the piano. Marty Kugell produced and issued the record on his own Standard label in 1956. It was then taken up by Ember Records and became a substantial Pop and R&B hit.

Names appeared on a record might not have been the actual songwriter of the song. Even though they were listed, they may had not been registered with BMI or ASCAP that collected royalties for artists.

Fred Parks should have made much money from the hit record "In The Still of the Night". However, due to his own lack of understanding, he didn't register with BMI until after the song had been recorded. Even though his name was on the label as the songwriter, the record company only offered him "something like $783.00" in settlement of all royalties. 164.

VINNY MAZZETTA

Photo courtesy: The New Haven Register

Fred Parris composed the song "In The Still Of The Night" while on Army guard duty one night. Back home in New Haven, Connecticut, in 1956, he formed a vocal group along with Wes Forbes, Lewis Peeples, Rich Freeman, and Sy Hopkins. They called themselves The Five Satins, and four of the five members recorded In The Still Of The Night in the basement of a local church, St. Bernadette's, on a reel to reel recorder. Vinny, who attended the church was asked to play the solo as a favor to a friend. Vinny told me that he continues to play in the area and enjoys the old standards. My thanks to Daniel Cipriano for putting me in touch with Vinny Mazzetta.

Vinny Mazzetta, a life-long parishioner at St. Bernadette, played saxophone on the original recording of "The Still Of The Night" on Feb. 19, 1956.

"If you did a take, you made a mistake, you went back," Mazzetta said. "Fred says we did 'In the Still of the Night' six times. Vinny stated, "I think we did it 12 times that day."

I called Mr. Mazzetta and asked why his name was not on the Internet when I first started my research. He stated that other sax players had claimed to have played the solo so he did not say anything because he did not want to cause any issues for his family.

The following courtesy https://www.all-about-vinylrecords.com/five-satins-oldies-music- lyrics.html;

"On February 8th, 2014 I called Vinny Mazzetta and talked to him for eight minutes and forty nine seconds.

I mention the time specifically because Vinny is a part of history and I appreciated those few minutes talking to a part of history more than Vinny could know.

The conversation with Vinny brought back memories of the prom dances with my first girlfriend, dancing to this very song.

And here I was, talking to the man who played that great saxophone solo on this wonderful old classic.

I asked Vinny if he had any photo's of him and The Five Satins in that recording. He said he did not.

I also asked Vinny if he toured with The Five Satins and he told me he was young at the time and had no interest in doing that.

He said he hardly knew the guys but wanted to do them a favor so they could record their music.

A final thought from Randall and Vinny.

Mazzetta is proud of what he set in motion; that recording also marked a breakthrough in race relations. "It was a first. You could tell I was only 21, I didn't know any better: bringing blacks into the Cove, into a church. But I just said, 'They're here to make a record.'"

Courtesy https://www.all-about-vinylrecords.com/five-satins-oldies-music-lyrics.html

"Vincent "Vinny" Anthony Mazzetta of New Haven died Sunday October 14, 2018 at Branford Hills Health Care Center. He was the beloved husband of JoAnn Giannotti Mazzetta.

Vinny was born in New Haven on February 4, 1935. He was the son of the late James "Tex" and Ellen Mazzetta. He lived in Morris Cove all his life.

He was a musician since the age of 16, playing the saxophone and clarinet. He played all around the greater New Haven area for 65 years as a member of the 3 Guys and a Gal and for 25 years as a member of the Top Hatters.

He was involved with the Five Satins and played the saxophone on the original recording of "In the Still of the Night." Vinny spent much of his working life in the grocery business and also served in the U. S. Army Reserves for 6 years.

After retiring, he continued to play music in local convalescent homes with a group called the "Misfits." He was a communicant of St. Bernadette Church, where he served as a collector, sang in the choir, and was also a member of the Knights of Columbus Rodrigo Council 44.

Influences and Legends

By Sax Gordon (Beadle)

https://saxgordon.com/

Maxwell Davis - The Father of West Coast R&B (LP Ace CHAD 239)

Maxwell was probably one of the most influential and important R&B saxists of all time, although one of the least known by name. His playing practically defines the sound of West-Coast R&B sax outside of the Honkin' school championed by wild men like Big Jay McNeely, Chuck Higgins and Joe Houston. Often working as session leader/arranger and player, Maxwell soloed and created the band sound behind hit recordings by Percy Mayfield (*Please*

Send Me Someone to Love, River's Invitation, Lost Love), Amos Milburn (*Chicken Shack Boogie, One Scotch, One Bourbon, One Beer, Bad Bad Whiskey*), Charles Brown (*Black Night, Seven Long Days*), as well for T-Bone Walker, BB King, Etta James, Lowell Fulson, Big Joe Turner, Clarence "Gatemouth" Brown and countless others. This LP features Maxwell soloing on instrumentals recorded in the early to mid 50s under his own name and with Gene Phillips and Lloyd Glenn.

https://www.discogs.com/Maxwell-Davis-Father-Of-The-West-Coast-R-B/release/3996617

Rock 'N Roll Stage Show - **Buddy Johnson and his Orchestra** (LP Mercury/Wing MGW 12111)

The baddest Rhythm and Blues Big Band ever. Pianist/composer/arranger Buddy wrote both rocking R&B and ballads, often sung by his sister Ella ("Since I Fell For You" is one of his well-known compositions). His powerful, blues-based arrangements really kicked into high gear when they unleashed tenor sax monster Pervis Henson.

https://www.discogs.com/Buddy-Johnson-And-His-Orchestra-Rock-N-Roll-Stage-Show/release/1160216

Slow Walk Rock - **Sil Austin** (LP Mercury 12168)

Although Sil became more famous for his ballads and easy listening records (much like R&B sax giant Sam "the Man" Taylor) his first LP's, in the mid 50s, were some of the greatest rocking sax ever recorded. His first hit *Slow Walk* utilized such techniques as double tonguing, and other records showed his incredible ability to get wild effects with tone, from extremely low growls to high screeches, all executed with incredible control. A compilation of his 50's R&B solo work is out on CD and if you're feeling adventurous I see that they've reissued *Battle Royale - Red Prysock & Sil Austin*.

https://www.discogs.com/Sil-Austin-And-His-Orchestra-Slow-Walk-Rock/master/522645

http://gocontinental.com/cdlist/evergreen_austin.shtml (Battle Royale)

Jazz As I Feel It - **Earl Bostic** (LP King 846)

Earl Bostic was simply the best. While better known for his muscular readings of 50's pop songs, his early work with Hot Lips Page and others shows an almost superhuman ability with the alto sax. His command of every aspect of playing, tone, fingering, melodic interpretation, improvisation and altissimo is unmatched anywhere. This hard-to-find album from 1963 with organist Richard "Groove" Holmes and guitarist Joe Pass is a departure from his usually more Pop-oriented fare. Anyone who starts thinking they're pretty good should sit down and listen to the rocking masterpieces *Telstar Drive* or *Don't Do It Please*. This won't be reissued, it's too dangerous. Earl's incredible altissimo epic *Up There In Orbit* may have made it to CD on an *EP Collection*.

Who's Muddy Shoes - **Elmore James/John Brim** (LP Chess 1537)

And

Black Magic - **Magic Sam** (LP Delmark DS-620)

Both of these records are by Chicago Blues guitarists/vocalists but feature sax players. I find that many sax players who are into Jazz, Funk, Fusion or Pop music end up taking gigs in Blues bands because they could use the work and it's considered easy. What most don't know is that there are many saxophone stylists in Chicago Blues that developed unique approaches to group playing either as a small section or by themselves.

On Black Magic, Eddie Shaw's solos show how to play background parts that fit with the rhythm section. While his many solo recordings feature more of his very unique solo style, his work in Magic Sam's band is a perfect example of how to fit in with an electric blues band so you don't end up standing there waiting for your turn to solo.

Who's Muddy Shoes features two artists, only one, Elmore James, using sax in his band. The saxist, J. T. Brown, plays sometimes alone, sometimes with a small section, once again showing the possibilities of the sax in a small electric Blues band situation. As a soloist J.T. is remarkable for his totally unique remarkable for his totally unique approach, as with Eddie Shaw, seemingly not influenced by the Jazz players of the day.

https://www.discogs.com/Elmore-James-John-Brim-Whose-Muddy-Shoes/master/409544

Bus Stop - **Oliver Sain** (LP Abet 406)

After a career starting in the 50s in St. Louis band leading, recording, arranging or playing for Blues and R&B greats like Ike Turner, Little Milton, Howling Wolf, Elmore James, BB King, Fontella Bass and his own groups, Oliver updated the R&B sax sound in the early 70s, putting his long, blues-drenched, insistent, clear and singing phrasing over more modern rhythm section sounds. His ability to get the most out of moody or funky vamps (sometimes on just one chord) led to some minor hits like the title song of this LP.

An overview of his work on Abet records has been reissued on CD.

Sax Gordon: Bio

"No other performer on the scene today brings to life and pushes forward the great tradition of American R&B Sax like Sax Gordon.

From an early start in garage bands, church groups, jazz combos and big bands in northern California, Gordon graduated to work and record with Bay-Area Blues giant Johnny Heartsman. After relocating to the East coast, five years and many recordings with Luther "Guitar Junior" Johnson established Gordon on the international scene. With Luther's encouragement, Gordon continued to develop his signature style, hard-blowing, exciting, gutsy sax steeped in the traditions of Blues and Soul.

Gordon then recorded and toured extensively with Matt "Guitar" Murphy as well as with the Duke Robillard Band with whom he also backed Blues and Swing greats Jimmy Witherspoon and Jay McShann on tours and recordings.

International tours with Roomful of Blues, Junior Watson, John Hammond, Sherman Robertson, Toni Lynn Washington, and Soul legend Solomon Burke followed, while at home Gordon was being called upon to play with a who's who of American Blues and Soul music greats, including Clarence "Gatemouth" Brown, James Cotton, Junior Wells, Little Milton, Ben E. King, Hubert Sumlin, Sam Moore (of Sam & Dave), Johnny Johnson, Howard Tate, Martha Reeves, and Johnny Copeland among others.

Modern masters have also benefitted from Gordon's unique sound, as heard on CDs by Kim Wilson, Bryan Lee,

Paul Oscher, Jerry Portnoy, Watermelon Slim, Ron Levy, and David Maxwell.

But perhaps it is Gordon's ability to conjure up the style and feeling of past R&B sax masters that led to his being featured as soloist on albums by legends such as Champion Jack Dupree, Jimmy McGriff, Charles Brown, Pinetop Perkins, Billy Boy Arnold, and Rosco Gordon

After releasing his first CD - *Have Horn Will Travel* (Rounder/Bullseye) Gordon began leading his own bands and appearing as a special guest in the USA and Europe and has now been featured at clubs and festivals in Italy, Spain, Germany, Holland, Portugal, Belgium, Luxembourg, Switzerland, France, Russia, Denmark, Croatia, Slovenia, Lithuania, Scandinavia, Chile, Brazil, and the United Arab Emirates."

Cannonball — Duane Eddy

Steve Douglas Tenor

#22 R&B #15 Pop #2 UK

Photo courtesy HOTLICKS from the VHS "Rock and Roll Saxophone"
HOT LICKS PRODUCTIONS, Inc,
P.O. Box 337, Pound Ridge, NY 10576 USA

Steve Douglas was an integral part of the popular music scene from the dawning of rock 'n' roll in the 1950s through the 1990s. Along the way he built an impressive list of credentials as a sax and flute soloist, composer, producer, arranger, and record company executive. His lengthy credits include playing with superstars, from Elvis Presley to Bob Dylan, as well as developing long-term working relationships with Phil Spector, Brian Wilson & The Beach Boys, and Ry Cooder.

Douglas's trademark saxophone sound was first developed on early rock 'n' roll, R&B, and blues recordings. As a teenager growing up in Los Angeles in the 1950s, Douglas got to play concerts backing Richie Valens, Johnny Guitar Watson, Thurston Harris, Don & Dewey, and The Sharps.

Right after graduating from high school, Douglas joined instrumental guitarist Duane Eddy and The Rebels to record two albums and tour extensively. In the following years, Douglas was in demand as a session sax player for Phil Spector and put together two studio bands, The Wrecking Crew and The Wall of Sound Band.

TIMELINE-Courtesy http://rockhall.com/inductee/steve-douglas September 24, 1938: Saxophonist Steve Douglas is born in Los Angeles.

1958: Steve Douglas begins a two-year association with guitarist Duane Eddy that will result in a run of instrumental hits, including "Cannonball," "40 Miles of Bad Road" and "Peter Gunn."

1963: Phil Spector moves his base of operations from New York to Los Angeles, enlisting Steve Douglas to contract sessions and play sax on such records as "He's a Rebel," a #1 hit for the Crystals.

1963: Steve Douglas begins working with the Beach Boys as a sideman, contributing sax to all their albums from Surfin' U.S.A. through Pet Sounds. He also becomes a regular on Jan and Dean's sessions, playing on "Surf City," "Dead Man's Curve," and others.

1964: Steve Douglas is hired to work in A&R (artists & repertoire) at Capitol Records, where he'll produce and play on sessions for such acts as Bobby Darrin, Billy Preston and Glen Campbell.

1967: Steve Douglas runs the West Coast office of Mercury Records, where he signs such acts as Blue Cheer ("Summertime Blues") and Asylum Choir (featuring fellow Phil Spector sideman Leon Russell).

1976: Steve Douglas releases The Music of Cheops, recorded in the King's Chamber at the Great Pyramid at Giza in Egypt, on his own Cheops label.

1978: Steve Douglas joins Bob Dylan's band for a year of touring and recording with Bob Dylan. He can be heard on Dylan's Live at Budokan album, recorded on March 1, 1978.

April 19, 1993: Steve Douglas dies of heart failure.

March 10, 2003: Steve Douglas is inducted into the Rock and Roll Hall of Fame at the eighteenth annual induction dinner. Paul Shaffer is his presenter.

"Back in the '80's and 90's I was privileged to play several gigs in the Bay Area with Steve Douglas and Lee Allen. Steve was in awe of Lee. He really loved and appreciated Lee's playing. He had listened to Lee when he was a kid. The other player he liked and mentioned to me was Big Jay. And Sam

Butera. He asked me to drive to Reno with him where Sam had a gig. Unfortunately, I couldn't make the trip: it would have been fun and enlightening. Steve was an interesting sax player in that he didn't listen to the usual "jazz" players the rest of us are influenced by. He listened to rock and roll and r&b players. I don't think he cared for jazz saxophone. He preferred the short little solos saxophones took in that era. He went out of his way to distance himself from King Curtis. I'm thinking he got tired of people comparing him to King or something along that line?...I do distinctly remember he didn't care for Clarence's Clemons name coming up as a comparison. If anything Steve was an influence on the way Clarence was utilized on recordings etc."

"A funny thing about Steve Douglas. He owned one of Ornette's Grafton altos. I played it a few times. I know it was OC's because I had seen the same sax for sale in NYC, etc.. Here's the funny part. Steve heard Ornette at the Hillcrest Club when he (Ornette) started out in LA. he wasn't impressed at all. But he became a huge fan of the electric harmolodic bands OC had in the '70's. Exactly the opposite of most long-term Ornette fans. Steve liked the rock and roll Ornette...

He made me aware that there truly was a rock and roll school of sax and very few guys could do it or figured it out".

-John Firmin

Highly Recommended: STEVE DOUGLAS: THE WORLD'S GREATEST ROCK AND ROLL SAXOPHONIST: a three part look at the recording history of Steve Douglas, with many great solos.

http://opensourcemusic.com/steve-douglas/

Douglas can also be heard on the following soundtracks and TV shows: Fast Times At Ridgemont High, American Hot Wax, Streets of Fire, Gremlins, Top Gun, Brewster's Millions, The Blues Brothers, Moonlighting, and The Twilight Zone.

Steve Douglas passed away from heart failure in his studio in the mid-1990s.

Equipment:

Selmer Mark VI Baritone Sax, King Super 20 Tenor Sax, Buescher Straight Alto Sax, Selmer Mark VI Alto Sax, Grafton Plastic Alto Sax, Buffet Soprano Sax

Haynes C Flute Artley Piccolo

Artley Bass Flute

Discography:

1962 Twist—Crown

Music of Cheops—Takoma My Kind of Music—DPI Beyond Broadway—Essdee Hot Sax—Fantasy

Reflections In A Golden Horn-Mercury

At My Front Door—El Dorados

Red Holloway (solo) Tenor

McKinley Easton Baritone

#1 R&B. #17 Pop

Formed in Chicago in the early 1950s with the name Pirkie Lee and The Five Stars. Pirkle Lee Moses Jr. (lead vocals), Louis Bradley, Arthur Basset, Jewel Jones, James Maddox and Richard Nickens.

 "Vivian Lee signed them to Vee-Jay Records. After a series of recordings and misses, they recorded "At My Front Door" which put the phrase "crazy little mama" into the vocabulary of every kind with a radio in 1955. Inexplicably the lead singer, Pirkle Lee Moses never made the transition to soul star in the 1960s that his talent would suggest. Right after recording 'At My Front Door', The Eldorados moonlighted by backing Hazel McCollum on an answer song 'Annie's Song' to the Midnighters' infamous 'Work With Me Annie'."- *The Vee-jay Story 1953-1993; Collector's Edition;* Liner Notes.

James Wesley "Red" Holloway (May 31, 1927 – February 25, 2012) was an American jazz saxophonist.

Born in Helena, Arkansas, Holloway started playing banjo and harmonica, switching to tenor saxophone when he was 12 years old. He graduated from DuSable High School, where he had played in the school big band with Griffin and

Eugene Wright, and attended the Conservatory of Music, Chicago. He joined the Army when he was 19 and became bandmaster for the U.S. Fifth Army Band, and after completing his military service returned to Chicago and played with Yusef Lateef and Dexter Gordon, among others. In 1948 he joined blues vocalist Roosevelt Sykes, and later played with other rhythm & blues musicians such as Willie Dixon, Junior Parker, and Lloyd Price.

In the 1950s he played in the Chicago area with Billie Holiday, Muddy Waters, Chuck Berry, Ben Webster, Jimmy Rushing, Arthur Prysock, Dakota Staton, Eddie "Cleanhead" Vinson, Wardell Gray, Sonny Rollins, Red Rodney, Lester Young, Joe Williams, Redd Foxx, B.B. King, Bobby Bland, and Aretha Franklin. During this period, he also toured with Sonny Stitt, Memphis Slim and Lionel Hampton. He became a member of the house band for Chance Records in 1952. He subsequently appeared on many recording sessions for the Chicago-based independents Parrot, United and States, and Vee-Jay.

From 1963 to 1966, he was in organist "Brother" Jack McDuff's band, which also featured a young guitarist, George Benson. In 1974, Holloway recorded The Latest Edition with John Mayall and toured Europe, Japan, Australia and New Zealand. From 1977 to 1982, Holloway worked with Sonny Stitt, recording two albums together, and following Stitt's death, Holloway played and recorded with Clark Terry.

Red Holloway died in Morro Bay, California, aged 84 of a stroke and kidney failure on February 25, 2012, one month after Etta James, with whom he had worked extensively. His interment is at Forest Lawn Memorial Park in the Hollywood Hills of Los Angeles.

McKinley Easton was an American jazz and blues saxophonist (baritone). Easton worked with: Big Joe Turner, Gene Ammons, Buddy Guy, Bobby Parker, T-Bone Walker, Magic Sam, Dinah Washington, Bill Henderson and others.

Eddie My Love-Teen Queens

Plas Johnson Tenor
Maxwell Davis Tenor
Jewell Grant Baritone
Jackie Kelso Alto

#3 R&B #14 Pop

"**Eddie My Love**" is a 1956 doo wop song. The singers were sisters Betty and Rosie Collins.

According to BMI and ASCAP, the song was written by Maxwell Davis (BMI), Aaron Collins, Jr. (ASCAP), and Sam Ling (BMI). Maxwell Davis played sax on the Teen Queens record.

Courtesy https://en.wikipedia.org/wiki/Eddie_My_Love

Per Gaye Funk; regarding "Eddie My Love" by the Teen Queens, Plas said that Maxwell Davis was in the booth on that session, and that it was him (Johnson) on tenor, and maybe Jackie Kelso on alto.

As it was playing, Plas remarked, "oh-three horns…himself on tenor, Jewell on bari, (and after listening a little longer) maybe Jackie Kelso on alto. Maxwell was in the booth on that session and that's me on tenor. After I arrived in town, Maxwell rarely played, unless he had to- he was too busy writing."

"According to my information, it is definitely Maxwell Davis who has a part of the writer credits, and according to the ACE CD of the Teen Queens, CDCHD 581, it was the

Maxwell Davis band that was in the studio cutting the record".

Brian
12/28/2012

"The Teen Queens were one of the early precursors of the Girl Group sound, but the thing that makes "Eddie My Love" one of 1956's memorable songs is its fine horn section.

It has an unusually rich and complex arrangement for a pop track- probably because it appeared one of the best R&B labels on the West Coast.

Three saxophonists appear on the track. Plas Johnson plays tenor sax. Jewell Grant plays tenor sax and the alto sax is provided by Jackie Kelso. The saxophone was a favorite solo instrument in the early days of rock and roll, but the way it is used on this track is utterly unique. It transformed what would otherwise have been a fairly pedestrian love song into something special. It was also a surprise hit, rising as high as #14 on the pop charts."

Another site;

Eddie My Love" is a 1956 doo wop song. According to BMI and ASCAP, the song waswritten by Maxwell Davis (BMI), Aaron Collins, Jr. (ASCAP), and Sam Ling (BMI). Maxwell Davis played sax on the Teen Queens record.
Courtesy https://en.wikipedia.org/wiki/Eddie_My_Love

MAXWELL DAVIS

Maxwell (Thomas) Davis was born Jan 14, 1916, in Independence, Kansas, and died inLos Angeles on Sept 18, 1970. He played alto saxophone and violin as the leader of his own band in Wichita, Kansas, for four years, then in 1936 moved to the West Coast. After changingto tenor saxophone, he played with the Woodman Brothers (1936-7) and in Seattle with the drummer Gene Coy (1939-41). He led his own bands in the 1940s and 1950s and worked as anartists and repertory agent and arranger. He played on a large number of R&B recordings with such musicians as Helen Humes, Lloyd Glenn, Pete Johnson, Jimmy Witherspoon, Red Callender, and the electric guitarist Gene Phillips, and he wrote arrangements for Jimmie Lunceford (early 1940s) and for a series of big band recordings for the Crown label (1958-60). Davis's style of Southwest jazz is well represented by his fiery performance on Jay McShann's Soft Winds (1949, Swing Time 205). He shows a more gentle approach on Rainy Weather Blues(1948, Metro-Goldwyn-Mayer 10397), which he recorded with Joe Turner.

Tony Valdez of KTTV Fox News in Los Angeles added a note that most of Davis's workas an A&R man in the 1950s was for the Bihari Brothers' stable of labels, notably Modern, Flair,RPM, and Crown, then later Kent as a re-issue label. Maxwell Davis was also A&R man/arranger/bandleader for most of B.B. King's original recordings for the Biharis.

444

Mr. Lee—The Bobbettes

Jannie Pought, Emma Pought, Reather Dixon, Laura Webb, Helen Gathers.

Jesse Powell   Tenor

#1 R&B #6 Pop #1 Pop Canada

The group wrote about the legendary "Mr. Lee" who was actually a teacher of some of the Bobbettes. The group's first single was released in June 1957.

Although the lyrics speak glowingly of "Mr. Lee," the original lyrics were not the least bit flattering. The girls had an immense dislike for the teacher and the song was originally written as a put down. At the request of Atlantic's A&R executives, the group revised the lyrics to make it more commercial or possibly less controversial.

"Mr. Lee" became the best known teacher in America, as the record went Top Ten in July 1957. "Mr. Lee", the record, spent for weeks at the top of the R&B charts and made it to the Top 10 of Pop, the first girl group to do both at the same time. http://www.history-of-rock.com/bobbettes.htm

THE BOBBETTES: *Emma Pought, Jeannie Pought, Helen Gathers, Laura Webb, Reather Dixon (vcls), King Curtis (ten), Reggie Obrecht (pno), Kenny Burrell, Everett Barksdale (gtrs), Lloyd Trotman (bs), Joe Marshall (dms), Teddy Charles (vbs).*
New York. February 16, 1958

A-2965   Um Bow Wow   Atlantic 1194

A-2966   The Dream   Atlantic 1194

THE BOBBETTES: Emma Pought, Jeannie Pought, Helen Gathers, Laura Webb, Reather Dixon (vcls), King Curtis (ten), Reggie Obrecht (pno), Allen Hanlon, George Barnes (gtrs), Lloyd Trotman (bs), Joe Marshall (dms).
New York. March 13, 1958

A-2995   Rock & Ree-A-Zole   Atlantic 1181
A-2996   Zoomy Atlantic 1181
A-2997   Skippy Doo-Wah   unissued

THE BOBBETTES: Emma Pought, Jeannie Pought, Helen Gathers, Laura Webb, Reather Dixon (vcls), Leon Cohen (alt), King Curtis (ten), Reggie Obrecht (pno), Allen Hanlon, George Barnes (gtrs), Wendell Marshall (bs), Sammie "Sticks" Evans (dms).
New York. February 20, 1959

A-3366   Don't Say Goodnight Atlantic 2027
A-3367   You Are My Sweetheart   Atlantic 2027
A-3368   I Shot Mr. Lee Atlantic 2069. **#52 Pop**
A-3369   Untrue Lover Atlantic 2069

-Roy Simonds- "King Curtis Sessionography"

JESSE POWEL - TENOR & ALVIN "RED" TYLER - BARITONE
Courtesy "The Sax & Brass Book"
JESSE POWELL

Jesse Powell was born February 2, 1924, in Texas. He joined Count Basie's band in 1946, replacing the great sax player Illinois Jacquet. Powell performed on blues recordings in the late 1940s with Brownie McGhee, Willie Jordan, Doc Pomus, Champion Jack Dupree, and Dizzy Gillespie. During the 1950s Powell was in demand by many R&B artists. In the early 1950s, he recorded as a leader for Federal and with the Josie label, which included groups like The Cadillacs. His R&B work includes a number of singles and studio work with Atlantic/Atco. Powell eventually returned to recording jazz in the early 1960s. He died October 19, 1982 in New

York, NY. The following link has more history about Jesse Powell. Courtesy of Tad Richards;
https://opusforty.blogspot.com/2020/07/listening-to-prestige-498-jesse-powell.html

Poor Boy—Royaltones

George Katsakis (solo) Tenor
Ken Anderson- Baritone

This rock 'n' roll instrumental band came from Dearborn, Michigan, USA. With its honking saxophone-dominated records, the Royaltones typified the sound of rock 'n' roll bands of the late 50s, before the guitar sound became dominant. The band was formed in 1957 as the Paragons, and comprised George Katsakis on tenor saxophone, Karl Kay on guitar, and two brothers, Mike Popoff on piano and

Greg Popoff on drums. "Poor Boy" was a US Top 20 hit in 1958. "Flamingo Express" went to number 82 in 1961. The Royaltones broke up in the mid-60s.

The info below comes from the liner notes (by Dave Burke and Alan Taylor of Pipeline magazine) for the Royaltones CD "Detroit Rock 'n' Roll Began Here!"

(Ace CDLUX 001), released in 2009.

Dik 10/19/2017

(August 20, 1958: The instrumental group THE ROYALTONES has its first session, at Carmen Towers Recording Studio in Dearborn, Michigan. The resulting single, "Poor Boy"/"Wail!" (Jubilee 5338, September) will reach a peak position of # 17 on the Billboard charts. Personnel: George Katsakis, Ken Anderson (saxes); Dave "Bob" Sanderson (guitar); Mike Popoff (piano); Greg Popoff (drums). The studio owner Stuart Gorelic expanded the group for the recording by adding the second sax (Anderson) and guitarist (Sanderson).

George "Kat" Katsakis

George was an original founding member of the Royaltones, a group that charted hits in the top 100 around the world. His solo on the song "Poor Boy" is listed in a book of the greatest sax solos of all time. The song charted for 17 weeks - the all time record for an instrumental hit. Other hits included "Flamingo Express" and "Our Faded Love." Kat was the saxophone soloist on all the Carlton recordings by Jack Scott. The Royaltones were the backup recording band for Del Shannon and a crowd favorite in venues far and wide. This lifelong entertainer brings his "A" game to every show.

Maybe it's his somewhat, uh…quirky personality (this is one crazy Kat) that separates his horn playing and entertainment style from the rest. Whatever it is, it works! Kat and his horn have found their way to NBC Today and

American Bandstand, as well as other local television and radio shows around the United States. Although his primary choice of horns is a classic Selmer Mark VI tenor saxophone, he also knows his way around the baritone and soprano. Kat is fluent on clarinet and flute as well. So much music, so little time... This much is certain: when this Kat gets goin', the dance floor will be flowin'.

Over the years George has appeared at Caesar's Palace, Harrah's, The Fountain Bleu in Miami, and The Latin Quarter in Japan. He has played one of the greatest stages of all - the Apollo Theater in New York, and various other stages across the planet. Sometimes we think a little space travel along the way may have influenced his musical senses. For those stuck on this planet though, Kat and fellow flyers in the Bluescasters have the jet engines heating up, a full tank of high octane nitro-methane, blues rocket fuel, and plenty of room on board...

-John,
"I have no problems with you using the bio and/or photo from the Bluescasters web site. I would be happy to receive a copy of your work. Thanks for your interest and diligence."
Sincerely,
George Katsakis
"The horn I play is a Mark VI 12000 series with a Guardalla mouthpiece and Barri hard plastic reeds. I just bought a Stephanhauser baritone, which looks a lot like a Selmer and plays great. I use a Lawton 8* with the plastic reed. I've gotten so used to the plastic reeds and I like the consistency and they don't sound like plastic. The horn I used on the early sessions was a Martin with a stock hard

rubber mouthpiece. I hope you find this information useful. If you get a chance let me know about your set up.
Thanks again,
George "Kat" Katsakis, Mon, Nov 8, 2021 6:50 pm

11 Pop Leroy- Jack Scott   George Katsakis Tenor
A two sided hit "My True Love" hit #3 Pop.
https://www.youtube.com/watch?v=MlTqbdUEBn8
https://www.youtube.com/watch?v=LEzJ_QHsfnY

A versatile, best selling singer/songwriter (19 US singles), Jack Scott, who sold more singles in a short time period than another other musical artist with the exception of Elvis Presley, Connie Francis, The Beatles and Fats Domino, has been largely forgotten.

Other Top 40 Billboard hits of Jack Scott include:
 "Goodbye Baby #3 Pop;
https://www.youtube.com/watch?v=7T9IWU13Rog
(innovative vocal arrangement)
 "The Way I Walk #35 Pop;
https://www.youtube.com/watch?v=OaoRmc2B4Tk
#5 Pop "What in the World's Come Over You;
#5 Pop Burning Bridges -another two sided hit backed with "Oh Little One #34 Pop
https://www.youtube.com/watch?v=z7FzcVVYHAE
https://www.youtube.com/watch?v=OKJZsPjJlek (Oh Little One-the classic 2 minute "love lost" ballad typical of the 1950s-early 60s).

John:

"I'm sure you picked it up by reading the bio, I was the sax soloist on all the Jack Scott recordings on Carlton and I played the solo on "Leroy", which by the way was my first recording session.

https://www.youtube.com/watch?v=wMo5atmhcrg

If I get a good scan I will send you a photo taken at the rehearsal before that session."

-George

John,

"Thank you for your dedication to the project. I am currently playing with a ska band.."

George

www.killerdillerska.com

The complete recordings of pioneering Detroit band
The Royaltones

featuring legendary musicians
GEORGE KATSAKIS, DENNIS COFFEY and **BOB BABBITT**

L to r: Dave Sandy, Bob Babbitt, George Katsakis, Dennis Coffey, Marcus Terry

Ask any music fan what they most associate with Detroit and the answer is sure to come back: Motown Records. And while the record label that Berry Gordy formed in 1959 came to be the colossus that bestrode Michigan's main industrial centre, its huge success has also obscured the other major waves of music that swept the city before its ascent to glory. In the 40s John Lee Hooker brought the blues to Detroit, while in the 50s it was the turn of black vocal groups such as the Royals (who later mutated into hitmakers Hank Ballard & the Midnighters) and then R&B singers Little Willie John and Jackie Wilson to rule the roost. As the 50s progressed, white rock'n'roll also began to emerge led by vocalist Jack Scott and Detroit instrumental band the Royaltones. One musician, George "Kat" Katsakis, linked both acts as he not only led the Royaltones but also played sax on most of Scott's early recordings. The Royaltones provided the rock'n'roll heart that pumped in Detroit clubs and bars and kept fans dancing from their first beginnings in 1957 through to their demise in 1964. With master musicians Dennis Coffey and Bob Babbitt also within their ranks, the Royaltones just never stopped rockin'. This is their story.

456

WOMEN IN ROCK N' ROLL
By Neil Sharpe

Have the women who helped to create rock n' roll in the 1950s been given appropriate recognition? That's the question asked by Leah Branstetter Ph.D (https://www.leahbranstetter.com/) . Which is appropriate given that a 2019 survey reports that less that 7.7 percent of inductees are women in the Rock n' Roll Hall of Fame. In 2018, a #GrammysSoMale text was started about the gender gap.

Evelyn McDonnell (2019) The Manhandling of Rock 'N' Roll History
https://longreads.com/2019/03/29/the-manhandling-of-rock-n-roll-history

"The reality is, however, that hundreds—or maybe thousands—of women and girls performed and recorded rock and roll in its early years."

The growing importance of rhythm and blues and rock n' roll resulted in experiments in production and formats that exploded in the 1960s with new styles of music that swept away much of what had gone before. The following selections includes songs released with limited success in the 1950s but were a critical influence in the 1960s. The following reviews notable artists and styles, however, this is a representative sample and is not intended as a complete summary.

Also, please see the following links.

https://www.openculture.com/2019/05/new-web-project-immortalizes-the-forgotten-women-who-gave-birth-to-rock-n-roll-in-the-1950s.html

http://www.womeninrockproject.org/introduction/

https://tymstevens.blogspot.com/2016/06/women-of-rock-1950s.html

https://apriltucker.com/timeline-women-1930/

https://www.womeninmusic.org/

https://www.womeninmusic.ca/en/

April Tucker (2022) *Finding Your Career in the Modern Audio Industry*. Focal Press; 1st edition (July 29, 2022)
***

The Boswell Sisters- their song from 1934 is one of the earliest entitled "Rock And Roll".

Marion Keisker – Elvis recorded his first demo, "My Happiness" at Memphis Recording Service. Marion Keisker says that she was the engineer.165

Elvis, 19 years of age, had walked in without an appointment to make a record for his mother. Marion happened to be there and recorded him. Sam Phillips later disagreed, arguing that he was the one who did the recording and was the first to see the raw potential. However, Sam Phillips also acknowledged that Marion Keisker spoke to him often about Elvis and had encouraged Sam Philips to record him again. When a follow up, three hour recording session, on June 26, 1954, went nowhere, Marion again argued that Sam Phillips should give Elvis another try. The resulting session, on July 5, 1954, produced the cover song "That's All Right Mama" (by January 1955, the record had sold over one hundred thousand copies; however, in Florida, some radio stations wouldn't play it because the record was "too racy" 166). That night after the session, Sam would tell his wife Becky that "nothing would ever be the same again." 167 The B Side of "That's All Right Mama" was "Blue Moon In Kentucky", recorded on July 7, 1954.

As to who first recorded Elvis, the obvious question is, if Sam Phillips had first recorded Elvis, why was it that Marion had to continue to champion Elvis and argue with Sam Phillips that Elvis should be given another opportunity after both the initial session and the failed session on June 26, 1954?

Zelma "Zeli" Sanders- manager of one of the first all female groups, The Hearts (that featured Baby Washington- e.g. their single "Lonely Nights") in 1956, she founded J&S Records. "Over the Mountain; Across the Sea" by Johnnie & Joe was a major hit in 1957 (#3 R&B #8 Pop) and featured Zeli's daughter, Johnnie Louise Richardson.

Her label was notable for releasing songs by The Hearts, The Jaynetts, The Clickettes, The Poppies, The Z-Debs, and more, all made up of the same female singers!

J&S Records ran into in financial trouble in the 1960s, however, with the help of Chess Records, a new label was formed, Tuff Records, a subsidiary of J&S. The Jaynettes had a hit in 1963 (#37 R&B #2 Pop) on this new label, with the controversial, and highly influential, song "Sally Go Round The Roses"; controversial because of the mysterious, haunting production and opaque lyrics (credited to Abner Spector but actually written by Zelma Sanders and Lona Stevens) which some have claimed refer to drug use OR illegitimate motherhood OR suicide OR "lesbianism". Although the session notes are unclear, at least ten vocalists were included in the recording which took over a week to record, rolling up unusual high costs for a single record. "Sally Go Round The Roses" has been covered at least 47 times, including by The Ikettes, Grace Slick, Tim Buckley, Donna Summer, The Pentangle and Judy Collins.

(https://secondhandsongs.com/work/27944/all)

The Top 100: 1955-59

The Top 100 Pop hits for each year from 1955-59 indicate that female artists whether single or in groups had numerous hit records; however, covers of r&b artists were common and resulted in Ruth Brown's and Lavern Baker's allegations of plagiarism.

1955

8 *Sincerely* The McGuire Sisters

10 *Dance with Me, Henry* Georgia Gibbs (a cover of Etta James' *"Wildflower"* originally titled *"Roll With Me Henry"*
https://www.youtube.com/watch?v=mmJkt10FMDM (Etta James)
https://www.youtube.com/watch?v=58NVzNlN-Os (Georgia Gibbs)

15 *Hearts of Stone* The Fontane Sisters

16 *Tweedle Dee* Georgia Gibbs (cover of LaVern Baker's original with the same title)
https://www.youtube.com/watch?v=GoqmtBKp1tY (LaVern Baker)
https://www.youtube.com/watch?v=K4sVwnTB-qE (Georgia Gibbs)

Lavern Baker, one of the most successful female artists in the 1950s-early 1960s, tried to sue for copyright violations arguing that the cover by Georgia Gibbs copied her arrangement and vocal style note for note. Congress investigated "song theft" but nothing meaningful resulted.

18 *Mr. Sandman-* The Chordettes (#1 Pop) -Multiple cover versions were released in 1954 including by Chet Atkins, Four Aces, Buddy Morrow and His Orchestra, Vaughn Monroe, Les Elgart & His Orchestra, Les Brown, to name a few.

Members of the Chordettes included, from time to time, Janet Ertel, Alice Mae Spielvogel -Janet and Alice were sisters, Alice later replaced by Carol Bushman with members

her sister-in-law- Dorothy "Dottie" Schwartz, Jinny Osborn, Lynn Evans, Margie Needham, Nancy Overton.
https://www.youtube.com/watch?v=CX45pYvxDiA
19 *Let Me Go, Lover!* Joan Weber
26 *Hard to Get* Gisele MacKenzie
28 *All I Want From You* Jaye P. Morgan

1956
4 *My Prayer* The Platters (Zola Lynn Taylor)
5 *The Wayward Wind* Gogi Grant
(widely covered including by Neil Young, Patsy Cline, Frank Ifield, Anne Murray, Sam Cooke)
https://www.youtube.com/watch?v=bW52i3iHQzg
10 *Rock and Roll Waltz* Kay Starr (#1 Pop #1 UK)
24 *Allegheny Moon* Patti Page
26 *Tonight You Belong to Me* Patience and Prudence (McIntyre)
32 *Ivory Tower* Cathy Carr
46 *A Sweet Old Fashioned Girl* Teresa Brewer
49 *A Tear Fell* Teresa Brewer

1957
12 *Tammy* Debbie Reynolds
29 *Dark Moon* Gale Storm
46 *Old Cape Cod* Patti Page (later covered in the 1990s with a haunting version by Groove Armada)
https://www.youtube.com/watch?v=a34kIKVideI
https://www.youtube.com/watch?v=wzCt7ABUU9Y
47 *Mr. Lee* The Bobbettes

1958

18 *Got the Whole World in His Hands* Laurie London
27 *Sugartime* The McGuire Sisters
37 *Lollipop* The Chordettes
39 *Who's Sorry Now* Connie Francis
43 *When* The Kalin Twins

1959

7 *The Three Bells* The Browns
8 *Come Softly To Me* The Fleetwoods
10 *Mr. Blue* The Fleetwoods
15. *Pink Shoe Laces* Dodie Stevens
16. *Smoke Gets In Your Eyes* The Platters
28 *Lipstick On Your Collar* Connie Francis
37 *Kookie Kookie Lend Me You Comb* Edd (a.k.a. Edward) Byrnes, Connie Stevens
39 *My Happiness* Connie Francis
43 *Don't You Know* Della Reese
45 *What A Difference A Day Makes* Dinah Washington
https://www.youtube.com/watch?v=nWSlm1sNB90
She had 27 R&B top-10 hits and was one of the most popular singers of the 1950s.
"Am I Asking Too Much" (1948) and "Baby Get Lost" (1949) reached Number 1 on the R&B chart; "I Wanna Be Loved" (1950) crossed over to hit Number 22 on the US pop chart.
51 *Broken Hearted Melody*- Sarah Vaughan
https://www.youtube.com/watch?v=ypwe0ZIsDFQ
A million seller, the song reached #7 on Pop #5 R&B. Sarah "The Divine One" Vaughan was one of the great jazz vocalists. Winner of two Grammy Awards, including the Lifetime Achievement Award, she was nominated a total of nine times and won NEA Jazz Masters Award in 1989, to

mention just a very few of the awards she won over her career that began in 1943.

Those who had hits, but didn't sell enough to make the Top 50 List for an *entire* year include, in no particular order:

The Chantels
Maybe
#2 R&B #15 Pop
Their famous hit 'Maybe' made them the first African-American girl act to sell a million copies in 1957 as well as gain national recognition.

Their signature "Look In My Eyes" is one of their classics with a memorable opening.

While being remarkable singers, the girls played their own instruments.

Ruth Brown
Lucky Lips
#6 R&B #25 Pop

Patsy Cline
Walking After Midnight
#12 Pop #2 Country

The Poni-Tails (Toni Cistone, Karen Topinka and Patti McCabe-Karen Topinka was later replaced by LaVerne Novak)
Born Too Late
#11 R&B #7 Pop

The Poni-Tails. 'Born Too Late', released in 1958, reached the number 2 in the Billboard charts, The Poni-Tails didn't enjoy the same level of success in the years that followed.

However, they were a source of inspiration for many female acts.

Nina Simone
I Love You Porgy
#72 R&B #18 Pop

Kitty Wells
"It Wasn't God Who Made Honky Tonk Angels"
Initially banned from radio play, hit #1 Country #27 Pop.

The Skyliners (Janet Vogel)
Since I Don't Have You
#5 R&B #12 Pop

Shirley (Goodman) & Lee
Let The Good Times Roll
#1 R&B #2 Pop
Lee Allen Tenor-tenor sax

The Davis Sisters (Skeeter Davis, Betty Jack Davis-they weren't related)
I Forgot More Than You'll Ever Know (About Him)
20 Pop #1 Country

Jodie Sands
With All My Heart
#15 Pop

Jean Shepard, Ferlin Husky
Dear John:
Youngest female artist at age 20 to have a Number 1 Country Record.
#1 Country #4 Pop

Mary Ford, Les Paul
Mocking Bird Hill
#2 Pop

Shortly after this record was released, a cover by Patti Page was rushed to market. The story is she was about to catch a connecting flight to New York when a telephone call from the record company told her that a limo would be waiting to take her to the recording studio to cut this one song. It also hit #2 on Pop.

In the 1950s, if you had released a song, you had better be fully armored and ready for battle, because the cover attacks could come from all sides.

Wanda Jackson
"The Queen Of Rockabilly"

"Let's Have A Party"- #37 Pop (recorded on the album "Wanda Jackson" 1958; released as a single 1960; originally recorded by Elvis Presley as "Party" # 2 U.K.)

https://www.youtube.com/watch?v=867uXhDzG8I (Elvis)
https://www.youtube.com/watch?v=7ksBcV-qrgo (Wanda)

She's enjoyed a long career in rockabilly, country, and gospel.
https://www.discogs.com/artist/321332-Wanda-Jackson
Released successful albums in the 1990s.
In 2011, with Jack White, she released the album "The

Party Ain't Over"- #17 Billboard Top Rock Albums. Inducted into the Rock n' Roll Hall Of Fame.

Kathy Linden
Goodbye Jimmy Goodbye
#11 Pop

Sparkle Moore
A pioneer in early rockabilly. Toured with Gene Vincent but stopped her career in 1957. In 2010, she released a 22 track CD.
https://www.discogs.com/release/10435928-Sparkle-Moore-Spark-A-Billy

The Tune Weavers (Margo Sylvia, Charlotte Davis)
Happy, Happy, Birthday Baby
#4 R&B #5 Pop
Frank Paul Orchestra, alto sax unknown,
The group formed in Woburn, Massachusetts, and originally was comprised of lead singer Margo Sylvia, tenor Gilbert J. "Gil" Lopez, bass singer John Sylvia and Charlotte Davis. Margo and Gil, who were sister and brother, sang as a jazz and pop duo together in clubs, before being joined in 1956 by Margo's husband John, and her cousin Charlotte, to form the group. They originally were called the Tone Weavers, but when they were mistakenly announced as the Tune Weavers the new name stuck.

Mickey & Sylvia
Love Is Strange
(Groove 78rpm & 45rpm singles, 1956)
No 1. R&B No. 11 Pop

'Love Is Strange' was written by Bo Diddley and was recorded by him in late 1955 but not released. The song was substantially covered by Mickey & Sylvia, whose version spawned others, including by the Everly Brothers. The duo disbanded in 1959. Guitarist Mickey Baker returned to session work. Sylvia Robinson hit the big time in 1979, when she founded Sugarhill Records and released the Sugarhill Gang's 'Rapper's Delight' and Grandmaster Flash's 'The Message' both major, and widely influential, hits.

MICKEY & SYLVIA: *Mickey Baker, Sylvia Robinson (vcls/gtrs), King Curtis (ten), Haywood Henry (bari), Ernie Hayes (pno), Abie Baker (bs), Panama Francis (dms). Piano, saxes omitted, and both vcls are female (Sylvia overdubbed?) on –1. Saxes omitted on –2. Prod. Bob Rolontz.*
New York. October 17, 1956

G5WB-7872	Two Shadows On Your Window –1	
	unissued	
G5WB-7873-3	Love Is Strange –2	Groove 0175
G5WB-7874-7	I'm Going Home	Groove 0175
G5WB-7875-6	(I've Got A Feeling) In My Heart	Vik LP 1102

Note: Take 2 of 7872 and take 1 of 7873 issued on (German) Bear Family CD 15438).
    -Roy Simonds- "King Curtis Sessionography"

The Shirelles (Shirley Owens, Doris Coley, Addie "Micki" Harris and Beverly Lee)
This Is Dedicated To The One I Love

#83 Pop

A cover of the original song by the 5 Royales, the Shirelles' version was re-released in 1961 and became a major #2 R&B and #3 Pop. The Shirelles would go on to become one of the all-time best-selling groups with major hits like "Will You Still Love Me Tomorrow" and "Tonight's The Night".

https://www.youtube.com/watch?v=0Z4FbRi2Rgk (Shirelles)

https://www.youtube.com/watch?v=y335E8mfBAU (5 Royales)

Additional Artists, Styles and Hits

- Down the Aisle of Love-**The Quin-Tones**
  #5 R&B #18 Pop

- *In Paradise*-**The Cookie**s (a group that went through numerous member changes-in the 1960s, they provided backup vocals for many artists including top 10 hits, and had their own hits, such as "Chains" that was covered by The Beatles
  #18 R&B

https://www.youtube.com/watch?v=c2tCx9dGhkg
https://www.youtube.com/watch?v=2_f9lrXd_48 (Chains)
https://www.youtube.com/watch?v=rJOhavaeJYk (Chains-The Beatles)

- *Move On*-**The Blossoms** (Fanita Barrett, Gloria A. Jones, Jewel Cobbs, Pat Howard and twin sisters

Annette and Nanette Williams. Nanette Williams was later replaced by Darlene Love).

Plas Johnson tenor sax

A group who hit their peak in the 1960s, including being the group who really recorded the #1 Pop smash "He's A Rebel" that was credited to The Crystals. They received only a session fee for their recording.

They were backup singers for many of Phil Spector's hits (such as "Be My Baby"), as well as for other artists, including James Brown, The Righteous Brothers' "You've Lost That Lovin' Feeling", Arthea Franklin, Marvin Gaye, Doris Day, and Ike & Tina Turner's "River Deep – Mountain High".

- *Black and White Thunderbird*-**The Delicates** (Denise Ferri, Arleen Lanzotti, Peggy Santiglia)

This minor hit triggered numerous T.V. appearances (including American Bandstand and Alan Freed's "Big Beat"), commercial and backup session work with other artists including Connie Francis, Neil Sedaka, Jose Feliciano, Kitty Kallen, Frankie Lymon, and Lou Christie (e.g. his #1 Pop hit "Lightning Strikes)

- *Lullaby Of The Bells*-**The Deltairs**
https://www.youtube.com/watch?v=eOq22JoURr0

- *Oop Shoop*-**Shirley Gunter & The Queens**
- *All My Love Belongs To You*-**The Joytones**

- *La Dee Dah* - **Billy & Lillie**

  - *Black Cadillac*- **Joyce Green**

- *Shake A Hand* - **Faye Adams**

- *I Need a Man*-**Barbara Pittman**

- *Wassa Matter With You*- **Jo Anne Campbell**

- *Oh Julie*- **The Crescendos featuring Janice Green**
  #4 R&B #5 Pop

- *Cry Baby* - **The Bonnie Sisters**

- *Bang Bang* -**Janice Martin "The Female Elvis"**

- *Heartbreak Harry*- **Alis Lesley**

- *Kiss Me*- **Laura Lee Perkins**

- *Mercy Mr. Percy*- **Varetta Dillard**

- *Party*- **Collins Kids**

- *Jump Jack Jump*- **Wynona Carr**

- Baby Sitters' Blues- **Bunny Paul**

- *Ambrose (Part 5)* - **Linda Laurie**
  #52 Pop
  A unique, one-of-a kind record.
  Linda's only Hot 100 chart entry. There were no Parts 1 through 4, but two sequel records followed: "Forever

Ambrose", and "The Return Of Ambrose". An instrumental "Just Keep Walking (Ambrose)" was also released.

- *Roll over Beethoven*- **Live Jerry Lee Lewis and his sister Linda Gail Lewis**

- *Love Your Rock n Roll* -**Cordell Jackson** and *Rock n' Roll Christmas*

Cordell Jackson
Cordell Jackson was recognized as an exceptional guitarist. Her father had led a local band and encouraged her to learn the guitar, piano, and upright bass. By the age of 12, she was performing with her father's band and appeared on his radio show in Tupelo. She later added mandolin, banjo, and harmonica. Rejected by Sun Records, she was encouraged by Chet Atkins to start her own label. Moon Records became the oldest continuously operating label in Memphis until she passed in 2004.

Crossfire—Johnny And The Hurricanes

Johnny Paris Tenor

#23   Pop

Johnny and the Hurricanes comprised a rock 'n' roll group of the late 1950s and early 1960s that had its own unique sound and produced a number of instrumental hits, one of which made the top ten and is closely associated with the group.

The group was formed in Toledo, Ohio, in 1958, and was at first known as the Orbits. The original members were saxophonist Johnny Paris (real name: John Pocisk), Paul Tesluk on organ, Tony Kaye on drums, Dave Yorko on guitar, and Lionel "Butch" Mattice on bass. The group started off recording with rockabilly artist Mack Vickery.

They soon went to Detroit to look for work as a back-up band for aspiring recording artists. Two music promoters there, Harry Balk and Irving Micahnik, signed the group to a recording contract of their own. (Micahnik later worked as Del Shannon's manager.)

In 1959 they made their first recording on the Twirl label, which was owned by Balk and Micahnik. It was a dance song that had been written by pianist T. J. Fowler called *"Crossfire."* Loaded with reverb, the recording was leased to the Warwick label and reached number 23 on the charts in 1959. Johnny and the Hurricanes were on their way.

The group's leader was nineteen-year-old Johnny Paris, and his hard-driving saxophone playing was prominent on a number of the group's recordings. Their next record, however, would feature Tesluk's Hammond organ and would become the group's biggest hit ever: *"Red River Rock,"* a reworking of the old standard "Red River Valley" that the group had transformed into pure rock 'n' roll. It was a huge success, reaching number five on the national pop charts. Don Staczek sat in for regular drummer Tony Kaye on "Red River Rock" and drummer Bo Savich took Kaye's regular spot in the band late in 1959.

The group continued to use rocking versions of familiar old songs as its formula. The Army bugle call of Reveille became *"Reveille Rock."* In 1960, Burl Ives' "Blue Tail Fly" was turned into *"Beatnik Fly"* by the group. Both songs made the Top 40. "When The Saints Go Marchin' In" became *"Revival."* Another song that was an original composition by Fowler called *"Rockin'*

A lot of the material they had used was out of copyright. Balk and Micahnik claimed credit as having written many of their songs, using the names Tom King and Ira Mack. Johnny and the Hurricanes had a total of nine chart entries from 1959 to 1961. They toured extensively. Eventually, the hits were not coming anymore, there were rumors that they were unhappy with the way the band was managed, and they became fatigued from being on the road so much. The band split up in 1961.

Johnny Paris went to Europe and settled in Hamburg. He played there at the same time as the Beatles, just before the Beatles became international superstars. In 1965, he started his own label which he called Attila, and for which he recorded the album *Live At The Star Club*. In 1970 he closed Attila. Paris formed a new Hurricanes group and toured in the 1970s and 1980s.

8/5/2008

"Dear John,

Thanks so much for you kind words and for contributing to our book about my late husband!!!
Sincerely,
Sonja"

EMAIL FROM A CLASSMATE;

"If you're not already aware, John Pocisk, a.k.a. Johnny Paris, died May 1, 2006 in a Michigan hospital. Johnny and I grew up in the same town, went to school together, and played in the high school band together. If memory serves me, one of the smallest genesis for Johnny and the Hurricanes was a Dixieland band we put together for a high school football game halftime show. Three of the founding members of the Hurricanes were part of it – Johnny, Paul Tesluk (organ, but trumpet back then), and Don Staczek (drums). The rest of that little group was Mike Wood (trumpet), Roland Lehr (E-flat bass), and myself on trombone. I still have his original 33rpm and 45rpm records in a closet.

I forgot to mention --- I'd dispute the contention that Tony Kaye was the original drummer for Johnny and the Hurricanes. I think if you look on the back of their first album, you'll find the drummer is Don "Butch" Staczek, a neighbor of Johnny's, and also a member of our high school band, as was keyboardist Paul Tesluk, who played trumpet in the band. Nobody knew he could do keyboards, but his melodies were so simple anybody could have played them one-handed with two days training. And that's fine – it was his organ lead that carried the tune. Johnny's raspy sax was just the filler. I really don't remember the name Tony Kaye, but I'd suspect he didn't join the band until maybe 1961, when Staczek quit to (I think) go to college.

Johnny was really a nice guy. He was also a very bright student in school and earned a four-year college scholarship, all expenses paid by his father's employer, Libbey-Owens-Ford Glass (later Pilkington glass) but elected to go into rock 'n roll instead.

As a musician in The Rossford High School band, (a 3,000 population suburb of Toledo, Ohio), he was a very competent musician. Not the absolute best one in that area but he knew what he was doing with a tenor or baritone sax. And he was confident enough in his abilities to improvise sometimes, as we all did.

By the way, some websites, and the Manchester Guardian's obituary on Johnny say he went to Rossford Catholic High School. It was a public school, not a Catholic one, except by default since about 90% of the residents of our village were Catholic."

Dave Arnold

"John: Here's a reply I just got from my old friend, Dr. Mike Wood, re. the earliest history of Johnny and the Hurricanes."

Dave Arnold

"We were the Black Cats (how trite that now sounds) and wore all black. In addition to RHS assemblies, we played Friday and Saturday night sock hop gigs around the Toledo area, mostly east and north Toledo as I recall. My "signature" trumpet piece was the slow dance to "Blue Moon," which I might even remember if I was pressed and still had an embouchure. I think I was making something on the order of 8-10 bucks a job (band usually split $30-$50 for the night, which was typically about three hours with a twenty minute break). It was Johnny, Donny Staczek, Paul Tesluk, Dave Yorko and I. That, plus the Blade paper route, basically put me through college."

Hello John.

Johnny Paris passed away last year around this time. (John M Pocisk), musician, born August 29 1940; died May 3 2006.

Any chance we here at his Hurricane Shelter Office can get a copy of that book of yours? We have an autobiography of him coming out soon as well. Thanks for citing him as a favorite.

Contact me anytime at the ad's below.

Thanks John, and God Bless.

https://imoneofthe3002020.wordpress.com/

https://en.wikipedia.org/wiki/Johnny_and_the_Hurricanes

"One of my early inspirations was "Crossfire" by Johnny & the Hurricanes."

-David Leibman (1999)

The Circle Is Unbroken

Detroit Gary Wiggins
By Neil Sharpe

"I was born in Detroit, Michigan during the early 50's and raised within the black American culture and community. The music that we choose to listen to and enjoy was mostly the music of my culture. This included all different rhythms, expressions, and moods. Every generation had and have their way of expressing the music they play and we all have a personal style that we represent.

Every generation had and have their way of expressing the music they play and we all have a personal style that we represent. There did come a point in time that I decided to focus and travel a certain musical path and that was when my life long friend, keyboardist, Kenny Jackson, of Detroit, told me that an old man told him "that you should find what you really like and what feel you are good at and lay in it". I realized that I preferred playing blues and gospel (the foundation of popular American music) and with a slight rhythm change it translates to soul and r&b and of course just like the song says "It don't mean a thing if it ain't got that swing".

When I was about 7 or 8 years old, during the fifties, I can remember seeing saxophone players on a television show maybe once or twice and that image of suit and tie wearing sax men stuck with me and when I attended the family church every Sunday and witnessing suit and tie wearing Brother Lawhorn sit in a row of seats, situated behind the Hammond organ, with his tenor sax brought this image closer to reality.

There has been many influences but when I think about the very early influences that may have began to shape my musical taste and playing direction I think of the organ trios that played in the night clubs of my Westside Detroit neighborhood or the preacher who has a roll going on and is basically singing his sermon with tone and rhythm. I also think of Ken Knox, who was the sax player in the Impacs and a member of the vocal group "Chairmen of the Board". Ken played the sax solo on our first recording of "That Good Ol' Funky Feeling". As for my most important early influence I must acknowledge the late Mr. Jack Perkins of Detroit, Michigan.

My major influences were:

ARNETT COBB, a man who played in a way that he deserves his entire name spelled in capital letters.

James Brown and his quote: "Appearance 75% Performance 25%".

And especially Big Jay McNeely. Touring with Big Jay was like a Doctorate from a University and the course was Show-Time 101." (Published with the permission of Pascale Wiggins)

Eddie "Cleanhead" Vinson played an important role in my early development as a player and performer by being the good role model that he was and by giving me certain advice which is second nature to me now.

My school training was very basic and not in the higher education, however, through practical experience and listening I should hold a P H D (*pretty heavy dude*). My tip for the younger players is to learn and practice as must as possible. This will increase your vocabulary when it is time to put it into practice and listen to everybody, especially the older players from the 30s and 40s for the foundation. Don't forget that at the time that they made the recordings they were also very young men and somewhat rebels of society being innovative on their horns.

Stanley Turrentine once told me, over lunch in Tokyo, that when he was coming up "it was a sin to sound like anyone else". That was the day that I realized and accepted the tone of my voice on the saxophone.

In Detroit, I began working with the Living Room Blues Band led by guitarist, Gary Meisner. We would play the Soup Kitchen every Wednesday and I would read the press releases posted about the musicians coming on the weekends. I then discovered that the blues was alive and well in Chicago and that these musicians also toured Europe.

May 1982- I took a trip to Chicago in search of the blues and all I knew was that I did not want to go to the south side of town (yet) and I had heard of clubs being on Rush street. I followed my map until I was far enough north to exit the Dan Ryan freeway at Diversy street. Driving west on Diversy, I came upon Halsted street and I had just heard that street mentioned on the radio. I made a right turn heading south and within a few blocks I saw a club on my left with a big sign that read "B.L.U.E.S".

I found a place to park my vehicle, after a 30 minute search, then I took my horn and went to the door and saw that Sunnyland Slim was playing. After a brief conversation with the owner, who sat at the door collecting admission, he allowed me entry without paying. And within a few short minutes I was on the bandstand playing with the band. I can remember that it was Steve Freud on guitar, Bob Stroger on bass, the late Fred Grady on drums and Sunnyland Slim on piano.

The day that Muddy Waters was buried I was playing in the Kingston Mines with Louis Myers on vocals, guitar and harmonica, Bob Stroger on bass, Chris Rannenberg on piano, Bob Levitz on rhythm guitar and Robert Covington on vocal and drums when Sunnyland Slim came into the club with Robert Jr. Lockwood and Odie Payne.

The younger musicians soon made way for these veterans to come together and play.

Sunnyland Slim at the piano, Robert Jr. Lockwood, guitar and vocals, Bob Stroger, bass, Louis Myers, guitar, harmonica, vocals, and Odie Payne, drums.

The experience of witnessing this collaboration of rhythms carry on a musical conversation between each player, at once, reminded me of being in my family church (when I think about the sounds and rhythms of Sunday afternoon) except they were playing the blues. This night has had a lasting effect on me on the importance of feeling the music as you play it.

Detroit Gary Wiggins, a great player, was the definition of stage image, presence and style.

Awarded the Berlin Jazz and Blues Award in 2001, he was an advisor for the Institute For Cultural Diplomacy (Berlin, New York City), and spoke about Jazz and Blues in Europe at Harvard University.

Johnny Ferreira
By Neil Sharpe

From traveling the frozen winter hinterlands of Canada doing 300 plus gigs a year, to being featured on *Billboard* Top Ten hits and winning gold and platinum albums, Johnny Ferreira has cut his own distinct musical path. He's done it by staying true to the music he loves best- rock n' roll.

"You have to love what you're doing. Playing blues, r&b, and rock n' roll isn't a recipe for getting rich quick. Although I know that many musicians have struggled, I can only tell you what it's been like for myself. You have to be stubborn and stick to it and look for that break that will make all the difference."

As a teenager, Johnny ran head on into people "who wanted you to be a plumber or a mechanic or whatever and had that attitude that if you didn't follow their suggestions, what would you have to fall back on? I hate that line, because you only need something to fall back on if you plan on falling back. I never thought of getting into something and 'falling back.' I always go forward.

That's what happened to me, and here I am all those years later."

"Earl Bostic is one of my favorite alto players for the big tone. Actually, I'd also have to put Louis Jordan in this category and Cannonball Adderley for his sweet tone and dexterity. As for tenor, King Curtis was a big influence. For example, he does 'Guitar Boogie' with Al Caiola that is a simple, 12 bar blues, but his tone and playing is amazing; same thing with his song 'Soul Twist'."

AL CAIOLA (gtr), King Curtis (ten), unk. pno/org, 2nd gtr, bs, dms.

New York. 1962

>   Guitar Boogie United Artists LP 3180
>
>   Foot Stompin' United Artists LP 3180
>
>   I Walk The Line   United Artists LP 3180

Note: It has not so far been possible to check the whole LP ("Solid Gold Guitar"), and it is possible there are other tracks featuring King Curtis.

"Guitar Boogie" was also issued on 45, U-A 545, and it is unknown if the reverse ("Kalinka") is from the same session(s). -Roy Simonds

"We were playing 300 gigs a year. Every month, the manager would hand us the itinerary. Sometimes, it seemed like we were playing every little town on the map, including towns that weren't on the map and that no one had ever heard of!

By 1988 –89, we'd recorded our first album for Virgin records in America. It was recorded at Criteria Studios in Miami, Florida with the legendary producer Tom Dowd (who also had recorded John Coltrane and King Curtis) and finished in Los Angeles with Danny Kortchmar."

It became the fastest-selling album in Canadian history. A single off the album, "Voodoo Thing", reached #30 on the "Mainstream Rock Charts" of Billboard.

Thom Omens of the *All Music Guide,* writing for *Billboard*, described the album as "an impressive collection of high-octane blues-rock that, at its best, explodes with the intensity of a keg of dynamite".

"Keith Richards had a real impact on our band. We had just finished up a two week tour with the American band "Little Feat" in North Carolina, and flew directly to Boston to start another tour with Keith Richards and his band 'The Expensive Winos'. It was The Fox Theatre and it was a real thrill for us. We were like giddy high school boys. It was kind of surreal, actually being there with this guy Keith Richards. We were all big Rolling Stones fans, and this guy was the heart and soul of all of that. It turned out to be a very valuable experience for us as musicians, and it had a definite and positive impact…it was like going to 'Rock & Roll School', and we had a class with Keith every day!'"

Then, Colin James decided to return to REAL rock n' roll, the jump and swing blues, with the album "Colin James and The Little Big Band", featuring a selection of late-forties and early-fifties jump-blues tunes. Produced by Chis Kimsey of The Rolling Stones, the album featured Johnny Ferreira and Greg Piccolo on tenor saxes (Gordon "Sax Gordon" Beadle later stepped in for Greg for some of the tours), Rich Lataille on alto, Doug James on baritone, the Roomful of Blues horn section, and Reese Wynans on piano, drummer John (The Fly) Rossi, and organist Chuck Leavel.

Entertainment Weekly called the CD "... a side trip into pre-rock blues and jump tunes...this album is an uninhibited love letter to an era when music was for dancing, not thinking..."; *Rolling Stone* wrote, "The music is swinging stuff, too rarely heard...reactivating this particular jukebox is one cool move...."

"That's where it all comes from- jump and swing blues. I grew up on rock & roll, or as we call it: 'Rock'.

Rock & Roll lost its roll sometime in the 60s. I mean Led Zeppelin is Rock but not Rock & Roll. I'm talking about before Elvis Presley in the 1950s. I've heard R&B records from the late 40's and they're singing, 'Let's rock, let's roll' etc. Did they call this 'Rock & Roll'? No, because the term hadn't been coined as of yet, but, it was Rock & Roll. The roll means just that, it's the swinging element of the music. Back in the 40s, the drummer would be swinging and the bass & piano would rock over top of him...this was the REAL rock & roll.

Growing up on Motown, Funk, R&B, I liked it all, but at the end of the day, I find the swing/rock & roll style to be the most expressive and the one that lends itself to fun and crazy lyrics. Just listen to Louis Prima or Louis Jordan or 'Little Charlie & the Nightcats'."

Try playing along with Red Prysock. He really raises the bar! The LP 'Battle Royale' between Red Prysock and Sil Austin really opened my eyes.

I've been a professional musician since around 1985. It's the only field I've worked in during that time, and I have no thoughts or plans of a career change, quite the opposite.

I have supported my family, bought a house, car, all the normal type things other working people do. So, yes it certainly is possible to do it. As for being typical or atypical, I don't really know. I do know many musicians who just do gigs to make their money, and some do well at it and others don't. I have been writing music (some of my songs have been used in movies and TV) and selling albums so this has created multiple money streams. Sometimes, there will be a very slow month for gigs, but then a royalty cheque shows up...

Things are getting more interesting and busier for me, especially with when I step into the studio and how digital technology now enables me to reach people around the world, even attracting 600,000 plus views on my YouTube channel.

People in the music business are always looking for labels and trying to slot you into genres. It can get frustrating. I've looked at all the so-called genre choices, and out of the dozen or so they've created, the only one that comes close is the blues. But, I feel like I'm different, a continuation of the swing and jump traditions but more focused and defined.

They wanted a label for me. Now, I had one to give them. It was the title of one of my albums- *Johnny Ferreira- Rock & Roll Saxophonist.*" HowToPlaySaxophone.org

John Barrow
By Neil Sharpe

The Swinging Laurels

In 1982, John Barrow's group, the Swinging Laurels hit the Number One on the English independent chart with their debut release "Peace of Mind." They played with stars including The Clash, Boy George, Culture Club, and Iggy Pop. John has a unique perspective. He was in the forefront of the ska, punk, and the "New Romantic" synth revolution in England during the late 1970s and early 1980s that triggered "a sea change in the way music was played and recorded."

What does a dust clogged C melody, a disastrous audition, and a street full of broken milk bottles get you?

How about The Clash, Boy George, Culture Club, Iggy Pop, and top ten chart success!

Not bad? Right?

Lots of fame and fortune?

Not quite.

Dedication, hard work, and lady luck might get you a chance to nod hello to the first but put one large hold on the second.

That's according to John Barrow, in *How NOT To Make It In The Pop World*, a fascinating, insightful guide to the magical, dream driven, roller coaster, shark filled world of rock n' roll. How against all odds, a young sax player's dreams came true but with one large price.

https://www.amazon.com/Make-World-Diary-Almost-Has-Been-ebook/dp/B0791LFDZF/ref=sr_1_1?dchild=1&keywords=john+barrow+how+not+to+make+it&qid=1613753266&s=books&sr=1-1

Rehearsals in a closet with an elderly neighbor pounding on paper thin walls, a lucky advertisement, life out of a suitcase, topless dancers, adoring fans, broken marriages, shattered egos, agents drenched in gold jewelry, hitting the big time playing a song that wasn't quite what it seemed to be, in a band that wasn't quite what it seemed to be, with a pay cheque that never was what it should be.

And that was only the beginning.

Although the first part of the book provides a fascinating overview of the growing pains every musician goes through, the book's real strengths are John's hard-won insights about the music business- and what a ruthless beast it can be. These tips, about what to watch out for and why, should be considered mandatory reading for every young musician aspiring for a career in the music industry.

"If it was all just about making music then fine but when you are saddled with all the legal and contractual technicalities, it gets as far removed from music as you could possibly imagine…it's enough to knock the creative stuffing out of any young aspiring musician".

Which brings us to the core question in John's book.

If, as John writes, "Music is 10% exhilaration and 90% utter disappointment", then what keeps one going?

What's the gravitational pull?

What is it that causes one to swallow nerves and shyness, climb up on stage, into the spotlight, and say, "Here I am"?

What keeps one playing 3 a.m. gigs for next to nothing, then reporting to that demanding, 8 a.m. job the next morning?

What makes one happy to be jammed shoulder to shoulder, equipment piled high on all sides, in a cheap, bitterly cold, exhaust fume-filled van?

What makes one willing to live in a brutally demanding way of life, through all the twists and turns, the friendships and betrayals, with no guarantee of either success or even survival?

If it's an ambition fueled by an appetite for money, success, and fame, that's fine. But that tells only part of the story.

If music is your lifeblood, if you are prepared to sacrifice everything for it, then that impulse makes everything possible, including moments of transcendence that can forever change a life.

"I saw friends establish themselves in well-paid jobs and enjoy the benefits of a regular pay cheque. During my time in music, many of them slogged away in the same jobs, but have any of them visited Oslo, San Sebastian, Vienna, or even Bannockburn? Money couldn't pay the stunning times music has given to me."

It can be a magical world, where anything is possible, where one can rocket from obscurity to international recognition overnight... and sometimes burn out just as fast. "One moment you appear to be riding the crest of a wave, only to have the rug pulled away from you, bringing you back down to earth with a sickening thud."

Musicians who want to soar from zero to the top have to be exceptionally resilient. Failures and setbacks are part of the game, a necessary part of the learning process.

John has a unique perspective. He was in the forefront of the ska, punk, and the "New Romantic" synth revolution in England during the late 1970s and early 1980s.

Out of those experiences, John shares invaluable lessons on what it takes to get ahead.

"It's not what you play but what you leave out that makes the difference", goes to the heart of it.

How many players today, for example, are familiar with the great jump blues and rock n' roll sax players from the 1950s like Lee Allen and Joe Houston? They could take just two or three notes and transform them into a sound so memorable that it seemed without limit.

Ultimately, perhaps the most important factor of all is the producer, whose mix can take you to the stars or sink you like a stone.

"Sometimes you feel isolated and vulnerable in a studio with headphones on having to peer at studio staff through the control room window...Often you recorded your parts after waiting around for hours, so it was difficult to inject life into it. After several takes, you started to worry and a sort of paranoia set in. You could see the wagging tongues in the control room but couldn't hear a word they were saying."

The common thread, underlying all of this, is financial survival. In 1979, at the fabled Hope and Anchor pub in Islington London, one weekend's lineup featured the breakout bands Madness, The Police, and The Specials. Yet, each band was paid only 20 pounds. Throw in traveling expenses etc., and bands soon were swimming in red ink. Even top flight acts had to play provincial pubs to pay the bills; "...we were still a pretty high profile band, still getting good service from the national music press, playing large prestige venues to thousands of screaming girlies, yet we were all stony broke. You only can live on adrenaline for so long; one thing is for sure, it doesn't pay the bills".

Stage success doesn't always translate into financial success. John's band opened for top acts like Culture Club but "People assume that because you have graced the same stage as the star act, in front of thousands, you must be reaping similar financial rewards. This is a complete fallacy."

In 1982, John Barrow's group, the Swinging Laurels hit Number One on the English independent chart with their debut release "Peace of Mind." The group picked up national exposure on radio, television, and the media.

https://www.youtube.com/watch?v=yl_T0xTq-YY

"Releasing a record is only the tip of the iceberg when it comes to the promotion of the product, but you have to play the game if you are to have a chance of competing in the marketplace."

So, be ready to run. If you want to survive as a musician, be prepared to play whatever you can whenever and wherever you can.

While attention and praise were rolling in, John still had to run for every dollar. In addition to countless live play dates, here's a partial list of John's hectic schedule, all powered by his beloved 1962 Selmer Mark VI with nickel plated keys:

-Released the four track EP "A Taste of ... "

-Played session on the Fun Boy Three hit "The Telephone Always"

-TV appearances including England's number one music program, "Top of the Pops "

-Video produced Ultravox vocalist Midge Ure with appearances by: Bananarama, Madness, and Ultravox

-Session musician for 2-Tone Records

Tracks on an album by Worldbackwards

-A session with chart toppers Musical Youth

-Work on the Fun Boy Three hit "Summertime".

-Recorded a track with Boy George that was overseen by top producer Steve Levine. WEA Records 1983

Our second single for Warner Brothers - produced by top producer Steve Levine -notable because it features Boy George on backing vocals – "Lonely Boy" - https://theswinginglaurels.bandcamp.com/track/lonely-boy-12

"However, the version that surfaced was minus George's vocal due to his label Virgin Records. There are white label test pressings out there that show how close we came to getting it out there before it was pulled! The release date was timed to coincide with a sellout UK with Culture Club but

because of delays in re-recording George's parts, the whole promotional pushed was out of synch.
https://theswinginglaurels.bandcamp.com/track/lonely-boy-12

In later years, John supported chart acts, like The Clash, Culture Club and Iggy Pop
-Played on tracks with Sinead O'Connor, Suggs (Madness), Ali Campbell (UB40) and Beverley Knight
-The Fun Lovin' Criminals' track that I played on was 'Daylight' featuring Rowetta of Happy Mondays it was a single and was also featured on the album 'Another Mimosa' - the album reached number 16 in the UK Independent charts - Both were on De Fontaine Records.

Fun Boy Three

This track is an instrumental called "Stranger Than Fiction" - https://theswinginglaurels.bandcamp.com/track/stranger-than-fiction

Here is what we did with Sinead O Connor.- It was included in a project by Radio Riddler (fronted by Frank Benbini and Fast of the Fun Lovin Criminals) from the album Purple Reggae - It is the Prince song "I Would Die 4 U" - https://www.youtube.com/watch?v=NX1D1MdcpiM

But you'd better understand that even if you have written and played the greatest song in the world, if the person on top decides to look in a different direction, no one may ever hear it.

"One of the major factors that convinced us to sign was that he was a real fan of the band. Now we were faced with the prospect of a newcomer taking control of our careers...from the beginning we formed the impression that he wasn't a fan...One lapse of judgment can cost and talent isn't everything. A huge slice of good fortune in needed to make it to the top, and without that element of luck, you've no chance."

In the end, some critics may say that John fell short.

"Flirtations with the music industry doubtless cost me in a financial sense...I persevered for as long as I could always telling myself 'this is the year', unfortunately that year never materialized. I came so close so many times..."

But did he fall short? Signing with a major label, chart success, television appearances on England's number one music show, and sharing the stage with some of the world's great bands, would be called a wonderful career by many musicians.

http://theswinginglaurels.co.uk/

More importantly, John reminds us that before we criticize ourselves for what we could and should have done, let's first acknowledge what we've accomplished and experienced.

John's great journey may not have resulted in financial rewards, however, his dedication, perseverance, courage, and "that lump of metal that I call my saxophone has been my passport to some unforgettable experiences and capers. It helped me to achieve many of my childhood dreams and for that I am very grateful... You see I believe 'If you never try, you'll never know what you are capable of'."

Editors' Note: John's updated version of "How NOT To Make It In The Pop World" continues to sell well. In 2020, his book was named to Amazon's Musicians Biographies List, sitting next to bios of Paul McCartney, Elvis, and Pink Floyd.

500

Deke McGee
By Deke McGee

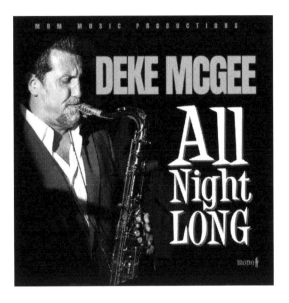

A 13 year old walked into a record store to buy the latest 12" vinyl pop song, had it in his hand when he looked over and saw the "most colourful looking LP" he'd ever seen- a bunch of musicians in straw hats, sitting in front of an old bus, blue sky and yellow stars flying all around them, with the strange title "Gon Doggett". He had no idea who they were, but hey with a cover like that how could he resist…or know that the album would change his life.

"The band was led by Bill Doggett who was completely unknown to me at the time but the LP just looked really interesting and the liner notes on the back had names of all these unknown Tenor, Alto and Baritone players...I bought it."

Which was more than a little surprising, since at one point, he had no idea what "Swing, Blues or Rhythm n' Blues" was and had little interest in it..."stupidly I thought that was old people's music I suppose."

"I took it home and put it on the turntable, wondering what was going to come out of the speakers...Track One played, followed by Track Two...'Honky Tonk Part 1' and 'Honky Tonk Part 2'... I was sold!

That was the way I wanted to play saxophone and that was the music I wanted to play. I didn't know who the tenor player Clifford Scott was, but I just loved his sound, notes and style. From then on, I wanted to know more about this really under-rated style of music…"

Flash forward to the 21st Century where Deke McGee's, album "All Night Long" has won widespread acclaim in the saxophone community.

' There have been so many players that I've listened to over the years that have influenced me in both style and sound. Listening to recordings by Fats Domino, Little Richard, Tiny Bradshaw, Count Basie, Lionel Hampton and many more, I would try to emulate the solos and stylings of the tenor players without knowing who they actually were. You then do a little research and find out it's players like Lee Allen, Red Prysock, Sam 'The Man' Taylor, King Curtis, Illinois Jacquet, Arnett Cobb, Lester Young… this leads you to their own recordings as the main name and not as sidemen to other performers.

All the solos of these great artists tell a story, playing repeated riffs and building a solo so it has a start, middle and end, not just 55 notes over 4 bars of music...Melody and Tone.

'Honky Tonk' played by Clifford Scott was the solo that set me off, but I remember hearing 'Memphis Soul Stew' by King Curtis and just fell in love with his sound and complete control of the instrument.

Earlier recordings like 'Blue Harlem' by Ike Quebec taught me that your solo should tell the same story as the song it's in. There is a wonderful live recording on DVD by Arnett Cobb playing in a venue in New Orleans in the mid 80s; he plays a song 'Texas Blues'. It starts with him and the double bass player for the first 24 bars; it's full of style, swagger, melody and all played with a beautiful tone. It's an absolute masterclass on how to build the song from start to finish.

Those musical roots continue today, keeping this wonderful music and style alive. One of my all time favourites is Greg Piccolo from Rhode Island. His style and in particular his sound are both just perfect, but I'm sure Greg would cite the great original horn players from the 30s, 40s and 50s as major influences. Great showmen like Terry Hanck and Ray Gelato are wonderful exponents of Blues, R&B and Swing as well as being fine singers and band leaders.

I also listen to players like Joe Sublett, Doug "Mr. Low" James, Marty Grebb, Ron Dzuibla, Bill Holloman and Jonny Viau...you'll hear them play with many different Bands such as Roomful Of Blues, Junior Watson, Kid Ramos, Taj Mahal, Duke Robillard and Jimmy Vaughan.

There are so many wonderful modern tenor, alto and baritone players that make my personal list too long to print, but so much can be learned from studying and mimicking these legendary saxophonists.

Players and teachers talk a lot about practicing technique and I agree it's very important. Learning your scales, breath control, trying to get a library of songs in your head and not just off the dots in front of you, effects like vibrato, practicing at different volumes and also various tempos, learning to play with and without a metronome, tuner practice, making sure the low notes and high notes sound just as confident as all the other notes...

The one thing people don't do enough of is to practice tone, especially in the early stages. There is technique in Sound and Long Tone practice that is very important; what's the point of being able to play a note for 36 beats if it doesn't sound nice and isn't consistent.

As far as playing Rhythm n' Blues Saxophone, it's important to listen to other players and take time to work out by ear and learn some of the patterns they are playing-you'll need inspiration from other places and not just from your own head...Picasso must have had a look at Da Vinci!

Plus, it's not only working out the patterns, but how these great players are playing the patterns. Are they falling off the note, using dynamics, bending the note, using growl or vibrato and other effects and stylings that players can use.

One question I always get asked from students, 'Why don't I sound like the saxophonist on the record'. The answer is the players on the record are doing a whole lot more than just playing the physical notes, it's how they are actually playing the notes, using various effects and techniques. I used to pick a particular player and try to mimic their tone, style and patterns, then move onto another player, then another. I found that by doing this, I wouldn't become a clone of one player; instead, I was taking a bit from everyone and also adding some of me into the mix. This may sound strange, but copying other players helps to find your own voice. Finally, too many beginners work on too many things in practice rather than focusing on things a step at a time. If you want to accomplish your goals, focus, repetition, discipline and hard work are the keys.

I'm Leaving Town

I've toured Europe and North America playing at Blues clubs and Blues and Jazz festivals. As well as loving playing with the band, I also got the chance to meet and play with many different musicians. Since that first musical break 33 years ago, I have made my living solely from playing my saxophone; of course, it's had its ups and downs, but I feel very lucky and also very proud to be a working professional musician.

Some Recording Studios have a list of players they can call if a certain instrument or style was needed. You turn up, meet the band or the main songwriter, and hear the song.

A lot of times it can be a young Indie band who might not know what they want in terms of parts, but know they want a sax somewhere in the song. If you're lucky, the studio engineer may have a few ideas, however, in most cases it's left up to you. Most of the bands ask you to play 3 or 4 slightly different takes and they will either pick one or cut and paste their favourite bits from each take into one solo. I can't tell you how many times I've received the final mix and thought that's not what I played or that's how I would have pieced my solo together, but it's *their* song.

It gets a bit more pressure if it's a TV or Radio jingle; there's more money involved and they want the work done quickly. That's always the thing with most musicians in recording studios...the first take. Everyone expects you to get it right in one go, and if you don't, you think they are all talking about you in the control room. For me, it took a bit of time for me to able to manage that; yes, you want to get the job done quickly, but you also want it to be right and what the band wants.

If you are going to hire yourself out to different bands whether for live work or studio work, you have to listen to all different styles of music- you never know what you might have to play to pay your bills. I hear a lot of young players now saying that they are Session players; I don't think they actually understand what that term actually means. Their idea of a Session player is playing in two or three bands that are playing the exact same music every take. A real Session musician has to play anything and everything that comes their way...by ear or using the dots. It could be an advert with Pop music or Classical in one session, the next might be a rock or soul band wanting a horn line in the style of The Memphis Horns or Motown- that is what a real Session player has to be able to do and that's what they get paid for.

Years ago, I remember my teacher telling me never to take a job for money that you don't think you have the right style or ability to do, your reputation is worth more than the session fee. That was great advice.

It all goes back to technique, why I learned scales, why I learned how to growl, why I learned to play by ear, why I learned to read music, why I listen to most styles of music...you never know what you are going to get asked to play until the phone rings or you turn up in the studio.

If you get a chance to listen to the song beforehand use it wisely, practice the horn line, practice the solo, make sure the phrasing is right, that's it the sound and feel they are looking for. That's is what makes a Session musician a Session musician. It's like any other profession, be prepared, be professional whether it's Take 1 or Take 27!

I remember a very important lesson that I was taught. The band that I was touring with was playing an open air show at the Montreal Jazz Festival on the Labatt's Blues stage. There must have been at least 20,000 in the audience. Again, I was younger and less experienced than the rest of the guys in the band, the drummer had played with many artists on World tours.

As nervous as I was, I was really looking forward to it. We got out of the shuttle bus that had picked us up from the hotel and dropped us off backstage. I got my saxophone out of the case and started to walk up the stairs at the back of the stage, just as the announcer introduced the band. The drummer said to me 'Remember you can't do this every night'. I had no clue what he meant or why he would say those words, however, the show that night was amazing. Three nights later, we were 200 miles away in a different city and playing at another venue. There couldn't have been more than six people in the audience at any one time and two of them were probably staff! I now knew what the drummer meant.

Some bands and musicians I've played with would treat touring and playing like a party every day, yet others treat it like any other professional job...really enjoyable but hard work. It's quite easy to get caught up in the nonsense, but at some point you need to treat it like any other profession- turn up on time, be rehearsed and do the job you are getting paid to do. I'll give you an example.

After I had worked with the above band and toured all over Europe and North America, I was asked to join a younger and really talented up and coming blues band from

Scotland. They were starting to do some of the same Festivals that the previous older band had played. I remember my first show with them, it was a beautiful sunny Sunday afternoon and we were about to go on stage at Antwerp Blues Festival in Belgium- huge stage and an equally big crowd. I was about to walk on stage with my saxophone and some bottles of beers, enough to see me through the show. The main man in the band said 'Where do you think you're going with them?...You are here to work...water only'. I left the beers, went on stage with bottles of water and am glad that I did. The band really put on a show. I came off absolutely exhausted and ready for a lie down. I soon realized that the audience pay their hard earned money to come and see a show, they don't really want to see someone gulping down bottles of this and that in between the songs. I know it's music and I absolutely love doing it, but for me it's like any other career, you need to be professional if you want to make a living at it. Like most musicians, there are too many wild stories from years of shows and travelling. Luckily for me, there have been a lot of highs and not that many lows, it's been a great job and long may it continue.

The Road

One practical reality is 'the road'. It can be a long day, up early and sitting in a van travelling to the new city or town or even a to a local gig. To be honest, it's never been a problem for me focusing on a show once I've arrived, sound-checked and ready to go on. However, if it's been a rush and we are late arriving at the venue, the sound-check takes longer than normal and all of a sudden you have 30 minutes till the show starts. I like to get the sound-check over with and then relax if I can. I never play my saxophone or practice after the sound-check unless there are new songs being brought in at the last minute. There are some musicians I've played with that like to leave the venue and come back just before show time. I have my routine for getting set up at the gig; one is finding my own wee corner in the dressing room to hang up my stage clothes and somewhere to drop my bag and sax case. By the time the sound-check is over, I'll have my Set List on the floor beside the monitor, have a spare reed case for any emergencies and some bottles of water at the microphone stand. Other than that, I don't have any other routine before the show, apart from relaxing if I can.

Like most people, over the years you eventually get used to the travelling and hanging around waiting for the show to start…and sometimes that can be a lot of hanging around. It's not as glamorous as people think, compared to some jobs, I am a very lucky person to be doing what I love and get paid for it. For me, it was always a lovely feeling getting picked up on a rainy weekday morning in Glasgow and knowing by late evening or next day I would be somewhere in Europe or North America.

I've been lucky to play in bands where most of the players are full time musicians, which means you are free to tour and don't have to work schedules around people with day jobs. This *doesn't* always mean though that players that are full time and the players that are part time are miles apart in terms of talent and experience.

As well as flying, you also spend time on boats (which I hate) and a lot of time on the Tour bus. Travelling on a Tour Bus sounds very grand and sometimes it was, but you also had the small van from your local Hire company that was modified into your Tour bus for shows in England, Wales, France, Belgium, Holland and other European countries. You had to fashion seats out of bass speakers and drum cases, it was always freezing in the back, and you'd designate a shotgun passenger that had to stay awake through the night to help keep the driver awake, all of us eating rubbish at the service station because it's 4 a.m. and you are still awake and hungry...everyone has their own versions of these kind of trips but again, it's always an adventure.

Accommodation would depend on the actual gig or who was paying or promoting the Tour. I spent a whole summer touring around the Province of Quebec in Canada, playing at Blues festivals sponsored by Labatt's Beer, so the gigs were great, the hotels were all very comfortable since they used the same chain of hotels for the entire Tour. That's the upside. I've also played gigs where the promoter puts you up in their own home, a bed each if you were lucky or sleeping bags, mattresses and couches. When young, you don't really care that much as you are in another country playing music with you buddies.

Dressing rooms also varied depending on the size of venue; some were unbelievably dirty with last night band's rubbish still lying on the sticky beer stained floor, but some dressing rooms were huge and welcoming. It was always lovely to walk into a nice dressing room after travelling most of the day and night and see a 'rider'...a flask of tea or coffee, some sandwiches and some beers cooling in the fridge, just like we were royalty.

Sound checks can be painful and boring for some musicians, it's something I've never really had a problem with. The trick to a sound-check is just to set-up and wait for the sound engineer to call you onto the stage, play-test the microphone, get the level in your monitor, shut up, leave the stage and let the next instrument do the same. Some players (drummers mostly in my experience) like to try and play-along with the next player as they are doing their sound-check, it is noisy and just wastes time. The quicker you do your test and keep quiet, the quicker you can sound-check as a band, iron out any problems with stage levels or songs and have a run through some of the set.

The Business Of Music

Promoters come in all shapes and sizes with different levels of experience. Most of the Festivals are very well run and the Venues also have mostly experienced personnel doing this job. Only a few times have I, or the band, had to argue for payment or get into a debate about certain contractual differences but I've never really had issues in this department. Most bands with the same regular personnel split the fee between each other after expenses have come off the top.

When hiring yourself as a sideman, the band will either tell you what they can pay you for the gig or tour or ask you what you charge for your normal fee. I always make sure I price myself depending on the actual gig or gigs, whether it's in the same country or abroad, how many rehearsals are involved and whether I am playing on 5 songs or 25.

I once took on an Acoustic Duo Tour, vocals, guitar and me, travelling in his car and staying in very small hotels. It started in France, then Belgium and Holland, back into France, over to London and we worked our way back through the UK and finished in Scotland. I was told I would be paid £100 per show (expenses paid), there were 13 shows over two and a half weeks, and this would be the same whether there was an audience of 10 people or 500 people. It wasn't my name on the posters, I wasn't taking the risk, so I said yes...the audiences turned out to be big and small. It was none of my business what the person who hired me earned, I had agreed to the deal and I came home with £1300 for 17 days work playing my saxophone and touring Europe. I was okay with that.

I would advise to get your saxophone serviced or at least checked over by your repair-man at least once every 12 to 18 months, especially if they are getting used constantly like mine are.

Customs can sometimes be troublesome, but as long as you have the right paperwork it is normally okay. I can remember once heading into Montreal with a band, we had return tickets for six months but only had secured gigs for the first three months and Customs wanted to know what we were planning to do for the rest of the trip. They let us into the country and stamped our passports for the first three months, but we were told to report back to them on the specific stamped date. Luckily, we managed to start working with other promoters and they secured us more Festivals for the second half of our tour. Unfortunately, we still had to find a lawyer to sort it out even though we now had contracts and the proper documents, but it did end up being a bit costly and troublesome.

The best advice I can give if you are starting touring, whether it's near or far, is to be as organized as you can. This means being both musically prepared and rehearsed as well as having your instrument and also your baggage packed properly. Try to be on time for your colleagues, don't keep people waiting and lastly have patience.

Recording

"As for my CD "All Night Long", some songs had been sitting there unfinished for years before I actually had a chance to go into the studio and finish them. The guys I used were all friends and they knew exactly how to play this style of music, so it worked without any issues.

https://www.dekemcgee.com/audio

The guys had asked me about a year before to arrange the horn parts and help them record their own original CD. I didn't ask for payment for this, but said I might get them to return the favour, and they did. I used drums, double bass, piano and two guitars. We went into the studio on a Sunday afternoon about midday and recorded the rhythm section live, they played 11 tracks and we were done by five o'clock.

We would run each song about two or three times so the guys got used to the arrangement, who was soloing where, and then record it. I wasn't putting a guide vocal down, I would just signal 1st verse, 2nd verse, chorus and then point to the player for his solo, quite simple really, but when you have good musicians it does become a slightly easier process.

About a month later, I went in to start recording the horn parts, using baritone and tenor. I'm old fashioned in my approach. I had already worked the parts out and recorded them separately on an old Tape Dictaphone. There were two horn-lines per song and each one had a baritone and tenor line on it, so it took a bit of time. As there were so many parts to remember, I would be in the recording booth, play back the baritone part on the Dictaphone, record it, then the same with the tenor parts. It was all low tech. I wanted to take my time to get my sound sorted out for the baritone and tenor and keep the same sound right through the complete CD, with the same mix for the horn-lines...keep it simple.

As for the actual songs, I had written 'That's Love' a few years before but in its most basic form, just voice and piano, recorded again on my old Dictaphone. With this in hand, it was just a matter of letting the guys know the tempo, feel, and arrangement of the song, they did the rest.

https://www.dekemcgee.com/audio

'Jumpin' Jesus Holy Cow' was actually another song of mine called 'Gravy Train', one I had played many times live. The night before the horns were being recorded, I decided to freshen it up, sat down at my kitchen table and came up with new horn parts with some new lyrics. When the guys heard the finished CD they didn't recognize 'Jumpin' Jesus' because they'd heard it and recorded it as 'Gravy Train' on the day, but now I have two songs out of one!

Playing Rhythm n' Blues and recording shouldn't be a big Hi-Tech affair, that's why I decided to do the rhythm section live. If the players are all well versed and listen to the same style, it shouldn't be a problem-luckily for me it wasn't.

As for the singing, I'm using that term 'singing' loosely here. I only started singing lead vocals at the time of the recording, which was 2016. I've always sung backing vocals but never ever dreamed I would be out front doing it, that's too scary when you have been a sideman for so long and watched other real singers doing that job.

When the recording was getting to the point where everything was basically done, I had to think about the vocals, who was I going to ask and who suited this style. I had led bands before, but only instrumental ones or ones where I had a singer in place; I led from the back where I felt more comfortable. I've worked with some great vocalists, but I got to thinking if I added another body, it would be one more person to pay and organize, and besides, who knew the songs better than me? For this style, you don't need to have a wonderful voice just be able to sing in tune.

As far as singing influences, again, there are many, but people like Eddie 'Cleanhead' Vinson, Greg Piccolo, Ray Gelato, Sam Butera and Terry Hanck, are all great saxophonists but also sing lead and play great. Because I never ever thought I would be out front, any kind of training never entered my mind, I was just doing the occasional backing vocal. But I'm glad that I've started singing lead. Singing your own songs is real fun, having a band where the vocalist is also the saxophonist is not that common, so it's another selling point plus one less hotel room and wage. As scary as it was at first, and believe me it really was, it showed me that sometimes things that seem huge, aren't that big after the fact.

Most of the bands I've been with have played Blues, Rhythm n' Blues, Rock n' Roll or a mixture of all three. I have never really seen any difference in audience response in any city, town or country. It's good time music and people respond pretty much the same all over; obviously, it originates from the United States but it's been around long enough for it to have travelled all over.

What you do find is that some of the audience might not have any idea the actual song the band is playing, but the rhythm, swing and instrumentation do the job time and time again. There are many great bands playing this style in the UK, France, Holland, Germany and many other European countries, not just the USA. The audiences are getting the chance to see and hear some wonderful players worldwide and the crowds are growing because of it.

In terms of playing this style, for sax players you would be hard pushed to tell the difference in a blind test between some of today's players and the players from the original era. We all know the originators of R&B saxophone and love them, but I've listened to loads of modern players on CD and also live on stage; they have studied this style for years and it shows in their performance and recordings.

I suppose we learn from them all, and Rhythm n' Blues saxophone is such a wonderful style and sound. Like any study, there is so much to learn and it can be hard work, but that's the challenge and also the fun.

Finally, I remember a short clip from an interview with ex-Beatle Paul McCartney; the young interviewer asked him when he would retire, and his reply...'retire from what'."

Courtesy Deke McGee

Short Shorts-The Royal Teens

Bill Crandall   Tenor

#2 R&B #3 Pop

"Bill Crandle, Bill Dalton, Tom Austin, and Bob Gaudio formed the original band, known as the "Royal Tones", in Fort Lee, New Jersey, in 1957. Crandle (Crandell) left the band and was replaced on sax by Larry Qualiano, and in 1958, Joe Francovilla (aka Joey Villa) joined the lineup as singer. A name change followed, and the Royal Teens got a shot at recording on the tiny Power Records label.

Their first two singles, "Sitting With My Baby" and "Mad Gas," didn't chart, and they were in the process of cutting a couple of new singles in 1958 when their producer, against the wishes of the band, decided to use some leftover studio time to cut an instrumental jam that they had done on stage, to which they would improvise some words. Out of that session, "Short Shorts" was born.

⌐Bob Gaudio has been a member of two well-known groups: the Royal Teens (1957-1960) and the Four Seasons (1960-1969). According to Bob, it was at Bergenfield High School, with some classmates, that he founded an instrumental group which was called the Royal Tones. Because all members were teenagers, their name was quickly changed to The Royal Teens.

With Gaudio on piano, the others were Tom Austin (drums), Bill Crandall aka Buddy Randall (saxophone), and Billy Dalton (bass). The quartet also featured a female who strutted around the stage wearing short shorts, which was the rage at the time. Her name was Diana Costello but no one seems to know anything more about her or where she is now.

Although the song "Short Shorts" had been co-written by Bob Gaudio and Tom Austin during the summer of 1957, it would not be released until November, which isn't really an appropriate time to be wearing short shorts! Released on the small Power label, ABC Paramount had picked up the master and the song entered the charts in January of 1958, rising to the #3 spot. Not bad as the song only took about 20 minutes to record! Bill Crandall left the group and was replaced by Larry Qualiano."

The above from http://spectropop.com/archive/digest/d1281.htm

Interview with Tom Austin, one of the founding members of The Royal Teens.

TA: We were scheduled to be in the recording studio that night with The Corvelles, The Three Friends, some other groups, and two girl singers. That night, we recorded the instrumental track. The engineer and soundman said we created a new beat with the sax solo. A major saxophone artist at the time, King Curtis, was in the studio and said, WHO is playing that SAX?? It's unbelievable! And, here it was, this skinny little 14-year-old Bill Crandall.

TA: Yes, that's how it happened. We were now on ABC Paramount Records. All of this took place in a month. We were at CYO dances one week and the next, we left on the Florida tour with Bill Haley and the Comets, Jerry Lee Lewis, Buddy Holly and the Crickets, the Everly Brothers. This was a major leap for us! We were like scared little rabbits. Bill Haley and the Comets took a liking to us and our music and showed us the ways of the road.

Bill Crandall had to leave the band. Since he was only 14, his dad wouldn't let him go on the road. Bill was replaced by Larry Qualiano, who was 17 and had just finished at the Manhattan School of Music."

Courtesy http://jerseyboysblog.com/jbb-exclusive-interview-with-tom-austin/2493#.XbzggzNKg2w

"1958 was a very good year for rock 'n' roll—Elvis was hot; The Danleers cooled us off with "One Summer Night"; The Elegants beamed through our transistors with "Little Star"; Bobby Darin rocked our Saturday nights with "Splish Splash"; Jerry Butler and The Impressions kept us dancin' close with "For Your Precious Love"; "Let's Rave On," we shouted with the unforgettable Texan, Buddy Holly.

"Rock was still young, fun, and dreams sometimes came true during this magical excursion through our musical youth. You could form your own street corner group, practice the harmonies of Dion and The Belmonts with your neighborhood pals, play your Fender guitar at full treble while picking out lead parts from Chuck Berry and Dale Hawkins recordings.

"We all move in cycles through this world, but the dreams of youth never felt better than 1958 when you could form your own band and get lucky just like the kids from New Jersey with the really neat name—the Royal Teens.

"I think I'll play it one more time…" Jim Pewter, Program Director, American Forces Radio Network.

However, a question that had gone long unanswered: Did Al Kooper [who has played with Blood, Sweat and Tears, Bob Dylan (Al did the famous organ on "Like A Rolling Stone"), Mike Bloomfield, Stephen Stills, Jimi Hendrix, The Rolling Stones, B.B. King, Lynyrd Skynyrd…to name a few), ever play with The Royal Teens?

https://www.youtube.com/watch?v=R6hJeZbNepI (Blood Sweat and Tears)

https://www.youtube.com/watch?v=IwOfCgkyEj0 (Like A Rolling Stone)

"Question: "This group name doesn't appear on your website, Al, so could you please confirm or deny that you were in the Royal Teens 'Short Shorts'? If you were involved with them, do you know who did the sax parts?

Answer: I did my time in The Royal Teens. Starting in 1958 at the ripe old age of fourteen. Bob Gaudio and Leo Rogers gave me my pro start!!! The sax player of note was titled Larry Qualiano - he played the parts on the records. A 16-17 year old Jersey lad.

Hope this helps."

Al Kooper

http://www.alkooper.com/

Oh What A Night — The Dells

Lucius "Little Wash" Washington (Solo) Tenor
McKinley Easton Baritone

#4 R&B Vee Jay. Re-released 1969 Cadet-#1 Soul #10 Pop

Courtesy
http://hubcap.clemson.edu/~campber/club51.html

https://www.youtube.com/watch?v=UMlzMUGwSRk 1956 compare to:

https://www.youtube.com/watch?v=DP2tjK0gdkc 1969

Lucius Washington was born in Memphis, Tennessee, on June 18, 1926. He began on guitar but soon moved to the tenor saxophone. In 1942, frustrated by the lack of music schools in Memphis, Washington moved to Chicago, where he stayed with a cousin and finished high school at Wendell Phillips. He served in the armed forces in 1944-45, then returned to Chicago where he attended Metropolitan School of Music. In 1949, he started his own group with help from drummer and bandleader Jump Jackson. In an interview with Robert Campbell (18 July 2001), he recalled that "Little Wash" was his hasty suggestion for a marquee name when Jackson was assembling promotional material for the group. He later regretted the choice, because he considered himself a jazz musician and his handle made fans think he was a blues man.

Washington really established himself playing weekends at Ada's Chicken Shack (5114 South Prairie) with a "battle of the saxes" format that included Grady Johnson (tenor sax), Louis Carpenter (piano), and Walter Perkins (drums). Contracts filed with Musicians Union Local 208 indicate that his group was in residence at Ada's from May 1952 through September 1954.

Thereafter, Little Wash led bands at the Victory Club, the Cotton Club, the State Theatre Lounge, the Crown Propeller Lounge, the Stage Lounge, the Pit, and the Strand Show Lounge (where he was working at the beginning of 1956). Washington got a major break when Al Smith, who had been heavily reliant on Red Holloway for tenor sax work, was looking for a "new sound" on some of his studio sessions, and Lefty Bates recommended him. Lucius Washington appeared on something like 20 studio sessions for Vee-Jay between May 1956 and May 1958, backing singers and vocal groups; he also participated in two for States (1956) and this lone session for Club 51.

From 1957 to 1959, Washington held down a high-profile engagement at McKie's Disc Jockey Lounge, in a battle of the saxes format with Tom Archia; McKie Fitzhugh broadcast parts of the proceedings on his radio show. He cut a local LP in 1969 in a group under the leadership of drummer Billy Mitchell.

526

Of Special Note
By Neil Sharpe

SONG WRITING: The melody for Tommy Edwards' Number One hit in 1958, "It's All In The Game", was written in 1911 by the Vice-President of The United States, Charles G. Dawes.

***

SOUND: Bill Putnam is generally credited with being the first to use reverb with his recording of "Peg o' My Heart" by the Harmonicats at Universal Studio in Chicago 1947. Putnam said that he used the men's room as an echo chamber!

***

PRODUCTION: Toni Fisher- "The Big Hurt" (Number 3 Billboard Top 100, Number 16 Billboard Hot R&B)- the first record to (inadvertently) use phasing (splitting an audio signal into two audio paths). Two tape recorders were played simultaneously by engineer Larry Levine in order to "double" the sound of her voice. The two tapes stayed in synch for most of the recording, but occasionally one would move ahead of the other, creating a phasing effect. When finally released, some DJs reportedly wondered if it had been recorded in an airport!

***

SOUND-Inducted into the Rock And Roll Hall Of Fame, the Blues Hall Of Fame, and Rhythm and Blues Music Hall Of Fame, Bo Diddley's distinctive "clave" rhythm and the harmonic tension of his shimmering tones continue to be a touchstone in rock, pop, and hip hop.

***

SOUND- Jackie Brenston & His Delta Cats recorded the vastly influential hit "Rocket 88" (actually done by Ike Turner and the Kings of Rhythm). The guitarist's Willie Kizart's amp fell off the roof of a car and burst a speaker cone. When the amp was turned on, it made static and fuzzy sounds. On a tight schedule, he couldn't get the amp fixed and tried to repair it by stuffing paper where the cone had burst. The amp now worked but made a strange sound like a saxophone. Sam Phillips of Sun, the record producer, decided to record with the amp. "I never listened to the sound of one instrument. I listened for the effect, the total effect."

Jackie sang, Ike Turner tore it up on piano, Raymond Hill blew a killer tenor sax solo, and Kizart's distorted guitar sound doubled the bass line. When released, "Rocket 88" exploded, hitting Number One on the R&B charts and became one of the biggest hits of the year 1951.

***

PRODUCTION c.1955-c.1958: One of the little-documented phenomena in the U.S. was the so-called "**song-poem labels**". Essentially, these outfits would accept songs written by amateur songwriters, record and release them and charge a fee to the writer for doing so – much the same concept as vanity publishing in the book trade today. One of these companies was Tin Pan Alley Inc., which operated out of 1650 Broadway and was a slight cut above the rest in that it tended to use better class artists to record the songs submitted (such as The Mello-Harps) and a "real" arranger, in the shape of George "Teacho" Wiltshire. More about these companies can be found at the website of The American Song-Poem Music Archive, www.aspma.com, where you will find this quote: "(Jack) Covais (Tin Pan Alley's owner) was charging his customers roughly $300 to produce their song-poems, double and triple what his competitors were able to get. Although he cut corners by recording only at ricky-ticky semi-professional studios, the steep fee enabled him to use six-piece combos including some of the top session players in New York. Guitar legend **Mickey Baker** and tenor sax giants **King Curtis** and **Sam "The Man" Taylor** were among the musicians who worked numerous sessions for Tin Pan Alley." To date, no details have emerged of items on the label they can be found on.

-Roy Simonds- "King Curtis Sessionography"

***

SINGING: Connie Francis (multi-Top 40 million selling records): "Some songs, there is no insight whatsoever. It's like standing in front of a microphone, with a full orchestra behind you, in the spotlight and now you're worried about how to sing the song and I just can't see it. For me, writing a book and doing an album the objectives are the same. The objective of writing a song or making a record is to show how the heart feels and to touch the people in some way."

Connie Francis's first big hit was "Who's Sorry Now" a song her father, a record producer had wanted her to do for some time but she had repeatedly refused until late in a session, she finally relented. It sold over a million copies.

"' Stupid Cupid' has never been listed in terms of a sessionography as far as I know. But the sax players who worked with Connie in the late fifties/early sixties have. They include Al Klink, Jerome Richardson, Seldon Powell, King Curtis, Bernie Kaufman and Artie Kaplan. Both Artie and Bernie K also worked extensively with Neil Sedaka and they are ex big-band players and play in a more mellow fashion. It's not King Curtis, but my ears tell me Seldon Powell. If not Seldon, then Bernie Kaufman. I asked Connie herself once but she couldn't remember."

- Norm "B" Blakely- tenor sax, DJ, nickname courtesy of King Curtis.

***

THE BUSINESS: Waylon Jennings

" I was in the hotel lobby of Moorehead Minnesota when I heard the news [the plane crash that killed Buddy Holly, Richie Valens and The Big Bopper] and didn't know quite what to do. I was awfully young. There was never a coin flip [the rumor had circulated that Waylon Jennings and The Big Bopper flipped a coin about who would take the plane ride], that's a big bunch of bull. No one ever flipped coins. Big Bopper came to me and said he had the flu. We'd been riding on a converted school bus, and he came to me and asked if he could take my place on the airplane and I said 'Yea'. That's how simple it was. But you know Hollywood or Hollyweird, they got to get weird with everything.

We played the next night and it almost ruined my whole attitude toward the music business. They begged us to play and promised all kinds of things, so we played the show and after the promoters decided they should dock us for Buddy Holly, Richie Valens and The Big Bopper. And we told them, of course, you can go ahead and dock us but you won't have a building left."

WAYLON JENNINGS (vcl/gtr), King Curtis (ten), Buddy Holly (gtr), George Atwood (bs), Bo Clarke (dms), The Roses: Robert Linville, Ray Rush, David Bigham (bkgnd vcls) overdubbed on –1 (prob. on September 12, 1958). Prod. Buddy Holly.
Clovis, New Mexico. September 10, 1958

107120	When Sin Stops –1	Brunswick 55130
107121	Jole Blon	Brunswick 55130

Note: There were at least seven takes of "When Sin Stops", four of which were without Jennings' vocal. One of these four appeared on Nor-Va-Jak LPs 816 and 963, along with a vocal version (without overdubs) that is a take with a different sax solo to that of the 45rpm issue. R. Serge Denisoff's 1983 biography of Waylon Jennings cites an interview with Waylon's brother, Tommy, who claims that The Roses were in fact The 4 Roses, so one more name belongs with that lineup. He also shows Tommy Allsop replacing George Atwood.

On the Buddy Holly session, he gives Bob Montgomery, Sonny Curtis, himself and Waylon as all being part of Buddy's band.

Some contemporaneous notes suggest that Buddy had put "Prism Recording Company" as the production company for the Waylon sides: although Waylon said Buddy told him he was going to record him for a label he was going to start to be called "Taupe" – which was the colour of his Cadillac.

BUDDY HOLLY *(rn: Charles Holley) (vcl/gtr), King Curtis (ten), Joe Maudlin (bs), Jerry Allison (dms).*

Clovis, New Mexico. September 10, 1958

112352 Reminiscing   Coral 62329

114367 Come Back Baby   Coral LP 57450

Note: Master numbers allocated in NY on June 19, 1962 and January 15, 1964 respectively.

-Roy Simonds: "King Curtis Sessionography"

***

PRODUCTION, SOUND: Link Wray's controversial "Rumble", the only instrumental to be banned from radio, with its use of feedback and distortion (courtesy of Link Wray jamming a pencil through the amplifier's cone), would influence generations of musicians such as Jimmy Page of Led Zeppelin, Iggy Pop and punk rockers Teenage Head.

https://faroutmagazine.co.uk/link-wray-rumble-only-instrumental-track-to-ever-be-banned/

https://www.npr.org/2017/08/06/541676283/-rumble-celebrates-rock-n-roll-s-native-american-roots

***

INSPIRATION: Eddie Cochran's "Summertime Blues"- Potentially one of most creative talents to emerge from the 1950's, this multi-instrument artist (blues guitar, piano, bass, drums, vocals) and songwriter's career was cut tragically short by a car accident in England in 1960. Inducted into the Rock and Roll Hall Of Fame, his songs have been covered by a wide range of artists. For example, "Summertime Blues" has been recorded by Blue Cheer, Beach Boys, Joan Jett, The Who, T Rex, Olivia Newton John, Brian Setzer, Rush, Downtown Blues Band, The Black Keys, and country music stars Buck Owens and Alan Jackson, to name just a few.

https://secondhandsongs.com/performance/2835

***

PRODUCTION, MIXING, ARRANGEMENT- The Flamingos' "I Only Have Eyes For You" (Number 11 Billboard Top 100, Number 3 Billboard Hop R&B) was first heard in a dream! "I was so tired that I fell asleep, and in my dream I heard 'I Only Have Eyes For You' just the way it came out on our record… As soon as I woke up, I grabbed the guitar off my chest and it was like God put my fingers just where they were supposed to be…

Note: The opening is an interesting production. What appears to be a bass line, buried deep in the mix gradually emerges to be a male chorus.

Buskin Richard (2009)
https://www.soundonsound.com/people/flamingos-i-only-have-eyes-you

***

SAMPLING: In 1956, song writer Bill Buchanan and producer Dickie Goodman used samples from other hit records for their production of "The Flying Saucer Part 1" (peaked at #3 on Billboard), followed by "Buchanan and Goodman On Trial"; in 1957, "The Flying Saucer Part 2" (#18 Billboard) and "Santa And The Satellite Parts 1 and 2" (#32 Billboard).

Goodman earlier had been sued for a rewrite of Orson Wells' "War of the Worlds". The court ruled that his sampled work was a parody and not a breach of copyright. Goodman continued to make use of samples in various records into the 1960s.

Speedo — Cadillacs

Jesse Powell   Baritone

#3 R&B #17 Pop

Artist Biography by Michael Erlewine

Texas tenor man Jesse Powell was born February 2, 1924. There is very little biographical information about his early years, other than his working with Hot Lips Page, Louis Armstrong, and Luis Russell. He joined Count Basie's

Band in 1946, replacing the great sax player Illinois Jacquet, which says something about his abilities.

Powell appears on a number of blues recordings in the late 1940s with people like Brownie McGhee, Willie Jordan, and Doc Pomus. He also worked with Champion Jack Dupree and continued to play jazz, touring France with Howard McGee in 1948. He played bop and recorded with Dizzy Gillespie in 1949. During the 1950s, as bebop fell out of favor, Powell found steady work with a variety of R&B artists.

He recorded as a leader for Federal in 1951 and 1953 and had established himself with the Josie label by 1954, which included groups like the Cadillacs. His R&B work included a number of singles, and studio work with Atlantic/Atco in the late 1950s. His work can be seen on the classic single "Mr. Lee," by the Bobbettes, where he takes the tenor solo and especially with Bobby Darin.

Powell was back recording jazz in the early 1960s. In 1961, he recorded Party Time for a subsidiary of Prestige. In his later years, he worked in Harlem and made only a few recordings. Those wishing to hear Powell's work are recommended to the Prestige album "Texas Tenors", produced by Bob Porter.

#3 Pop SPLISH SPLASH—BOBBY DARIN   JESSE POWELL   TENOR

Bobby Darin, vocals, piano; Al Caiola, guitar; Billy Mure, guitar; possibly Wendell Marshall, bass; Jesse Powell, tenor sax.

#12 QUEEN OF THE HOP—BOBBY DARIN   JESSE POWELL   TENOR

Bobby Darin, vocals, piano; Al Caiola, guitar; Billy Mure, guitar; possibly Wendell Marshall, bass; Jesse Powell, tenor sax.

Slow Walk- Sil Austin

Sil Austin   Tenor
43 R&B #17 Pop

R&B tenor saxman and bandleader **Sil (Silvester) Austin** was born September 17, 1929, in Dunnelon, Florida. He taught himself to play tenor sax at age twelve. Four years later, he played "Danny Boy" on the Ted Mack Amateur Hour in St. Petersburg, Florida. Austin also won a talent show at the Apollo Theater in New York City for a version of "Danny Boy." Mercury Records decided to sign the teenager to a contract and persuaded his mother to let Austin go to New York to refine his technique at the Juilliard School of Music. He was inspired by the music of Coleman Hawkins and Lester Young.

In 1949, he worked with Roy Eldridge and then with Cootie Williams from 1949 to 1952. From 1953 to 1954 he was with Tiny Bradshaw. Austin also performed with Cootie Williams in the house band at Birdland. During the years with the house band, he performed with Charlie Parker, Miles Davis, Lester Young, Max Roach, and Dizzy Gillespie.

Ella Fitzgerald recorded Austin's composition "Ping Pong" and then gave him the title as a nickname.

He later signed with Mercury and recorded with his own band. While under contract with
Mercury, he performed on 32 albums. "Danny Boy" reached #59 for twelve weeks in 1959, and the album" Plays Pretty For The People" is now considered a classic.

Sil Austin performed all over Europe and Asia. He moved from New York to College Park, Georgia in 1973 where he owned a successful car wash and continued to perform until cancer took his life on September 1, 2001. I met him while he was performing an acoustic gig with piano at the Perimeter Mall in Atlanta. -John Laughter

Discography:

1956 Slow Rock—Rock Wing
1957 Everythings Shakin'—Mercury
1959 Battle Royal!—Mercury with Red Prysock
1960 Plays Pretty—Mercury Soft Soul—SSS
Honey Sax—SSS Silver Screen—SSS
1995 Great Sax—Sun
Go Sil Go—Mercury
Sil Austin Plays Pretty for the People—Mercury Songs of Gold—SSS
1999 Swingstation—Polygram
1999 Sax Moods: Best Of Sil Austin—Polygram

Bonnie Came Back – Duane Eddy

Jim Horn   Tenor

#26 Pop

Photo courtesy Warner Bros. Records, Inc.

Jim Horn was born in Los Angeles, California. Like so many sax players in the early 1950s, he started playing at junior high school dances. He then started playing nightclubs while still in high school. He enjoyed the music of King Curtis, Plas Johnson, Clifford Scott and Hank Crawford. Jim started performing with Duane Eddy in the 1960s. As you will see from this history of Top 40 solos, Jim Horn has played with the best.

His nightclub experience and a friendship with fellow saxophonist Steve Douglas led Horn to Duane Eddy. He eventually became a member of Eddy's road band, The Rebels. Jim joined the band on TV's Shindig! and was in Phil Spector's Wall of Sound recording sessions.

During this period of the 60s, he played with countless artists including The Beach Boys, Van Dyke Parks, The Carpenters and The Mamas and The Papas. He played oboe and English horn on all of The Carpenters' records.

During the 70s, Horn recorded albums with Leon Russell, George Harrison, and Joe Cocker. He was invited by Cocker to play on the Mad Dogs & Englishmen tour, and Harrison's 1971 benefit Concert for Bangladesh and the 1974 Dark Horse tour.

"I've traveled all over the globe with John Denver and learned so much about life from the experiences we had out there on the road. I walked on The Great Wall of China, saw the Pyramids of Egypt and tasted the foods around the world." He played on the Black and Wy (Clint Black-Wynonna) tour and in September of 1997, Jim was a part of the massive Garth Brooks in Central Park HBO special.

"John,
I happened to remember the sessions I played for "The Pussycats" with John Lennon &
Harry Nilsson (tenor sax). Also, "Don't Go Where The Road Don't Go" with Ringo Star (tenor saxes), "Rockestra Theme" with Paul McCartney & Duane Eddy (tenor sax).
That's all I can think of right now".
Peace, Jim
4/5/15

"Hey John:

I think you left out Jose Feliciano which I played flute on all of his records. Also, I played flutes and saxes on The Beach Boys records. Remember Pet Sounds?

The Carpenters, Canned Heat "I'm Going Up The Country" (3 flutes), Stevie Wonder "Ebony Eyes" (Alto Sax solo), The Stones (Goats Head Soup), Elvis Presley, Boz Scaggs "Low Down" (Flute & Bari Sax) "Georgia" (Alto Solo), Toto "Rosanna" (Tenor & Bari Sax), "Africa" (Recorders) Lynyrd Skynyrd "What's Your Name" Tenor & Bari Sax.

I'm sure there's a lot more but I just can't think of all of them John. Good Luck with the book.

Send me one when you finish it!!"

Peace, Jim

Rebel Rouser—Duane Eddy

Gil Bernal Tenor
#6 Pop (#19 UK)

"Rebel Rouser" was recorded in a Phoenix studio that had an echo chamber that originally was a 2,000 gallon water tank. A speaker was placed at one end of the tank, the microphone at the other, and the guitar "twang" was piped in there.

Gil Bernal has been working professionally since the age of 19, and his startup job was with Lionel Hampton, no less. His string of credits in the years that followed indicate not just diversity but the ability to flourish in an amazing variety of situations, from the intense brooding blues of John Lee

Hooker to the completely not serious musical mayhem of Spike Jones and his City Slickers.

#8 (R&B) DOWN IN MEXICO—COASTERS   GIL BERNAL   TENOR

"I know who played the sax. It was Gil Bernal. Thank you and good luck with your greatproject".
Claus Rohnisch 12/7/12

#8 YOUNG BLOOD—COASTERS   GIL BERNAL   TENOR

Credit has been given to both Plas Johnson and Gil Bernal. According to Plas Johnson, it was Bernal who played the solo.

The recording Spike Jones' "Spoofs the Pops" featured an incredible send-up of Dean Martin's hit "Memories are Made of This," supposedly performed by Gil Bernal and the Canine Nine. It was Bernal alright, but the music he was playing along with was actually a bunch of pooches recorded on a field trip to the dog pound.

In 1957, he was part of the newly revised Spike Jones and the Band That Plays for Fun, representing a slight but noticeable toning down of the lunacy factor. Fellow players joining Bernal in this venture included trumpeters George Rock and Cappy Lewis, fellow saxophonists Clyde Amsler and Brian Farnon, trombonist Phil Gray, the banjo team of Freddie Morgan and Jad Paul, and accordion player Carl Fortina, among others.

Bernal was blowing tenor seriously on all manner of rhythm and blues sessions during the same period, including some classic sides by the Coasters. One of Bernal's great rock sax performances is on the original recording of "Rebel Rouser" by twangy guitarist Duane Eddy. Listening closely to this recording, one can hear that producer Lee Hazlewood used only three tracks: one is Eddy, his guitar's sound altered considerably by the presence of a 2,000 gallon water tank in the studio; another is the clever handclapping track; and the third is Bernal's rip- roaring sax licks.

Following the period with Jones, Bernal hooked back up with another alumnus from the old Hampton days, none other than arranger, composer, and trumpet man Quincy Jones. He collaborated with Jones on some of that artist's finest film soundtracks, usually various fusions of rhythm and blues, jazz, and film music.

Bernal's blowing can be heard on the soundtracks to Banning, In the films "Cold Blood", and "In the Heat of the Night"; the latter film also features the flute sounds of Rahsaan Roland Kirk. Later Bernal appearances on soundtracks include the film "Primary Colors "and the 1997 Wim Wenders film "An End to Violence", the latter part of his involvement with another busy Hollywood film scorer, Ry Cooder. The Wenders film may have been a disappointment, but the soundtrack has some very interesting moments involving an unusual combination of musicians.

Bernal plays alongside the accordion player Flaco Jimeniz as well as avant garde jazz guitarist James "Blood" Ulmer. Bernal recorded two albums with Terry Evans in the 90s and once again was invited by Cooder to play tenor sax on the overwhelmingly successful soundtrack to "Buena Vista Social Club" by Ibrahim Ferrar and a host of other Cuban jazz musicians.

According to Gaye Funk, "I know he had one gig at a club in Gardena for something like 18 or 19 years. A friend of mine, that sang with a group called The Turks, told me that there was a concert at the Shrine Auditorium in LA in the early 50s (they were on the bill), and Gil played - he was introduced as Sex on a Sax!"

"I think my real roots were with the black style of playing, the black musicians," Bernal said in "Land of a Thousand Dances: Chicano Rock 'n' Roll from Southern California" by David Reyes and Tom Waldman. "I felt there was more soul, more energy in that music. I like the sound, the attack, that's the way I played."

Raunchy- Bill Justis

Bill Justis   Alto

#2 Pop #6 COUNTRY

In September 1957, Bill Justis recorded the instrumental "Raunchy".

Three cover versions were released in the next three months, three more in 1958, and nine more in the next year and a half!

In the 1950s, competition for record sales and chart position was a slash and burn, kick and stomp, all out war...

However, legend tells us that because a young George Harrison could play the song "Raunchy" perfect, note-for-note, on guitar that convinced John Lennon to let him become a member of The Quarrymen, forerunner to The Beatles.170

https://secondhandsongs.com/performance/97074

Courtesy http://www.spaceagepop.com/justis.htm

Courtesy http://www.history-of-rock.com/instrumentals.htm

Bill Justis, upon hearing that a certain rock 'n' roll musician made a lot of money, put down his trumpet for a saxophone, bought $80 of rock 'n' roll records, and set his sights on stardom. His May 1957 hit "Raunchy" gets its title from a magazine article on current teenage slang. Justis and Sid Manaker concocted the song in Justis' home while making fun of rock n' roll, convinced that they too could do it well if only they tried.

Justis was older than most teenage rock fans and had little interest in rock as a musical style. He soon realized, however, that rock's simple sound actually was harder to achieve than he first thought. "Raunchy" (teenage slang for "dirty" or "messy") became the first rock 'n' roll instrumental song.

"Raunchy" was a little Southern tune that Justis just couldn't get out of his head. Originally named "Backwoods," it was a tune that he recalled from his childhood in Birmingham, Alabama.

There was nothing sophisticated about "Raunchy," which came out in November 1957. It consisted of Sid Manaker playing a short guitar riff over and over, alternating with Justis leading the Sun house band on tenor sax. The only thing remarkable about the recording was the riff and the unorthodox way Manaker played it. Rather than play in the middle string range, as most rock and country guitarists would, Manaker used the bass strings, further exaggerated by the studio echo.

Part of the charm of his hit version of "Raunchy" was the off-tone of his saxophone. Justis had called another sax player to do the session, but he begged off at the last minute, forcing Justis to play the lead part himself. He hadn't played the sax for a while, and his rusty playing accounted for the strange tone.

"Raunchy" shot up the Billboard charts, just missing becoming #1 and staying in the Top 40 for fourteen weeks. The record became a classic, one of rock's first true instrumentals, but Justis ultimately would have only one other charting record, "College Man" (#42)

Unlike other Sun artists, Justis was well-educated, from a well-to-do family, and he had formal musical training. In 1957, Justis became music director for Sun, arranging hits for Johnny Cash and others. Justis eventually left Sun after a fight with Sam Phillips, and for a brief time produced for his own label, Play Me Records.

He moved to Nashville in 1961 and became a successful arranger and producer for everyone from Ronnie Dove to the Dixiebells.

Before his death from cancer in 1982, Justis wrote the musical scores to the Burt Reynolds film *Smokey andthe Bandit* and later produced major hits for Bobby Vinton.

Neither Justis nor Manaker, who remained a session man at Sun, capitalized on the uniquely original guitar sound they had created. That would fall to an enterprising deejay, Lee Hazelwood in Phoenix, Arizona, and his nineteen-year-old protégé Duane Eddy.

Raunchy-Ernie Freeman

Plas Johnson Alto

#1 R&B #4 Pop #11 Country

By PFC Henry Smith

PLAS JOHNSON

Raunchy-Billy Vaughn

Justin Gordon Alto
#10 Pop

Justin Gordon also recorded with Laurindo Almeida, Pat Boone, Benny Carter, Rosemary Clooney, Nat King Cole, Bing Crosby, Connie Francis, Barney Kessel, Frankie Laine, Peggy Lee, Dean Martin, Ella Mae Morse, Louis Prima, Peggy Lee and Elvis Presley.

From "Sail Along Silvery Moon" onwards, it's usually him doing both sax parts. "I could overdub an album in an hour", Gordon says. (Bear Records). Gordon continued recording with Vaughn and retired from the music business in 1985.

More from Bear Records:

"It was Milt Rogers who brought Justin Gordon into the [Billy Vaughn] fold and it was Gordon who provided the distinctive twin alto harmony that would make help Billy Vaughn a household name. Born in Cleveland, Ohio, Gordon was a professional musician by the age of fifteen. Moving to New York in 1939, he soon found steady work on radio and in nightclubs. After military service in World War II, he moved to California in 1946. In 1949 he signed a contract with the music department at Paramount Pictures and rapidly solidified his reputation as one of the most accomplished and versatile studio musicians in town."

Gordon: "When Dot started recording in Los Angeles, the first thing I did for them was the Gale Storm session when she recorded "Ivory Tower" (this was probably in January 1956 - Dik). The first time I worked with Billy Vaughn was a Pat Boone session, the time he recorded "Friendly Persuasion".

"We had to cover a record called "Raunchy". Randy Wood thought it was going to be a big hit. I played the sax solo. It was going to be put out on a little 45 rpm single, and we were wondering what the hell to put on the back. Billy said, "Well, I've got a little old song here called 'Sail Along Silvery Moon' and I think it would go just great. I'd like to have it with two saxophones and I'd like to have Justin play both parts."

Justin Gordon explained at length how the twin saxophone sound was created: "We had it down to a science. First, we would record the songs and I'd play the melody. Then after everybody had left, I'd stay for perhaps an hour or so and overdub the things we had recorded. We didn't waste any time. Sometimes we'd do twelve tunes in one session. It was easy if I had a competent engineer who knew what he was doing and could set it up to suit me. I could not play wearing earphones, because I couldn't hear myself. What he had to do was set up a small speaker next to me that I could hear and play the music very low. I could hear what I had done on the first session, and then match it. I very carefully marked all my parts, like where did I take a breath, how long did I hold this note, how long did I hold the last note, and so forth. I got to be pretty efficient at it. I could overdub an album in an hour. Occasionally, when they were pressed for time, they would have one of the other guys play the second part, but they really preferred the sound of one guy playing both parts, which was fortunate for me."

"I'm not sure if Gordon is still alive. There is an entry for one Justin S. Gordon in the Social Security Death Index, born in 1917 who died in San Diego, CA June 15, 1998. That could be our man."

Best,
Dik
https://tims.blackcat.nl/

"Get A Job"-Silhouettes

Rollee McGill Tenor

#1 R&B #1 Pop

ROLLEE McGILL
By Phil Davies

Rollee and the Rhythm Rockers hit the national R&B charts in 1955 with the great "There Goes That Train" on Mercury. The recording was originally on Philly based Piney Records. However, Mercury quickly picked up the national rights to both the single and Rollee McGill. It hit the Billboard charts in August 55 and reached #10 on both DJ and jukebox charts. Rollee plays fine solos on the hit and the flipside, "You Left Me Here To Cry." His next session was in LA in June of 55, with Chuck Norris on guitar and the superb Ernie Freeman on piano.

Rollee wrote all four songs but none of them charted which is not a reflection on the quality of the songs especially the great "Rhythm Rockin' Blues."

Rollee returned to NY in on January 24th 1956 (the same week that Elvis first shook up America on the Dorsey/Gleason television Stage Show). He cut the cracking "Oncoming Train", "I'm Not Your Square" and two more sides. Neither charted in the rock n' roll boom year of 1956. Mercury and Rollee eventually parted and he returned to Philly. In 57 he cut the two part "People Are Talking" which was later leased to Cameo.

In October 1957, he cut the great blasting sax solo on the Silhouettes classic "Get A Job," originally released on Junior before being leased to Ember (Cameo and many other labels turned it down). Rollee couldn't read music and his songs and solos were usually head arrangements made up on the spot. What Rollee played wasn't written by the arranger Howard Biggs, instead Rollee just winged it.

More Rollee sessions followed in 1958-59 including a Sam Cooke styled ballad. He did two sessions in 1963 (featuring fine sax by Rollee) and 1965 (soul style). He remained on the music scene in Philly apparently was working well into the 1980s, playing locally and on various sessions by other artists. On November 1, 2000, Rollee McGill died at the age of 68.

Highly recommended CD:
Rhythm Rockin' Blues BCD 15926 AH Bear Family, released 1999.

leadership influenced a subsequent generation of ensemble players.

Real name: Marshal Walton Royal. Born: May 12, 1912 in Sapulpa, OK. Died: May 8, 1995 in Los Angeles, CA.

Frank Wess- /Frank Foster

Frank Wess (born January 4, 1922 in Kansas City) is an American jazz musician, who has played saxophone (both alto and tenor) and flute. In 1953, he joined Count Basie's band, playing flute and tenor sax. He reverted to alto sax in the late 50s, and left Basie's band in 1964. Courtesy http://en.wikipedia.org/wiki/Frank_Wess.

FRANK WESS

Although best known for his work in the Count Basie Orchestra (and as the composer of the Count Basie hit, "Shiny Stockings"), Frank Foster's saxophone playing owes more to the bebop of Charlie Parker and Sonny Stitt than the swing of Basie.

Foster began playing clarinet at 11 years old before taking up the alto saxophone and eventually the tenor. By the time he was a senior in high school, he was leading and writing the arrangement for a 12-piece band. Foster studied at Wilberforce University in Ohio before heading to Detroit in 1949 with trumpeter Snooky Young for six weeks, becoming captivated by its burgeoning music scene.

Drafted into the Army, Foster left Detroit and headed off to basic training near San Francisco, where he would jam in the evenings at Jimbo's Bop City.

After being discharged in 1953, two life-changing events happened to Foster: he sat in with Charlie Parker at Birdland and he was asked to join Count Basie's band, where he stayed until 1964. Foster's fiery solos contrasted nicely with Frank Wess' ballad work, providing Basie with an interesting contrast.

Foster, already an accomplished composer by this time, learned from Basie how to simplify arrangements to make the music swing. He soon was providing compositions and arrangements for the band ("Blues Backstage," "Down for the Count," the entire "Easin' It" album just to name a few), with his most popular number being "Shiny Stockings."

He also was an extremely successful freelance writer, creating a large body of work for jazz, including works contributed to albums by singers Sarah Vaughan and Frank Sinatra, and a commissioned work for the 1980 Winter Olympics, Lake Placid Suite, written for jazz orchestra.

In the 1970s, Foster played with contemporary musicians such as Elvin Jones, George Coleman, and Joe Farrell and began expanding his compositions. He led his own band, the

Loud Minority, until 1986 when he assumed leadership of the Count Basie Orchestra from Thad Jones. While playing the favorites, Foster also began introducing original material into the play list.

Foster resigned as the musical director of the orchestra in 1995 and began recording albums again. In addition to performing, Foster served as a musical consultant in the New York City public schools and taught at Queens College and the State University of New York at Buffalo.

June Night- Jimmy Dorsey Orchestra

Dick Stabile Alto
#21 Pop

This song was recorded five days after Dorsey's death.

DICK STABILE
https://en.wikipedia.org/wiki/Dick_Stabile

Dick came from a Musical family. His father was a featured violinist with the Vincent Lopez Orchestra for many years. It was Lopez who advised him to play the sax also, as it seemed to be gaining popularity. When his dad brought home a brand new Selmer saxophone, it was the young son, Dick Stabile, who took to the instrument. He did take some lessons and also learned to play the piano.

Dick Stabile learned the big band business from his time as featured saxophonist with the Ben Bernie Band, where he served for many years. He had joined Bernie in the early 1930s when Dick was only 15 years old.

He formed his own orchestra in 1936, later hired, and in time married, vocalist Grace Barrie. The band's highlight was a sextet of reeds, ranging from clarinet to bass sax.

Near the end of his career and the big band era, Dick was leading an orchestra at the Hotel Roosevelt, in New Orleans, LA., and was also acting as musical director for the Dean Martin and Jerry Lewis show.

Dick Stabile was known for playing a full octave above the top range of the saxophone. He had his own unique fingering and a sound that was his alone!

Jimmy Dorsey was an excellent musician and specialized on alto saxophone and clarinet. He was one of the top bandleaders of the swing era. His father was a music teacher and marchingband director. Dorsey received early music instruction from his father and by the age of seven was playing cornet in his father's band. Two years later he switched to alto saxophone and clarinet. In the 1920s he performed with the California Ramblers, the Jean Goldkette

Orchestra, and Paul Whiteman's orchestra. His younger brother followed him into each of these bands.

When the brothers moved to New York, they worked as session musicians, appearing on records and radio. The Dorsey's started a touring band in the 1930s and signed to Decca Records. Dorseywas diagnosed with throat cancer at age 53 and died in 1956. His last recording session for Fraternity Records included "So Rare."

https://en.wikipedia.org/wiki/Jimmy_Dorsey

"At the time of his death on June 12, 1957, Jimmy's final hit song, "So Rare", reached the number-two spot on the *Billboard* charts, becoming the highest charting song by a big band during the first decade of the rock-and-roll era. With an arrangement heavily influenced by R&B saxophonist Earl Bostic, it marked Dorsey's attempt to acknowledge rock music and marked a significant departure from his earlier work." They also talked about Clifford Scott's tone on "Honky Tonk" by Bill Doggett. The arranger stated: "that's what we want".

Photo courtesy "Big Band Swing" LP-221

Tea for Two Cha Cha Cha-**Tommy Dorsey Orchestra**
Joe Lopes- Alto

#7 POP (#3 UK)

"John, I joined the Dorsey band in the summer of 1958 and Joe Lopes was the alto soloist. "Tea for Two" had been recorded earlier that winter. Joe had left the band by that summer so I never met him nor do I know what happened to his career. The players did tell me "Tea for Two" was an afterthought and was played without a chart as a head arrangement. When the tune became a hit, they had to hire someone to write out the parts that had been improvised at the recording session. There were no trombone parts because the trombone section supplied the Latin instrument parts. I played claves while I was in the band. So, I don't know who could give you anymore information. John Dodge was playing lead alto when I was in the band."

-William Shepherd

Experiments With Mice-Johnny Dankworth

Johnny Dankworth- Alto
Pete Warner- Tenor
Alex Leslie- Baritone

#7   (UK)

    Born in 1927, John Dankworth showed early proficiency on the clarinet and by the age of seventeen had entered London's Royal Academy of Music. Benny Goodman was his first idol, but he soon became impressed by the work of the great Charlie Parker and took up the saxophone as a result. He was voted Musician of the Year in Britain in 1949, the beginning of a succession of such honours, which included top composer, arranger, and leader of both small and big bands. His success was to continue unabated for the next fourteen years in Britain. Later the accolades took on different and often more international forms. During this period Dankworth's recording activities included two hit records, "Experiments with Mice" (1959) and "African Waltz" (1960). In 1985 Dankworth founded the London Symphony Orchestra's Summer Pops, with which he continued to be associated as Artistic Director until 1990. He conducted symphony orchestras throughout the world, including the majority of the great American and Canadian organizations, as well as in Hong King, Singapore, Australia, New Zealand, Holland, and Great Britain.

In The Mood- Ernie Fields
Plas Johnson- Tenor & Baritone
4 Pop #13 UK

Photo courtesy Plas Johnson

According to Mr. Johnson there was no other sax player in that session so he apparently overdubbed the bari part; "Yeah, sounds like me". Plas Johnson, 10/8/2011

Ernie Fields led one of the better known territory bands of the southwestern United States during the 1930s and 1940s, but did not become nationally famous until the 1950s. His brand of music was typical of the territory band scene - exciting, driving music that was designed to carry away the troubles of poor southern audiences at ten-cents-a-head tavern dances and open-air carnivals. Throughout the 1950s, the Fields group stuck with their successful formula of R&B and pop tunes and small group versions of familiar big band era hits like "Tuxedo Junction" (#18 Adult Contemporary, #5 Dance -1978) and "Begin The Beguine." Finally, Ernie's long-awaited gold record arrived in 1959, with his remake of the Glenn Miller hit "In The Mood."

Kissing Time - Bobby Rydell

George Young- Tenor

#11   #29 R&B

"**The Best Of Bobby Rydell**" on ABKCO Music & Records Inc. credits **GEORGIE YOUNG, BUDDY SAVITT, FRED NUZZILLIO.**

"Joel Whitburn (Top Pop Singles 1955-1999) credits **Georgie Young** and the Rockin' Bocs as the backing group. (They had a hit with "Nine More Miles")
    Which would mean that it's George Young. I think I hear more than one sax, though."

Regards,
Dik

"Hello John,
Jeff told me about the work you are doing concerning saxophone solos and etc. on various hit recordings over the years. I think it's wonderful of you to do all of this work, and believe me, I can imagine what a task it is!

Some of my work, that I can remember, is:

1- "Kissin' Time" (Bobby Rydell's first hit on Cameo) I played the tenor solo.
2- "Let's Twist Again Like We did Last Summer" (Chubby Checker's second hit on Cameo-Parkway) Again, I played the tenor solo.
3- "I Can't Sit Down" (The Dovells) Tenor solo
4- "Some Cats Know" (Peggy Lee) Flute solo
5- "Stuff Like That" (Quincy Jones) Alto solo
6- "Tie a Yellow Ribbon" (Tony Orlando and Dawn) Alto solo
7- "Casanova Brown" Alto Solo
8- "Dancin' In The Darkness" (Coco Du Jour) Alto solo
9- "Read Me Like A Book" (Chubby Checker) Tenor solo
10- "Everywhere You've Never Been" (John Krugh) Alto, Tenor and Soprano
11- "Since I Quit Drinking Coffee" (John Krugh) Alto, Tenor and Bass Clarinet
12- "Turn The Beat Around" (Vickie Sue Robinson) Tenor solo

13- "Bridge Over Troubled Water" (Michelle Le Grande) Soprano solo

14- "Double Fantasy Album" (John Lennon) Tenor solos

15- "Lightening Strikes Again" (Lou Christie) Tenor Solo

16- "Swear To God" (Frankie Valli) Alto Solo

These are just a few of the many solos I've played on recordings and as more come to mind, I'll be happy to e-mail them over to you. The span of time on the above information covers from the late '50's thru the late '90's.

If you check my web-site at ... www.georgeyoungmusic.com ... you might find more information that can be helpful to your quest.

Thank you for all the hard work you are doing to make known the saxophonists who performed on all of those tons of records.

Best wishes and all good things, George Young ♪ " 5/2/09

"Hello again, John ...

Just in case you're interested, I just learned that a CD project that I was involved with just recently was released by my good friend's group which I helped him with. His name is, Burt Conrad. The name of his group is: The Burt Conrad All Stars. The titles of the songs where I had tenor solos were: "Until Then" and "It's Up To You".

If I can remember any other work on which I've performed solos, I'll e-mail them on over to you.

And again, thank you for the wonderful work you're doing.

Sincerely, George Young ♪ " 5/2/09

"Yes John,

Please feel free to use the photo on my site. It's totally cool, in fact, thank you for being so thorough with the work that you're doing.

I hope that some day we can have the opportunity to meet in person so that I can shake your hand for your wonderful energy that you're spending on behalf of all the wonderful unsung saxophonists you are documenting!

Please let me know when your book is finally published. And once again, many many thanks!!

Sincerely,

George Young ♪ " 5/2/09

George Young is one of the most frequently heard musicians of our time. Young plays over ten instruments, including the tenor, alto, soprano, and sopranino saxophone, clarinet, alto flute, c flute, East Indian and ethnic flutes, and the piccolo.

George has played with Pavarotti, Mick Jagger, John Lennon, Madonna, Gillespie, Brown, Sinatra, Tony Bennett, and many more.

Young has contributed to many television and motion-picture soundtracks, including Miller's Crossing, My Blue Heaven, My Name is Earl, Naked Gun 2 1/2, New York, New York, Silent Movie, The Simpsons ('03/'04 Season), Sleepless In Seattle, Tootsie, Working Girl, You've Got Mail, Adam Sandler's 8 Crazy Nights, Animal House, Brighton Beach Memoirs, A Chorus Line, Fame, GI Joe The Movie, Ghostbusters, Great Mouse Detective (Walt Disney Pictures), Hair, Meet Joe Black, The Object of my Affection, All that

Jazz, Silent Movie, When Harry Met Sally, Ferris Bueller's Day Off and more.

George Ernest Opalisky Jr. aka "George Young", professional reed player since the late 50's, is one of finest technicians in fusion, jazz, swing, bebop, rock, studio and concerts, and although he is one of the most heard, he is one of the most unknown.

A virtuoso in most of the reeds, he specializes in the tenor and alto sax when in recording sessions with such artists and musicians as George Benson, Ron Carter, Jack DeJohnette, Martin Mann, David Sanchez, Earl Klugh, G.E. Smith & The Saturday Night Live Band ('91-96), Jay Hoggard, Dean Friedman, Dave Holland and Toots Thielemans and so many others. George has also recorded solo; recorded in the combos of the great Steve Gadd, Jay Leonhart and John Tropea; in the big bands of Louis Bellson and Benny Goodman, and as a leader for both the Chiaroscuro and Paddle Wheel Studios, working with the dozens of artists that went through their doors. George is very respected throughout the world's music industry and by all the heavy saxophone & reed players.

* Special thanks to Jeff Peterson, Los Angeles Atelier, Yamaha Corporation of America for contacting Mr. Young.

Hi again John,

First of all, thank you for sharing your information regarding the saxophone artists in your attachment. Your information certainly brings back many fond memories regarding some of my contributions to your list.

Just in case you aren't aware of a few more of my solos that were used on various recordings, I'm happy to share them with you below.

There was the Len Barry's recording of "Lightning Strikes Again", which as best I can remember was a tenor solo. "Casanova Brown" by Gloria Gaynor, possibly an alto solo. Then, a tenor solo for Vicki Sue Robinson's "Turn The Beat Around", and an alto solo for Frankie Valli's "Swearin' To God". John Lennon's Double Fantasy album which featured a short tenor solo on "Clean Up Time".

Also, there were a series of tenor solos on an RCA recording of a group called The Brothers which was formed by Warren Schatz of which Artie Kaplan was the contractor.

There was an Atlantic recording of a solo album by Robert Plant on which I performed several tenor solos.

I hope you don't mind my sharing all of the above with you.

Thanks again! George ♫ 4/3/15

Buddy Savitt
In a 1968 photograph

BUDDY SAVITT

Born Burton Swartz, in 1930 or 1931, probably in Philadelphia, Buddy Savitt began playing professionally while he was studying at Matbaum High School in Philadelphia. At first he worked around Philadelphia. Then he joined Elliott Lawrence's Orchestra, probably in 1948.

Buddy Savitt played with Woody Herman's "Second Herd" taking the place of Stan Getz, in March 1949. Al Porcino recalled that when he rejoined Herman in 1949 that "the [Four] Brothers were Gene Ammons, Jimmy Giuffre, Buddy Savitt—with Serge Chaloff the only remaining one of the original four."

Savitt is credited on some of the "Second Herd's" Capitol recordings and was in the band until it disbanded mid-way through 1950. In the fall of 1950 Savitt re-joined the Elliot Lawrence Orchestra. All indications are that he stayed with Lawrence into the beginning of 1951, probably through the winter.

Buddy Savitt settled down in Philadelphia in the 1950s, working casual jobs, including some at the Blue Note in the company of Charlie Parker, Dizzy Gillespie, and Gerry Mulligan, among others. He taught saxophone at Ellis Tolin's Music City and played on many recording sessions.

The Lord Discography of jazz recordings lists Buddy Savitt on 17 recording session between 1949-1960, on either tenor or baritone saxophone. In addition to the sessions with Herman, he recorded extensively as a sideman for the Philadelphia-based label Cameo/Parkway (many of which are probably not listed in Lord).

He also recorded for them under his own name: Buddy Savitt - Smoke Gets In Your Eyes / Come Blow Your Horn (Cameo 857), 1961; and, Buddy Savitt - Most Heard Sax in the World (Parkway SP-7012), 1962.

Savitt played baritone sax in The Salsoul Orchestra between 1975 - 1977. In 1978 or 1979, when gambling became legal in Atlantic City, NJ, Buddy joined the house band at Caesar's Boardwalk Regency Hotel-Casino. In 1980 or 1981 he joined the Paul Mann Orchestra at the Sands Hotel - Casino, also in Atlantic City.

Buddy Savitt died on Monday, April 18, 1983 in hospital, in Somers Point, NJ. Buddy was, and is, remembered fondly by his contemporaries and former students.

A few of the many hits Buddy Savitt played at Cameo-Parkway Records:

THE TWIST—CHUBBY CHECKER
BUDDY SAVITT TENOR

MASHED POTATO TIME—DEE DEE SHARP
BUDDY SAVITT   TENOR

YOU CAN'T SIT DOWN—THE DOVELLS
BUDDY SAVITT   TENOR

THE WAH WATUSI—THE ORLONS   BUDDY SAVITT (?) TENOR
Credits per *The Best of the Orlons-1961-1966*;
GEORGE YOUNG, BOB SCHWARTZ, BUDDY SAVITT, DAN DAILEY & FRED NUZZULLIO
However, BUDDY SAVITT is credited on his Parkway L.P. recording of "The Most Heard Sax In The World."

SOUTH STREET- THE ORLONS   ? TENOR
Credits per *The Best of the Orlons-1961-1966*;
GEORGE YOUNG, BOB SCHWARTZ, BUDDY SAVITT, DAN DAILEY a/k/a FRED NUZZULLIO

Dave Appell Writer/Arrange/Producer

The name Dave Appell will probably be associated first with the Cameo-Parkway label. In which he played a substantial part. Prior to joining the label, which was founded by Kal Mannand Bernie Lowe over a Christmas party in 1956, Dave worked as an arranger for several big bands dating back to his wartime service in WW2.

You would think today a man born on March 24th, 1922 that has worked hard in the music business for over 60 years would be relaxing in the sun and not doing much of anything. But that is not even close to reality. Dave wrote and produced brilliant smooth jazz music at his home studio with some of the best and brightest young musicians in the Philadelphiaarea.

Dave started his music career at an early age playing guitar and trombone. Between hisstint in the Navy and joining Cameo-Parkway, Dave started to gig around town and formed a group called "Dave Appell and the Applejacks". Before long he landed the job of musical director on the Ernie Kovak Show which was an NBC Network show out of Philadelphia. In addition to the group's duties on the show they worked as backup musicians for John Zacherie on his Top 10 hit *"Dinner with Drac"*.

The Applejacks broke into the national charts undertheir own name with the instrumentals *"Mexican Hot Rock"* (#16) and *"Rocka-Conga"* (#38) both in 1958.

Dave and his group went on to become the house band at Cameo-Parkway backing such artists as Chubby Checker, Bobby Rydell, The Dovells and Dee Dee Sharp whose records he also arranged and in many cases co-wrote with Kal Mann, such as "Let's Twist Again", "The Bristol Stomp", and "Mashed Potato Time".

Dave left Cameo-Parkway in 1964. In the seventies he had great success with his productions for Tony Orlando and Dawn, including the #1 hits *"Knock Three Times"* (1970) and *"Tie A Yellow Ribbon Round the Ole Oak Tree"* (1973), on Bell

Records. His co-producer was Hank Medress, who had been a founding member of The Tokens in 1956 and also sang in the reformed Tokens of *"The Lion Sleeps Tonight"* fame.

The team, based in New York City, also produced gold and platinum records for MelissaManchester, Frankie Valli, Mac Davis and The Richard Simmons Exercise Album among manyothers.

It's incredible to think that in the Mid-Forties, Dave, who wrote charts for such famous bands as Earl "Fatha" Hines, Benny Carter, Boyd Raeborn, Sam Donahue and Clean Head Vinson, later on the radio a, listeners could hear Bobby Rydell sing his song *"Wild One"* or the Orlons singing Dave's classics *"South Street"* and *"Don't Hang Up"*. Only a few years ago he wrote a beautiful jazz instrumental which was recorded and released on Columbia Records by the late great Grover Washington, Jr.

580

The Big Bands- 1950s

In the 1950s the glory days of the big bands were over, however, they did not fade away quietly but had one last run in the sun with hits in the Top 40 Pop Charts...

April In Paris-Count Basie

Marshal Royal Alto
Frank Wess - alto, tenor, flute, clarinet
Frank Foster - tenor, clarinet

#28 Pop

The title track was included in the soundtrack of the 2008 video game release Grand Theft Auto IV.

AllMusic awarded the album"April In Paris" 5 stars calling it "one of those rare albums that makes its mark as an almost instant classic in the jazz pantheon" and noting "*April in Paris* proved Count Basie's ability to grow through modern jazz changes while keeping the traditional jazz orchestra vital and alive."

For close to 20 years (early 50s-70s) the characteristic sax sound of Count Basie's big band was topped by the clear, vibrating lead alto of Marshal Royal. Royal was, by all accounts, a competent swing-based soloist, but his strength was first and foremost as a team player. Royal's style became the prototype for swinging a sax section; his slightly behind-the-beat phrasing, pronounced vibrato, and aggressive

Tall Cool One-The Wailers

Mark Marush- Tenor

#24 R&B #36 Pop

Photo courtesy Golden Crest Records

The Wailers recorded their national hit while still in high school. They were soon called to the East Coast for appearances on the *Alan Freed Show* and *American Bandstand*. Although they were offered major tours, they returned to Tacoma, Washington, to dominate the local entertainment scene. Mark Marush was a member from 1958-1962. The band lasted for ten years.

Mark Marush (1958 - 1962) the original sax player in the Wailers came from the school band side of music. Another trained musician. He dropped the stiffness associated with school players and dug in with the heart and soul of King Curtis, Red Prysock and Blackwell. The raw timbre and melding of sound that Mark added to the guitars with his underlying support in the mix made a unique and special voicing that became an important part of the Waiters sound. Mark also attended Stadium High school in Tacoma and lived in the north end. Occasionally the Wailers would rehearse in Mark's living room, where some of the material on their Castle album was put together. Mark played in the Wailers until 1962. He left to pursue interests in his family's business.

http://www.louielouie.net/blog/?p=306

"Mark Marush, the original saxophone player of the Wailers, passed away recently (2007). I don't have a lot of information about his death, or even what he's been doing all these years, but I've been told that he died in Aberdeen, Washington. I never had a chance to interview him, unfortunately. He was the original sax player on the 1961 version of "Louie Louie" by Rockin' Robin Roberts and the Wailers, which was a major influence on The Kingsmen and Paul Revere & the Raiders." August 19, 2007

584

You're So Fine- The Falcons

Sax Kari- Tenor

#2 R&B # 17 Pop

Members; Mack Rice, Eddie Floyd and Robert Ward per one website.

Under the musical direction of Isaac Columbus Toombs, Jr. a/k/a/ Saxton Kari, Isaac "Sax" Kari, Candy Yams, Ira Green, Texas Red and Dirty Red Morgan.

SAX KARI (Musician, bandleader, songwriter, record producer, vocals, guitar, piano, organ, saxophone)

"Good morning John.

Eddie Floyd here. The Falcons' members on the song 'You're So Fine" were Eddie Floyd, Mac Rice, Lance Fenny, Willie Schofield and Joe Stubbs. SAX KARI he played saxophone. Robert Ward played on the song "I Found A Love". Anyway all the best. And good luck".
11/6/19

Night Time Is The Right Time-Ray Charles

David "Fathead" Newman- Alto

#5   R&B. #95 Pop

David "Fathead" Newman got his famous nickname from a high school music teacher who caught him playing his horn with the music turned upside down. He joined Ray Charles on baritone saxophone in 1954. He later switched to alto and then tenor saxophone. Newman worked steadily with Charles' small and big bands for the next dozen years, soloing on such immortal sides as "Night Time is the Right Time," "Talkin' 'Bout You" "I Got a Woman," "Let the Good Times Roll," and "Rockhouse."

588

Home Of The Groove

Prominent saxophonists in the 1950s also included (in no particular order): Don Wilkerson, Rusty Bryant, Henry Hayes, Bull Moose Jackson, Haywood Henry, Johnny Pennino (known as "The Tenor Sax King of New Orleans"), Jimmy Cavallo (out of Syracuse N.Y.) who, with Joe Marillo, played the title track of Alan Freed's movie, "Rock, Rock, Rock", plus a few of the many exceptional players out of New Orleans:

-Jimmy Cavallo & His House Rockers - Rock, Rock, Rock (1956)

https://www.youtube.com/watch?v=YS3EN7qnz24

https://www.discogs.com/artist/2048391-Jimmy-Cavallo

-Harold Battiste

"Back in the late 1980's, I got the chance to buy a sealed, four LP box set put out by Harold Battiste in 1976 that contains jazz recordings from 1956 to 1966 by him and other founders or close associates of AFO Records in New Orleans… the label was established in the early 1960's in the Crescent City by musicians for musicians in an effort to cut themselves in on some of the real record business money that, as session players, leaders, arrangers, producers or songwriters, they did not get…"

https://homeofthegroove.blogspot.com/search?q=Harold+Batiste

https://www.youtube.com/watch?v=2Ai5iM6Y3Mk&list=OLAK5uy_nIbbW-1Uqh2c_9hlYF_5u37zZHE6so0u0&index=5

https://www.youtube.com/watch?v=JZwea3rP2uE&list=OLAK5uy_nIbbW-1Uqh2c_9hlYF_5u37zZHE6so0u0

-Johnny Pennino

"...performed for the Rat Pack at the Factory in Los Angeles, NBC Studios, Millionaires Club, Sahara Tahoe and Las Vegas Sands. Johnny has played with dozens of recording stars from Freddy Fender, Ernie K-Doe, Professor Longhair to Sam Cooke, Aaron Neville, Frankie Ford, Kenny Rogers and others. Johnny has recorded in New Orleans, Canada and Nashville..."

http://www.johnnypennino.com/

-Nathaniel "Nat" Perrilliat

""You Better Say Yes" (Johnson) Willie Tee, Atlantic 2302, 1965- When I first heard this song, maybe fifteen years ago, after finding the record in one dusty bin or another, my first thought was that King had "borrowed" the main repeating riff in the song, played on guitar by George Davis, from Cannonball Adderley's jazz hit, "Mercy, Mercy, Mercy",.. Cannonball Adderley, along with his cornetist brother, Nat, and bassist Sam Jones, came to New Orleans to record a jazz album, In the Bag, at Cosimo's studio, using three fine young local players in the sextet on the date: Ellis Marsalis on piano,

Nat Perrilliat on tenor sax, and James Black on drums. Those three were at that time also recording jazz and R&B sessions with Harold Battiste for AFO, the musician-owned label he headed..."

https://www.youtube.com/watch?v=U8DL6LmaF0Q

https://www.youtube.com/watch?v=H7jqyBq9hes

https://homeofthegroove.blogspot.com/search?q=Perrilliat

James Rivers

"In the brief notes to the Mardi Gras CD, Best of New Orleans Rhythm & Blues Volume Three: James Rivers (link follows) which compiles 14 of James Rivers' JB's tracks... the saxophonist is quoted by Jeff Hannusch talking about the Senator Jones sessions...pretty much nothing was written out. 'Head arrangements' were worked up by the players around the basic melody lines provided by Rivers. There is a long tradition in New Orleans recording of giving the players latitude to develop their own parts..."

https://www.youtube.com/watch?v=riTTyJ62318&list=PL9RJmKoi3egQMJIft1MqCbsKvVeIS0hDB

"Best Of" CD tracks:

https://www.youtube.com/playlist?list=OLAK5uy_nSCTi_rYbR3LAcHHRbl1eDOCElcJ8irBk

https://homeofthegroove.blogspot.com/2009/12/james-rivers-it-aint-over-yet.html

Noble "Thin Man" Watts

"Noble "Thin Man" Watts was one of the hottest tenor saxman on the 1950s R&B scene. This was the era of honking tenor sax, when sax players, not guitarists, led the transformation of R&B into rock 'n' roll. Saxmen like Big Jay McNeely, Joe Houston, Plas Johnson and Noble Watts were early rock superstars. Watts was one of the greatest exponents of that honking tenor style."

https://www.alligator.com/artists/Noble-Thin-Man-Watts/

https://www.youtube.com/watch?v=RBvF9YZhWJ0

Above excerpts are from the blog "Home of The Groove", courtesy of Dan Phillips

"Based on the premise that the true Home of the Groove, at least on the North American landmass, is the irreplaceable musical and cultural nexus, New Orleans, Louisiana and environs, this audioblog features rare, hard to find, often forgotten, vintage New Orleans-related R&B and funk records with commentary. I currently host a weekly show, "Funkify Your Life", on KRVS 88.7 FM in Lafayette which includes music covered on HOTG and more."

Collections of Blues, R&B, Rock n' Roll Sax

Atlantic Honkers: Rhythm & Blues Sax Anthology (2 LP set)
https://www.discogs.com/release/13790079-Various-Atlantic-Honkers-A-Rhythm-Blues-Saxophone-Anthology

Have A Ball: Screaming Saxophones Vol. 1- Black Roots Of Rock & Roll
https://www.discogs.com/release/2758989-Various-Have-A-Ball-Screaming-Saxophones-Vol-1

Honkers and Bar Walkers Volumes 1-3
Vol. 1
https://www.youtube.com/watch?v=PyVKKHlMLYE&list=OLAK5uy_ng_rSv_sE_iSGCbZhixl_AAV_xyzJ30sk

Vol. 2
https://www.youtube.com/watch?v=z5ASOEHvwBc&list=OLAK5uy_khkA4TS9ZLoiBKF1630JKuY6ZDr3sVjeM

Vol 3.
https://www.youtube.com/watch?v=JREWtBPO4rE&list=OLAK5uy_lvVqxQ7UvoOebqqhKOy1nSZKdStfM37VI

Honking The Boogie: Hot 40s & 50s Saxes
https://www.discogs.com/release/13355351-Various-Honkin-The-Boogie

Tornado: Hot Screaming Saxes From Los Angeles 1945-1947

https://www.discogs.com/release/8479192-Various-Tornado-Hot-Sreamin-Saxes-from-Los-Angeles-1945-1947

The Big Horn (The History Of Honkin' & Screamin' Saxophone)

https://www.discogs.com/release/2921763-Various-The-Big-Horn-The-History-Of-Honkin-Screamin-Saxophone

Tequila- The Champs

Chuck Rio- Tenor
#1   (#1 R&B)

Photo courtesy Chuck Rio
CHUCK RIO

Chuck Rio was born Danny Flores in Santa Paula, California. His parents migrated from Mexico in the 1920s. "Little" Danny Flores was playing guitar in church at age five and was singing and playing with a Mexican trio by age fourteen. In the late 1940s, he moved to Long Beach and formed a group called the 3-D Ranch Boys. They played local bars at night and were in great demand as studio musicians.

In 1957, Flores teamed up with guitarist Dave Burgess, head of A&R and the first artist signed to Gene Autry's Challenge label. They recorded "Train To Nowhere" and used Flores's band to record it. They needed a "B" side of the record so they used a song that Danny wrote. They didn't have a title for the song yet, but everybody knew that Flores drank a lot of tequila and one of the musicians said, "Call it Tequila," so they did. Flores also introduced a technique to a new generation of sax players when he added the "flutter tongue" to the melody. He said it is like spitting watermelon seeds!

The studio band consisted of Flores, Gene Alden (drummer), Buddy Bruce (guitar), Cliff Hills (bass) and Dave Burgess (guitar).

Challenge told Flores that he would have to change his name because he was signed to Modern Record Company as a vocalist under his real name Danny Flores. So he took his mother's middle name (Carlos) and his father's middle name (Del Rio), and Challenge signed him up as an instrumentalist. However, as soon as "Tequila" was released, Modern sued Rio. He said one word on the record—"Tequila!"—and they said that was vocalizing! The touring band was named the Champs, after Autry's horse, Champion.

"Tequila" is a timeless classic and has become an international standard. In 1957, "Tequila" received the first Grammy Award ever awarded for the best R&B category.

Chuck Rio, age 77, passed away on September 19, 2006 of pneumonia in Westminster, Calif He had resided in Orange County, California, and continued to perform with his wife Sharee, who is also a singer and musician.

Chuck's appearances include the Greek Theatre in Los Angeles, Taj Mahal in Atlantic City, Angel Stadium, Lake Tahoe, Hawaii, Puerto Rico, Bahamas, *American Bandstand*, *Ed Sullivan Show*, *Dick Clark Show*, and the *Al Jarvis Show*.

"Tequila" has been used in movies such as *Pepe*, *Overboard*, *Peggy Sue Got Married*, *Ninja Turtles*, *The Freshman*, *Pee Wee's Big Adventure*, and many radio commercials.

(2006—I spoke with Danny's wife several times this year. According to Sharee, Danny had Alzheimer's disease. He was no longer able to perform but really appreciated his "fans" staying in touch.). Sharee put Danny on the phone in my last conversation with her and Danny said: "Tequila".

Discography:

1998 *The Tequila Man*—Ace

Other members of the band included:
- Buddy Bruce — "Tequila" lead guitar.
- Dave Burgess — rhythm guitar — Lancaster, California.
- Dale Norris — lead guitar — Springfield, Mississippi.
- Cliff Hills — "Tequila" upright bass.
- Chuck Rio — sax — Rankin, Texas — replaced by Jimmy Seals eight months after "Tequila" was recorded.
- "Van" Norman — upright bass — replaced by Bobby Morris — Tulsa, Oklahoma.
- Gene Alden — drums — Cisco, Texas — replaced by Dash Crofts.

"Hi John,

I really enjoyed reading the story about Danny, except for the fact that he died Sept. 19, 2006. You're a great writer and have a lot of talent and knowledge. I also enjoyed reading about the other "Sax Greats".

Sorry I don't keep in touch more often, but you know that I have NO computer skills. So, I wait for my daughter to come over and she does it for me. I guess it's about time that I learn, but I don't have much patience for it. I hope all is well and that you are doing wonderful, as well as your book. Stay in touch.

Love to hear from you!"
Love, Sharee Flores 1/10/2010

Some errors, I think, in John's post.
1) Dave Burgess wasn't lead guitar but rhythm guitar; lead was Dale Norris, but not at first, in "Tequila" recording lead guitar was Buddy Bruce, Norris came months later.
2) "Ben" Norman was "Van" Norman and he wasn't on bass guitar, but on upright bass (quite sure); anyway, he wasn't into "Tequila", that time bass player was Cliff Hills.
Regards
Posted by **Maurizio** on April 14, 2008

Huelyn Wayne Duvall (August 18, 1939 – May 15, 2019) was an American rock and roll and rockabilly musician. He is noted in a Wikipedia website stating, in part, about the "Tequila" recording session that he "contributed to the backing vocals and Flores, also a saxophonist, suffered a jaw injury the night prior to the session in a brawl at a local establishment. He (Flores) was unable to play saxophone for the session so another saxophonist was called in to play the trademark "dirty sax" solo at the last minute". This statement appeared in his old website titled (Huelyn

Duvall. "Memories of the Tequila Recording Session" Retrieved August 21, 2006.).

Huelyn's name DOES NOT appear in ANY online articles about The Champs and his name has NEVER been in a list of members of The Champs. Every article about The Champs gives the recording credit to Danny Flores a/k/a Chuck Rio.- John Laughter

Sat, Jan 15, 2022 8:11 pm - Per Dave Johnson;

I inquired on Facebook messenger posing the question to Dash Crofts. Here is Dash's response to me; "We didn't join the Champs until after Chuck Rio left. Chuck Rio wrote the song "Tequila".

600

Blues, R&B, Rock n' Roll Teaching Links

*****

R&B, Funk & Pop Saxophone Styles Clinic
Jeff Harrington (Berklee College of Music)

https://www.youtube.com/watch?v=4u5BqhMvXKQ
https://college.berklee.edu/people/jeff-harrington

https://www.jeffharrington.com/

D'Addario Performing Artist
Professor, Berklee College of Music
Massachusetts Institute of Technology (MIT) Affiliated Artist
Harvard University MLSP Instructor
LESSONS in jazz improv for all instruments & all levels. Teaching students worldwide & in Boston, Newton, Needham, Brookline, Belmont, Wellesley, Weston & Watertown, MA.

*****

Blues Riffs and Licks
Pete Thomas

https://tamingthesaxophone.com/theory/impro/blues-riffs-licks

Transcribing Blues Saxophone

https://tamingthesaxophone.com/saxophone/players/blues-transcriptions

"One of Pete Thomas' first professional gigs was with Fats Domino, both as a soloist and as a member of the legendary horn section. It was this connection that led to a musical partnership with Joe Jackson as co-arranger and saxophonist on records and world tours…A one time member of award winning fusion band Swift he has also featured with the Thad Jones Orchestra, Loose Tubes, Slim Gaillard, Jimmy Witherspoon, Jon Hendricks and Laverne Baker.

He works with producers such as Adamski, Flood, Rod Argent, Pete Wingfield, Gus Dudgeon, Robin Millar, Stuart Colman, and Marshall Jefferson on projects for artists including PJ Harvey, R.E.M., Cliff Richard, Elton John, Richard Thompson, Robert Cray, Keziah Jones and Kim Wilde."

That Old Black Magic-
Louis Prima, Keely Smith

Sam Butera- Tenor

#18 Pop

"Sam Butera is renowned as one of the most impeccable players of the tenor sax of this or any other musical era. Butera, with his distinctive sax playing and his powerful vocals, has thrilled millions in performances from Las Vegas's major showrooms to the famed Copacabana in New York City. With his recordings, television, and motion picture appearances, Butera went on to reach and thrill millions more."

Butera was born on August 17, 1927, in New Orleans, where his father Joe ran Poor Boy's Grocery & Meat Market. His mother was Rose, and he had a brother, Joe, Jr. Butera always loved music and at a young age, his father gave him a saxophone. At the age of eighteen, in a contest held at Carnegie Hall in New York City, Sam was voted the Outstanding Teenage Musician in America by Look Magazine.

Upon graduation, Butera went on the road with Ray McKinley, with whom he made his recording debut on McKinley's versions of "Civilization" and "Celery Stalks At Midnight." After stints with various bands including Tommy Dorsey, Joe Richman, and Al Hirt, Butera returned home. Once home, he played at Leon Prima's 500 Club, where he and his five-piece band backed bad comics and strippers.

In his spare time, Butera jammed with the band of one of his father's customers, Paul Gayten, who had one of the top bands in the city. In 1951, a recording was made of Sam with Paul for Regal Records. Eventually, Sam formed his own group and produced such hits as "Easy Rockin'" and "Chicken Scratch" for RCA Victor.

When Louis Prima was looking for his Vegas band, his brother reminded him of Butera. In 1954 Butera joined Louis Prima and Keely Smith in Las Vegas, and the rest is musical history. Together they recorded several albums, appeared on many TV shows, starred in several movies, and broke attendance records in every showroom and lounge in the country.

Butera recorded for Cadence under his own name and for subsidiary label Prep as Sam Butera & The Witnesses after the Capitol signing. The group was also given billing on all Prima recordings.

https://www.youtube.com/watch?v=Y1oh3vSDoJo (Bim Bam)

Butera appeared with Frank Sinatra across America from Caesars Palace in Las Vegas to the Latin Casino in Philadelphia. The two recorded the song "Stargazer," which was written by Neil Diamond and was released through Reprise Records.

Sam has also appeared with Danny Thomas, Jerry Vale, Sergio Franchi, Jimmy Roselli, and Sammy Davis, Jr., with whom he recorded an album "Sam Meets Sam, When The Feeling Hits You."

On April 3, 1998, the Augustus Society gave Sam the "Lifetime Achievement" and the "Entertainer of the Year" awards. In 1999 the Tropicana Casino and Hotel inducted Sam Butera into the "Las Vegas Hall of Fame."

Copyright © Las Vegas Review-Journal, June 03, 2009-Sam Butera, whose saxophone kept the Strip swingin' for 50 years, died Wednesday in Las Vegas. He was 81.

"SAM BUTERA and THE WILDEST"
Photo courtesy Sam Butera:

606

Notes/References

134. Shaw op cit. pg. xxiv

135. Dawson Jim (1994): *Nervous Man Nervous*; Big Nickle Productions. Milford New Hampshire. A fascinating review of the flamboyant swing, jump blues saxophonists and their critical influence on rock n' roll and rhythm and blues. This book includes bios of Big Jay McNeely, Joe Houston, King Curtis, Chuck Higgins, Hal Singer, Big Al Sears, Sam "The Man" Taylor, and more, with a special look at Big Jay McNeely and his influence on future generations of musicians, including Jimi Hendrix. The quote about the psychiatric board examining Big Jay is at pg. 125.

136. Gillette op.cit., pgs. 20-22, pg. 71 Billy Rose quote at pg. 19

137. Kelley (Editor) Reebee Garofalo op. cit. Gillette op.cit., Billy Rose quote at pg. 19

138. Dawson op cit. pg 134

139 https://www.courant.com/news/connecticut/hc-xpm-1996-06-16-9606140042-story.html

140. David Mac *BLUES JUNCTION* http://bluesjunctionproductions.com/big_jay_from_la_has_something_on_his_mind

Marc Myers (2018) Big Jay McNeely (1927-2018)

https://www.jazzwax.com/2018/09/big-jay-mcneely-1927-2018.html

141. Harrington, Richard. (1984) "'A Wopbopaloobop'; and 'Alopbamboom', as Little Richard Himself Would Be (and Was) First to Admit." The Washington Post 12 Nov. 1984, Final ed., sec. C1.

142. https://theconversation.com/the-1950s-queer-black-performers-who-inspired-little-richard-138658

143. https://www.loc.gov/static/programs/national-recording-preservation-board/documents/Jerry%20Lee%20Lewis--FINAL.pdf
https://500songs.com/podcast/episode-59-whole-lotta-shakin-goin-on-by-jerry-lee-lewis/

144. http://www.rebeatmag.com/songs-made-rock-n-roll-big-mama-thornton-elvis-unleash-howling-hit-hound-dog/
Zollo Paul (2020) *Behind The Song "Hound Dog" by Lieber and Stoller*. American Songwriter. https://americansongwriter.com/behind-the-song-hound-dog/

145. Lauterbach op cit. https://oxfordamerican.org/magazine/issue-87-winter-2014/sympathy-for-the-devil

146. The litigation- https://www.americanbluesscene.com/blues-law-hound-dog-vs-bear-cat/
http://preslaw.info/valjo-music-publishing-corp-v-elvis-presley-music-1957); https://www.americanbluesscene.com/blues-law-hound-dog-vs-bear-cat/

147. Lydia Hutchinson (January 10, 2016) "Heartbreak Hotel". Performing Songwriter;
https://performingsongwriter.com/heartbreak-hotel/

148. Richards K (2010) Life. Little Brown & Company. New York. Pg. 58.

149. https://timscoverstory.wordpress.com/2015/03/23/hound-dog-big-mama-thornton-freddie-bell-and-elvis-presley/
https://www.culturesonar.com/big-mama-thornton-and-hound-dog/

150. https://secondhandsongs.com/performance/1730

151. https://www.nytimes.com/1956/06/06/archives/tv-new-phenomenon-elvis-presley-rises-to-fame-as-vocalist-who-is.html

152. Gillette op.cit. pg. 36

153. Palmer, op cit. pg 241

154. https://theaudiophileman.com/crudup/

155. Etta James (1998) Rage To Survive: The Etta James Story; Da Capo Press; page 64

156. Noah Berlatsky (2014) "Getting Elvis' Legacy Right". Atlantic Magazine
https://www.theatlantic.com/entertainment/archive/2014/07/whats-so-great-about-elvis-he-didnt-invent-or-steal-anything/374081/

157. James Brown with Marc Eliot (2005) I Feel Good: A Memoir Of A Life Of Soul. New American Library. Pgs. 66-68

158. https://americansongwriter.com/dont-be-cruel-otis-blackwells-triumph/
https://www.billboard.com/pro/music-streaming-royalty-payments-explained-song-profits/#!

159. King Bill (1989) *Interview With Otis Blackwell*. The Jazz Report. June 23, 1989.
https://www.shrout.co.uk/JazzRInt.html; Otis Blackwell songwriter- https://secondhandsongs.com/artist/3379/works

160. Broven J. (1978) Rhythm and Blues In New Orleans; pgs. 86-95; 1978- subsequent printings through 1995, revised, updated version. Highly Recommended

161. https://www.nancywrightmusic.com/tracks-playdate/
https://www.nancywrightmusic.com/store/

162. https://www.rstrathdee.com/bio3.htm

163. https://adp.library.ucsb.edu/index.php/mastertalent/detail/105513/Taylor_Sam?Matrix_page=5

164. Norman Kelley Editor Dr. Reebee Garofalo (2005) R&B (Rhythm and Business): The Political Economy of Black Music. Akashic Books (Aug. 1 2005)

165. Guralnick P (2015) "Sam Phillips-The Man Who Invented Rock n' Roll". Back Bay Books. Little, Brown and Company, New York, New York.

166. Ibid pg. 221

167. Ibid 213.

168. Ibid. pg. 681

169. Forte, Dan (1991). Guitar Player Presents Legends of the Guitar – Rock: The '50s, Vol. 2 (CD notes). Various artists. Santa Monica, California: Rhino Records. *R2 70561.pgs. 2-3.*
170. Philip Norman (May 2011). Shout!: The Beatles in Their Generation. Simon & Schuster. p. 91.

References

Photographs have been generously donated by Paul Harris, who was a regular contributor to *Juke Blues* magazine, Bristol, England and to *Now Dig This* magazine, Gateshead, England.

paulharrisphotography.blogspot.com

American Bandstand: Puckett JL. Going National: Dick Clark and ABC's American Bandstand
https://collaborativehistory.gse.upenn.edu/stories/going-national-dick-clark-and-abcs-american-bandstand

Berlatsky Noah (2014) Getting Elvis's Legacy Right. Atlantic Magazine. July 8, 2014/
https://www.theatlantic.com/entertainment/archive/2014/07/whats-so-great-about-elvis-he-didnt-invent-or-steal-anything/374081/

Bertrand Michael T (2004) Race, Rock, and Elvis. University Of Illinois Press.

Broven J (1978) Rhythm and Blues in New Orleans; Pelican Pub Co Inc; (First Editon; January 1, 1978); 3rd Edition; Revised and Updates.

https://www.pelicanpub.com/proddetail.php?prod=9781455619511

Guralnick Peter (1995) Last Train to Memphis: The Rise of Elvis Presley. Back Bay Books (September 1, 1995).

Howard David N. (2004) Sonic Alchemy- Visionary Producers And Their Maverick Recordings. Hal Leonard Corporation. A comprehensive, insightful, discussion of innovative producers from the 1950's to early 2000's.

Palumbo M. American Bandstand. http://20thcenturyhistorysongbook.com/song-book/the-fifties/american-bandstand/

Recording "C.C.Rider" by Chuck Willis- https://www.dailydoowop.com/chuck-willis-c-c-rider/

Recording "The Stroll" by The Diamonds. – Merey A (2004) Rock And Roll Diamonds. http://www.min7th.com/diamonds/andymerey2004p2.html

Thompson H. S. (1979) The *Great Shark Hunt*, Summit Books, New York, New York. pg. 96.

Ward Brian (2017) Champion or copycat? Elvis Presley's ambiguous relationship with black America. The Conversation. https://theconversation.com/champion-or-copycat-elvis-presleys-ambiguous-relationship-with-black-america-82293

Zollo Paul (2020) Behind The Song "Hound Dog" by Lieber and Stoller. American Songwriter. https://americansongwriter.com/behind-the-song-hound-dog/

9
Stardust

Billy Ward and The Dominoes

The multitrack arrangement (one of the first), plus outstanding production, lyrics and vocals helped "Stardust" to peak at #12 on Billboard's Top 100 (originally written/performed by Hoagy Carmichael in 1927; has been covered nearly 1200 times).

https://www.songfacts.com/facts/hoagy-carmichael-his-orchestra/stardust;

https://secondhandsongs.com/work/19677/versions

In the Digital 21st Century, streaming services attract a worldwide audience, but whether these services translate into music sales and royalty rates sufficient to earn a living for a musician is far from certain. Especially when an estimated 60,000 music tracks are uploaded every day!

Musicians complain that some streaming services pay only a fraction of a cent for each play, and/or pay a royalty only *after* 30 seconds of a song.

In the opening chapter of this book, the music industry in the 1920s was described as both demon and angel. Over a hundred years later, some critics choose to describe streaming services in the same manner.

Before streaming services, artists could earn, on average, $1.00 to $1.50 for every album sold. Streaming service royalty rates are always changing, however, in 2023, it is reported that "Spotify's per-stream rate has settled at $.00348 per stream, which is roughly one-third of a penny.

A notable exception has been Bandcamp, "one of the few economic success stories of the past decade: a direct-to-consumer marketplace for artists and labels to sell physical releases, merch, and digital downloads to listeners, at rates far exceeding streaming platforms' paltry payouts…"; however, Bandcamp's founders sold the company to Epic Games, the software developer behind *Fortnite*…"171

171. Sherburn P (2023) Is Bandcamp as We Know It Over?-Oct. 17, 2023 https://pitchfork.com/thepitch/is-bandcamp-as-we-know-it-over/

The following free form cento (a collage poem assembled from various sources) originally written by Tim Price (jazz artist, author, teacher) was edited by me at Tim's request. It has equal application to every decade whether in the 1920s, 1950s, 1970s or today.

I spent decades
doing the "chittlin circuit"…with organ groups,
staying in a " flea bag" was an honor compared to
"hit & run"…
shaving/cleaning up in the bathroom before the gig.
Trying to find food worth eating that wouldn't kill you
mid-set. But…
that playing day to day was burnin' proof from dues'
sidelines.

The road rat musician-in-the-trenches, at heart of their
talent,
a hipper point of departure, traveling
in a band bus, always moving towards
the next city, chasing the sun.

There was an energy then.
Seemed to be a much more vibrant subculture in the air.
TIME
was much more important.

Life and times today are very different-
I've done some "high profile" gigs with leaders who imho
had huge reps and names, worldwide
& never filled 1/2 the auditorium.
So,
I'll take any gig, play a wedding and just roll with it.

Musicians always have led two lives: playing the dance,
wedding-bar mitzah-club date
for cash & the after-hour
jam/jazz gigs for a more inner urge artistically.
The only way... just KEEP ON.
Remember your
PURPOSE,
the ideas flying.

When I was with Jack McDuff- we traveled 8 months
doing music that was
BURNING...
6 nights a week- sometimes 4 sets per. Bashing
FUN jazz.

People in the clubs standing up screaming and partying!!!
We went to record and...
the PRODUCER...
wanted NAMES. So half way thru the date...
NAMES
were brought in. The road band quit on the spot.
Execs...Producers...Biz ears...NEVER came out
to the clubs in Newark, Chicago, Detroit, to hear
MUSIC.

The "powers that be"...
just don't know/or care to know.
The media/jazz press...just don't have a clue.
The record companies...just don't exist within
these musical worlds.

NONE know TIME, how it feels
inside and driving hard,
a music that brings a place to silence,
like a vapor coming in, freezing
everyone with their mouths wide open.

NYC........one week I just saw a sax player...who had a
brand new deluxe auto-bio out
...with BIG credits w/Miles etc...going "Birdland"...
the whole diamonds/diamonds procession. Two weeks
later...
he was playing a dump
for $10 door charge. Along with a $50 buck per man thing
for band.

I just saw Bergonzi there- Cheap beer, winos,

on the other side
a Hunter Thompson flick, joint
smells like stale beer and Mr. Clean and piss.
Some of the BEST
musicians in the world go there, NYC, *just* to play.

GO.
Watch look and listen. Sit in,
With GREAT players.
and some
good players.
AND…a lot
of players who you'd be surprised at how
shitty and sad
they are,
course that's way
in any business.

GO.
THE city that you can play jazz in- IF…
you're willing to play for the door
and for nothing.
That includes most everyone-unless you're Pharoah or
Lovano or Potter.
It's just like walking on
glass.

Bob Rockwell…HAD…to split.
He was driving a cab in NYC…while playing w/Thad
Jones n' Mel.
How depressing is that?

Jenny Hill in NyC who will funk ya outta the room with
her LIQUID HORN...
Wildman Rob Shepps or Sue Terry.
Claire Daly plays great- and she has NO manager, nadda.
And she won
the Down Beat poll. Nobody returned her calls. SOS.
WHY?
Ya dig?

That BIZ focus is what gets people
"lost".
Ya try to lead a normal life- pay bills, get medical
coverage, own a car.
Ya gotta hustle 24-7
Ya just keep shedding.
And so
IT GOES
and so in
ESSENCE
you do what you do...be glad you're alive & can
play.

Our mind and our body and all around us is music.
We live and move and have our being in it.

To be out here
all these years is
a blessing.

I create
if someone hears it

cool…

The Authors

John Laughter

John Laughter joined his high school band in 1956 to play the saxophone during the heyday of Rock & Roll and R&B and was soon playing Top 40 music in dance bands in Florida and Virginia. He joined the US Air Force in 1963 through 1967. In addition to regular military duties he formed dance combos in the U.S. and in Italy.

He earned his BA degree at the University of South Florida in Instrumental Music Education in 1973 and taught elementary and high school band for ten years. During this time he was asked to join the Tampa University Jazz band for summer concert series backing jazz artists Maynard Ferguson, Dizzy Gillespie and Don Ellis.

John and his wife, Lee, moved to Atlanta in 1975 where he taught concert and marching band at Headland high school. His students maintained superior ratings in concert festivals. He also formed the "Area Stage Band" (20 piece show band) including band students, singers and dancers from surrounding Atlanta high schools.

He moved to Macon in 1980 and continues to perform with party bands that play for wedding receptions, high school reunions, corporate parties and conventions in Georgia, Florida, South Carolina and Alabama. He has played in the backup bands for the Temptations and Four Tops for local concerts and for dances sharing the stage with the Swinging Medallions, The Tams, Chubby Checker, Clarence Carter and The Temptations.

John has two books/CDs published and distributed by Hal Leonard Corporation titled "Rock & Roll Saxophone-2nd Edition", "Contemporary Saxophone", and the 607 page "The History of Top 40 Saxophone Solos-1955-2020" which is free. In 2021, MD Records in England re-released John's 1969 45 rpm recording of "It's Our Time" and "Dreams of a Child" for sales in Europe.
https://www.mdrecords.co.uk/product/john-laughter-and-third-generation-in-our-time-picture-sleeve/

Neil F. Sharpe

After breaking a leg in three places at the age of 10, while in hospital, Neil picked up a superbug that, at the time, no one knew how to deal with. Blood samples were taken every day; his arms and legs were soon covered with needle tracks, until one morning a nurse exclaimed "There's nowhere left to shoot!" The doctor finally allowed a radio in the glass-walled isolation room. Neil found a radio station that only played blues and r&b. Close the eyes and the music took everything away. Neil's been playing blues and r&b ever since.

Neil has served as:

Senior Contributing Editor:

- *Blues, R&B, Rock n' Roll Sax Teaching Resource*, distributed for free internationally (over 500,000 downloads), with contributions from (in no particular order) John Laughter, John Lull, Pete Thomas, Johnny Ferreira, Joey "The Saint" St. John-Ryan, Andrew Campbell, Curtis Swift, Paul Harris.
https://web.archive.org/web/20070914032140/http://www.saxontheweb.net/Rock_n_Roll/

Senior Editor:
-*New Orleans Musicians' Relief Fund*-a fundraiser to assist with the rebuild in New Orleans following Katrina, with musical contributions from (in no particular order): Big Jay McNeely, Lee Allen, Pete Thomas, Lionel Prevost, Oozie Blues Show (Joe Houston), Powder Blues Band, King Biscuit Boy, Sonny Del Rio, Johnny Ferreira, John Barrow, Gaz Birtles, John Firmin, Johnny Pennino, Jimmy Cavallo, Pat Carey, David Wilcox, Tom Wilson and Rosanna Cash, Blackie and The Rodeo Kings, Joe Topping, A Fragile Tomorrow.
https://archive.li/5qIaU

Neil's records with multi-instrumentalist/producer Greg Ulrick as "The Weekend Staff". E.g. https://theweekendshift.bandcamp.com/track/step-back-santa

Neil is the author of *In Control: Making The Most Of The Genetic Test For Breast Cancer*. Prentice Hall, 1997, and Co-Contributing Senior Editor of the clinical text *Genetic Testing: Care, Consent, and Liability* with contributions from over 40 clinicians, counselors and researchers, John Wiley & Sons Inc., 2006.

Printed in France by Amazon
Brétigny-sur-Orge, FR